Advance praise for
Agents of Change: The Problematic Landscape of Pakistan's K-12 Education and the People Leading the Change

Education reform in Pakistan has been pronounced dead—but here comes a comprehensive suggestion for an all-inclusive national discourse. The atrociously high fertility rate causes an alarming increase of youth out of school. We must do our bit to help change the tenacious, conservative beliefs of our people. There is hope that redemption can be earned by keeping the candle lit.
> – HAAMID JAFFER, social entrepreneur, philanthropist, and co-founder The Citizens Foundation

The book chronicles the story of TCF which needs to be better known—a remarkable journey of impact, innovation, and integrity in a noble effort to provide quality education to a large number of Pakistani children who would otherwise follow their parents in unrealized potential. In the broader context of education policy and reform in Pakistan, the book shows also just how much more needs to be done to provide equitable and quality education to the millions of children still being deprived of it.
> – MASOOD AHMED, President, Center for Global Development, Washington DC

The author combines scholarly research, ethnography, and personal narrative, built on a lifetime of experience and decades of service, into a comprehensive yet pragmatic blend of policy proposals for educational reform in Pakistan. It is refreshing to see genuinely constructive engagement with madrasas, balancing their integral nature to Pakistani history, society, and culture, with the need for meaningful change. [...] Offering concrete recommendations, the book argues that —for those who possess power at all levels of society—the most important ingredient for reform may be the simple act of commitment with sincerity.
> – MAHAN MIRZA, Executive Director, Ansari Institute for Global Engagement with Religion, University of Notre Dame

Agents of Change is a widely applicable best practices guide and an excellent resource for understanding and reforming the educational landscape of Pakistan. The book examines the state of literacy standards in public schools, the role of NGOs and madrasas, along with the stifling effects of feudalism on reform. It highlights the necessity for a shift in language policy, pedagogy, and technological literacy along with the need for bridging resource gaps between public and private education to transform the country's education towards creating a society free of wealth, gender, and health inequalities. Let us all embark upon this noble journey by joining hands and becoming *Agents of Change*. Development of Pakistan's education system is vital for the future of the country's healthcare infrastructure.
> – ZEBA VANEK, MD, Emeritus, UCLA Assoc. Prof. Neurology

Like many other public policy dilemmas, Pakistan's educational challenges are seldom addressed in a meaningful way. This is not tenable in a country where the failure to spearhead real education reform has such troubling and far-reaching implications—for the economy, for public health, security, and much more. *Agents of Change* makes a vital contribution to this longstanding debate by outlining a clear, practical, and actionable way forward. It warrants a close read globally – and from all Pakistanis.

> – MICHAEL KUGELMAN, South Asia Program, Woodrow Wilson Center

Agents of Change is an incredible story of commitment and resolve placed within the larger historic and material context. It is an important compendium of informed and reflective commentary on education policies and practice in Pakistan. The authors have successfully initiated a deeply political conversation. However, to borrow from Antonio Gramsci, they promote a 'politics of consent' in the realm of education.

> – HARRIS KHALIQUE, poet and author, Secretary-General, Human Rights Commission of Pakistan

A good school is never an island of good practice. It is nested in and supported by a complex system. There will not be any good schools without effective institutions that deliver curriculum, teaching and learning materials, teachers, and school leaders. There will be none of the above without a vibrant public sphere, including both civil and political actors. In the absence of these elements, a high demand for education will only promote private, not public good. Amjad Noorani goes beyond serving us with a jolting reminder of the dysfunction of our civil and political spheres by also suggesting viable remedies to revitalize them. Read and pay heed!

> – IRFAN MUZAFFAR, educator, independent researcher, and consultant to education reform programs; co-author of *Educational Crisis and Reform: Perspectives from South Asia*

The state of school education in Pakistan calls for extensive discussion. The authors have done a service by highlighting the lessons derived from the TCF initiative. They have suggested what difference new ideas can make to public education while being realistic in pointing out that the barriers to better education go beyond the lack of good ideas. The book provides a much-needed opening to re-imagine the movement for reform.

> – ANJUM ALTAF, social economist; former Dean, LUMS

In its 25 years, The Citizens Foundation (TCF) has become a remarkable model for low-cost, high-quality childhood education in Pakistan. Its acceleration of equity and justice works to eliminate barriers of gender, class, and privilege to enable all citizens to become agents of positive change. Amjad Noorani and Nadeem Hussain show how TCF has created a pathway to prosperity in a challenging and complex landscape through education reform and an insistence that equity of opportunity is an unquestionable human right.

> – DONALD GIPS, CEO, Skoll Foundation, Palo Alto

The power of this narrative comes from the passion invested in it. A first-hand account of the amazing story of TCF is in itself a most valuable contribution. But by bringing in multiple voices, personal experiences, and an unrelenting focus on the education challenge in Pakistan, the authors have produced an important addition to a literature that needs fresh ideas and approaches.

> – ADIL NAJAM, former Vice Chancellor, LUMS; Dean and Professor, School of Global Studies, Boston University

The book holds great value for policy research organizations, think-tanks, and development practitioners globally. It roots the debate on delivering quality education to all children in Pakistan in the context of elite capture, institutional challenges, inequity, and marginalization. It argues that the education challenge is not only technical in nature but also deeply political; and reforms that fail to establish a vibrant interface between the technical and the political are likely to be short-lived. Political yet non-partisan advocacy embedded in robust data and evidence is the key.

> – SALMAN HUMAYUN, Executive Director, Institute of Social and Policy Sciences, Islamabad

'When the world is silent, even one voice becomes powerful.' So says Malala Yousafzai, the youngest Nobel Prize laureate, who understands the challenges of making societal changes in Pakistan better than most. In *Agents of Change*, the authors paint an unerringly accurate portrait of Pakistan's broken education system, but more, much more, than that—they offer a pathway forward with detailed, informed ideas to bring all the voices—political and public—together to advocate real change. They see their book as just the beginning. It is now up to us, their readers, to pick up the baton.

> – DAVID GARDNER, US Editor, *London Standard*

Agents of Change offers deep insights into Pakistan's enormous challenges to educate tens of millions of its children—insights acquired through years of work done with teachers, planners and administrators serving at schools in the most underprivileged neighborhoods of the country. The author has shared his knowledge of these challenges and the book explains the enormity of the task. It also gives reasons to hope for a better tomorrow. A must read for anyone wanting to learn about education in Pakistan.

> – RIAZ HAQ, high-tech entrepreneur, writer, and blogger in Silicon Valley

Agents of Change is an audacious, labor of love which brings a uniquely human lens to the seemingly impossible challenge of reforming education in Pakistan. This is more than a book; it's a dramatic, hopeful Call to Action which seeks to rally agents of change, engaging them to push for and sustain education reforms. A must read for anyone interested in understanding or reforming Pakistan's education sector.

> – M. BILAL LAKHANI, writer, columnist

When classrooms are open to women, you open their minds to the possibilities that await them. My camera has often captured the strength and resilience of women who are fighting to create a better tomorrow for their neighborhoods, communities, and for Pakistan. Education has allowed them to have a voice enabling them to be better citizens. The next revolution will almost certainly be powered by these lights seeking to torch out ignorance.

> – SHARMEEN OBAID-CHINOY, Academy Award winning storyteller and women's rights activist

A thoughtful assessment of Pakistan's education challenges. A call to action. And an inspiring story about an amazing organization that has overcome all those challenges.
  – SHASHI BULUSWAR, Assoc. Prof. International Development, UC Berkeley;
      CEO-Founder, Institute of Transformative Technologies, Berkeley

Agents of Change is a unique and in-depth work on education in Pakistan. Within its pages are serious scholarship but also much needed hope. It charts out a difficult journey but without just pointing fingers—which has often been the norm. And it encourages conversation instead of argument. It points not to a 'them' but a collective 'us' as future catalysts for the change and effort that is required to ensure a more educated and prosperous country.
  – RAS SIDDIQUI, writer, Pakistan Link newspaper (USA)

Discussions about education in Pakistan typically focus on the very top-down role of the government and international actors. *Agents of Change* provides a rare window into Pakistan's vibrant civil society, their efforts to provide quality education in the country that has the world's second largest out-of-school population. Reform will require leadership from Pakistan's elites, activists, intellectuals, teachers, and students. This book provides the author's perspectives directly. It outlines the potential for collective action, drawing from local experience, to put Pakistan on a path to positive change.
  – NADIA NAVIWALA, independent writer on education policy; advisor to TCF;
      Fellow, Wilson Center

We are often told that the only solution to all of Pakistan's problem is better education. We have also seen that some of Pakistan's most chronic problems are caused by people who are educated. This book captures the myths surrounding education in Pakistan and also brings us face to face with civic leaders and organizations trying to bring about that change. It is a must read for educators and policy makers.
  – MOHAMMED HANIF, author of *A Case of Exploding Mangoes*

This book lays out the enormity of the problem that Pakistan faces in educating its youth, together with an inspiring account of efforts made by brave and dedicated individuals to put our out-of-school children into schools. One hopes that such examples will lead to more such initiatives.
  – PERVEZ HOODBHOY, Professor of Physics, Islamabad and Lahore

TCF by all accounts is perhaps the most remarkable story in creating a confluence of providing a fundamental service, i.e. primary education, raising the consciousness of an entire society regarding education, mobilizing wide spread community ownership and philanthropy for a crucial cause and now finally providing incisive insights for comprehensive response and rational policy making. Amjad and Nadeem cohesively bring forward the scale of TCF's 25 years of intervention, that provides both qualitative and quantitative basis to decisively shape the direction of primary and secondary education in Pakistan, laying the foundation for development of individuals with civic responsibility and consciousness to address challenges humanity is globally facing.
  – WASIF A. RIZVI, President, Habib University

The book is a thought-provoking, engaging, and moving read. Amjad and Nadeem have given a humane narrative to the notion of a level playing field in education.
    – AIJAZ A. QURESHI, Founding Director, Sindh Development Study Center (SDSC)

Agents of Change is a unique effort to initiate debate around K-12 education reforms. It is a conversation that access to quality education can transform lives of under-privileged and working classes. The authors have reminded our ruling-elite that investment in education will set the course for national progress and prosperity.
    – FAISAL EDHI, philanthropist, Chairman, Edhi Foundation, Karachi

Agents *of* Change

The Problematic Landscape of Pakistan's K-12
Education and the People Leading the Change

Agents *of* Change

The Problematic Landscape of Pakistan's K-12
Education and the People Leading the Change

AMJAD NOORANI
and
NADEEM HUSSAIN

Foreword by
Shashi Buluswar

OXFORD
UNIVERSITY PRESS

OXFORD
UNIVERSITY PRESS

Oxford University Press is a department of the University of Oxford.
It furthers the University's objective of excellence in research, scholarship,
and education by publishing worldwide. Oxford is a registered trade mark of
Oxford University Press in the UK and in certain other countries

Published in Pakistan by
Oxford University Press
No. 38, Sector 15, Korangi Industrial Area,
PO Box 8214, Karachi-74900, Pakistan

ISBN 978-0-19-070550-3

Typeset in Minion Pro
Printed on 55gsm Book Paper

Printed by The Times Press (Pvt.) Ltd., Karachi

Acknowledgements
Rendition of Abdul Sattar Edhi's photograph
© Rabia Adil with permission from Faisal Edhi (Edhi Foundation).

To

Abdul Sattar Edhi

The iconic humanitarian who
introduced the first nation-wide,
non-profit ambulance service in Pakistan.

The Edhi Foundation provides loving care and schooling for
orphaned youth, free health clinics for the communities, and
respectful disposal of unclaimed bodies of the homeless.

Contents

Postscript

Foreword

The years 2020 and 2021 will likely go down as perhaps the most difficult in recent memory. Even before Covid-19 struck, countries everywhere were electing autocrats who valued greed and power over peace and human rights. Communities around the world are retrenching into the 'Us vs. Them' doctrines that had torn the world apart in eras past; Islamophobia in many parts of the world has reached toxic levels; the 'Me Too' movement is reminding us exactly how egregiously men exploit their structural power over women; and all the while, the effects of climate change rage on. Pakistan is beset by its own share of problems, when it comes to development, inclusivity and religious tolerance; and the rise of nationalism across the border in India—my home country— is not making matters any better. No matter where you look, it can be hard to find reasons for optimism. That is why writing this foreword gives me so much joy.

I work in global development, and one of my occupational privileges is the chance to travel all over the world and meet remarkable people and institutions. It was during an unlikely visit to Pakistan fifteen years back that I was introduced to The Citizens Foundation (TCF). Since then, I have advised and analyzed over a hundred of the world's leading NGOs and international institutions working on health, education, food security, human rights, and other pressing issues. I can say— objectively, and in no uncertain terms—that TCF is among the most effective NGOs anywhere in the world working on any issue; arguably, it is the world's single most effective NGO in Education. This is because TCF has a profoundly thoughtful methodology, laid on a foundation of deep-rooted ethics and followed up by exceptional execution. TCF's methodology has many facets which are explored later in this book. Here are some of my own observations: every teacher is handpicked and goes through rigorous, ongoing training; the fees are on a sliding-scale basis so that even the poorest of the poor can afford education while also enjoying a sense of agency by virtue of paying for it; and 100 percent of its faculty members are women, which dramatically increases the trust parents (especially parents of girls) place in the schools. TCF insists on—

and invests in—a culture of education in the families and communities it serves. Most importantly, it has an intensive performance assessment system which allows the management to keep an active finger on the pulse of its vast network of schools, teachers and students.

The results speak for themselves. TCF has grown into one of the largest private non-profit education systems in the world with over 250,000 students actively enrolled across more than 1500 schools, virtually all of whom come from Pakistan's poorest communities. It costs TCF only $120 per student per year (25 percent less than government-run schools), but its quality metrics are even more impressive: an 86 percent attendance rate (compared to a nationwide average of 62 percent); a 95 percent of secondary school graduation rate (compared to 50 percent across Pakistan); and over 40 percent of TCF graduates attain higher education (compared to only 6 percent nationwide). Remarkably, nearly half of its students are girls many of whom go on to get productive jobs, take care of their families, and break intergenerational cycles of poverty and long-held gender stereotypes. In one of the toughest contexts for education—particularly for girls—TCF has accomplished what would be considered remarkable even in contexts that are significantly more supportive. As impressive as these results are, I have every reason to believe that the arc of TCF's journey is long, and it will continue to become a formidable force for equity, inclusion and social justice in Pakistan.

Still, for all its accomplishments, TCF is not very well known in the wider world. This is because the global media's coverage of Pakistan is narrowly skewed towards the country's troubles with fundamentalism and militancy. The other reason is that the TCF community and leadership are far too modest to toot their own horn. In recent years, as word of this remarkable institution has gotten out, awards and accolades have soon followed.

That's why I'm so glad that my friend Amjad took it upon himself to share the TCF story. In this book, Amjad thoughtfully weaves the larger political and policy challenges faced by Pakistan with the powerful human stories behind TCF and the fight for education. We learn about the people who make TCF work; the parents who place their trust in this institution; the children whose lives are forever transformed by the journey; and what all this can mean to the country. The stories in this book demonstrate the fundamental role of quality education in alleviating poverty and boosting development. Amjad makes the case that TCF's ability to offer quality education at such a large scale offers a template for Pakistan's public education system. His analysis is based on sound research, conversations with many members of the TCF community, interviews with several experts in the field, and deep first-hand knowledge of the many challenges within Pakistan's education system. He also offers a number of suggestions for reform, geared specifically to the Pakistani context. One particularly innovative suggestion, for example, is on the value of integrating the vast number of informal *madrasas* into the mainstream education system. In discussing the essentials of such a reform process within Pakistan's policy ecosystem, Amjad makes a forceful appeal for broader public support and strong civic leadership to shape and oversee potential reforms over the long term. He argues that, while TCF has been an inspiring catalyst for bringing about change, it will take much more on the part of Pakistani and international supporters in terms of public participation and political advocacy to achieve effective and deep systemic reforms. Perhaps the most important point the book underscores is the critical role of education—particularly girls' education—to the future of a country struggling to find its place in the world.

One of the more remarkable geopolitical events of recent decades has been the rise of India as a global force. Every analysis of India's emergence highlights the critical role education has played in unlocking the technical and entrepreneurial potential of its people. Pakistan has an equally rich cultural history and institutional appreciation for education, a deep well of local talent that is hungry for opportunity, as well as a global diaspora willing to invest in its uplift. There is no reason Pakistan cannot build on this foundation and make education a pillar of its own emergence onto the global stage. Getting there, though, requires the types of broad engagement and policy reforms that this book describes.

I am profoundly grateful to Amjad for opening this window into a remarkable institution and how TCF—and the rest of us—can help improve education in Pakistan.

SHASHI BULUSWAR
PhD, University of California, Berkeley

On a Personal Note

My parents, Abdul Khaliq and Aziza, were 16 and 14, respectively, when marriage was arranged for them, as was common in pre-Partition India (and still is, in that part of the world). My eldest brother Obaid was born when Mother was not quite 16. By age 27, she had three more children—Hamid, Niloufer, and me. Both my parents were minimally educated to a 5th or 6th grade level, as was also common but only in the 'progressive' families of that era. Mother was from a relatively affluent family and privately tutored at home. Father went to a madrasa school in a Bombay (now Mumbai) *mohalla* (neighborhood). A parent at 18, he had to support a family. Both parents were avid readers. Mother preferred Urdu and Father took to English. Books and magazines were in abundance at home. Father became impressively knowledgeable on his own. His knowledge of current affairs, history, classic literature, and Urdu poetry were equal to the best readers and highly educated persons.

In Bombay, Mother was a proud volunteer and activist for independence and the creation of Pakistan. She was about 32 when the family moved to Karachi, with dreams of prosperity and a peaceful life in a harmonious Pakistan. Without much formal education or capital for a business start-up, Father got off to a rough beginning and it remained a bumpy ride for several years. Our dream migration was turning out to be a nightmare, saved only by the kindness of the Ahmed and Ali Mulla family (Arab-Indian friends from Bombay who had also migrated to Karachi) and we were given refuge for two years in a single room about 10 by 12 feet, above the garage in the spacious home of the Mulla brothers. Despite difficult times and meager resources, our parents apparently had a clear vision for our future: *they would find the best education affordable.* Young Obaid was sent to an air force cadet school. Hamid got into the prestigious BVS Boys School, sister Niloufer went to St. Joseph's. I went to Happy Home School, run by a kindly lady who operated the school in her home and charged just two rupees a month.

In 1952, we moved from the Mulla's single room over the garage to a three-room flat in Patel Para for 150 rupees per month in rent. And we lived there for eleven years. Our modest flats were surrounded by slum dwellings and gave us a graphic view of the daily struggles of the neighbors. After a rainstorm flooded the area, I vividly remember the mud walls, the straw roofs, pots, and pans from some of the huts being swept away. I recall Mother taking me to admission tests at St. Patrick's, St. Paul's and St. Lawrence's schools. One lucky day, I was accepted in second grade at St. Lawrence's where the fees were 12 rupees per month, a big jump from Happy Home. But Mother had a modest stream of income through sewing, embroidery work, and part-time jobs. Father struggled with work and had a health crisis which put him out of work for two years. I think we probably got by with financial assistance from relatives and I am sure my brothers pitched in too. Both parents were socially progressive, especially Mother, who had made connections with elite families that were good for her business of selling quality household linen to the affluent ladies.

Mother was the entrepreneur and had a 'business plan' to move from the Patel Para area to the nicer PECHS area of Karachi and encouraged Father to take the plunge. Our rent went up from 150 to 450 rupees a month, but Mother attracted more clients and the family income went up. I was 16 then and had just finished 10th grade matric from St. Lawrence's. Father set up a small bookstore with brother Hamid's help and kept himself busy but the cash flow was only just enough to pay the store rent and some home expenses.

After serving thirteen years in the air force, brother Obaid managed manufacturing plants in Dhaka and later in the UAE. Hamid, the family genius, went to UC Berkeley at age 16 on a private scholarship, thanks to a benevolent community leader, Mohammed Ali Rangoonwala. Obaid and Hamid sent money home for family support. Niloufer pursued her creative talent and became a professional commercial artist. And I've had a most satisfying career as a physical therapist and safety consultant in the US.

This ordinary history chain of my family's minor struggles is not unique. I present it here only to illustrate how education in my family resulted in short cuts to attain middle-class life standards. Succeeding generations have done better than previous ones, gone further in education and in professional or business achievements. Yes, we have seen struggle, but it was made easier only because of the education we received, and the values instilled in us. Like most parents, Mother and Father took risks to give us the gift of education, which has paid dividends. At the end of the day, I have had a cool family of siblings, cousins, aunts, and uncles and we are the first generation of college graduates!

> **My Father, our neighborhood activist…**our Patel Para neighborhood and flats were improved in many ways by my father's efforts: multiple trips and letters to the Karachi Municipal Corporation to convert a 200-yard dirt strip into an asphalt road; stopping and reminding the donkey-cart owners (our neighbors) to clean up after the animals; paying a sweeper to keep the compound of our flats swept clean, with equal contributions collected from the eight tenants (not a small feat); paying a man to monitor the water supply and storage tanks, and operate the water pump, again with equal contribution from the tenants; installing better stairs and safety handrails for the upper level flats. He made it more livable and cleaner for us and our neighbors. Every neighborhood needs a civic-minded activist like my father.

My Family

Time marches on. New stories replace older ones. Najma, my amazing life partner for more than fifty years (counting the sweetheart years of courting), deserves all the credit for raising our family of three wonderful children. Born in the US, our kids fill us with pride and all have college educations. Ali works very hard with incredible focus and heads a national non-profit for immigration policy and advocacy. Zeba is an educator; she is a mother-teacher, home schooling her two smart and adorable daughters Aysha and Zenaya, as well as professionally coaching[1] California teachers in math pedagogy. Farah is a remarkably talented and acclaimed performing artist and teacher of *kathak*, a classical dance form; she has a smart and spirited daughter Aziza.

The underlying point in extending the story to us, our children, and grandchildren is that my parents had no formal schooling of any great duration, but the tradition was established by them that children must have a good education. It was only a generation ago in my large extended family that college education was not a very common thing. The present tradition is one of college education being the norm.

I live a charmed, blessed, and idyllic life. Enjoy the book. Support education. Be an agent of change. Rome wasn't built in a day. Finally, Saint Francis of Assisi reminds us: *For it is in giving that we receive.*

Here's a fond homage to a very dear friend and Silicon Valley neighbor, Don McDonald, whose encouragement to write the book was priceless. Passing at 99, he lived well and was a wise mentor. We had in common our love for poetry, music, and aviation and I have great memories of morning walks with him, coffee stops and occasional games of chess. A good man, great friend, and a generous supporter of education in Pakistan. Cheers, Don…

Among the many blessings I enjoy is an incredible bond with my dearest friend of many years, Mumtaz Feroz (Chunnu to the family). He has always been there and made life easier for me. Generosity and fairness are in his veins. In his unique ways, he's changing Pakistan for the better. I am grateful. Be happy, my *yaar*.

Note

1. Zeba has also conducted math teacher training at TCF on two of her visits to Pakistan.

Introduction

Pakistan has its share of problems, but it also has possibilities.
Munis D. Faruqi, Associate Professor, History, South and South East Asian Studies;
Director, Pakistan Initiative, University of California, Berkeley

The institution that needs immediate attention is Pakistan's broken K-12 education system. It is not hopeless or beyond redemption. It can be fixed. But can it be salvaged and reformed without a strategically planned political advocacy and public demand campaign? Dealing with this requires that we look in the mirror and face some unpleasant facts. Procrastinating will not change anything. To simplify the challenging process, we must focus on actions to rebuild a durable, equitable and progressive education ecosystem. We must identify and mobilize the stakeholders, bring together people from civil society, put heads together to develop an action plan and roadmap, with open communication and eagle-eye focus on actionable priorities.

This book aims to energize open discourse on the education landscape and initiate civil society action for sustainable change. From the historical to the present state, the book vividly describes the feudal and dysfunctional environments which have impeded reforms. It addresses sensitive areas such as the politics of language, the curriculum content, quality improvement measures and inclusive education; the misunderstood and maligned *madrasas* (Islamic seminary schools); the struggles of transition from poverty to a middle-class position; and the need for organized political advocacy. It interlaces bold ideas and proposes civil society ownership for implementation of reforms. It proposes that the influential elite should lead as committed stakeholders and recommends long-term public engagement to uphold the changes. It urges action to reduce inequities and promote policies and practices that will even the playing field for the underprivileged. Addressing the important area of quality education, it proposes achievable measures of improvement in academic inputs as well as management efficiencies in the school systems. I believe that Pakistanis are capable of implementing the technical changes needed for reforms but we must employ more effective ways to resolve the complex underlying issues. My optimism is based on first-hand experience over the last twenty years, diligent research, and wide-ranging conversations with numerous educators, activists and reformists of education.

The central character of the book is the quintessential underprivileged Pakistani child. The unrelenting focus is the prevailing social inequity in the country. Deprived of the right to quality education in a feudal system, the disadvantaged child struggles in a divisive, conflict-ridden, principally patriarchal and unjust society. Tyrannical practices persist— not only those of suppression of thought and oppression of rights—but the ongoing injustice of language discrimination, education apartheid, and the inequities of class-based *quality* of education.

Pakistan seriously lacks an effective system of education for its population of children from underprivileged households. Roughly, 80 percent of child-citizens are in this segment of the underprivileged population and only the fortunate ones go to *public* schools in a system which anyhow generally delivers low-grade literacy or mediocre learning at best. The highest quality education is reserved exclusively for the affluent and privileged in private schools which have costs ranging from low to expensive. Combined, the provincial education departments and the Ministry of Federal Education and Professional Training are the largest employers of public servants in the country.[1]

Sadly, there appears to be no urgent mobilization by members of civil society groups to propose viable solutions. Tactically planned, politically smart, citizen-led demand and voices for education reforms are almost entirely missing.

Whether in the media or in casual conversation, the mention of Pakistan evokes an image of a country with many dilemmas: a volatile nation, a burgeoning population, a struggling economy, sporadic violence, endless poverty, poor health services, atrocious environmental practices, governance plagued by corruption of scandalous proportions… and a severely stressed education system with high levels of illiteracy and millions of children not in schools. Regrettably and painfully, those images are accurate. The negative perceptions are a reality. Despite all of that, Pakistan has robust possibilities.

In the chronicles of nations, Pakistan is a young country with a complex historic past. It is a country severely hampered by political, religious, ethnic, and social challenges. Additionally, it has been plagued by mismanagement, poor governance, malfeasance, and erosion of resources by both civilian and military administrations. These realities have shaped Pakistan into a dysfunctional state. In many respects, it is a difficult country to govern and turning it around after decades of mismanagement will not be an easy task. But it also has tremendous potential if the problematic challenges are confronted and seen as opportunities to make change.

In the last decade, Pakistan has been heading towards institutionalization of its democratic civilian governance and recent changes are heartening. But it remains to be seen if good governance and efficient management will take hold or will we have another roller coaster experience. Instant romance with a new set of political leaders, putting them on pedestals, prematurely singing their praises before they've proven themselves worthy of public trust, and having unrealistic expectations of their performance: these traits have been a longstanding weakness in our national culture. Instead, for a change, we should expect our elected leaders to work *for* the citizens and demand better performance, not mere promises of action. Their job is to serve the public good. They must contribute to good policies for social reforms and they must earn our support, or they should be replaced democratically by someone possibly more capable.

'Every country has the government it deserves.' These words are attributed to Joseph de Maistre, an eighteenth-century French lawyer, diplomat, and philosopher. Our expectation should be that Pakistani youth deserve good stewardship. It's time we raised our expectations and directed our leaders to serve the needs of the people, instead of the people being driven like sheep. It's time for social justice. It's time to expect a sound education system grounded in the best values of our cultures, our local languages, and a contemporary curriculum that provides learning of life skills and a path to incremental prosperity. Government leaders and administrations may come and go. But the education system must remain unaffected, steadfast and solid.

At the outset, I acknowledge that I'm an emigrant American citizen from Pakistan, and I include myself in the 'we' both as a Pakistani of origin and as a global citizen. I also include myself among the fortunate and affluent. I am extremely concerned about the bleak future of a large number of Pakistani children. At the same time, I am exceedingly optimistic about the many possibilities of my remarkable home country. Even as we in the Diaspora remain intensely involved citizens of the adopted country, being away does not diminish the love and sincere concern we have for Pakistan. In fact, being away probably drives many of us to do even more with the idea that 'giving back' to our country of origin is an obligation and that our prosperity must be shared. When we are critical, we do not mean to be cynical, hurtful, or condescending. We express our feelings and our views with empathy, because we want to help.

THE ROLE OF CIVIL SOCIETY IN EDUCATION

The principal purpose of the book is to initiate a non-political conversation on primary and secondary education (and to some extent, the entire education ecosystem), to explore how effective voice and civil society action can lead to proposed solutions. These should be considered, debated, implemented, and *sustained* by participation of all segments of Pakistani society led by the elite and middle-class, and including the grassroots ranks. Our education system is in a state of chronic illness. Remedies have been attempted but perhaps not enough, or not the right ones. A question we must ask ourselves: are we ready to apply some uncomfortable remedies to the sick education system? If we have the expertise to execute the technical steps for reforms, then what's missing? Is it resources (answer: maybe), or is it the political will, or is it because we haven't effectively demanded for it to be fixed? In these pages, we will look for answers to those vexing questions through the views of well-informed persons with expertise in the fields of education and development. We will also look for clues in samplings of the work that has been done in the context of reforms, learn which of these efforts are enduring, what's in progress and what can be built upon. We must learn and adopt more forceful ways to deal with the issues and the politics of education.

In recent times, there has been greater global awareness of and emphasis on quality education. Improving quality is probably the supreme challenge within reform and admittedly negligible progress has been made in this area. There is evidence of effort in reform, but perhaps it has not been aggregated into neat building blocks. Though valuable groundwork has been taking place, the momentum has been sluggish and sporadic. Relative to the scale of the problem, the achievements have been modest. The reform efforts have also gone largely unnoticed by average citizens and Diaspora-supporters. Many have become disappointed and hopeless, feeling that the malaise is permanent, that Pakistan's education is doomed forever. The book presents bits and bytes of good news, and also reveals the reality that there is a tremendously difficult task ahead. With time, the monstrous problem is almost guaranteed to grow unless the right steps are taken in short order. Strong civic leadership and a large base of support will be needed to see that those steps are taken and the momentum is sustained into the future.

As the book unfolds and its content is absorbed, you will agree with some information and views. The fact that you're reading this is evidence of your curiosity to learn more through a diversity of opinions. But I urge you to be critical and to challenge anything. Please do not hesitate to offer constructive suggestions for solutions. Explore the references and sources shared here, read up on what's going on in the sphere of education reform, speak with friends and family and motivate them to act by supporting the campaign for better education. It's a never-ending task and we must prepare for the long haul.

First, we can all start by becoming mindful of the suffering of marginalized communities. Walk the dirt roads of the *katchi abadis*— the communities of 'unauthorized' homes in the city slums and the rural countryside. Meet the people who live there. Learn of their aspirations. Explore and study the various initiatives for education. Identify the initiatives that have the vision, the infrastructure and the capacity to create lasting, large-scale impact. Ask how you can support[2] them with volunteer action and grassroots political advocacy, not only with donations. Learn how you can help disadvantaged communities through education, how you can get more children into schools, how you can make the schools deliver better education. Find out where and who the local education bureaucrats are, learn what they do and what more can be done by citizens in the local area to demand better public education. Mobilize support in the community to join in these efforts. Spread the word about your findings and successes. Pursue your leads to create unemotional, objective impact. Ask friends and family to start similar efforts. These are just few examples of how we can build upon civil society action to transform Pakistan's education.

This book is an important project to challenge our assumptions about Pakistan's education landscape. Gleaning from the research of academics, agencies, and think tanks and viewpoints of knowledgeable journalists, and social scientists, I have assimilated diverse perspectives for discussion. Nothing is intended as the final word. This book is not a prescriptive manual of do's and don'ts, nor a collection of concrete policy suggestions. I have tried to create a framework of ideas and aspired goals. I speak for like-minded colleagues and it is our collective hope that this compilation will stimulate discussion and serious study of specific areas such as language issues and quality education.

The promise of the ideas contained in the book is in the hands of its readers as citizens of Pakistan, its well-wishers and supporters of its prosperity. I hope that every person finds information and insights of value because the momentum and direction of future reforms will depend on our collective political will and actions. I am convinced that we will need well-directed advocacy and constructive activism for effective change in policy and it must involve leaders from civic society. I reiterate these points to be deliberately redundant and drive home their importance. So, what is the aspired takeaway from the book? There's more than one:

1. Please do not be overwhelmed by past failures of the governance and mismanagement as it affects the education system. There are also many good things happening. Learn about them.

2. Please do make constructive suggestions, but please don't jump to hasty conclusions or offer advice impulsively. Explore all aspects of the issues with patience and an open mind. Learn the facts, especially at the policy and political level. Learn how the politics affects the system and what everyone can do to advocate for a sound, sustainable education system. And please be especially courteous to people you may not agree with. For the bigger goal, we must learn to differ with respect and grace.

3. More money *is* needed but more money is not the only answer. The solution must begin with greater involvement and commitment of every parent, every citizen, and all supporters far and near. Education must be valued for its own sake and for the development of every child in preparation for life as a tolerant and balanced adult, regardless of the choices she makes in life.

4. We must believe that education provides the best possible tools to achieve a way out of the vicious, multi-generational cycle of illiteracy and poverty.

5. Learn and be confident in the belief that poverty can be overcome with equitable opportunity for every child to receive quality education and achieve her potential in life.

WHY THE BOOK, AND WHO SHOULD BE WRITING IT?

Reasonable questions, both. Because I straddle Pakistan and the US, I feel I can present the issues of Pakistani education on both sides of the world. But let me begin at the point when the very idea for the book germinated. It was in a conversation at The Citizens Foundation (TCF) a few years ago. A short list of US writers was briefly discussed but nothing came of it because there was too much going on at TCF. As always, decisions couldn't be made, and the book idea was shelved.

My moment of commitment to writing the book was in the summer of 2015 on a six-day hike with my son Ali, about 15,000 ft up in the Hindu Kush-Karakoram mountains north of Chitral. (I love to be in the mountains). Over breakfast at camp with Ali, I shared my audacious thought of writing the book. Given my interest in education reform and a twenty-year history with TCF, I felt confident that I would be able to take on the project. Little did I know that it would be a long, three-year period of learning and writing. The ideas began to rapidly incubate, and the excitement mounted. I shared my thoughts and outline for the book with friends and I know I surprised TCF leaders by announcing that I was going to write 'the book'. I began to gather content and record conversations. As I dove into the research and writing phase, it was satisfying to experience the increasing scope of the book to include the broader landscape of the K-12 education system. On several trips to Pakistan, I met with key people in academic circles of Karachi, Lahore, and Islamabad and also travelled to Khyber Pakhtunkhwa, Gilgit-Baltistan, Balochistan and remote areas of Sindh to see the rural landscape at first hand.

I assumed I knew a fair amount about education in Pakistan. Even as I completed the writing, I realized how little I knew. I discovered that there's much more to learn about the complexities of education and my desire for information has been aroused to a greater degree. I am energized by new knowledge of the issues and also feel a sense of responsibility that the multi-dimensional perspectives I have gathered must be shared with others. In my learning, several sources and references led me to a maze of more trails of information and the challenge was to decide where to draw the line and what would be of value to readers. I've also become a keen student of social sciences and what began as writing about education, soon became a quest for more knowledge about the sociology of education and the intense historical, social, and political aspects of education.

I can assume that there are thousands of ordinary people (like me) who would like to support improvements in education but probably don't know where to start or how to join in the action. To these readers, I say: with the book in your hands, you are now a part of the conversation. Your interest in education is evident and so is your desire to help steer it on the right course. Read and share the ideas contained here, whether or not you agree. Change begins with thoughts. I encourage you to voice your thoughts. Spread the word. Act with compassion for the children of Pakistan.

The fascinating personal stories and conversations I collected gave me inspiration. And I hope the message and stories will touch your heartstrings as well. I am also grateful for the freedom to express my own thoughts, perhaps naïve at times. But I firmly believe in my thoughts as I have laid them out. And I should add a writer's disclaimer that, in many sections of the book, the thoughts and opinions are entirely mine and do not reflect the policies and beliefs of the TCF organization, its leadership or management or, for that matter, the policy and thoughts of any other organization.

THE STORY OF THE CITIZENS FOUNDATION (TCF)

Without leaps of imagination…we lose the excitement of possibilities.
Dreaming, after all…is a form of planning.
Gloria Steinem, feminist journalist and social political activist

Is TCF a dream journey, an emotional response to a need, or a planned initiative? Is the story of TCF a study of a wild experiment in correcting the flaws of a dysfunctional society? Probably all of these.

The stories of people doing good work must be told, because such stories don't always make news. Like folklore and legend, the story of TCF is worthy of being passed down through generations. The TCF family is relatively young, getting close to twenty-five years old now. But history has been made already. The story will continue to evolve and likely be the subject of conversations in the future. The most important reason for the TCF story to be included in this book is because the story needs to be preserved in the annals of Pakistan's educational history. The impact of TCF has been to take education to where there were no schools or very poor schools. There is also no doubt that TCF has significantly influenced public consciousness about the inequities in education. It has created national awareness that education is a human right for all children and their families, that social change for uplift of living standards begins with good education, and that depriving disadvantaged families of their right to education is a grave social injustice.

Writing the book has been a voyage of immense personal fulfillment. I gathered several books, reports, and documents, plus information and recordings from visits to dozens of schools and the TCF head office, and from conversations with global TCF leaders and several experts working in education reform. I must have recorded more than a hundred hours of interviews, translated many from Urdu, and edited them for length and clarity. A profound regret is that I was unable to contact a few notable persons that I had wanted to, especially Dr Pervez Hoodbhoy. Also, because of space limitations, the other regret is that I had to be selective and drop some interviews that were recorded and transcribed. The important thing is that we will end up with a book which serves the long-term needs of education reform.

ORGANIZATION OF THE BOOK

The book begins with the foreword written by Shashi Buluswar, an expert in global development and a strong advocate for education and development in Pakistan. Chapter 1 contains historically significant markers and events, including landmark legislation in 2010 which made education mandatory for 5 to 16-year-olds (but not for the first time) and pledged that primary and secondary K-10 education was to be provided by the state, at no cost. More than a decade later, the state is still struggling with universal education as the number of out-of-school children (OOSC) remains a huge challenge. Also, in Chapter 1 is an overview of the various systems of education running in parallel and somewhat autonomously in an unregulated, disorganized environment. These systems include the public schools, the low-cost private schools (LCPS), a fairly sizable layer of medium-cost private schools, the 'A Level' Cambridge-British K-12 schools system and finally, the *madrasa* system of Islamic seminary schools. Chapter 2 is exclusively about the fine work of The Citizens Foundation, a non-profit which has structured its model for education management in a national network of 1567 schools (as of 2019). Chapter 3 highlights the bright side, the fascinating personal stories of star achievers and illustrates that quality education is changing families and communities and helping to reduce the gender gap and disparities when comparable education opportunities are made available. Chapter 5 makes the case for equity—essentially, the opportunity for education on a level playing field. The sections on poverty to prosperity should be of interest to all and are followed by an essay on inclusive education. Intensely moving is a conversation with an education activist and planner with Teach For Pakistan. There are select excerpts from *The New York Times* columnist Nicholas Kristof and his wife Sheryl WuDunn on how compassionate action can produce change in the development trajectory of mismanaged countries. The madrasas, and the influence of Islamic culture in Pakistani society, particularly their impact on education, are of personal interest to me. Chapter 6 includes commentaries on the role of the madrasa as a social institution; a report on my visits to madrasas and my conversations with scholars (*ulama*) and students (*talaba* or *talibaan* in Persian); my views on why madrasas should be acknowledged as institutions of education; and how they can be helped to improve the quality of teaching of the non-religious components of education. The discussions also address the culture of charitable giving in Islam, and how *zakat* can be redirected to supporting education for social change. The essentials of education reform are detailed in Chapter 7 and include suggestions for quality inputs such as training and content knowledge of teachers, textbooks, curriculum, pedagogy, assessment and systems management. There is discussion of a proposed national agency for mandatory registration of all schools in the country. I am proposing that the same agency should also have the capacity and mandate to monitor and rate the quality of education in all schools. Additionally, the agency should have the capability to drive improvements in quality. I expect these ideas to stimulate lively discussion and I look forward to the debates. I shall defend my thoughts respectfully, and I am always open to learning. The chapter closes with discussion on the perceptions of quality in Pakistani K-12 education and high expectations in the schools of Silicon Valley, California. The three appendices have been contributed by dedicated Pakistani academics to whom I am deeply indebted. I am confident readers will find their writings to be enlightening and of immense value. In the Postscript, I share how you can be a participant in the campaign for change in education but for that first you need to know the landscape and the complexities of the challenges. We do not need passive spectators. Active participation is important, and we will need enthusiastic 'change makers' to join ranks.

Most chapters are divided into numbered sections for easier reading. The sections are essays pieced together on subjects that I hope are of relevance to readers. Occasionally, the narrative and conversations in the book take a distressing deep dive into disturbing social dilemmas such as the unthinkable living conditions, cruel corruption and unconscionable treatment of the marginalized poor in Pakistan. Like most people, I strive to be sensitive to the plight of the poor and disadvantaged. But it has shocked me to the core to learn more of the cultural marginalization, social exclusion and relegation of the disadvantaged poor to the fringes of our society. At times, the discussions are poignant and intense, perhaps to the point of anguish. (Read Tooba Akhtar's thoughts on poverty in Chapter 4). The discussions are intended to provoke debate on the state of social injustice and to put human faces on the statistics. In interviews, I have tried to pose leading questions to stimulate a discussion. In some instances, the questions and conversations have given me an opportunity to make a statement, speak my mind or present useful information.

It is my hope that the book will be of global interest for readers everywhere. It is also expected that the book and more writings on education reform will be discussed, examined and debated in formal forums and informal chatrooms as well as in college classrooms, in cafes and living rooms, at family dinners—and, eventually at the influential executive boardrooms in the country.

In a broadcast message very shortly after the birth of Pakistan, Mohammed Ali Jinnah, the revered first head of state, said, 'Without education it is complete darkness and with education it is light. Education is a matter of life and death to our nation. The world is moving so fast that if you do not educate yourselves you will be not only completely left behind but [you] will be finished up. [...] No sacrifice of time or personal comfort should be regarded too great for the advancement of the cause of education.'

With that somber message, I welcome you to *Agents of Change*. I am hopeful that, as you flip the pages, you will have an awakening discussion with yourself, and through that introspection, you will have views to express and constructive suggestions to offer. I hope that you will feel an urge to get involved and support educational reforms. Those of us who have worked in support of education may feel a degree of satisfaction in what's been achieved thus far but this is not the time to pat ourselves on the back, not yet. There's much more to be done. Just as important, I hope that your first thoughtful takeaway from this book will be an earnest desire to find out more of what's happening both on the surface and behind the scenes in Pakistan's education. In other words, how can you—and each one of us—be an 'Agent of Change'.

Notes

1. Nadia Naviwala, *Pakistan's Education Crisis: The Real Story* (Wilson Center, 2016), p. 8.
2. Financial contributions are valuable when they are directed to a larger social need, like education. And giving to the right initiative is important for the organizations to carry out their mission and sustain their strategically planned programs. We should rethink contributing because it 'feels good' and give thought instead to how the funds are utilized and the social impact they create.

Chapter One

Fixing the Problematic Education System

A COMMITMENT AND CELEBRATION

The labor of research, compilation, and scripting of this book is dedicated to the plight of underprivileged Pakistani children and the disadvantaged communities affected by the dismal state of the education system. This book is an open invitation for dialog to adopt solutions. It is also a signal and commitment that the poor and uneducated are not forgotten. If the national conscience is stirred, we can hope that this effort will turn into a rallying point for social change led by education reforms.

We salute student achievers who have climbed the grueling academic ladder. The book is a celebration of their success. We are especially proud of the accomplishments of achievers from underprivileged families who have overcome the barriers of class and persevere to make it out of the cycle of poverty. They have defied the heavy odds of meager resources, class bias, gender disparity, and cultural struggles. Their achievements have been made possible by their own hard work and by opportunities provided by generous benefactors. Gaining the proverbial level playing field in education has given them a fair chance to improve their future economic and social status. These achievers are Agents of Change who will keep the ball rolling for future generations. Their teachers and benefactors are the *Angels* of Change who set the ball in motion with compassion and the vision that education is the essential institution needed for nation building. This is where Pakistan's national reorganization must begin.

The numbers of educated Pakistani youth are growing but not fast enough, relative to the growth in population numbers. The achievers are the few in a small minority who have received the gift of education and have a head start in the race for better opportunity. But it is the huge number of victims of illiteracy and endless poverty who will need our continuing compassion and mindful attention. The uneducated and

13

poor don't have a voice. They don't know how to use their voice. We, the elite and the educated, must be a surrogate voice and the force for changes in education of the underprivileged.

1.1 Whose Problem...*and Who Will Fix It?*

In our context, 'fix' is a concise, three-letter verb that has many positive associations—like repair, mend, correct, renovate, resolve, overhaul, and restore to the ideal state. Regardless of how we perceive fixing it, I propose that we should settle for nothing short of fixing Pakistan's education by rebuilding the broken system. As we have seen from past experience, patch-work cannot fix it. The piecemeal approach insidiously and selectively feeds the corrupt, self-serving bureaucracies of public education while the twin problems of school shortage and poor quality of education continue to grow and fester.

With regard to who will fix it, clearly the obligation is incumbent on Pakistani problem solvers: its public leaders, policy makers, citizens, civil society organizations and its empathetic worldwide Diaspora. Fixing it is not the responsibility of the rest of the world. Should we be grateful to development partners for aid and initiatives which have had mixed or unsustainable results? The failed reform efforts have been expensive in time and resources and responsible for contributing to major setbacks in development. Future partnerships for development should be selected and tailored to project-specific requirements rather than for political benefit or diplomatic visibility.

Some reform efforts in education are making progress but clearly not fast enough, perhaps only in sporadic spurts of activity. It is an understatement that social change is needed in many areas of Pakistani life. To accelerate social change, educational reform must be driven by a select group of innovative leaders[1] and social entrepreneurs, with major support coming from the elite. A large number of citizens must join the effort for the long haul with a solid foundational understanding of the complex issues and be capable of patiently, persistently working on reform solutions and ongoing oversight of the system. We should be looking for incremental and consistent progress in the reform process. There is no quick fix.

1.2 Select Milestones in Pakistan's Education History

Pakistan is a nation with a choppy history of institution building. Ever since its birth, the process of constructing a sound public education system has just not gathered steam or gained sufficient traction. As a result, the system is broken and dysfunctional. Restructuring a broken system and establishing a balanced, modern education system is a complex challenge, especially in a multicultural environment with strong feudal leanings. So, for purpose of the book, it is prudent to start with a few historical milestones and a brief account of events that took place along the way. The history tutorial is an overview of salient events and lays a foundation for better understanding of the complicated past challenges. The list of events is not complete by any measure, and the actions illustrate that the failed and awkward efforts lacked the strength of building blocks upon which a comprehensive system could be constructed. The embarrassing outcomes also affirm the obvious, that not enough was done—due to bad circumstances, political upheavals, disappointing let-downs, or whatever reason. In any case, despite numerous policy statements, conferences, reports and studies, there isn't much to show as tangible results. On one hand, the pitiful fact is that little has been accomplished and a huge problem is staring us in the face. On the other hand, a moderate amount has been achieved in terms of reform but very little is publicly known about these efforts. In the following chapters, we will attempt to share where we are, what's been accomplished, and what more can be done.

Historically, education has been the foundation for economic progress and the scaffolding for societal advancement. But Pakistan's civil society and the government administrations have struggled to find reform solutions. Past governments have been in a daze, going in different directions and wondering what to do next. And all this while the powerful political machine of the education complex has continued to erode, obstruct, or weaken reform efforts to its own corrupt advantage. However, there are signs of a revitalized approach and there is renewed optimism for reform. For tangible evidence of improvement, we can hope that the rhetoric will translate into actionable results and education will take the top spot on the list of national priorities.

Invariably, all movements for new nationhood begin with hope and optimism. That was true for the creation of Pakistan as well. Unfortunately, the 1947 Partition of British-India and the birth of

Pakistan were marred by problems that linger to this day and have severely affected Pakistan's development in a number of ways.

Select Milestones[2]

14 August 1947: British India was partitioned. Pakistan became an independent state with two wings, East and West Pakistan. In 1971, East Pakistan would become the independent state of Bangladesh which is on a good trajectory of social change and progress.

24 September 1947: In a formal address, Mohammad Ali Jinnah, the first head of state, proclaimed: 'Education is a matter of life and death for Pakistan. The world is progressing so rapidly that without the requisite advance in education, not only shall we be left behind others, but we may be wiped out altogether.'

1947: The National Education Conference recommended that universalization of primary education should be achieved within a period of twenty years. The Conference formed a special committee on primary and secondary education which considered it 'essential that a national system of education should be based on the strong foundations of free and compulsory primary education.' It also addressed the issues of medium of instruction (language) and teacher training. Another Committee suggested setting up a system of Adult Education, closely linked with compulsory primary education.

1951: The National Plan for Educational Development, 1951–57 was adopted at an education conference.

1957: The First Five-Year Plan 1955–1960, was launched in December 1957 and stated that '...a system of universal primary education is imperative. Primary education is essential to prepare citizens for the discharge of their democratic and civic responsibilities and to provide them with equal opportunities for economic and cultural advancement.' The Plan proposed adding 4,000 more public schools to the 15,602 in existence and addressed the organizational and management aspects of primary education at the local level 'constituting local school management committees and district advisory boards [to be] elected by members of the community.'

1958: A Commission on National Education was appointed by the Government of Pakistan.

1958: The first military coup took place.

1959: The Report of the Commission on National Education and the Education Policy chastised citizens for their poor perception of public service workers and government and lamented that less than half the children of primary-school age were enrolled in schools. It recommended eight years of compulsory education to make the child 'functionally literate' and set a target of achieving universal enrollment by 1975. The Policy also called for curriculum reform, for religious education to be made compulsory, and for teaching in the 'national languages' of Urdu and Bangla.

1960: The Second Five-Year Plan 1960–65, allocated Rs 990 million for primary education. The Plan was critical of the disappointing results of the previous five years: of the 4,000 additional schools planned, only 2,400 primary schools were added; no significant improvements occurred in the quality of school education; primary school enrollment increased by only 440,000 when the Plan had intended to increase enrollment by one million. The Second Plan provided for opening of 15,200 additional primary schools to the 18,000 existing schools. These efforts were expected to increase primary school enrollment in West Pakistan by 1.2 million, raising the primary enrollment rate from 36 to 56 percent. Improving curriculum content and teacher training were emphasized. The education of girls received special attention: '...of the 4.7 million children presently attending primary schools (1960), only 1.1 million [less than 25 percent] are girls.'

1965: The Third Five-Year Plan, 1965–70, allocated Rs 2,652 million to primary education and recognized '...education as a vital national investment and a major determination of the nation's economic growth.' It claimed that 2 million more children were brought into primary schools during this period, against a target of 1.2 million. The Third Plan proposed to increase enrollment from 45 to 70 percent with the additional enrollment of 2.8 million children in primary schools by 1970. The Plan proposed 42,500 new schools in West Pakistan. Attention was also focused on improving teacher retention, teacher training, teacher salaries, teaching aids, and the physical condition of schools. The Third Plan was effectively abandoned with the outbreak of major civic disorder in 1968, leading to the fall of the government in March 1969.

1970: The New Education Policy 1970, reaffirmed the government's commitment to universal elementary education. It lamented that Pakistan had one of the highest rates of illiteracy in the world, stressing that the challenge of '…sustaining and accelerating economic development would remain unfulfilled' and aimed for universal primary enrollment by 1980, with emphasis on achieving gender parity. The 1970 Policy was never implemented due to outbreak of war with India, secession of East Pakistan, and the collapse of the military government.

1972: The Education Policy 1972–1980, aimed to eradicate illiteracy through universalization of primary and secondary education and an ambitious adult education program, with equal access to education for women and underprivileged groups, and programs of inclusive education for the challenged population. The Policy would be interrupted mid-stream in 1977 by another military coup, leading to a significant shift in education priorities.

1973: The Constitution of the Islamic Republic of Pakistan (Article 37-B, 1973) proclaimed: 'The state shall be responsible for eradication of illiteracy and provision of free and compulsory education up to secondary level, within minimum possible time.'

1973: After the separation of East Pakistan (Bangladesh), the Fourth Five-year Plan had been abandoned in the commotion and political confusion of the time. Under Z.A. Bhutto, only annual plans were prepared, and they were largely ignored. The Five-Year Plan was replaced with a program of nationalization, which featured a high level of government ownership and management of private entities and schools.

1975: Private schools were nationalized by the Z.A. Bhutto civilian administration and operated as public schools, with exemptions granted to most elite schools including all private schools which subscribed to the Cambridge system. The government take-over of private schools was reversed after a few years.

1977: Another military coup. General Zia-ul-Haq took over and imposed an ultra-conservative religious ideology that has had a significant and lasting impact on the curriculum. Education suffered a major setback.

1978: The Fifth Five-Year Plan 1978–1983, bemoaned the past neglect of primary education and proclaimed '…a fundamental reordering of national priorities in favor of primary education' and aimed at 'a comprehensive approach towards primary education; augmentation of physical facilities; measures to reduce the drop-out rate (from 50 to 40 percent); improvement in the quality of teaching and better supervision.' The Plan proposed allocation of 33 percent of development expenditure for primary education. High priority was given to rapid expansion in girls' enrollment (from 33 to 45 percent) and 12,641 additional primary schools.

1979: The National Education Policy and Implementation Program 1979, repeated the lament that '...nearly half the nation's children and two-thirds of the girls do not go to primary schools.' The Policy proposed an Implementation Program which included the opening of 13,000 new primary schools, establishing 5,000 'mosque schools' for boys, and 5,000 *mohalla* (neighborhood) schools for girls.

1982: An Academy of Educational Planning and Management was established and charged with the responsibilities of 'capacity building of educational planners and managers, consolidating and collating education statistics, maintaining comprehensive national database, and conducting policy research to facilitate preparation of educational policies.'

1982: The Sixth Five-Year Plan approached primary education with 'serious efforts to institute universal education' and a target to increase enrollment in primary schools from 48 to 75 percent by 1987. This implied, unrealistically, that more than 5 million additional children were to be provided with primary schooling, an increase of 80 percent over the base-year enrollment of 6.8 million children.

1984: A National Literacy Plan 1984–1986, was launched at a cost of Rs 317 million to raise the literacy rate from 26.2 to 33 percent. The Plan envisioned opening more than 25,000 literacy centers for adults.

1988: The Seventh Five-Year Plan 1988–1993, stated: 'Primary education facilities are available to only 60 percent of the children in the age group of 5 to 9 years. Primary schools lack physical facilities; about 29,000 primary schools have no buildings and 16,000 schools have only one classroom. Rural primary schools are beset with a shortage of trained and qualified female teachers and teacher absenteeism is high.' The Plan acknowledged that '...there is no substitute for formal education.' It estimated that the literacy rate would rise to about 80 percent by the end of 1999 and proposed to provide every child in the age group of 5 to 9 access to a school within a radius of 1.5 km by 1992–1993, '...so that no child is deprived of basic education due to unavailability of a school within a reachable distance.'

1990: The National Education Management Information System (NEMIS) was established to 'collate, consolidate, and analyze national education data and generate useful information for policy makers, planners, education managers and decision makers.' Since 1992, NEMIS has published the annual Pakistan Education Statistics Report and also provided planning data and indicators to the government, international agencies, and other stakeholders.

1992: The National Education Policy 1992, complained of disappointing outcomes due to limited financial resources, poor definition of educational priorities, inadequate delivery system, rapid population growth, and vacillating policy on the medium of instruction.

1999: Another military coup.

2007: LEAPS Report[3] was published. The survey covered 1,200 schools in Punjab and monitors enrollment, learning outcomes, and other factors over a four-year period 2003–2007. Significant conclusions of the report were: national enrollment increased by 10 percent, from 51 to 61 percent (2001–2005); the number of private schools increased by 32 percent from 32,000 to 47,000 (2000–2005); in the period 2000–2005, enrollment of girls in Punjab schools was up by 14 percent; there was a proliferation of private schools in villages and small towns. The survey stated that every third child in school was enrolled in a private school and that was interpreted as 'increased demand for better quality'.

2009: The Enhanced Partnership with Pakistan Act of 2009, better known as the Kerry–Lugar Bill, was signed into US law by President Obama, allocating $7.5 billion to Pakistan from 2010 to 2014 at $1.5 billion per year, to be invested in healthcare, education, social services, and humanitarian assistance. Generally, the US media reports left out specific restrictions and omissions within the Bill. In the days following signing of the legislation, controversial reactions to the legislation erupted in Pakistan as the language and spirit of the Kerry–Lugar Bill were interpreted by the Pakistan Army as being derogatory, restrictive, and possibly having sinister 'motives of control'. The sentiments and stance of the military leadership forced the Pakistan government to decline the aid. This period was tumultuous for Pakistani politics as it followed the resignation of President (General) Musharraf in 2008 and the uncertainties of transition to democracy. The Kerry–Lugar Bill enjoyed significant support in some circles and was eagerly anticipated because the funding was to bypass dysfunctional government institutions in favor of grassroots programs, NGOs, and local institutions, intending to bring tangible benefits directly to the people. Specific outcomes of the Kerry–Lugar Bill and funding were unclear as my research did not find conclusive data. The programs and funding were probably cancelled, covered up, and forgotten: an opportunity lost for education and for Pakistan because its civil society was not ready to deal with the politics of the situation at that time.

2010: A Pakistan Education Task Force was formed, jointly by the Pakistan and British governments. In the words of co-chair Sir Michael Barber, 'Its work is…given high priority by the UK DFID [and] represents a concerted effort to bring together seven eminent leaders of Pakistan's education system with major business and civil society representatives [including TCF co-founder Ahsan Saleem], donors and global experts to enhance the chance of success. The challenge of education reform in Pakistan is not a lack of ideas or experiments; it is one of scale, capacity to deliver and political will to tackle some longstanding binding constraints. The Task Force has no intention of writing yet another report; it is working…to assist provinces with the task of implementation and of ensuring that intent at system level translates into results at classroom level.'

2010: Constitutional Amendment for Universal Education: Article 25A of the 18th Amendment to the Constitution, was signed into law, stating 'The State shall provide free and compulsory education to all children of the age of five to sixteen years in such manner as may be determined by law.'

2011: The Annual Status of Education Report 2011 (ASER) was published as a household-based national survey led by Idara-e-Taleem-o-Aagahi (ITA), assessing the learning outcomes of children aged 5–16. It was conducted in 3,642 public and private schools in 84 rural and 3 urban districts. The ASER 2011 survey collected information on enrollment, achievement, and learning quality for 143,826 children (41 percent girls) from 48,646 households in 2502 villages in rural Pakistan. ASER 2011 also collected data on literacy from 50,473 mothers.

2013: Sir Michael Barber published an essay 'The Good News from Pakistan' and expounded on how a revolutionary new approach to education reform in Punjab showed the way forward for Pakistan and for development aid everywhere. He famously stated, 'This time it's going to be different,' but conceded: 'Early in my involvement with Pakistan's education system, I called the country the biggest education reform challenge on the planet.'

2017: Annual Report: Pakistan Education Statistics 2016–17 was published by NEMIS.

2019: A preliminary 2018[4] Annual Status of Education Report (ASER) was released in February 2019. It reported that learning was improving but not fast enough. The ASER data from 2014 to 2018 for grade 5 showed improving trends at the national level in Urdu, mathematics, and English. Quality of teaching was emphasized again, and the report stated: 'One intervention alone will not raise standards in teaching across Pakistan; a range of tools and approaches that support better teaching are required. Good teaching is intrinsically linked with good school leadership, which applies and monitors standards and targets.' The report proposed setting targets and monitoring progress with 'more and better-quality data on how well children are learning…' and added that 'The Citizens Foundation has demonstrated how this can be done effectively in Pakistan'.

Author's note: The historical events and education conferences resulted in elaborate planning, formation of agencies, and stacks of policy statements. Reports produced were complete with essential jargon of bureaucratic and development expertise but lacked actionable items, realistic goals, or accountability.

1.3 The Systems and Inequities in Pakistan's K-12 Education

K-10, Matriculation: Generally, the K-10 Matriculation system is the domain of the public schools, and the low-cost and medium-cost private schools, which typically offer Urdu as the medium of instruction. To be competitive in the private school market, some 'English-medium' schools are upgrading from the K-10 system to the Cambridge 'A Level' system.

A typical schooling experience for the Pakistani child may start at the age of 4 when she/he enters a pre-school nursery classroom, also called KG-One or *Katchi* One. The following year, she will move up to kindergarten, KG-Two, or *Katchi* Two. The next jump is to Class One, or first grade, at the age of 6, serially progressing thereafter to grade 10 or Matriculation. The public schools start at grade one without pre-school or kindergarten programs. In broad strokes, this describes the K-10 Matriculation or Matric system of the government schools and low-cost private schools (LCPS). The network of TCF schools are K-10 with a pre-kindergarten (nursery) class for the 4-year-olds in more than 200[5] primary schools. The most common medium of instruction (MOI) and textbooks are Urdu, the widely spoken *lingua franca* which is the national language. Use of regional, native, and mother tongue languages varies considerably and may be adopted in the early grades in some regions or provinces, depending on local community demand. With few exceptions, the books and classroom interaction are in Urdu regardless of the child's first language (L1) or mother tongue spoken at home. Provincial language policy[6] and practices are unsettled and have gone through several changes.

Urdu is generally taught either as the first language L1 or as the second language L2 if a native language or mother tongue has been used earlier. Orally, English is sprinkled in with traditional nursery rhymes and very basic reading-writing skills. English is taught as a language L2 or L3, typically starting in grade 3 or 4. The acute shortage of English teachers and the absence of uniform language policy contribute to inconsistency and confusion in the curriculum, books, pedagogy, and student learning. For parents who can afford to send the child to medium-cost schools (from Rs 1,000 and above, per month), the faulty perception is that learning in English means overall better quality and is a factor in the selection of a school that claims to offer 'English medium' teaching, though in reality the school may be a hybrid Urdu-English environment with very limited English in the mix. The MOI is English in very few mid-tier private schools.

Tuition Fees: The public schools are free, nationally. Private school fees vary considerably depending on the location and other factors. The low-cost private school (LCPS) fees typically range from as low as 25 to 1,000 rupees per month. Medium-cost private schools have a wider range and may charge between 1,000 and 10,000 rupees, again depending on several factors; the tiers are not clearly defined. Schools for middle-class families may charge between 10,000 to 25,000 rupees and the top-of-the-line elite private schools are 25,000 rupees and even as high as 50,000 rupees per month.

Quality, Language and Curriculum: Perceived quality of the education delivered is often based on whether or not English is the MOI. In the absence of a quality-rating system or reliable criteria to evaluate school quality, a higher tuition fee influences another possibly erroneous assumption that higher cost means better quality. At the floor of the education quality scale is the free education in public schools and its presumed poor quality. The benchmark is often set by the family at whatever is affordable or seems most reasonable. Most parents, especially if they haven't received much formal education themselves, lack the ability to evaluate or compare important quality inputs of teacher training, books, curriculum, facilities, management or extra-curricular programs at the schools being considered. If a choice is to be made, the decision factors are usually the family budget, which school is conveniently located and whether the school is 'English-medium'.

TCF has consistently and wisely stayed with Urdu as the MOI in its schools and offers a model of good school infrastructure, efficient management, quality education inputs (curriculum, books, teacher training), easy access in the neighborhood (short walking distance), and affordability based on a liberal sliding fee scale. There is an all-women faculty of teachers and principals at all TCF schools which gives a sense of security to parents and encourages enrollment and retention of girls. TCF introduces rudimentary English in the earlier grades and teaches English as a language, starting in 3rd grade.

Primary and Secondary grades: K-5 is the primary school and grades 6–10 are in secondary school. In rural areas, there may be a 'middle school' where 6th to 8th grades have been added to a primary school.

Assessment: In the K-10 Matric system, the standard testing and assessment are done in the 9th and 10th grades, with examinations conducted by the local secondary boards of education. There is no standardized or system-wide testing at the end of primary school.

The Intermediate College (grades 11 and 12): After grade 10 Matriculation, there's the two-year Intermediate College for grades 11 and 12, technically the 'higher secondary certificate' or HSC, also called 'Inter'. These are typically free-standing college institutes, perhaps a vestige of an archaic system inherited from British India, which serve as the bridge between secondary school and college or university education. It is a mystery why the typical college bachelor's degree can be obtained in only two more years after grade 12 or Intermediate College, although there are some exceptions to this, such as the four-year bachelor's program at IBA and other universities, and the five-year professional programs in medical universities. The tracks or branches of study in Intermediate College are the arts and humanities, science or commerce (business) that determine the professional track a student will follow in a bachelor's or master's program, which makes Intermediate College and the grade 12th test scores critical for obtaining university admission and for career options. Testing and assessment at this level are carried out by the local Higher Secondary Board of Education, now called the Intermediate Board. In most cases, the quality of education in 'inter' is not the same as the superior quality of the 'A Level' diploma of the Cambridge system, which is an easy ticket to the best universities. The 'A Level' student bypasses the Intermediate College and goes directly to a college or university program.

Language of Instruction in the Intermediate College: When the Urdu-medium matric graduate enters Intermediate College, probably with poor skills in English, math and computer usage, she immediately faces a serious problem because the MOI abruptly changes from Urdu to English and all teaching and books are in English. The Matric graduate aiming for acceptance at a top university almost always has to supplement her learning with extra tutoring in English and other subjects to boost her chances of doing well in the SAT-equivalent entrance test for a Tier 1 or Tier 2 university program.

The Cambridge System, K-12: In the early 1970s, there were a handful of private K-12 schools subscribing to the British-Cambridge system and these were in the major cities where affordability was not an issue. There was a major shift in the 1970s led by growing affluence and parental concerns that the Matriculation certificate and secondary education standards were inadequate and not readily accepted by colleges and universities in other countries. That is probably what started the proliferation of the 'A Level' phenomenon of the Cambridge K-12 system and there are presently hundreds of these excellent, expensive, elite private schools, which are affordable only by the affluent in Pakistan.

The cost of a Cambridge system K-12 education can run to over Rs 25,000 per month, and even higher, plus the premium admission fees and extras added on. The education quality is the highest in the country with management controls, curriculum, testing, teaching and assessment standards set and supervised by the Cambridge examining and accreditation authorities in the UK. English is the MOI and Urdu is L2. Additional languages are also offered such as French, Mandarin, and others. These elite private schools are experiencing high demand from the affluent and growing upper middle-class. The glaring disparities in quality between the K-10 matric and K-12 Cambridge systems have further increased the inequities in the national education landscape.

The Madrasa System: Contrary to media images of madrasas, they are not unique to Pakistan and they are not a recent phenomenon. A madrasa system of Islamic seminary schools had been in vogue for over a century in pre-partition India and several larger and smaller madrasas still exist for the huge Muslim Indian population which, by most reports, is relatively lesser-educated and in a lower socioeconomic demographic primarily because of lack of education.

In addition to traditional Islamic teaching and recitation-study of the Quran, the madrasa schools in Pakistan provide general education to varying degrees in the local native language or in Urdu. Madrasas may also teach Arabic to facilitate Qur'anic study and a few include English as an add-on language in the later classes for senior students who may aspire for university programs. The madrasa system generally caters to the poorer and more conservative communities and many or most madrasas subscribe to a *wafaq* or board similar to the boards of education for traditional schools.

1.4 Education Inequalities and Social Imbalance

Talent is universal, but opportunity is not. Expanding
opportunities benefits not only those individuals
but also enriches the entire society.

– Nicholas Kristof, author and columnist, *The New York Times*

It is estimated that less than 20 percent of the school-going youth are receiving fair-to-good (and in some cases, excellent) education, but these are children from middle-class and affluent families who can afford the high tuition fees in the expensive private schools. Except for tiny pockets and small networks of reasonably good quality schools in the LCPS[7] group (including the TCF network), the other 80 percent of school-going children are generally getting a poor-to-mediocre learning experience, either in the public system, the LCPS, or medium-cost private schools. Do these inequities in education accentuate and potentially increase the prevailing social imbalance between the rich and the poor? Over time, the stark differences and inequities in education do create a serious social divide and cultural imbalance, which is increasingly apparent in everyday life. The schools and the education systems have become a virtual division and line of social distinction between the haves and have-nots of Pakistani society.

The students and youth are not the wrongdoers in creating the gulf and class-based systems. The responsibility must be pinned squarely on the thoughtless actions or inactions of those accountable for the neglect and slackness in the K-10 Matriculation system. They did not foresee the social inequalities and drastic widening of the opportunity gap between the well-educated and the poorly-educated. And why should this be of any serious concern? Because inequalities in opportunity create tensions and struggles between social classes, whereas efforts to level the playing field and offering of equal opportunity result in social advancement[8] of the underprivileged, building of social capital, and harmony between socio-economic classes.

But, how did this disparity happen? Did proliferation of the superior system of elite K-12 Cambridge schools create the disparity, or did the mediocre K-10 Matriculation system allow the disparity to get worse by not delivering improved quality to the population segment it serves? Both phenomena probably happened in tandem, not sequentially. In all fairness, the affluent have the absolute right to subscribe to a system that they desire and are willing to pay for, such as the K-12 Cambridge system, as long as the higher-cost system does not ostensibly harm the population segment that is left out due to affordability, and the superior system does not receive any public monies.

Many of my friends of Pakistani origin are from the affluent elite, who are generous givers to social and charitable causes. However, our culpability may lie in the underlying fact that as long as children from our affluent homes receive the best education available, we (the affluent) probably have little or no sensitivity to the disparities in the education systems, or the wider social inequities that are made worse by the difference in schooling systems. Should we have anticipated that the K-10 Matriculation system was incapable of incrementally improving its quality and management, and that the expanding social split created by the education gap would only get worse with time? Should we have intervened on behalf of the underprivileged and aggressively advocated for better education also for the poor children? What probably happened is that we, the elite, were content that a superior Cambridge system had become more readily available for our own children. The plight of the poor was neglected. No thought was given to the declining quality of education in the K-10 Matriculation system. In this, I regret that I was one of the culpable elites who lacked that sensitivity. But, it's never too late to make amends and do the right thing.

At the other end of the issue, the policy makers and the education hierarchy are equally at fault because they too did not realize that with the rapid growth of the superior Cambridge system, the K-10 Matriculation system would be left further behind and the inequity between the systems would only be made worse, unless greater investment was made in education reforms to the K-10 Matriculation system.

Intrinsically, personal wealth and assets are a blessing that have been rightfully earned, in most cases, by hard work, prudent investment, and good financial decisions. Inherited wealth too is a blessing. Being rich is a matter of being lucky in the lottery of life and it comes with the responsibility that good fortune and prosperity should be generously shared with those who haven't been that fortunate. So, how can we reduce 'the opportunity gap' and equalize the field of opportunities? Answer: by creating equity in education.

1.5 Reducing the Equity Gap: Ideas for a K-12 System and College Education

Pakistan has a serious problem of inequity in education. That said, what can be done to reduce the equity gap? The gap must be bridged by us, the fortunate wealthy, with empathy for the poor, through acts of compassion, and through support and strong advocacy to enable equal opportunity for quality education on a system-wide level. A good line of action for us, the elite and affluent, is to abandon the position of entitlement that 'Our kids deserve the best education because we can pay for it.' Such a narrow view must be replaced with the empathetic belief that 'Our kids benefit from the best education because we can afford

EDUCATION IS *BIG* BUSINESS!!

Private elite schools are thriving in Pakistan's cities where the demand exceeds capacity. International networks of expensive private schools have established strong brand recognition and are paying off handsomely for the investor-owners. While the schools deliver excellent education, they are prohibitively priced for most segments of the population.

Beaconhouse School System is a privately-owned network of schools in over 30 cities, offering pre-school to 12th grade classes and preparation for the international GCE examinations. The system subscribes to the Cambridge International Examinations board and has independent divisions in Pakistan, the UK, Malaysia, Thailand, the Philippines, Oman, the UAE, and Belgium. Tuition fees in Pakistan range between 15,000 and 25,000 rupees (or twice as much), depending on the school location. All instruction is in English.

The Educator is a less expensive, franchise model of about 800 schools owned by Beaconhouse that cater to a market that can afford 5,000 to 15,000 rupees. 'Educator' schools are in 225 Pakistani cities and student enrollment is 175,000. Again, all classroom instruction is in English.

The City School is another network brand that operates 'English medium' primary and secondary schools in forty-nine Pakistani cities with 126,000 students enrolled (2018 figures). It has joint venture projects in UAE, Saudi Arabia, the Philippines, Malaysia and other countries. Average monthly fees are about $200 or Rs 25,000. Its primary school curriculum is derived from the UK National Curriculum and secondary school education is divided between the local Pakistani curriculum and the Cambridge regulated programs.

Sources: Beaconhouse and The City School websites, and Wikipedia - May 2018.

it—but we must not ignore the education needs of the poor child. We must work to urgently help reform the K-10 public education system and reduce the inequities.'

Next, reform efforts must include concrete steps to reduce the equity gap both in terms of access and quality of education that prepares young students for university education. The widening gap between elite and public schools must be addressed first, with a structural change in the present Matriculation system, which terminates in 10th grade. Upgrading the secondary school system to a twelve-year program should be a fairly easy transition. Ten years is just not sufficient for the student to gain the foundational knowledge in preparation for university education and it is common practice worldwide for the college preparatory period to be twelve years. The 'intermediate college' should be phased out and eliminated over a period of four years. Secondary schools should be upgraded to a 12th-grade high school system.

The typical undergraduate bachelor's degree programs should be standardized to four years after 12th grade, eliminating the disparity between various college programs. (Professional degree programs may be exceptions to this). Liberal Arts programs must be added as a requirement for college graduation. Quality control and ratings of school and college programs should be transparent and available to the public through a federally mandated system of rating[9] and quality improvement. Students and parents invest large amounts of money and time into education. They should not have to rely on half-baked and subjective word-of-mouth recommendations, or 'roll the dice' with the child's future. Regardless of how it is sugar-coated, education is never truly free, or cheap. The costs are paid by some portion of the treasury and by all citizens, through taxes or direct fees. Additionally, quality in education can only be achieved at added cost. There's a critical window of time for education in every child and young person's life that should not be squandered by poor decisions based on misinformation about the curriculum and quality of teaching.

1.6 The Quick Fix?...there is none!

How will Pakistan extricate itself from this quagmire of illiteracy and increase its capacity to adequately educate its people? The solution to our national woes must begin with reform. Let me repeat: there is no quick fix. But the essentials of reform can be very simply listed in the following five points. Of course, the devil is in the detail. These steps cannot be sequential. They must be acted on, all at the same time, with equal vigor and appropriate resources for each. Nothing short of an all-out campaign can succeed. And, failure will result in the certain extension of injustice on the next generations of uneducated and underprivileged families who will continue to suffer in poverty.

1. ENROLLMENT AND CAPACITY-BUILDING FOR UNIVERSAL EDUCATION: the catastrophic state of out-of-school children must be addressed. School capacity must be increased, both primary and secondary. More institutions must be added for quality tertiary education and certifiable vocational skills training.

2. CURRICULUM, LANGUAGE AND TEACHING ENVIRONMENT: the critical elements of *what* is being taught and *how* it is taught must be addressed and reorganized. Language policy must be resolved by national mandate with provincial consent and cooperation. Quality teaching in a healthy, stimulating environment must be the normal expectation in all public and private institutions.

3. TEACHERS AND INSTRUCTION: recruitment and pre-service training of professional teachers must be managed efficiently. Evaluation of content knowledge and pedagogical skills of teachers must be ongoing in public and private systems. Continuing professional development must be streamlined.

4. MANAGEMENT OF QUALITY INPUTS AND EVALUATION OF OUTCOMES: best learning outcomes are achieved only when the inputs of the best resources are injected into the system. Building of efficient systems for delivery of quality education, excellence in management, and testing and assessment of outcomes must be standardized and streamlined. (See Chapter 2 for how these steps can be structured and implemented).

5. MONITORING AND OVERSIGHT BY THE PUBLIC: advisory, monitoring and oversight role—with authority to demand and enforce correction—must be with civil society organizations. Effectiveness and quality of inputs and outcomes in the entire system of public and private education must be a function of civil society though organized, local citizen groups. (Much more on this in Chapter 7).

1.7 Language Issues add to Inequity

A fair and consistent language policy is essential to education reforms. The challenging issues of language that separate socio-economic classes add to the equity gap because education in the elite English-medium schools is undeniably of superior quality to that in Urdu-medium schools. This is primarily because of the meager resources and poor-quality inputs allocated to the dysfunctional public education system, where close to 80 percent of children get their schooling. The expensive and medium-cost private schools cater to the remaining student population in urban centers and affluent communities. We inherited the English language from our colonial past and we are married to English for business and governmental purposes. College and university education is in English. But does this have to be the only way, going forward? Or, is there room to consider other options?

For most Pakistanis, English is a foreign language. The British colonial imposition of English as the dominant language in education, business, and government has caused irreparable damage to these institutions and we are paying the price in education quality, as well as the communication inefficiencies in commerce and government. The dominance of English for instruction in post-secondary education has crippled and severely affected the growth of our youth and social capital. We prepare the majority of our secondary school students in Urdu and then break their spirit and confidence by expecting them to abruptly switch to English for college. We have been 'teaching' in the wrong language, a beautiful but *foreign* language, English—instead of the beautiful and *local* languages of our own environment. For these reasons and others, our system is broken and dysfunctional. I believe that reform must include significant change in our language policy as one of the first few essentials.

Up to this point, we are discussing the equity gap made worse by the language discrepancy. Experts warn that it is a far bigger problem than it appears to be at first glance. Because numerous challenges of education are linked to the issues of language, experts also caution that it will be nearly impossible to make advances in education unless there is agreement on language policy. Let's agree first that all regional and native languages are deemed important for their cultural value and no native language should be ignored. In fact, a consistent and uniform language policy in education must give greater impetus to development of regional and native languages. Let's also get past the squabbling and politicking. Let's allow the language debate to be brought to the surface and some serious longer-term alternatives to be discussed in the open. It's unavoidable that there will be phased and nuanced solutions. There is no immediate, painless answer to the tricky problem of language policy because the issues are plagued by regional and linguistic politics. The need is to rise above these differences and find a language solution for the children and for future generations.

By reasonable estimates, nearly 95 percent Pakistanis speak *some* Urdu, along with perhaps a regional or native language. A high percentage of people—even if not formally educated in schools—can read and write some Urdu. It is also generally accepted that Urdu is predominantly the 'language of the environment' (LE) and, for all practical purposes, it is the commonly spoken language of business and government and in daily life. The irony is that almost all written language of business and government is in English, which adds to the confusion and conflicting opinions.

I reiterate with emphasis that regional and native languages should be recognized equally in early education and efforts made to retain them for cultural value and social identity. However, the vast majority of school-going youth are receiving education up to grade 10 in Urdu. As discussed in 1.4 above, the sudden switch to English in intermediate college causes the Urdu-medium student (or the Sindhi-medium student in Sindh) to have a difficult time getting into good university programs, making the disparity abruptly worse at this juncture. And, primarily because English is a stronger ticket to better jobs, the personal and societal importance of Urdu is of less relative value compared to English. Another amusing fact is that though Urdu is taught and tested at the intermediate college level, the scores in Urdu are not aggregated into the overall grades for pre-medical or pre-engineering students because it is assumed that engineers and doctors 'will not need Urdu'. Such weak rationale and exemptions have further denigrated the importance of Urdu as a language when the reality is that engineers and doctors do need to communicate in Urdu with clients and co-workers. A suggestion is that Urdu test scores should be included for pre-engineering, pre-medical, and all other tracks as well. To extend this a step further, serious thought should be given to making Urdu a required subject through all undergraduate and graduate university programs, including engineering and medicine, because of societal and personal value in learning rich classical Urdu literature and poetry at all levels. The social benefits of Urdu as a required class, even if just a few times weekly, would become evident in increased cultural sensitivity among the graduating professionals. A pilot study could easily be conducted to test the idea.

In conversation with three recently graduated professionals (a physician, an accountant-auditor, and a computer science engineer, who had studied in Urdu-medium schools and completed English-medium university programs), the consensus was that from a student's perspective, inclusion of Urdu in university programs would be easy to adjust to and a good step to enhance the cultural significance of Urdu as a language. They also supported the idea of a pilot program to study the benefits versus any drawbacks.

As long as we have a system of college education in English language, an immediate intervention to reduce the language-equity gap for the Urdu-medium student is to significantly increase the intensity of English language teaching in grades 6 through 10. This will enable better English language competency by the time the student reaches grade 11. Also, the English-medium student (in the elite, private schools) should be put on notice that greater skills in Urdu will be required of them—to be phased-in over a period of five years—and that Urdu will be taught and tested in all college and university programs. The English-medium schools should start preparing current entrants in early classes for the transition. This would not disrupt the normal curriculum or pedagogy the schools follow, except that it would add more serious preparation for their students to be proficient in Urdu at the higher education and university level.

This change would partially balance the scales for language and should be recognized as following the successful models of economic giants like China, Japan, South Korea, Germany, France, and a host of other countries that have retained their local languages as the pragmatic medium of instruction for education at all levels. Moreover, their local languages are a source of national pride, not a drag on the systems of education, international commerce, or normal daily life. These countries are comfortable using English terminology and technical explanations when necessary, without compromising the local languages.

In a personal communication, Dr Anjum Altaf eloquently summarized the transition of languages: 'My recommendation, keeping very clear the distinction between learning a language and learning in a language, would be to have the early years of education in the mother tongue, introduce Urdu second, followed by English. This would yield a sound educational foundation, a common language for communication, and a facility with English when the study of science and technology requires its use.'

Resistance to change is universal. But change should not be feared as the terrifying end of the world. When the benefits are considered and rationally weighed, the change becomes acceptable and, in fact, it can be appreciated as a good decision when seen in the rear-view mirror. Remember when we had rupee-anna-paisa for money?—and gallons-pints, and yards-feet and inches? We thought that converting to the metric system for currency, weights and measures was a bad idea and predicted that it would not work in Pakistan. That was fifty years ago, and it seems to be working just fine. Let us declare a cease-fire in the political skirmish of language, unemotionally debate the options and rationale, make smart decisions and initiate bold language policy changes to make radical, far-reaching improvements in the entire education system at all levels. We may have to learn to live with more than one language, be it Urdu plus a regional language like Sindhi, as an example for Sindh. Pakistan is not unique in this regard. There are numerous countries that function with more than one language: Belgium (Dutch-Flemish, French and German); Switzerland (Swiss, French, Italian), Canada (French, English) to name just a few. Most European, Asian, African and some Latino-American countries have combinations of languages and do not rely solely on English as the language for education, business or government transactions. The multi-cultural city-state of Singapore has four languages: English, Malay, Mandarin-Chinese, and Tamil. English is the language of business and government, and also the medium of instruction in schools.

The long-term transition in language could be twenty years out but, for a solution to language issues and inequity in education, the policies need to be directed to a 'single-language' system of education at all levels, and that single language may be Urdu, which is the practical language of the environment. I truly believe there will be relief when the language issues can be resolved for Pakistan's education future. The debate must begin and lead to a rapid, democratic solution.

1.8 An 'Elite' Initiative

Along the lines of a Corporate Social Responsibility (CSR) program, here's an idea of significant social value and one that can be initiated by the affluent elite as a positive step to reduce inequity on a small scale. It would be a great beginning if the affluent could demonstrate empathetic action for change and initiate the desegregation of elite schools. Patrons of the superior systems of elite private schools should promote a school policy that at least 20 percent of the enrollment in elite schools should be from underprivileged communities, with students selected on merit scholarships. A special fund should be set up in the schools to support tuition costs for underprivileged students and funding for this should come from affluent families who could easily pay 20 percent more in tuition fees. This practice of scholarships for underprivileged children is common in elite schools and universities in the US as it reduces the economic and cultural segregation in private schools. This benevolent gesture would benefit the students from affluent families by increasing their social sensitivity and awareness of the need for a level playing field for the disadvantaged. There is a great deal to be gained by everyone in developing a fair and equitable system of education. Read this from Tooba Akhtar (see section 4.3 in Chapter 4), a privileged young woman who had an awakening experience.

> It was a stark realization for me that our life paths were decided by where we were born. It kept nagging at me, unsettling me….Of course, there is abject poverty in Pakistan, you see it everywhere, but I had never thought about who 'these people' are, and what their lives were like, what do they like or dislike, who are they—and they look just like me but then our lives are so different, yet our lives are so connected. I think I had a deep, deep unsettling sense of how ignorant, and privileged and naïve I had been. I had never thought about this, or done anything about it, because of the power structures that continue to exist and the number of people that won't do anything about it. I belong to the privileged class in Pakistan, a privileged family. We are the kind of people who just turn away and never do anything about it, or anything that would affect us greatly. These were…the stark realizations that I couldn't shake off.

1.9   Civic Leadership Needed for Reforms to Succeed

In a *TIME.com* article,[10] co-authors Julia Gillard[11] and Wendy Kopp[12] commend the efforts of millions of dedicated professionals around the world who work diligently to help children succeed and shape a brighter future and because of their professional efforts, 'remarkable progress in global education has been made… especially around increasing enrollment and gender equity.' True, here also some strides have been made but Pakistan cannot claim remarkable progress. However, I totally endorse the view of the authors that, to make lasting change, it will take [civic] leadership to build and sustain successful education systems. This is confirmed in a report[13] by McKinsey & Company, which analyzed twenty education systems and found that 'leadership is essential not only in sparking reform but in sustaining it…improving systems to actively cultivate the next generation of system leaders, ensuring a smooth transition of leadership and the longer-term continuity in reform goals.'

Education reform is not a destination; it's a never-ending process. It's a relay, not a sprint. And there is no finish line, no end to the marathon. Past task forces and reform committees have not had lasting impact, probably because there has not been effective civic leadership to 'spark and sustain it...to actively cultivate the next generation of system leaders, ensuring a smooth transition of leadership and the longer-term continuity...' of education reforms.

To ensure progress and ultimate success, the process must be seen as a long-term progression chain that will require the commitment of a select blend of energetic, innovative individuals as the principal leaders supported by a large base of citizens. The collective commitment for transformational change should be merged together in a well-structured civil society organization—a broad-based coalition—that can be the primary public driver to monitor, advocate, and campaign for reform, with a high degree of mandated authority to enforce corrective measures.

The key leadership of the coalition should be drawn from the ranks of social entrepreneurs, the educated youth, college graduates and alumni, network partners such as the media, and educational organizations like Teach for Pakistan and others, to name just a few broad categories. We must reach out to the demographic of our influential elite and middle-class citizens, through the channels of service clubs such as Rotary, Lions, and similar social-professional groups in the local civil society. People of influence and wealth have social capital and are capable of reaching out to policy makers.

The twin focus of the coalition should be universal access and quality education. Global participation and investment should be invited and the proposals should be commensurate with reform projects as part of a comprehensive strategic plan. To move the needle in education, the organization should seek global partners who can support programs through local leadership and not depend entirely on state management for implementation of programs with international partners. Do Pakistanis have the capability for such leadership and the ability to reach out to collaborative partners around the world? I believe that we do.

As it relates to Pakistan's education, there is clear evidence of some progress in reform, even if it is not apparent or is not in tidy building blocks, but, disappointing as earlier failures have been, we must not be overwhelmed by the failures of the past. Our focus must be on learning of the positive happenings in reforms, sharing the information publicly with practical suggestions on how citizens can support the reform efforts. We should aggregate public demand from the underprivileged masses, especially from those who missed out on education, and convey the demand to the policy makers. This is where strong, astute leadership is needed because we should not risk another round of failures.

By global measures, the world is becoming increasingly prosperous: extreme poverty is down, productivity is up, personal income and wealth are rising, healthcare and education systems are improving. Yet, there are dark pockets of gloom that exist in some societies where change is not happening fast enough. It may be another decade before tangible change in life standards is recorded in Pakistan. With all its power and hubris, why is my homeland one of these 'slowly improving' dark corners of the world? Is it because quality education as a systemic solution has been missing and, to a large extent, our education systems have operated in a dysfunctional environment without public leadership and oversight? Are we ready at this time to face our problems, instead of turning away from them and hoping that they would magically disappear? It is not possible to change the past. But it is possible to plan the future and guard against making the same mistakes again.

Deliberate repetitiousness notwithstanding, these words are worthy of yet another iteration: 'Leadership is essential not only in sparking reform but in sustaining it…'. Unless we approach reforms with resolute civic leadership, restructuring education systems will be painfully slow and possibly ineffective, again.

1.10 Sustainable Goals

Global development goals are set as incentives for achievable results. Participating countries may merge the aspiration goals with their own strategic development goals but the reality is that few countries reach the goals within the timeline. More important is the journey and incremental progress of the effort towards the goals: did the participating countries establish the institutions to set the right programs in motion? Will they build upon and sustain that effort, or was it a flash-in-the-pan activity? Is timely progress monitored and are adjustments made, with serious resources allocated to achieve the goals?

In September 2015, the UN adopted the 2030 Agenda for Sustainable Development that lists seventeen Sustainable Development Goals

(SDGs).[14] Building on the principle of 'leaving no one behind', the new Agenda emphasized a holistic approach to achieving sustained development. Goal-4[15] strikes to the heart of our discussion: 'Ensure inclusive and equitable quality education and promote lifelong learning opportunities for all'. I cannot imagine anyone not in total agreement with the statement.

Pakistan was a willing signatory to the 2030 Agenda. That was in 2015, which means that a third of the timeline has already elapsed. Signing the Agenda...*Was that a joke?* Has anyone asked what progress has been made towards achieving the SDGs? Now, in 2020, can we take on and achieve the SDG by 2030? Can we provide the civic leadership to reach most of the SDGs?—especially Goal-4: *equitable and inclusive quality education for all by 2030?* Can we get on track, start building the institutional capacity to set the right programs in motion? Can we sustain that effort, monitor the progress, and make adjustments with serious resources to achieve the goals?

Historically, in the past seven decades, we have done poorly with goals. We missed the boat with the Millennium Development Goals of 2000. But with strong and judicious civic leadership, I believe the SDGs of 2030 are attainable. The good news is that we have only ten more years to get it done.

1.11 'So Much Aid, So Little Development'

The catchy title of Dr Samia Altaf's 2011 book says it all and not very much has changed in almost a decade. The Amazon.com write-up for the book adds, 'Pakistan has received more than $20 billion in external development assistance [till 2010] but has made little evident improvement in its social indicators.' The author, a physician and public health specialist, followed the Social Action Program which cost hundreds of millions of dollars and her book describes planning meetings in Islamabad, navigates the tiers of bureaucracy down to the village health-worker trainee, and then moves on to the US capital for the project's final assessment. At every stage, Dr Samia Altaf finds 'skewed incentives, misplaced priorities, and inappropriate designs diverting the project from its original intentions and ambitions.' It is at times a lighthearted read on the grim subject of misused resources and opportunities squandered in the futile exercise of a development assistance project.

In 2010, with fine investigative reporting on the effectiveness of assistance under USAID, the Public Broadcasting Service (PBS) produced a documentary by David Montero[16] and a series of video interviews of senior USAID officials and Pakistani persons of influence. The video conversations and reporting are a decade old but again, not much has changed. There is some learning in these conversations.

Of particular interest is a 2010 interview[17] with Randy Hatfield, director of USAID's education office in Pakistan between 2006 and 2008. Hatfield is asked specifically about funding for education. A few samples of his responses: 'There are a number of reasons why development hasn't [has not] been as successful as it should have been. One of the reasons why Pakistan never became an Asian tiger was its lack of investment in human resource development [...] For me, the education sector in Pakistan is an emergency. Here's a staggering figure: 79 percent of children between the ages of 10 and 16 are out of school; that's almost 24 million children. And the literacy rate in the adult population is about 50 percent. These are figures quoted by UNESCO and others.'

Addressing the anticipated Kerry–Lugar Bill (2009) and billions in funding, Hatfield added: 'With new funding coming in, there's a wonderful opportunity to open up dialogue again with Pakistan and try to understand all the issues about good governance, quality, and access [...] it's an investment that needs to be made through leadership in the country itself...develop a policy that's relevant to the country.' Hatfield advised against leaving it to 'contractors or development specialists' and suggested that '...both governments need to take stock and understand what has not worked and get beyond just applying money, building more schools, and sending more textbooks [...] Instead, ask 'How do we make things more efficient and put real muscle behind this?' You can't ask institutions that are already flawed to do this by themselves.'

When asked 'Who should get the money? And why?', Hatfield did not say outright that the money should be controlled or overseen by civil society leadership, perhaps because Pakistan's civil society was not capable of intervention at that time. However, Hatfield did say 'I think change could come if we put local partners up front.' As we know well, bureaucrats and policy makers are not inclined to have civil society groups take leadership or oversight roles. It can only be hoped that by 'local partners' Hatfield might have meant civil society groups, not some layer of bureaucracy. That's an interesting thought for the future.

Another 2010 conversation of interest is the one with Robin Raphel,[18] a high-level special envoy who was to 'manage' the funding under the Kerry–Lugar Bill. Regrettably, I find Raphel's statements and responses to be deflective, non-committal and vague. On the subject of risk avoidance and corruption, she says: 'No program of this size and scale is going to be problem-free on the financial side [...] But we are making a very conscious and deliberate effort to mitigate problems.' That sounds very bureaucratic and troubling.

Of the three Pakistani persons interviewed in this series by PBS, Mosharraf Zaidi states his position explicitly and in straightforward terms. In response to why Pakistan has a net primary school enrollment of only 52 percent (lower than India, Sri Lanka, and Nepal), Zaidi says it's because 'education is not a priority for the Pakistani state.' Zaidi adds that the feudal elite benefit from the sustained illiteracy of the Pakistani people and 'education, health care, clean water, social protection, police services—all the things that make life livable in a country like the United States—are the things that are seemingly the least of Pakistan's priorities.' Zaidi is an analyst, policy development adviser, advocacy leader (Alif Ailaan) and strong supporter of educational reform. His interview[19] dates back to 2009.

Going back to the $7.5 billion (some of it for education), Zaidi was unequivocal about how it should be spent. 'On public sector schools all the way, with very specific requirements and conditions [...]...it would have been really interesting to have conditions within the Bill that for example, said that X percent of Pakistan's budget will be spent on education, that X number of teachers every year will need to demonstrate Y qualities to keep their jobs, that civil service status for teachers will be transformed over several years into contractual relationships with the state, that communities will govern what happens in terms of the administration of their school rather than...a bureaucrat' and also that '...there isn't a country in the world that USAID supports that doesn't have a corruption problem.'

Zobaida Jalal was Pakistan's federal education minister from 1999 to 2003. Her PBS interview[20] took place in 2009. She spoke boldly, with criticism of the USAID program, saying there was 'nothing to show' for the $100 million already spent by USAID on an education project. 'The problem is we had no monitoring system in place; there were no third-party evaluations to check where the money was going, where the grants were going, or if they were actually being utilized or not.' She received strong conservative pushback when she proposed reasonable changes to the curriculum that related to a biology textbook having references from the Quran in Arabic, suggesting that, out of consideration for non-Muslim minorities, the Quranic phrases could be added as footnotes. Another controversial part of the curriculum she looked at was Islamic education, suggesting 'a more humanistic approach...talk more about human rights and tolerance and peace, rather than just about rituals.' It is apparent that Zobaida Jalal was frustrated by the futility of her work for curriculum reform. Her interview is good reading and also a distressing reminder that brave efforts like hers should not be in vain.

In 2010, PBS also interviewed journalist Badar Alam,[21] the Lahore bureau chief of *Herald* magazine, who said, 'In terms of our administration, we see no initiative. In terms of finances, we have hardly any money available for education [...] we have a curriculum that is very biased, extremely outdated and there are no serious efforts to revise it.' Alam lamented that the education system '...deprives people of their political, social, cultural, and economic contexts and turns them into something other than what they should be.' He also says that the curriculum is 'poisonous' against certain groups and the remedy should '...come from the community itself. People need to be concerned about the education that the younger generations are getting in Pakistan.' Alam adds that '...creating islands of excellence...has not helped. We need to address the sea of mediocrity that is surrounding those islands of excellence.' A decade later, we may ask ourselves: has anything changed for the better?

If tomorrow's headlines were to read, in bold caps and italics, '*TURBULENT TIMES AHEAD*', that would probably not faze us. Because daunting headlines in the past have not frightened us. (I remember the intense 'Education Emergency' campaign by Alif Ailaan, a non-profit organization). In the carrot-and-stick culture we live in, the doomsday fear of the stick has not worked. But the appeal to our collective compassion just might work. Or will it? Sweeter enticement of the benefits of a better economy with an overall healthier, more prosperous society—will that be more appealing in garnering support for education reform? Change is inevitable and it's coming. It always does. But will it be change for the better? That is entirely up to us.

State as well as philanthropic investment will be needed to prepare our youth for the world of the future. These are rapidly changing, highly competitive, and unpredictable times. So, what is our short-term goal for Pakistan and our future generations? Our focus and priority should be education. It will be important to accept a very different perception of the education landscape of the future. And we must equip the future workforce with life skills that will help them to adapt to the demands placed on them. Workers of the future will need to develop a competitive mindset for growth through first class, experiential learning as well as contemporary, cutting-edge technical knowledge. This is the new reality for which we should prepare—or be left further behind. As Quaid-i-Azam Mohammad Ali Jinnah said very fittingly in 1947,

> The world is progressing so rapidly that without the requisite advance in education, not only shall we be left behind others, but we may be wiped out altogether.

Seven decades later, those words still ring true.

Notes

1. See 1.9: 'Leadership Needed for Reforms to Succeed'.
2. Sources: Pakistan Education Statistics 2016–17 (National Education Management Information Systems); History of Educational Policy Making and Planning in Pakistan (compiled by Kaiser Bengali) Working Paper Series #40, 1999 (SDPI); Wikipedia: Five-Year Plans of Pakistan - https://en.wikipedia.org/wiki/Five-Year_Plans_of_Pakistan.
3. Tahir Andrabi, Jishnu Das, Asim Ijaz Khwaja, et al., *Pakistan: Learning and Educational Achievements in Punjab Schools (LEAPS): Insights to inform the Education Policy Debate*, 20 February 2007.
4. ASER report, http://aserpakistan.org/document/aser/2018/reports/national/ASER_National_2018.pdf
5. 2017 numbers.
6. Language policy and practices are addressed in other chapters.
7. Low-cost private schools.
8. See 5.1: 'Poverty to Prosperity' in Chapter 5.
9. Rating of quality education is discussed in Chapter 7.
10. Julia Gillard and Wendy Kopp, 'How to Help National School Systems Succeed,' TIME.com, 22 September 2016, http://time.com/4501405/national-school-systems/.
11. Julia Gillard is former Prime Minister of Australia and currently Chair of the Global Partnership for Education. GPE is working to support education in Balochistan. https://www.globalpartnership.org/blog/pakistan-using-technology-bring-education-most-remote-areas.
12. Wendy Kopp is co-founder and CEO of Teach For All and founder of Teach For America.
13. McKinsey report: How the World's Most Improved School Systems Keep Getting Better https://www.mckinsey.com/~/media/mckinsey/industries/social%20sector/our%20insights/how%20the%20worlds%20most%20improved%20school%20systems%20keep%20getting%20better/how_the_worlds_most_improved_school_systems_keep_getting_better.ashx.
14. Sustainable Development Goals (SDG): https://www.UN.org/development/desa/disabilities/envision2030.html#menu-header-menu.

15. Goal-4: https://www.UN.org/development/desa/disabilities/envision2030-goal4.html.
16. PBS documentary and interviews are available on FRONTLINE/World: http://www.pbs.org/frontlineworld/stories/pakistan901/video_index.htmle.
17. For complete interview, see 'Extended Interview: Randy Hatfield', Pakistan: The Lost Generation, *PBS*, January 2010: http://www.pbs.org/frontlineworld/stories/pakistan901/hatfield.html.
18. For complete interview, see 'Extended Interview: Robin Raphel', Pakistan: The Lost Generation, *PBS*, February 2010: http://www.pbs.org/frontlineworld/stories/pakistan901/raphel.html.
19. For complete interview, see 'Extended Interview: Mosharraf Zaidi', Pakistan: The Lost Generation, *PBS*, November 2009: http://www.pbs.org/frontlineworld/stories/pakistan901/zaidi.html.
20. For complete interview, see 'Extended Interview: Zobaida Jalal', Pakistan: The Lost Generation, *PBS*, November 2009: http://www.pbs.org/frontlineworld/stories/pakistan901/jalal.html.
21. For complete interview, see 'Interview with Badar Alam', Fixing Pakistan's Schools, Pakistan: The Lost Generation, *PBS*, February 2010: http://www.pbs.org/frontlineworld/stories/pakistan901/schools.html.

Chapter Two

The Incredible Story of TCF

'Everything is unprecedented, until it happens the first time.'
Captain 'Sully' Sullenberger of US Airways who landed an airliner in New York's
Hudson River when both engines failed shortly after takeoff, saving all 155
passengers and crew on board.

The unprecedented and incredible story of The Citizens Foundation (TCF) began with the founders taking off on an audacious flight to change Pakistan's education system. The country was in chaos in the mid-1990s, beset with horrendous regional and domestic strife. Crime and random shootings were rampant, civil law and order had broken down, and the worst affected was the metropolis of Karachi, the country's heartbeat, which seemed to be paralyzed and in shock. In the words of TCF co-founder Ahsan Saleem, 'Karachi was burning... and the rest of the country wasn't much better'. The best long-term solution, the TCF founders believed, was in rebuilding the public education system which had become a political game of football. Public confidence in the government to implement changes in the system were at an all-time low. Something had to be done to rescue the country from its downward spiral.

Is Pakistan better off now than it was at its lowest point in the 1990s? I believe the answer is in the affirmative but with the caveat that an enormous amount of work remains to be done in several areas of societal and infrastructure development. Along with investment in development efforts and infrastructure improvements, the momentum of education reform must be accelerated. Have education reform efforts been proportional to the huge challenge we face in Pakistan? Clearly not, but some foundational work has been done, upon which a framework of reforms can be built. It's going to need the total buy-in, pledged commitment, and energetic voice of the elite citizenry.

Has TCF made a difference, as a significant player in education reform? As the reader, it will be up to you to make that judgment.

I firmly believe that TCF has made a huge contribution to education reform by demonstrating that, with the right inputs, quality education can be delivered at scale and efficient management of a large system is possible at affordable cost. But first, I urge you to learn more about the education landscape, weigh the facts, and support quality public education for the underprivileged masses. If we fail to get past the purposeless rhetoric, we will only see more children added to the many millions already not in school. So, let's read up and do the math to stop the OOSC (Out Of School Children) epidemic.

The story about to unfold is best heard in the words of the people of TCF, who live the day-to-day grind of the challenges of the country, its woes and struggles. The early thinking of the TCF founders was to simply build primary schools, take children off the streets, and put them in schools— but it wasn't quite that simple. There were dozens of serious after-work meetings in 1995 to debate various ideas and address the concerns of the times, and to narrow down possible solutions until the right one was agreed upon. The final idea of creating an education non-profit with a national footprint was, after all, unprecedented. But there was never the illusion that TCF would itself become the national provider of education because there was consensus that responsibility for public education belongs with the government.

The initial ideas were a little rough around the edges, but the unpretentious aspiration of the founders was that TCF should be fashioned as an efficient model system of management for a nation-wide network of a thousand schools, with focus on quality schooling for the underprivileged in such severely underserved communities as urban slums and rural areas. The growing economic disparity between the well-off and the poor, the inequity in education opportunities, and the burgeoning population of the uneducated poor, were a sure-fire recipe for worsening social distress and challenges that may come to the surface over time if the injustice was prolonged. Something had to be done to remedy the inequity in educational opportunity and to level the playing field for the poor.

Starting with five TCF primary schools in 1996 and adding ten more the next year, there were encouraging signs of the growing patronage. By the third year, there were some thirty schools and the recognition that the organization could have wider impact as a national movement for education reforms. But the TCF Board was (perhaps wisely) reluctant to assert the role of 'reformist', to avoid the risk of an adversarial relationship with an authoritarian government. There was important work to be done and TCF stayed away from the volatile politics of the time. Democratic action and strategic political advocacy were unknown notions. Public advocacy for education reforms was not discussed at TCF for the same reason that advocacy would be associated with overt criticism of ineffective government policies and past inaction. Instead, TCF prudently adopted patience and an unobtrusive kind of advocacy which was demonstrated only through its actions and outcomes.

A few years later, there was the realization that the children finishing grade 5 would need secondary schools and that presented a different set of challenges. So, in 1999, TCF added secondary schools to its network. But there was surprisingly weak demand because of the high dropout rate between grades 5 and 6. In most TCF schools, an average of twenty-five children were finishing grade 5 but not all of them were signing up for grade 6 in secondary schools. This was attributed to cultural and economic reasons where girls were typically not continuing school after grade 5, puberty being cited as the chief reason, and boys needed to work to help with family income. Undeterred, the TCF Board continued to add secondary schools. The dropout tendency began to slowly change and secondary enrollments began to climb. The typical TCF 'cluster' of schools began to take shape, with typically four or five primary schools feeding into a two-unit secondary school. Communities began to feel good about the change. For the first time, K-10 education was getting established in some of the poorer settlements where there were no schools and parents began to dream that it may be possible to see their children enter college and commence professional careers.

By 2005, a future vision for TCF began to emerge and come into focus as the founders, leaders, and management teams shaped it into the existing model organization, and as a movement contributing to broader changes in the education system. Remarkably, TCF has maintained its principal focus on primary and secondary education and, within the framework of that commitment, it has been able to innovate and add programs of adult literacy and mentorship for students in many of its schools.

Steeped into the character of the management and staff is a passionate, almost fanatical missionary zeal to serve the cause of education. These enthusiastic individuals assume virtual ownership of their departments with outstanding teamwork and camaraderie. Remarkably, each one is at peace with the workload they carry and describe their responsibilities with pride.

Box 2.1 TCF School Units

School capacity and management infrastructure are best utilized when a TCF school structure (or campus) operates both morning and afternoon shifts wherever possible. This makes it a campus with two operating school units. Typically, afternoon shifts are added as needed. About 300 primary and 70 secondary schools operate afternoon shifts.

TCF adopted 252 government primary schools in 2016. By April 2017, there were 1,150 school units in its core network—800 primary and 350 secondary schools. The total number of schools operated by TCF in 2017 was 1,402. In April 2019, the number of school units (including adopted government schools) is at 1,567 and student enrollment is 252,000. Punjab has 697 school units, Sindh 704, Balochistan 81, Khyber Pakhtunkhwa (KP) has 75, and the autonomous Azad Jammu and Kashmir (AJK) area has 10 units. The number of adopted schools is in flux as more schools are added. As of May 2019, fifteen schools were added in Sindh and nineteen more were being negotiated. Some of the schools in Sindh were funded by USAID.

All primary schools are co-ed and have no more than 30 students per classroom. Secondary schools, grades 6-10, are typically built as two-units, sharing the computer and science labs, administration offices and library. Most secondary schools are co-ed except where gender separation is requested by the communities or required by law, as in Punjab and KP provinces. Secondary schools are co-ed in Sindh and Balochistan.

2.1 How TCF Operates

Videos and slides cannot be as effective as a personal visit to the crudely built communities where TCF schools are located. The school visit is a unique opportunity to gain better understanding of the intense work that goes into providing quality education and the management systems to support it. There were 16,000 unique school visits in 2018. Typically, visitors will describe their impressions by saying that the schools were clean, with spacious and well-furnished classrooms; children wore neat uniforms and there were books and learning supplies for all; there were a modern curriculum, professionally trained teachers, and more. But very few visitors would know about the complex operations of managing a network of 1,567 schools. The heartbeat of the organization is the TCF Operations Department, the least glamorous of all the departments, made up of teams that are happy just doing the grunt work without expecting recognition for the results to which they contribute.

In early 2017, I spoke with Vice President of Operations, Tauseef-ul-Islam for a revealing virtual tour of how TCF usually hums along without missing a step, another validation of how well things are planned and executed. As a seasoned manager, Tauseef's responses and remarks are on point. His commitment to the cause comes through clearly as an example of the remarkable work ethos of all managers and staff at TCF.

Q. When did you join TCF and how has the scope of the Operations Department evolved in recent years?

Tauseef: I joined in January 2016 and it has been a busy, very fulfilling year personally, and a very productive year from the perspective of the organization. A lot of new things have been initiated. The organization has taken on a different shape, the management structure has changed, and some consolidation has taken place. When I joined, Operations was managing the school network in the four regions. In March 2016, a decision was made to consolidate the teams of Engineering, Supply Chain, and Community Development Unit (CDU)[1] into the Operations department.

Merging the Engineering department with Operations made a lot of sense because the newly constructed schools built by the Engineering team are handed over to Operations when construction is completed. Engineering is also responsible for school maintenance. There was always a tussle between Engineering and Operations over school construction, whether it could be completed on time, and whether Operations had been informed of any delays. Now that it's all under one umbrella, it's an easy conversation between Regional Managers, Area Managers, and the Engineering team, which is very much a part of our management team. The head of Engineering is at our monthly team meetings and there's regular update and flow of information in both directions. So, it has become a very easy process for us to manage.

Similarly, we are the biggest users of the Supply Chain team's procurements. I think 95 percent of whatever they procure for TCF is for Operations—school vans, furniture, uniforms, books, notebooks, supplies, and many other items. So, it makes sense for them to be under the Operations umbrella for better synergy and alignment of processes and for better efficiency all around. For management efficiency, TCF has functioned as four regions for more than a decade. With adoption of the 250-odd government schools (see Box 2.1), we created two more regions. Now we have six regions in a very elaborate management structure. A Regional Manager (RM) heads a region with several 'areas' within each region. The Area Education Managers (AEMs) and school principals report to the Area Managers (AM), who are responsible to the RM, and the RMs report to me as VP Operations.

Area Managers are the key liaison between the principals and administration, providing immediate support and problem-solving capability. An AM has 30 to 40 schools in his area and routinely visits each school at least once a month, often traveling long distances in a difficult environment. An AM will also assist with donor visits to schools, conduct land surveys for new school sites, coordinate new school construction, promote and community involvement, as well as managing and resolving school maintenance issues. For logistical, safety and cultural reasons, only men are selected to be area managers.

Area Education Managers (AEM) coordinate teacher training, monitoring, and evaluation of teachers, and provide support to principals and teachers. All AEMs are women and many of them have come up from the ranks of teachers and principals.

Q. **The adoption of government schools in 2016 was probably the biggest logistical challenge taken on by TCF and it has impacted the organization in several ways. What is your take on the Government Schools Program (GSP) and how has it affected Operations and management?**

Tauseef: The most significant change in 2016 was the decision to participate in adoption of government schools. Initially, we took over 80 government schools in Punjab and created a new (the fifth) TCF region for these 80 schools. In a very short time, we completed the management takeover of these schools—hiring and training of school principals and teachers, the *ayahs* (maids) for each school and *chowkidars* (gate guards) and drivers. We commissioned the operation of these 80 schools with an entirely new school staff when the academic

Box 2.2 Public-Private Partnership: Adoption of Government 'Partnership Schools'

The Government Schools Program (GSP) comprises the public schools adopted by TCF, most of them in Punjab. The teachers and support staff are TCF employees. The Punjab government pays TCF a monthly subsidy of 715 rupees per child, less certain deductions which reduce the net subsidy—while TCF spends nearly 1,400 rupees per child, on average. The difference is supported by TCF donor funds. In Sindh, the subsidy amounts are better but the teaching staff is a combination of government and TCF employees. In Punjab, TCF invested in the restoration of the GSP schools that needed repairs, cleaning, painting, furniture and supplies. Waiting for the government to do the rehab would have severely delayed adoption of the schools. The signage on the GSP schools does not identify them as TCF schools but word spread quickly in the communities that the schools were under TCF management and average enrollment went up from forty-one in April 2016 to over a hundred students on average, in a year. Student outcomes have also shown good improvement. The GSP schools are all primary schools.

– Tauseef-ul-Islam

year started in April 2016. Most of the teachers hired are from the local areas. We decided not to transfer teachers from TCF schools to the adopted schools because that might have destabilized our own network. It was easier to have a fresh lot of teachers and train them, get them started as a new team. We considered the transfer of AMs because they were experienced, but in hindsight it was a good decision not to do that either because the GSP schools have a different organizational structure and the management activity is also different to a typical TCF region. Because TCF does not own the properties in the GSP regions, we don't have any donor management or donor visits to be coordinated, and we're not looking at new pieces of land or conducting land survey for new schools which would normally be the AM's task in the TCF core program regions.

From an organizational perspective, the biggest challenge was to set up two new regions to commission 250-odd government schools in addition to about 40 TCF schools that we normally commission every year. Starting nearly 300 schools in one year, the resourcing and hiring of new teachers was a huge challenge, not only in terms of adding new teachers and school principals but also the regional office staff, the AMs and AEMs, etc. The whole organization pitched in and it was a superb effort. No one complained or said it wasn't my job. Everybody from all the various departments was very positive, travelling to difficult locations to set up centers, letting the community know that we were hiring. The support was just great and that is the secret to success for this well-knit organization. An important decision made also was not to differentiate between the GSP and core TCF schools, applying the same standards and policies for the hiring of staff, salaries and benefits, and for student learning outcomes. The GSP schools are seen just the same as TCF schools despite the higher cost associated with GSP schools, and regardless of the low subsidy that we get from the government. Some other Education Management Organizations (EMOs) that have adopted government schools are trying to manage their costs to not exceed the subsidy payment, whereas we are putting in money from our own resources to ensure that the child in the GSP gets the same quality of education that we are giving at our TCF schools.

Q. But, can we say that we are giving the same quality of education when the teachers are new, the books are different, and the physical environment is not the same?

Tauseef: Yes, the physical environment isn't the same and there's not much we can do about it. In terms of the books, we are required to follow the Punjab textbooks, but we are supplementing those books with our own TCF books. We have initiated a remedial program at many of the GSP schools where we saw that the children were not able to cope with the class level. For example, a 5th grader was not able to comprehend or read a 2nd grade book, or not able to read at all. So, in addition to remedial programs at the government schools, we have established a baseline to assess and re-assess the children for learning outcomes and follow the same processes that we have in our TCF schools. There is no curriculum for kindergarten in Punjab, so we have provided our own KG books, at our own cost. These are some of the things we are doing in the government schools, because quality of education is important to us.

BOX 2.3 REMEDIAL PROGRAMS

TCF has two types of remedial programs: (1) *Uraan* (flight) for children who are lagging in class. They are not out-of-school children and could have come from other schools or they are just slow learners. These children are given extra help and coaching to get over the hump, usually as an after-school program. (2) *Aaghaz* (a beginning) and it is for children who have never been in school or they may have gone to school intermittently or dropped out. There's a different curriculum and set of books for this group and they are in this program for varying lengths of time with the intent to bring them up to speed and integrate them into an age-appropriate class.

TCF is planning to run the *Aaghaz* program as a pilot in Mansehra for children who haven't been to school and, in a few months, an effort will be made to mainstream and integrate them into the TCF school in an age-appropriate grade. This is along the lines of the *Aagahi* adult literacy program. – *Tauseef-ul-Islam*

Q. That must have been a very exciting period in 2016-17, the expansion and adoption program. So, what is the targe or optimal number of GSP schools?

Tauseef: Yes, 2016 was an exciting year, to say the least. We were looking to further expand our reach with the GSP, but we decided to first consolidate the first two phases with 250 adopted schools before we took on more government schools. We've been talking to government leaders in other provinces as well and, if we get a favorable response, we are very keen to venture into the other provinces to leverage our work and have an impact in all areas. As far as the target number of schools and where we see ourselves in a few years, the organic growth of TCF is about 35 to 40 new school units, every year.

Q. ...although we've exceeded that number in most years!

Tauseef: Yes, I think we'll be adding 45 TCF school units [in April 2017] but we may not take on any new government schools until we've consolidated and established the GSP on a sound footing, and we get a better response from Punjab Education Foundation (PEF) in terms of their support and collaboration. Right now, it's more of them telling us what to do rather than a partnership. That needs to change, the tone needs to change before we can be more confident that we can expand our presence and take on more schools, that it's not going to be a financial burden on us.

Q. And when you say 'government', do you mean the Punjab government or Punjab Education Foundation?

Tauseef: We deal primarily with Punjab Education Foundation (PEF), an autonomous agency created by the Punjab government, and its focus is on excellence, improving the quality of education. The Punjab Education Department manages its own schools, whereas PEF is doing something quite new and revolutionary.

Q. Please take me through the typical process of what happens when a TCF donor expresses a desire to donate land or fund a new school: the feasibility study to see if the school is viable in the location desired by the donor, how the community buy-in is initiated, the planning, the start-to-finish construction process and finally the handover to the school principal.

Tauseef: If there's no TCF school in the area, we begin with two surveys. The first is an operational survey which focuses on the location of the land, how far it is from the residential communities the school will serve, the number of households, the estimated number of children in the community, other existing schools in the area, and other factors to determine whether the children will have safe and easy access to the school. Distance from the homes is especially important for primary schools because it is not possible for very young children in the early grades to walk long distances. The survey also looks at where the teachers are going to come from, whether there is a sufficient number of educated women or experienced teachers in the community. We get some idea of that when we see other schools operating in the area, because those schools obviously have faculty, so we should be able to find local teachers too or attract teachers from a commutable distance for our schools. Our focus is first to find teachers who are local and part of the community because they wouldn't need transport, and they are also known in the community. Teacher attrition rate is lower with local teachers as compared to teachers who are brought in from other communities. Another consideration is the distance of the school from the area office because the school will need to be administratively managed. Then the engineering team steps in and surveys the condition of the land. We normally conduct the initial land survey jointly, with the Area Manager and the Construction Manager from the engineering team looking at the approach to the property, whether there are proper roads leading to the proposed school, the soil condition tests, the water table, and what is in the vicinity of that piece of land that can be important. The size and area of the land being offered is another factor to be considered. Ideally, the land should be large enough to build a cluster of schools in the future, as we have done in many locations. From a cost and long-term perspective, it is ideal for us to build and manage a few school units on one plot of land with a common administrative block, and one or two principals in charge of four or five school units. Generally, other staffing costs are also lower if we have several school units on one piece of land and also administratively efficient for our Area Managers. We also like to take our children all the way through secondary school and beyond, so we prefer to build a cluster of primary and secondary schools on one property whenever possible.

Q. So, this is all happening at the same time—the community survey, the fact-finding, the engineering study.

Tauseef: Yes, as the first contact in the operations survey, the Area Manager's team will often meet with community leaders to share with them that TCF would like to build a school in the area, enquire about availability of teachers and community attitudes regarding girls' education, to capture the essence of the community, whether they are keen to have their children educated. The community leaders are made to feel important and they are usually happy that a new school is coming to the area and we often get valuable information from them. Without exception, parents want their children to be in school. That is a huge change across all communities. There is no resistance to schools anymore and we are welcomed everywhere, so that is the least difficult part. Walking around or driving around, we see other schools and children going in and out. That's usually a pretty good indication of the student population that we are likely to get because whenever we open a new school, we not only get out-of-school children, we also poach several students from the private and government schools in the area, and that gives the TCF school a good start. And, in a very short time, the community can see some visible differences as well, especially in the discipline that our schools maintain. Our assemblies are very impressive, so is our infrastructure. A lot of parents will transfer their children from private schools or government schools and bring them to us.

Q. And, what are the steps in planning and completion of the school?

Tauseef: We also look at whatever data we have for information about the community. When the two surveys are completed and positive, we inform the land donor that we will be happy to accept the land and the transfer process starts. We must have clean title to the land before we go any further. Once we have title, then we inform our Resource Mobilization Department (RMD) that the surveys and transfer are completed, that they can look for a 'build donor' to fund the school construction. A detailed school proposal from RMD is sent to the prospective build donor, with construction and furnishing costs, the phases of construction and timeline for installments of donor payment required at various stages of construction. Once the signed commitment is received from the donor, the architectural design process and construction contract with a builder are set in motion. Our Human Resources (HR) department gets busy with hiring of the teachers, principal and other school staff who are trained and ready before opening day. Construction is usually completed in twelve months and the new school is handed over to the principal and Area Manager before the start of the academic cycle in April.

Q. All this activity must create quite a buzz and excitement in the community. What are the dynamics in a community where there are existing government schools and other low-cost private schools?

Tauseef: Interestingly, there is heightened excitement because of the reputation that TCF enjoys and the quality of education that is expected. The competition is good for everyone and the whole community benefits.

Q. A typical TCF primary school will start with three classrooms— KG, Class I, and Class II. What's being done to give children a head-start with early education in pre-kindergarten or a nursery classroom?

Tauseef: TCF schools built in the early years had a pre-kindergarten or nursery, plus a KG and five more classrooms, a total of seven classrooms. The pre-KG program was discontinued some years back as it was thought that it was perhaps not adding much value and was adding considerably to our building cost. But we have started nursery or pre-KG classrooms again, especially in communities where the children were struggling in first grade because they couldn't speak any Urdu, as they came from Baluchi or Sindhi-speaking families. We added a nursery class in about a hundred schools last year because these schools had a room to spare.

Q. Surely, the value of a pre-school or nursery classroom is well-established. Is it possible to add or build an extra room for a nursery classroom?

Tauseef: Adding an extra room for that expansion is expensive and we would need to find a donor because there is no extra cash lying around at TCF. The design also needs to be considered. We can add a room generally on the first floor, not on the ground floor, but there are considerable costs involved and, unless there is a donor, we must make some hard choices. An innovative solution we have tried in a few communities was to find a suitable teacher who could offer a nursery class in her own home, for a small fee. This gave the teacher some extra income and we supported her with training and learning materials. The teacher would prepare the children for a year and then transfer them to the TCF school. This worked and saved us the cost of the additional classroom, but I agree that it's ideal to have the pre-KG program in our own school buildings for better quality control and oversight. So, now we are expanding wherever we have the room, or we utilize the library or art room in schools where we don't have the extra classroom. The nursery class has shorter hours, about three hours in the day, so we can easily make the adjustment and make it work, utilizing the rooms that we have. This year, *Insha Allah*, the number of nurseries will go up to 200.

Q. Over lunch, I heard you say that a parent was asking you to change the school timings to the afternoon because his child must go to the madrasa in the mornings. Is that a common trend or a competitive issue?

Tauseef: Not everywhere, but most of the children who go to our schools, or to any school, also go to a madrasa. That's a common trend in the villages and *katchi abadis*. The madrasa in the masjid is a part and parcel of their lives but the madrasa may not be competing with our schools everywhere. In some locations, the timings may be the same and the family's priorities should be respected. The principals play an important role in communicating with the parents and with the people at the madrasa and try to convince them to alter the timing so that the child can come to school and also go to the madrasa. On occasion, we face criticism from the madrasa that the TCF school is not an Islamic school and that we don't teach the Quran, but we do have Quran or *naat* (poetry in remembrance and praise of Prophet Muhammad [PBUH]) recited at the assemblies and the principal will occasionally invite the madrasa teachers and show them the curriculum and the Islamiat books. So, our principals do respond and make sure that the community is satisfied.

Q. What are the considerations on the part of TCF when a privately-operated school is offered for a take-over because the original owners or patrons cannot operate it any longer?

Tauseef: Of course, each situation can vary quite a bit. But we go through a similar process, an operations survey and an engineering survey, and there can be a few things we look for very carefully, the first being the continuity of the school. In most cases, these are primary schools with virtually no options for expansion to the secondary level. We look at the structure itself, if there is any open space, or if the school was run in a small house with few rooms and no open space. After 5th grade, the children would be left with no choice but to look for another school. The other aspect we consider is the faculty. If they meet our criteria, we're happy to take them on and re-train them. Funding the operations cost is another issue. We ask the previous owners or patrons to continue to support the operating cost. We would not be concerned about the prior quality of education because there are a lot of interventions that we can do to bring the children up to speed. Finally, we would consider if this new school is close to existing TCF schools, if it could become part of a cluster in our network, feeding into our secondary school capacity. And, there's the transfer of the property itself. Ideally, TCF would like to have clear title and ownership of the property in which the school is located.

Q. Since Operations is responsible for coordinating between the teaching staff and the Head Office (HO), please take us through the frenetic exercise of the pay day.

Tauseef: We don't send out individual checks, so we have a huge task on our hands. Almost all TCF schools have a bank account, and the money is remitted to the school's bank account from the Head Office. The principal draws the money and pays the teachers and staff in cash.

Q. I presume the teachers and staff prefer their salaries paid in cash.

Tauseef: That's right. We should remember that many of our teachers and staff do not live or work in urban centers. Their preference is cash because not all of them have bank accounts and there's a sizable population that we deal with. Now, for the GSP staff, it's a totally different process. When we started with the GSP, staff salaries were dispersed in cash and we were struggling to get their school accounts opened at the banks, so we began to look for alternate methods for delivery of salaries, and we found a solution. We contacted a couple of banks and one showed interest in working with us. Branchless banking is expanding rapidly in the country. So, a customer opens an account with the bank and is given an ATM card. We contracted with the bank and accounts were opened for the first batch of principals who were issued ATM cards and the bank said they had the capacity to take on the rest of our faculty as well. For some reason, the first design did not work. Salary payments were getting delayed, opening of accounts was taking a long time due to paperwork requirements, or the teacher's National ID Card (NIC) not being valid, or due to other administrative issues. Also, teachers had to go to an ATM to draw their salaries, which was not always convenient for teachers in remote areas. Then we started discussions with another bank, which had a good program of 'mobile money', as all teachers do have mobile phones. We would transfer the money to the bank, give them a list of cell phone numbers for the teachers and their ID cards. The bank would send a text message to the teachers who would show the message to their appointed agent along with their ID and receive the cash from the agent. The agents are located across the country. He or she may be a shop owner in the village who gets a small cut as a service fee which is covered by TCF and the bank is charging us a very minimal amount for their services, just enough to break even. The program is called 'Easy Paisa' and that's how we transfer money for salaries. The moment the teacher receives the salary in cash from the agent, we are notified by the bank that the transaction has been completed. We are expanding the scope of this program and exploring other bank options as well. Teachers will have the right to select from an option that is best for them. So, that's how we are disbursing salaries for the GSP teachers. The plan is to stabilize the salary system, make sure that it works, and then expand it across the TCF network to all 14,000 employees, making the schools cash-free as much as possible. Parents could go to the same agents to make payments for school fees, books, uniforms, etc., and deposit the amount in the TCF school account. That will reduce the administrative work at the school, make the cash collection more efficient and streamline the tracking and accounting functions as well.

Q. So, the GSP has given TCF an opportunity to try out new and innovative processes. Besides salary disbursement, have there been other innovations that are being tested in the GSP?

Tauseef: The GSP has helped us to innovate in many ways. The ways in which we manage the government schools is very different to our own TCF regions in terms of the management structure and hierarchy. In the GSP, since we were starting with a clean slate, we had the luxury of trying out some new things. We have one Administrative Manager in each of the two GSP regions who is in the regional office and has support of administration coordinators. The Area Manager in our GSP is an education specialist unlike the Area Manager in our core program because the requirements are very different. In the GSP, we don't deal with donor management, operational or land surveys, the financial management is minimal, the property infrastructure does not belong to us, and it doesn't require that kind of effort to maintain it. So, we decided that a GSP Area Manager would be an education specialist with 95 percent of his focus on education and 5 percent on administrative issues only to the extent of identifying administrative problems during a school visit and reporting them to the Admin. Manager. On each school visit, we want the Area Manager to focus on education quality, make classroom observations, sit with the teacher, look at the school improvement plans, identify training needs, and assess student learning outcomes. It takes a lot of effort to manage the education aspects, so we don't want to dilute their attention by giving them additional administrative responsibilities. That's possible in the GSP because it's a structure with different requirements. In our core program, the administrative load is quite heavy. The number of school vans we operate, a fleet of about 800 vehicles, that in itself is quite a bit of administrative work in addition to the fee collections and reconciliation of cash taken in to make sure that there are no misappropriations.

Q. I understand you gave up a senior executive position at Shell to join TCF. What motivated you to make that career change— and, how is it that we have a quite few former Shell executives at TCF?

Tauseef: It's not easy to explain why I changed stripes because Shell was my only employer before TCF. I completed my Master's in Physics and joined Shell and had a very enjoyable career for twenty-seven years. It was a great learning experience and culturally enriching as well because I had the opportunity to live in other countries and travel frequently. I was based in Singapore. which is a wonderful country. and my territory was from the Middle East to New Zealand and Australia. When my Singapore rotation was completed, I had the option to move to either Oman or Hong Kong.

While in Singapore, my wife and I had started a family and we felt the need to raise our children in Pakistan and that's what we chose to do. People questioned my sanity, but we held firm and moved back to Pakistan in 2009 and I continued with Shell. Our children were 2 and 4 at that time, so I wanted to cut down on business travel and spend more time with the family and we were happy with our decision. In a few years, Shell wanted me to take on another assignment, but I wanted to continue to live and work in Pakistan. So, the need for leaving Shell and making a career change was becoming apparent. There were opportunities in other countries, but I didn't want to move again. I wanted to live in my own home and in my country of origin.

I've known CEO Asaad Ayub for many years and we joined Shell at about the same time in 1988. We have a common circle of friends that would get together for dinner occasionally in Karachi. I casually mentioned to Asaad that I may be looking for a job in a few months. He was surprised and asked me if I was serious. That led to more conversations with him and others in the TCF team and I began to give it serious consideration. As I learned more, I found TCF fascinating and felt that I may have found my calling, that I should join this wonderful organization. Money is obviously important but, at my stage, it's not the most important thing in life. Our children are still young, but I think they will find their own way and that, with God's help, we will be fine. Whatever God has destined for me, I'll get it done—and here I am.

The cause that TCF is supporting is truly remarkable and we have such an amazing set of people on the Board and on staff. The moment you go to a TCF school and interact with the children, it's so powerful. It brings tears to your eyes. It makes you wonder that maybe this is something I should have started earlier. In my assignments at Shell, I never had the opportunity to pause and think of making this switch. I always thought of doing some social, charitable work but only after I retired from Shell.

I listen to the moving stories of the teachers and principals, these young women who have achieved so much in such a short time. The hardships that they have overcome first to get their own education, then their determination and courage to become schoolteachers and to excel as principals. Their stories are mind-boggling. The rural environment that they come from can be so oppressive. Girls may not have been allowed to go to school in some families, yet they have overcome those hurdles and they have a desire to teach. For them to break down those hard traditions is such a game-changer in those communities. Many of them haven't been to formal college or universities but take their B.Ed. and Master's in Education privately through self-study and then take the Board exams for professional degrees. Why do they do this? Not for the paltry salary of a teacher, I don't think. The income cannot be the motivation. There are 12,000 teachers in our network who are doing this, day in and day out. For some of them, the reason could be the salary but for most of them, I doubt it's the salary. It must be more than just financial benefit.

I think these young women are far ahead of us who live in the major cities. We have a very easy life. Our parents sent us to school and to college and university. There's peer pressure and it's fashionable to go to business school, or medical school, or whatever. But, if it were left to us, I doubt most of us could do what these young women have done. These young ladies from small, remote villages are so determined. They want to excel, make a difference, and the kind of work they're doing is incomparable. If I was in that position, I don't know if I would have that determination and courage. So, you must be exposed to this environment and appreciate how hard these young teachers are working to transform the lives of underprivileged children.

Q. At the Global Chapters Conference (GCC), you introduced the Regional Managers, Area Managers and Area Education Managers as the unsung heroes of TCF.

Tauseef: At the GCC, I wanted to highlight how the Regional and Area Managers and their teams just go about their business unnoticed, without looking for recognition or any appreciation. These teams are out there in the field with very little contact with the Head Office. They don't get to come to Karachi very often so now we have created an opportunity for them to visit Karachi more frequently for administrative training, coordination, and team building. Obviously, there are cost concerns, and we must be frugal.

Q. And most of your RMs and AMs are former military officers. Is there a reason for that, and what are the advantages? How do they fit in with TCF?

Tauseef: You see, what we do isn't exactly rocket science. We need specialists in academics for the technical aspects of education, designing a curriculum, etc. but for the management of our schools and systems, we need good managers who understand policy. So, the former military officers bring excellent management skills because of their senior positions and institutional training in the military. All RMs are retired brigadiers and almost all the AMs are ex-military as well. They are self-driven, very good with people management and inter-personal skills, capable of resolving issues that come up in the field, especially any security-related issues that come up occasionally. They are strong, disciplined men who are resourceful and that's a good thing because we ask the AMs to travel almost every day and to some very difficult remote locations. They must be physically and mentally tough and capable of putting out fires. They bring a lot of strength and because they have retired from senior positions in the armed services and draw decent pension benefits, they don't have financial pressures and they can focus on the goals and mission of TCF. They do their jobs with heart and dedication. The salary we pay is obviously not the driving motivation. The change that they must adapt to is that we have a corporate culture where performance is important, unlike the military where performance issues may be handled differently.

Q. Are they helpful in working through any bureaucratic hurdles?

Tauseef: Yes, at the local government level. Because they have contacts in security circles, that can be helpful occasionally.

Q. Working with a widely spread team must take tremendous efficiency in communication with your network of people. How do you manage that?

Tauseef: That's something I learned at Shell, being a global organization. I was based in Singapore or Karachi and operating with teams in different countries halfway around the world. So, I learned to work with a virtual team and getting the job done and that's what I brought to this organization. I have regular contact with my teams. Mondays and Fridays are very busy days when I spend an hour on calls with my RMs and AMs and it's a structured engagement. Once a month, we have a conference call with all RMs on the call, so everyone is engaged. The engineers, supply chain people and finance teams are right here at HO, so we meet regularly. Then, I also travel frequently to the regions and schools and meet with the teams of AMs, principals and teachers. Everyone likes personal face-to-face visits and that engagement is extremely important. The regional offices organize meetings of the school principals and I attend as many as I can. It's important to stay connected with teams at all levels and at times I am on the road for weeks at a time. Occasionally, I've been on the road the whole month and attended the annual awards ceremonies for teachers. The smallest of the ceremonies had 300 teachers and the largest one in Karachi had nearly

3,000 teachers—in three ceremony sessions, with almost a thousand teachers in each session. That was an excellent opportunity to meet almost our whole population of TCF teachers and principals. So, I use multiple modes of communication from scheduled personal phone calls and regular team conference calls to personal visits. It's important to stay connected.

Q. What were some of the challenges in Operations that have been fixed with technological solutions, and are there any others in the works?

Tauseef: Governance and control were the weak areas and we're working hard to fix that. We're getting good support from Finance and we're getting good reporting coming in from the schools—both financial and other data—and making the RMs aware of the relevant pieces of information that they are responsible for and making sure the teams are aware of their responsibilities as well. We have a few other important projects coming on. We're implementing a new HR system and capital management system and that would revolutionize the way we manage our resources. Right now, it's all scattered with no central database. It's all manual and very labor intensive. We're also bringing in some automation, working on an Android application on a tablet, again using our government schools as the experimental model, providing all principals with a tablet with a customized application which they will use for data management, school enrollment, teacher management, and which will finally cover all aspects of TCF finance, education, you name it. So, we.hope to have student level information that the teacher can access, and that we can access at HO, and we can use to drive our Management Information System (MIS) including financial transmissions from the schools, areas and regions. Reconciliations of all financial data will be seamless, more accurate and much faster. The application is being developed and tested and we hope to launch it very shortly. If all goes well with the experiment in the government schools, we will roll it out through the TCF network very quickly.

2.2 Asaad Ayub Ahmed, President and CEO

Asaad joined TCF in 2009 as President and CEO. Prior to that, he had served in executive positions in the petroleum industry with Castrol,

British Petroleum, Exxon-Mobil, and Shell Pakistan. He has an MBA from the University of Texas at Austin and a Bachelor's in Civil Engineering from NED University of Engineering and Technology, Karachi. Asaad has effectually assembled a team of enduring, like-minded managers, several from careers with Shell. He is judiciously objective, fiscally tough as nails, and firmly declines to see things through a rosy lens. Soft spoken and humble almost to a fault, he has often said that the secrets of success at TCF are *niyyat* (intent) and the *pagalpun* (madness, passion) of its supporters and workers.

In his eloquent message[2] for the 2018 Annual Report, Asaad says that growth at TCF is tied directly to its 'culture of continuous improvement' and that 'making small, incremental improvements every day is the way to progress. Our biggest priority continues to be the quality of education [...] We are committed to making our education system stronger and more effective, day by day. TCF promotes a culture of observation, reflection, and continuous improvement. This practice... helps improve the quality of our programs [and]...also enables learning and sustainable growth.'

Q. What makes TCF different from other models of education networks in Pakistan?

Asaad: The TCF model is not unique and I believe that any model would have worked. Keeping focus on our mission and objectives is a high priority. Our bandwidth is always challenged and we're not fat at the top or even in middle management. The plate is almost always full, and we try not to add to it by taking on more than we can efficiently manage and deliver. Opportunities present themselves and it is tempting to grab the opportunities, but we have learned to restrain ourselves, keep focus on what's on the plate, what's in the works and what fits into our stated mission. For example, TCF in-a-Box,[3] the low-cost model of intervention that we were considering, was temporarily shelved when the opportunity to adopt public schools came up in Sindh, Punjab, and KP.

Q. How many more government schools could you take?

Asaad: We adopted about 250 public schools in 2016–17, mostly in Punjab, but we cannot really plan this. It is unpredictable because I don't think we can guess what the government is going to do. The fact that we were given these schools to manage is not necessarily related to our own performance but because Punjab decided to do this. So, the opportunity came along, and we jumped at it. Now, how big that program becomes obviously depends on the government. We believe that it is going to become bigger in Punjab because the provincial government is extremely focused on public-private partnerships in education and also in healthcare. So, I think the trend is likely to continue. As far as we're concerned, I think it is the right policy and the right approach on our side that we're going a bit slow to first learn how to deal with this beast called the government because we've never had to before. We have had a very comfortable life in our own shell and this is the first time we are dealing with government. Although we have a separate team to run the government schools, it's still within the Operations Department. There is a likelihood that we will change the way the organization is structured and, to provide more focus, we may have a totally separate unit to manage the government schools which uses the organization's expertise and resources. All of that will evolve in the coming years. It isn't possible to plan these things. In the first year of taking over the government schools, we added 21,000 students. I think starting at this pace is a good decision, learning as we go. My preference would be to take over more schools in Sindh because we would want to start that process in other provinces as well, the learning process of how to deal with them, because all provincial governments have their own ways of working. So, I do think that Sindh is also going this route. They are slower but it's going to happen and, in time, the public-private partnership space is going to grow definitely in Punjab, most probably in Sindh, perhaps not so in KP because I think their view is—and they have an absolute right to that view—that they will fix the system themselves, so they are not really interested in giving over government schools to the private sector, which is fine.

Q. The other parallel initiative of partnership with the Railways, adopting the one large campus in Karachi, and the possibility of taking over more Railways schools—how has that gone so far?

Asaad: The understanding that we have with Railways is that they would continue to pay salaries of the Railways staff and teachers. If their teachers retire or are replaced by our staff, then TCF would pay for new staff hired by us. I think the first objective for Railways is to improve the quality of teaching in their schools. They want to get out of running the schools. So, they had offered us to take over more schools, but we had not shown much interest because, unfortunately, their assurances are not really coming through that under-performing teachers would be replaced. We already have a small problem on hand and we are trying to manage their staff. We didn't want to take on more problems at this stage, now that we have the GSP running. Everything takes your energy and divides your focus.

Q. Can TCF mobilize rapidly to adopt more schools if the right agreement and terms are offered?

Asaad: In an ideal world, the government should be paying us the full cost, not just a portion of it. The subsidy paid by Punjab to TCF is 715 rupees per child, less certain deductions, so that the net subsidy we receive is around 600 rupees per child. But our cost is uniformly 1,400 per student and our deficit is thus nearly 800 rupees per child. The shortfall is made up by TCF donor funds. We feel that our cost is the minimum needed to do a half-decent job. The other consideration is whether we want to work with teachers employed by the government, although Punjab has shown this model of no government-employed teachers in the schools we have adopted, we are not sure if each province will have a similar model. The other part is the management and whether we have the bandwidth. I think the organization is well poised to create that bandwidth and it has the capability to strengthen itself in a fairly short time. So, I think we are in a robust position and we can mobilize fairly quickly to take on more schools for adoption.

Q. Of these partner organizations, the EMOs that are participating in Punjab, is there a cooperative or association between the EMOs for sharing of common learnings?

Asaad: Yes, we are trying to create that kind of an environment. We've had a couple of meetings, and we are sharing what we are doing and we're learning from each other. For example, the National Rural Support Program has a strong background in creating community support, so we're learning how to mobilize a community, how to get parents and community leadership involved for help with school enrolment, so there is an exchange of views and a better understanding of the different models.

Q. In the initial phases, how many schools have been adopted by EMOs?

Asaad: I believe there are about 2,300 schools that have been adopted by EMOs so far.

Q. With adoption of schools, do you see any alteration in the mission and the vision of TCF?

Asaad: The founders have said that, in the early years, there was both a demand side and a supply side issue. The demand side issue is not there anymore. We are convinced that there *is* demand for education and we see that in the communities where we have been operating for a while that there are lots of people who want their children to be educated. So, that is not an issue anymore, particularly when you look at the primary schools; they are practically full to the brim. I think what has happened over a period of time is that we have become more conscious of the quality that we are delivering. As more secondary schools have been added and our children have started to do their Matriculation, and how the children are doing in the Matric board exams—because that is of course our terminal point as far as we're concerned and under our control—we've become more conscious of how we're doing and whether we can improve in terms of quality. Internally, we are also trying to strengthen our systems and our understanding of what our quality is. So, we have put measures into place, such as developing our own books because we felt that was one way of improving the quality by improving the content and the delivery of the content, and that it would have an overarching impact on the whole system. We have found that to be true.

The type of discussions that are taking place in the schools are different; they are talking about creative thinking and critical thinking, more of that is now happening. Earlier on it was more a typical '*rutta-fication*' (rote learning) kind of approach in the government schools. That part is fairly well taken care of and now we are talking about the quality of the principals, the quality of the teachers—all of the inputs that go into producing a quality student. Then we are measuring the quality of student learning which earlier on depended on the

---

BOX 2.4 QUALITY EDUCATION: *WHAT IS IT?*

Like beauty, should 'quality' education be regarded as being in the eye of the beholder? I don't think so, because there are established criteria and standards of quality. And then there's the subjective scale of quality. TCF delivers good education in the communities it serves and within the limits of its resources. CEO Asaad Ayub says, 'We do not claim that TCF delivers "high quality" education comparable to expensive, elite schools. But we can comfortably say that we provide the best quality in the communities where our schools are present— certainly far better than the government schools or low fee private schools in the area.' I believe that quality of education should be measured by its thoughtful curriculum, the professionalism of the teachers, the pedagogical practices, the quality control measures in place, and the management efficiency of the system. Several other inputs also contribute to quality—such as good books, high quality learning materials and the school environment. Chapter 7 is a more detailed discussion on quality education. – *Author*

---

government markers of the Matric results, the 10th grade board exam… or, in Punjab's case, they even test their 5th grade students. But now we're talking about having more student competency measures in place. So, I think there is a move. not just towards quality assurance but also real improvement in quality, first trying to understand where we are and then trying to do something about how we improve that quality of learning.

So, in some ways, there is a gradual shift away from that earlier slogan of 'taking the children off the street and into schools' versus—okay, now that's really not the problem. We are trying to do the best we can with the limited resources we have. The resource question will always be there. If we have 10 percent more money to spend on programs, we will always be faced with the option of spending it on enrolling more children, or on the quality of education. That kind of discussion will always take place, but I think the consciousness today is greater for improving student learning quality.

Q. Has TCF successfully exposed the myth that poor families did not want their children educated?

Asaad: Perhaps things have changed. More parents are now realizing that they should get their children educated. Having said that, it's obviously not the same as in the middle classes. We should remember that we work with the less privileged, poor community. We see enrollments drop off after 5th grade, in the transition from primary to secondary school, though TCF numbers [for enrollment in grades 6 to 10] are much better than the national figures. We are clearly seeing an improving trend. Parents in less privileged areas look at the opportunity cost of sending an income-earning child to school. Often the feeling is that a 5th-grade education is good enough, the child can now go to work, there's no need to go to secondary school. Things are changing, and we see that wherever our school has been established for a while, say in 2002 or earlier, the enrollment figures are higher. If you look at our secondary enrollment figures in the five years from 2012 to 2017, average enrollment has gone up from 100 to 105. Not good enough, by any means, but edging slightly upwards. I think that trend is likely to continue. It's just something that takes time to see change in communities, but the movement is in that direction.

Q. The perception generally was that poor people don't—or can't— send their children to school.

Asaad: Obviously, I think it's still true in some cases where they cannot send their children to school for economic reasons, simply cannot afford it, or there is no access to a school. But 'don't want to' was true and it is perhaps not as true today as it was some twenty years back.

Q. How about 'don't want to send their girls to school'? Do you think that is still an issue, or a myth?

Asaad: I think that's also changing. To encourage girls' enrollment, you've heard of school principals who tell parents that we will admit your son only if you allow your daughter to come to school. So, we try to coax the parents to send their girls to school. But that's also changing. In fact, I have the latest reports on gender ratios here on my desk...it's

50-50 in secondary schools, which has always been our goal. Overall, primary and secondary combined, it's 48 percent girls—not bad at all.

Q. It's hard to track dropouts and find out why they dropped out in the first place. Do the principals or teachers know of the reasons why children drop out of school?

Asaad: I think for boys it's usually because at some point, usually 5th grade, the parents will say, 'That's enough school, he's old enough—time to get to work now.' We see the highest number of dropouts after 5th grade. For girls, some conservative families will have their daughters married at the age of 13 or 14. Or, they don't want their daughters to mix around with boys, or they feel that 5th grade is good enough. It's probably a mix of these reasons. Our overall enrollment gender ratio over the last few years has inched up from 46 to 48 percent girls. These are small gains but encouraging.

Q. 'Education for all' as a human right and also as mandated by law, requires inclusion of children with special needs, physical disability, visual impairment, or other needs. Does TCF have any guidelines or policy regarding inclusive education for children in TCF schools?

Asaad: The needs can vary considerably so we allow the principal and the community to resolve the situation on a case-by-case basis.

Q. For the global reading audience, what else would you like to say?

Asaad: I've said this on other occasions as well: I hope more people would understand the local ground conditions and the context within which we are operating, sometimes in very difficult circumstances. An area manager recently told me that he had a criminal complaint filed against him because he refused to hire a man as a *chowkidar* (gate guard). Some influential person in the community wanted this *chowkidar* to be hired for the school. So, we had to scramble to resolve the situation. I often visit some areas by terribly broken *kutcha* (bumpy, unpaved) roads, no electricity or running water supply in the community. And people talk about introducing digital literacy in that area. I feel they are unrealistic, and don't understand the daily struggles we go through just to provide this quality of education. I also feel that *Masha Allah,* we have an excellent team, particularly in our education department which I think is the best in the country, and that includes curriculum development, teacher training and professional development. The amount of internal thinking that goes in to developing staff is enormous. We have this full-time laboratory of TCF giving us feedback on what is working and what is not working and we are thus able to tweak and change to improve things. Also, there is the spirit of the organization, which is to try to continuously improve in whatever is being done, such as taking the teacher content knowledge score from a very low level to a very respectable level. I think these are things that set us apart, distinguish us from other organizations. We are really trying to do as well as we can despite a difficult environment, with literally no government support. We don't say that all the time, because politically it may not be a good thing to say, but frankly there's no support from anywhere and in that environment, being able to create what we have—and at a very low cost—I think we've done quite well.

Q. What kind of support would you like to see from government?

Asaad: I think, for one thing, financial support should be there.

Q. ...for the adopted government schools?

Asaad: Not just for the adopted government schools but also for our core program. We're basically doing the government's job.

Q. If we take funding from government, we would technically not remain a non-government organization.

Asaad: No, no. Many organizations get government grants and they remain independent. But, frankly, there's a lot to learn from what TCF is doing. One doesn't see that spirit elsewhere. There's a lot to learn from the way we've developed our books. The government could take our books and use them in public schools. Hopefully, one day, something like that will happen. I think we need to inform leaders in government about the environment in which TCF operates, and partly it's our fault that we don't communicate enough about what the circumstances are.

You know, every time I go to visit schools, my appreciation goes up for our teachers, our principals, and our area staff. I realize the very tough circumstances our Area Managers work in, going out sometimes hundreds of kilometers away, to check on a school on a regular basis. So, I feel that *Alhamdulillah* within our financial resources, we are doing a fairly decent job.

Looking back, Riaz Kamlani and I were discussing this the other day, that we have gone through things in a very methodical manner. We started with developing the textbooks—and that was a long process—and I'd say that was the strength of TCF. Rather than creating the books in a rush, we took our time, being very deliberate about it. Then we moved our focus on to principals and started improving the quality of the principals' cohort. The focus on principals is ongoing but now we have added the focus on improving teacher quality. Meanwhile, we are putting together the piece on quality assurance. So, in some ways—although I wouldn't say it was really planned that way—it was a very deliberate and phased approach that, if we try to fix the pieces one by one, then *Insha Allah* we will see the results in a few years. You can't see the results right away because, as they say, education has a very long gestation period.

Q. A few years back, there was a point person appointed as liaison between TCF and government. Is there still a point person, or was that a different phase?

Asaad: That was a different phase and that appointment was for a specific project. If you look at the government component, we also need to recognize that it is not out of the goodness of their hearts that the government is doing the school adoption program. They are getting funding from the World Bank, from aid agencies, who are specifically asking them for progress in public-private partnership, so they must show something. It's not that they suddenly decided that school adoption was the silver bullet. I think that kind of pressure or incentive is required, and it forces the government's hand to go this way.

I recently sat in on a meeting of our Education Committee and they were discussing the model and principles of TCF education, principles like gender equality with its ramifications of having an all-female faculty; building proper, purpose-built schools rather than low-cost *chapparr* (shade-tree) schools; or, as a lot of people ask us, why we build these expensive schools when we could have built them at much lower cost, or why we are catering only to the least privileged, or why we don't go a tier above, or why we don't have a school model that will recover its own cost and get over this constant need for fundraising. But we have specifically chosen a segment of the population that nobody else wants to go into. And, we have specifically chosen to provide a much better quality of education than they would otherwise get in that landscape. I think that was a great discussion about the principles of our model, to understand what we're doing and why we do it that way. We're also asked why we are Urdu medium, use Urdu as language of instruction, and not teach in English. We have a particular view of what quality education means and we try to follow that vision. Our view is that we must deliver a certain level of quality. We could have designed our programs to deliver a 400-rupee quality instead of the 1,200-rupee quality that we currently have and we could have had 4,000 poor quality, 'token schools' by this time.

We have proven certain myths to be far from the facts. The myth that parents don't want their daughters to go to school, for example. Given the right conditions of locating the schools within walking distance, making parents comfortable with an all-female faculty of teachers, keeping our costs down, and making the schools affordable for all children in a family to enroll—all these factors have helped to challenge this myth and prove it to be untrue.

Q. **Thank you for this great information for a better understanding of TCF from the CEO's perspective. There is a great deal of work being done in education, health, micro-financing and other sectors related to development. Can you name some other non-profits that are worthy of mention?**

Asaad: In education, CARE, DiL and Read Foundation (in Azad Kashmir) come to mind. Habib University has been a great addition. There are several one-off school initiatives that have good models but small impact. In micro-finance, Akhuwat is doing good work. In healthcare, there's SIUT, Shaukat Khanum Cancer Hospitals, Indus Hospital and Healthcare, ChildLife Foundation—all are doing very good work with great impact. We should give credit also to Shahbaz Sharif, the former chief minister of Punjab, who was a strong champion of public-private partnerships. We should recognize the willingness of certain government leaders to lead the change and be progressive.

2.3 Outcomes at TCF

Riaz Kamlani leads teams that focus on the impact of core TCF programs and, as Vice President of Outcomes, his responsibilities include several key departments. Riaz has an MBA from IBA and an MSc in Development Management, plus work experience in the corporate and social development sectors. He has served in senior management with Shell in Pakistan, the UK, South Africa, and the UAE before joining TCF in 2008, taking a hiatus between 2013 and 2016 to be with Sina Health. During time in Cape Town, South Africa, Riaz learned of a mentorship program and a business-leadership program for youth deprived of education because of apartheid. He was able to transplant ideas gained from the programs in South Africa and apply them to the *Rahbar* mentorship program and the TCF Intermediate College.

Q. We are very pleased that you're back in the management team. Please describe your portfolio as VP-Outcomes and reflect on what is the foundational basis of the TCF education program.

Riaz: I'm happy to be back at TCF. My responsibilities are Education, which is Academics, for example, what books we are going to use; Teacher Training; Quality Assurance, including monitoring and evaluation; all our Volunteer Programs; Alumni, which is managing and assisting our post-Matric students; and Human Resources.

The foundation of the TCF education program is the curriculum—the larger framework of what we want to do, with a sub-component of having specific year-end targets for all grades. Syllabus is the ways and means, the materials we use, things we do, to achieve those curriculum targets. But within the curriculum, there is an explicit curriculum, which is the books that we teach from, and an implicit curriculum of the things which are within that overall context. So, for us the starting point on the implicit curriculum is the actual school premises. We are often asked why we spend on the brick-and-mortar model instead of educating many more children. I think the answer is that the school institution, the building itself, is a starting point for the curriculum.

The second principle is language. We take pride in stating that we teach primarily in Urdu by choice, not because we must, or for economic or other reasons. There is overwhelming acceptance of research that early education should be delivered in the native language or mother tongue, or in the commonly spoken language of the community—in our case, Urdu—and that is why we are an Urdu-medium school network since English is neither a native language for our children nor is it a commonly spoken language in the country. The TCF language policy goes against the grain of everything that is happening in Pakistan's education. So, we firmly believe in our language policy of teaching in Urdu.

The next guiding principle of our system is the decision to employ only female teachers and principals, because it is culturally and socially important that we facilitate girls' education. As our core program, we currently have an eleven-year schooling system, Kindergarten through 10th grade (Matriculation), and we may expand that to higher secondary 12th grade, or intermediate college. We consciously chose to work with local boards instead of other credentialing systems, such as the International Baccalaureate (IB) or the 'O' and 'A' levels of the Cambridge system, both quite expensive. The choice is based on the rationale that we want to work nationally. So, working with local boards helps our student to easily transition from secondary to intermediate and college boards. Foundationally, these are the principles at the core of what we do and, evolving from that core, we move to academics and training and curriculum.

Academics is essentially what we want to teach in our schools. Here, we made a couple of fundamental assumptions based on what we have sensed in the environment, the first being that the typical teacher we employ is coming to us from the dysfunctional public-school system with all its issues of rote-learning and teaching-to-the-test practices and these come with the teacher. The heart is in the right place but the conceptual knowledge we like to see in our teachers could be missing in the newly employed teacher. So, there's a process of unlearning that needs to happen on the part of the new teacher. Second, for the new teacher coming in, her primary objective may be only to teach the whole textbook that she has to teach from. Third, in all good systems, planning the lesson is an integral part of good teaching. But the ability to develop a lesson plan may be lacking, and it is also difficult for the teacher to make the time for planning the lesson. So, because the new teacher is probably arriving with weak concepts, we have made it easier for her

---

Box 2.5 Curriculum and Examination Systems in Pakistan's elite private schools

International Baccalaureate (IB) originated in Switzerland in 1968 to provide an international standard of education for children of diplomats and foreign workers. It currently has nearly 5,000 schools in about 150 countries, catering to ages 3–19. There are two IB World schools in Pakistan.

Cambridge Assessment International Education is part of the University of Cambridge and offers international programs to learners from 10,000 schools in 160 countries. There are more than 400 private schools which subscribe to the Cambridge system in Pakistan.

The IB and Cambridge (12th grade) exams are recognized internationally as high-quality, high-cost preparation for university education.

Sources: IB and CAIE websites, February 2018

---

by creating an efficient lesson plan so the teacher can focus on the needs of each child. Moreover, we have also created workbooks related to the lessons. Each day, the teacher opens her Teacher's Guide binder which reads, for example: 'Today, I am teaching *Amali Science* (practical, physical), Book 4 and the chapter on Minerals, Teacher Guide page 57, Day 4.' So, that's the two-line lesson plan for Day 4 with details on how to do the 10-minute opening, how to deliver the lesson, how to do the consolidation, what activity to conduct, what props are needed, what is the homework going to be, what is the follow-up for the next day. All that is clearly spelled out in the lesson plan and teacher's guide.

When it comes to books, we embed everything we know into this and everything that we think ought to be done, both from the perspective of *taaleem* (learning) and *tarbiyat* (child development)—and these include conceptual knowledge, critical thinking, creative thinking and core values. Now, with that in mind, when we developed our books, we looked at the national curriculum and found there wasn't much wrong with that. We've compared it to curricula in Australia and Scotland and other countries. The things to think about are scope—the content of the curriculum, the sequence, and the slope. If the child is coming from the street and has no support at home, we may tweak the slope. We may change the grade-on-grade variations. We may also tweak down the optional content in the curriculum, but we may add things which ought to be added on. For example, when we were developing the math curriculum, we saw that patterns are conspicuously absent from the national curriculum. In studying the Canadian curriculum and others, we realized that to do algebra well, you need to be doing patterns at random. So, in our math book *Meri Riyazi* (My Math Exercises), we have embedded those patterns as part of the syllabus. Second, it's how we treat things in terms of the language issue. Our science books are all in Urdu, but the technical terminologies are in English, so the child does not suffer when it comes to switching at higher secondary levels. For math, we have actually gone a step further. The text of the word problem, and explanation is in Urdu. The digits, the signs, all the technical treatment are in English. So, rather than an ideological approach, we've taken the more pragmatic approach, because the child must be able to first understand, and this combination of languages is better for the child. Also, to augment the learning, the components of experiential learning that go with the lesson should be conducted at the same time. The physical activity related to a math or science lesson takes place in the same class period. For example, in a science class dealing with concepts of forces, the lesson plan suggests taking the children out to play a game of tug-of-war, then bring them back in the classroom and have them move furniture by pushing or pulling, open and shut doors and windows, to experience the forces involved in pushing and pulling.

Q. Even as they are going through that activity, do teachers insert some words in English?

Riaz: Yes, 'push' and 'pull' are used commonly.

Q. We know that children from TCF have difficulty in English and math when they take the college entrance tests. How is TCF dealing with that and how are we trying to resolve it?

Riaz: The issue with education is that the gestation period is long and it is going to take some time to see outcomes. You can't just insert something in the learning process and see the results right away. We are constantly trying to identify what is systemically wrong and address it at the front end. Since 2008, we have been working on designing and producing our own textbooks. We have completed the in-house work on our social studies books all the way up to 8th grade, including teacher's guides, lesson plans and workbooks. In science, we have completed up to 7th grade and *Insha Allah* next year we should be done with 8th grade. For our math textbooks, we should be completing 4th grade this year. We have completed the English books for grade 1 and hope to complete two grades every year and get it done. Prior to 2008, we were using a mish-mash of books from Oxford University Press and other sources. We didn't have the wherewithal then. But we are diligently—and patiently—working on it now, not rushing the book development process. Every chapter of every book goes through multiple drafts before it's completed and illustrated. It's a lengthy process. Systemically, I think we are now getting this right, because I can see the dialogs and the quality of conversations in classrooms is very different now. The issue in the short term is what we should do for the children currently in the secondary grades, how can we help them with their learning gap. There are changes we're bringing about in secondary schools as well but that may require addressing the needs of individual student and giving customized help to students who are struggling.

2.4 Strategic Development Unit

Rahila Fatima is one of the strategic thinkers at TCF. She came to the TCF Academics-Education Department fourteen years back and currently heads the Strategic Development Unit (SDU). Earlier, Rahila was with Aga Khan Education Services (AKES) for five years, first as a lecturer and later in curriculum development and training for the AKES school system. She has degrees in English Literature and Linguistics, and a diploma in Social Enterprise Management from LUMS.

Q. You've witnessed the maturing of TCF as an institution of considerable influence in the education landscape of Pakistan. In recent years, there has been frenetic activity at TCF. Please share with us what's been happening at a higher level in the SDU.

Rahila: Certainly. 2013–14 was an important year for TCF because the 1,000 school milestone was very much in sight. There had been discussions on a long-term course for TCF, but 2013 was the year when there were louder and longer conversations about 'What Next'. Do we add a thousand more schools? Or 2,000 more schools? Or just consolidate? Build only secondary schools, add colleges? Follow a different stream? Or what? Along with those ideas, we also began to think about something which was not there in 1995–96, when we got started, and that was information about out-of-school children (OOSC). We could *see* children on the streets during the day, obviously not in school. People generally had an idea that there were a fairly large number of OOSC but many of us thought that there were some 100,000 or maybe 200,000 OOSC. According to the higher estimates by Alif Ailaan[4] (an advocacy campaign), there could be as many as 25 million OOSC, so there was no possible way that TCF could solve this huge problem without government involvement and we had to look for ways to leverage our work through collaborative partnerships with the government. That itself could take huge resources and have many twists and turns, but we realized that we had to look for opportunities with the government.

So, we began to scratch our heads and wonder how that might happen. And, also what TCF could do to extend its reach and its impact if we were not successful in collaborating with government. That led us to think of other large players in the education sector, namely the low-cost private schools (LCPS) that had proliferated and were thriving with the increasing demand in that socioeconomic market. It was also apparent that quality was not of high importance to the school owners, that bottom-line profit was the driving force and motivation for an LCPS owner. It is a profitable small business, so there is no reason to add to the cost by introducing expensive features for the sake of quality. In most cases, parents could not tell the difference between quality schooling or not, as long as the children were learning *something* and appeared to be 'smarter'. Sadly, we were aware of the poor quality and that the children were not really learning very much.

We designed an intervention that was essentially a pilot funded by DFID and we aptly named it 'TCF-in-a Box' (TIB) and envisioned it as a self-contained package of easy-to-follow tools and practices of education delivery for LCPS. In addition to education tools, we included management efficiency tools such as easy-to-follow manuals on HR, basic financial management, and school administration.

Box 2.6 TCF-in-a Box (TIB)

TIB was designed as a 'package' of education tools and management practices developed at TCF for teacher training, textbooks, pedagogical techniques, HR, and financial management at schools. TIB was offered at no cost to subscribing low-cost schools. The objective was to improve management and pedagogy for quality education. In return, TCF required accountability in learning outcomes and evidence of improved management procedures.

Funded by DFID for two years as a pilot, the first six months of the project were spent in planning the program, and survey and selection of schools. TIB was rolled out and implemented in fifty of Karachi's LCPS in the second year. A couple of schools dropped out within a few weeks for reasons that they did not have management and staff to carry out the procedural and pedagogical changes required by TIB. At the halfway mark, it became apparent that many of the owners could not cope with the requirement of evidence-based reporting and that they may not continue with TIB after the pilot. Many school owners did not see value in quality improvement measures or better management practices, despite encouragement by TCF that the extra effort would result in increasing the enrollment, better student retention and increased profits.

TIB was shelved after the pilot program. There were however, two strong offshoots of this pilot: (1) an in-house publishing department for quality textbooks to be made available to all schools, and (2) professional development and teacher training services. TCF is now focusing on developing these services as quality catalysts.

– Rahila Fatima

Q. Was SDU formed as a result of TIB?

Rahila: Not really. TCF management leadership and directors thought that there should be a smaller strategic planning unit focused on 'What Next' for developing ideas; study feasibilities of enterprise projects; run pilots; explore 'partnership' schools with government versus flagship TCF schools (our core program), supported by government subsidy through vouchers or other programs; expand *Aagahi*, the adult literacy program, to include the population of young adults who had not gone to school at all or dropped out in early grades to go to work; testing a low-cost franchise model for the mid-tier market.

Interestingly, DFID had come in at about the same time, with a desire to explore the low-fee market schools. They had Ferguson, a local consultancy group, do a study to see if the LCPS would be interested in microfinancing to improve quality of education. Because of our learning and experience in that market, DFID then got in touch with us to explore if we could develop a package for anyone interested in opening a school who could take our set of procedures, books and learning materials and maintain a certain level of quality in the education to be delivered. These conversations were happening in parallel. That was the birth of TIB and SDU was created at the same time.

TIB was one of the pilots that we did with DFID. There were other feasibilities that we worked on, like forming an education board, marketing of teacher training services, the GSP, alternate methods of education via radio, distance learning, and other such projects. Some of these ideas were related to quality and others had impact both on access and quality. The government schools adoption program certainly has an impact on both access and quality. Teacher training services was for quality focus only. Alternate methods of education whether through radio or mass media, and generally adult literacy and life skills training, were also considered for providing both access and quality. These were the combination of areas and ideas that were pouring in. The SDU team was formed in April 2013 and announced at the Global Chapters Conference (GCC) where more ideas were kicked around. It was smart of the Board to form the SDU to keep these conversations alive, refine the ideas and narrow the focus to a few feasible ones which can be taken forward. Then, at the 2015 GCC, we had two or three clear things that we shared—the 1.5 million target was established and now, *Alhamdulillah,* we may soon have a publishing house and a teacher training service for professional development. So, that's SDU.

These 'enterprise' programs could be financially viable as they would have their own income streams, and at the same time, provide much-needed services to the education ecosystem. Most of the smaller, low-cost private schools are looking to fill the void in teacher training and good books, and TCF can contribute these services at an affordable cost to these schools. In the bigger picture, TCF would be giving them a hand in quality improvement through guidance and books for curriculum development and through sound pedagogical skills for their teachers.

Box 2.7 TCF Next?

'*What Next*' was a brainstorming exercise at the inflection point in 2013 when TCF was nearing its target of 1,000 school units. At that time, TCF schools had 150,000 children enrolled. Leaders at the Global Chapters Conference (GCC) decided that the next goal for TCF would be to expand its impact 10x, to reach 1.5 million learners. This number could include students in the TCF core programs as well as the programs managed by TCF such as adopted government schools, the Railways schools under TCF management, *Aagahi* adult literacy program, learners reached through radio or mass media, and other alternate education programs.

Since the GCC in early 2019, the new goal and rallying cry is '*Two Million by 2030*'. To achieve the target, TCF plans to continue expanding its effort for formal education through TCF 'flagship' and partnership (adopted public) schools, also increase its outreach through the literacy and life skills programs, to empower those who have missed their first chance at schooling.

TCF expertise in developing books and learning materials for children, leadership programs for principals, and teacher training programs can be used across public and private sector schools (especially, low cost schools), to enable delivery of quality education.

– *Rahila Fatima*

For many of the schools in the LCPS market, the teacher's job is to flip the pages of the textbook—and that is the extent of quality teaching. The book itself is the lesson plan. The teacher comes to class each day totally unprepared. There's no extra reading or activity-based learning for the students, hardly any effort to identify the slow learners or the root cause of the poor learning, and no extra help given to the student who falls behind.

Q. Since SDU was initiated in 2013, what are the projects or programs that have gone through the pipeline?

Rahila: Besides the feasibilities and ideas that we are working on, there were two major programs: TIB and the GSP which kicked off with

---

Box 2.8 Global Chapters Conference...A Biennial Forum

The GCC is a forum held every two years in Karachi for local and international TCF leaders. The two-day program is an opportunity for leaders to learn about recent happenings and future plans at TCF, to explore innovative ideas, and set financial and program goals. Just as important, personal friendships and relationships are rekindled and camaraderie is strengthened. – Author

---

the Railways school, then the five schools in KP, followed by the three Sindh-SEF schools, and then the huge chunk of 250 Punjab-PEF schools.

Q. Just to be clear, in the first round, we got 80 schools from Punjab. In the second lot, we took another 153 schools and the total is 253 government schools in Punjab.

Rahila: That is correct. These numbers could change as we are in frequent conversations with the governments of Sindh and Balochistan as well.

Q. Any sense of how many schools are being considered for adoption in Sindh and Balochistan?

Rahila: We need to consider a few things. First, what is the deal in terms of the subsidy we would receive, and the infrastructure and condition of the schools. TCF can do just so much with our own resources to rehab the government schools we agree to take over. That's an important element. Second, how much do we want to continue increasing our bandwidth by adding more adopted schools? Because then we have to sustain the management of those adopted schools. These are the two major considerations. I think, with Balochistan and Sindh, we want to start with a reasonable number, say fifty schools each in the first phase, see how things go, and then proceed to grow.

Q. TCF should be pleased that we have a foot in the door. We have yet to see if it is a feasible public-private partnership for the long term, but can we expect the provincial governments to give us better terms of subsidy payment that help us to recover our cost, and a little more?

Rahila: Exactly. From our perspective, we have finally crossed this barrier of public-private partnership (PPP) which we have been deliberating for the last 7 or 8 years. The question has been 'When will TCF be ready to partner with the government?' and we knew that eventually we would do it but it was just a matter of when. I think reaching the target of 1,000 schools gave us the confidence and the impetus to go ahead with it. Another thing to our benefit is that, in recent years, the provincial governments have also become more flexible and softened to the idea of public-private partnerships. Otherwise, only Punjab was agreeable to partnerships for adoption of schools. Other than that, there was no PPP or adoption program and there were no other organizations coming forward to adopt schools on a large scale—and, more important—to invest in improving the quality of education.

Earlier, we were talking about OOSC and people generally dismissed it as an 'insignificant' number of no more than 200,000…until Alif Ailaan's numbers were quoted in the UN Millennium Development Goals (MDGs) that there was in fact a very serious problem of 25 million OOSC. I think the Alif Ailaan messaging and persistent advocacy, plus the MDGs, had significant bearing on shaking up the governments and making them realize that something must be done in each province, and they became more agreeable to the PPP ideas and adoption program. So, it was a good point in time for TCF that we were able to reach our target of 1,000 schools, the confidence it gave us and the fact that we had met the expectations of our donors—all that put together positioned us well to take on the challenges of scaling up. The twenty years of experience, not only in education and academics, but also in areas of governance and management have added to our confidence to take over schools in large numbers for scaling up rapidly.

Q. What's in the SDU pipeline at this time—more government schools, or is that a given?

Rahila: That's a given…the way we have scaled up and the potential impact that we see with the GSP, our desire to expand across the

> ### Box 2.9 Public Advocacy for Education
>
> Alif Ailaan was an advocacy campaign for education reform funded by DFID. Launched in February 2013 and terminating in August 2018, it made a positive contribution by bringing education issues and survey data into public discourse and had an influence on policymaking through media campaigns and strategic communications. The campaign demonstrated that sustainable advocacy campaigns can have a constructive role in Pakistani civil society by highlighting the issues and promoting robust debate on education reform and public oversight. – *Author*

provinces, our ongoing dialog with Sindh and Balochistan. So, that's for sure, there's no stopping to the GSP now. The question obviously is how soon and how much. That will depend on the kind of deals we can negotiate with the provinces. But another couple of areas we would like to explore are really by-products or offshoots of the learning experience from the TIB pilot. As part of the pilot, we were working with 50 schools, but we had surveyed 500 low-fee private schools to obtain information on teacher training, curriculum, books and learning materials used at the schools. We discovered across all the schools that there is a huge void of quality material because good books are expensive. Thus, the schools will have one or two good books on any subject from quality publishers like Oxford University Press, but the rest of the books are very mediocre, low quality material. That way they can claim that they 'teach the Oxford curriculum'. So, there is very clear need for good material, but we will need to translate our books from Urdu to English, because the medium of instruction that prevails in the low-fee private schools is English and our books are in Urdu. Other than that, wherever we have sent our books—in the low-fee schools or the better private schools like Habib Public School—our books have been liked across the board. They want the books.

Q. Did you say Habib Public School? Their books and teaching are in English, and our books are in Urdu…

Rahila: Right. When the people at Habib saw our books, like the social studies book *Hamari Dilkash Duniya* (Our Beautiful World), they asked if we were planning to translate these books because they want the books we have developed. So, development of learning material—because that's a quality intervention—is one big area and we're looking at it as a project which is financially sustainable as well. A publishing house is one of the enterprise areas that we will expand into, as a long-term 'business', if you will. We're constantly adding to our menu of books and materials. It will be relatively easy to translate them into English for that market. There's a dearth of good story books, particularly in Urdu. So, there are multiple avenues to explore as a publishing house, and the best part is that it could be financially sustainable.

Q. ...perhaps even profitable?

Rahila: That's entirely possible.

Q. What's happening with the idea of creating a school board? Is it feasible, is it a dead issue, or on the shelf?

Rahila: It's still on the shelf, not dead. When we had it on the discussion table, we knew it was a far greater challenge than any other project we were exploring, the reason being that in Pakistan we have not been successful with private boards of education. The Aga Khan University Education Board (AKU-EB) is the only private board and they...

Q....but they haven't been able to grow.

Rahila: Yes, it's been a struggle for them to grow. Secondly, we can't have a board for our own schools because the optics will not be right. No matter how transparent we remain, we will never be seen as fair and transparent. So, this has to be in the public domain, like AKU. It can be time consuming and politically challenging. There was this desire and debate around it, but we don't foresee it happening any time soon, unless we see the AKU Board succeeding and growing.

Q. Is 'Curriculum Development' a separate team or department within TCF?

Rahila: Organizationally, curriculum development is part of the TCF Education Department which had three functions initially: Academics,

Training, and Monitoring & Evaluation (M&E). Monitoring & Evaluation was separated and has now grown further as the Quality Assurance (QA) department. So, currently, Academics and Training are part of Education, and Academics includes Curriculum Development—books, materials, learning targets, and so forth—and it's rolled out with the help of the Training Team which also manages any other training needs that emerge from the field.

Q. So, will the Academics Curriculum teams manage the creation and development of the textbooks?

Rahila: That depends on how rapidly we grow as a publishing house because it will probably be a bigger team, perhaps two teams—the publishing house, and the internal Academics and Training teams working together—because the materials need to be practically feasible for students in *all* schools, developed in both Urdu and English probably in parallel, or translated from one to the other. These things will take shape once we get going and this is what we plan to present to our Board in a couple of months. If we move ahead, *Insha Allah*, then our target for 2018 will be to have our own books translated [into English]. Then we'll see how it flows, what the sales are, what the demands are, and go accordingly.

Q. The textbook industry is competitive and quite protective of its turf. Isn't it known to operate somewhat like a 'mafia'?

Rahila: In some ways, yes.

Q. Have they attempted to block or sabotage the growth of TCF in the publishing market?

Rahila: They don't know of us because we don't have a presence in the market, and we may not be a significant competitor. But it's like any other business. We will try and grab our share of the market. We will go into it with that mindset and with that understanding because it must be a financially sustainable enterprise. We will study the competition and strategize against them, frankly, to do it right and in a business-like manner.

Q. Tell me about the Railways school adoption, how it came about and the challenges you faced, because the challenges were different to the GSP. Is there possibility of collaboration with other agencies that operate schools for employee families like the Railways—other nationalized systems, such as PIA, or the Customs service?

Rahila: Interestingly, the Railways school adoption happened at the time we were talking with the KP government and the ruling political party there was Pakistan Tehreek-e-Insaf, PTI. The Railways school was in the constituency of an MNA (Member of the National Assembly) with a PTI affiliation and he facilitated some of the conversations with KP. Now, PTI has a social welfare wing, the Insaf Community Welfare Society (ICWS) and they were exploring how to work with the Railways school because it had fallen into disrepair and was in bad shape. That's when ICWS suggested that we consider taking the school on as an adoption-management project. I think our challenge with Railways or PIA would be that their schools are scattered, located where employee residence colonies exist, and there aren't very many schools, so when we look at scale and clusters, this may not be a simple fit for alignment with TCF. Nevertheless, we wanted to experiment and try our hand at a PPP, so we came to an agreement and that's how it happened.

The biggest challenge we have is that the teachers are employed by Railways through union contracts. To some extent, we expected that to be a challenge. The school location is close to a very large residential colony of hundreds of Railways employees of the junior cadre. It is the largest campus in their network. When we took over the management, there were roughly 600 students, about 75 percent of them were children of Railways employees. The schools are subsidized for the employee families and they pay 130 rupees per child as tuition. The schools are also open to the community, but non-Railways families pay 450 rupees per child. Rehabilitation, renovation of the buildings and maintenance are paid for by the ICWS and the physical infrastructure is looking much better. Now, two years later, we have grown to 1,150 students, nearly double. It's a huge campus, on eight acres of land. The ground level is now fully operational, and work is going on for classrooms on the upper floor. When completed, the campus has a capacity of 1,500 students. It has several sections or school units which operate in two shifts, morning and afternoon.

A year down the road, the staffing situation is much better. When we took over, we placed two of our most experienced principals at the campus, one for each shift. More than half the teachers were the existing faculty employed by Railways. TCF provided the rest of the teaching staff. As enrollment has grown, we have added more teachers paid by TCF. There has also been some attrition of the Railways teachers due to retirements or resignations, so we have better balance in numbers, plus the existing batch of Railways teachers is blending in nicely with our staff and there is better harmony. In all aspects, we try to manage the school just like any other TCF school, providing teacher training, learning materials and other admin support.

This school was probably on the verge of closing down due to mismanagement and insufficient funding. So, this has been a successful rescue operation on the part of TCF. In terms of subsidy from ICWS or the Railways, they do not have the funds to pay us anything. We do collect the fees paid by all students, so there is some income, but it only covers about 30 percent of our cost. A great thing that has occurred is the support from the community and the parents. We have had regular parent-teacher meetings and gradually the community interest has grown. Initially, they wanted to know who we were, but they have started to see the change. We are running remedial classes, offering extra classes and free tutoring, so the results have been really satisfying. When we took over, the 10th grade results for girls were 21 percent passing; this has gone up to 88 percent in one year. For the boys, it was 19 percent and is now 40 percent, which is not a big increase but there were other challenges with boys, such as behavior and discipline issues. Some boys also go to work in the mornings and come to school in the afternoon shift, and that could have a bearing as well, because they are tired and worn out after several hours of work. The Railways workers' union is very appreciative of the work done by TCF in turning around this school.

Q. The increase in enrollment of nearly 600 more students – where did these 600 children come from? Were they in government schools or were they out-of-school?

Rahila: No, they were in schools. Quite a few of them are students who had left the Railways school after disappointing experiences because things had become so bad. The parents pulled them out and put them into private schools at a higher cost but brought them back when they saw things improving here. They probably did not enroll in government schools because that would have been a step down. But we're glad that we have turned things around and these children are back in their old school. So, this is the story of the Railways school that TCF is managing. It has been a great learning experience for us.

At the same time, we have introduced the *Rahbar* mentorship and *Aagahi* adult literacy programs at the Railways school and we're trying to embed these ancillary programs we have in our core TCF system. We see change taking place, but it is slow, and it will take some time. There is a noticeable difference between the participation level of our core TCF students and the Railways school students, but as we see the confidence level of children getting better at Railways we will see better participation and enthusiasm for the mentorship program as well.

2.5 Inputs: Resource Mobilization, Marketing, IT and SDU

VP of Inputs, Zia Abbas has been another great find for TCF. He joined in 2014 after a 17-year career in the banking industry. Zia did two years of schooling in Canada and has an MBA from LUMS. He exemplifies the selfless TCF managerial team of talented and dedicated people at the top.

Q. What are the departments and functions you oversee as VP-Inputs?

Zia: In the overall jig-saw puzzle of TCF, I manage four units. The two that require most of my time are the Resource Mobilization Department (RMD) and Marketing. The departments don't really generate the revenue resources we need because the volunteers do that globally, but these departments help in enabling those volunteers, sometimes planning and supporting their work and at other times aligning and directing it. That's the core job of RMD. Marketing obviously manages the brand and it is slowly getting to the point where it can support the fundraising efforts in Pakistan and globally. Apart from that, I oversee the Technology Department and the Strategic Development Unit (SDU) which is responsible for thinking about and incubating ideas which will get us to the aspirational goals we set for ourselves. That's the breadth of it. The senior management team, the VPs and the CEO, work very closely and my role within that team is to look at

Inputs, which are the money, the brand, and the technology that goes into it. There is one large 'input' which is Human Resource (HR) but that's managed within outcomes because that is closely aligned with the learning process. Teachers are the main human resource and TCF employs 17,500 people including 14,000 women—arguably making us the largest employer of women in the country. We employ more than 12,000 teachers, who are all women, and, because of their involvement in the learning process, we've always managed HR with 'Education' under the umbrella of Outcomes.

Within fundraising, we have the happy problem of growing at high double digits historically and in excess of 20 percent in the recent past, and that for any organization is a remarkably high pace of growth in terms of program expenses, which pre-determines our need for revenues to be raised. By and large, *Alhamdulillah*, we've been able to match that growth. Very broadly, half the money we raise every year is from Pakistan and the rest comes from abroad. Within that, there are four large overseas support groups—the US, UK, UAE, and Canada—who are the biggest contributors and far ahead of the smaller, emerging groups. We refrain from calling them TCF chapters because these are independent organizations that support us and they must be compliant with local and national laws in their respective countries.

Pakistan is interesting in that we have a very large organization here and half the funds are raised here. Yet most of that money comes from a very few domestic locations, actually mainly from Karachi. In that sense, we have the opportunity to really become a national brand from a fundraising aspect, not just from the impact aspect. Most of our schools are outside of Sindh now and we're investing in the capability to bring TCF to donors everywhere.

Q. What is the role of the Strategic Development Unit, SDU?

Zia: Because the organization is extremely focused on execution, and that is one of our strengths, it has done so by not getting sucked into a lot of conversations or proposals that have come to us over time. Many ideas are blue sky ideas—what is out there, what can we do beyond what we've done—and SDU is really a capability to handle that narrative, to organize it, to advise the Board on where investment of time and money are most likely to yield results. It is guided by aspirations of growth and scale but really it is more than that. It is to push the frontiers of scale and cost and delivering both at an even higher quality if possible. So, these three frontiers are in their hands and we have allied ourselves with the government wherever it has become financially and operationally possible and we've taken over 250 government schools with 20,000 students and we hope to increase that number. This is within the direct programming part of SDU, with the core TCF schools and the Government Schools Program.

But, beyond that, we are looking at interfacing with the ecosystem as a whole, to become a broad service provider pushing all three of the frontiers, to reach more and more children, to bring them a better quality of education, and do it at a cost which makes sense for the other players as well as for us. So, we feel that what we know can also be leveraged by many other players in the ecosystem. We are right now incubating enterprises—hopefully, financially sustainable ones—that can, for example, provide books and learning materials to government schools and private schools as a spin-off, a large publishing house enterprise. Similarly, we're looking at and toying with ideas of a training service which delivers teacher training and management training to the entire ecosystem. And, as you see, there is a whole range of work that people do in a school and we don't need to own a school to be able to upgrade that work and to enhance its quality. We are driven both by sustainability concerns as well as—and, primarily by—benefit to the lower strata of society, which is getting a very poor quality of education, if at all. Those are the immediate projects. Another is to look at the population who have missed the boat, so to speak, and see if we can provide a standardized, consistent, well-delivered and low-cost solution for men and women who are beyond the age of going to school—young adults, adolescents—and be able to provide not just literacy but basic life skills as well: how to open a bank account, how to deal with money, how to deal with the system, how to deal with government, and also how to run an enterprise perhaps and how to deal with technology. So, these are all themes which this population segment is not accustomed to or exposed to—and there is no enabling entity out there which provides information and guidance on this.

We have tried to structure solutions and we're talking to grantors and also figuring out how to create the internal bandwidth to be able to do all of this at the same time. Those are some of the most immediate projects. The SDU, then, is a unit that can think laterally and explore, toy with ideas which the bigger machine within TCF is not able to deal with.

Q. Since quality is a major concern, is there thought being given to the formation of an examination board?

Zia: It's something we keep coming back to. I think it's fundamental. Frankly, even in our system, we end up losing momentum in 8th grade because, in the end, we do have to get these children into an examination board and we deal with more than twelve examination boards, country-wide—it's not just one—and they have varying levels of quality but all of them need much improvement. Just in terms of scale, though, the examination board—if we ever go down that path—is a far larger enterprise than anything we have taken on so far. It would have huge impact on quality, but it also requires much greater investment and rigor. So, it's something we clearly keep coming back to but it's something for which we have to find the right time to really dive into.

Q. Other than the political elements, what would be some other ingredients that would spur that action?

Zia: If we approach it apolitically and there is enough trust placed in us, there is obviously the element of getting the government's authorization to do it which is not going to be easy. The other concern would be the management bandwidth which, in turn, would determine the money needed.

Q. Wouldn't it be supported by the revenues it would generate?

Zia: If TCF does it, we would do it for the lowest strata of the pyramid, the low-cost private schools who would be our potential subscribers. The closest comparison is the Aga Khan University Education Board (AKU-EB) and it is far more expensive than what we could afford. There are costs involved with the platform creation, monitoring of tests, the administration expenses and, finally, the cost of assessment and tabulation. If you can craft the story and develop a business model, the money often follows. So, it's really how many things you can pick up and manage at the same time and where does it fit into the roadmap, so to speak. But certainly, it will have a massive impact in quality improvement.

Q. Other than the virtually free current model of TCF schools, are TCF and SDU looking at other low-cost models for schools in the private-school market?

Zia: Sure. Within direct programming, the way we run the government schools that we have adopted and the way we've always followed for our TCF schools, the cookie-cutter model. The two are very different in the sense that the infrastructure is just not there [for the adopted government schools] and we have resolved to live with the same qualitative inputs even while the hardware and infrastructure is not there, and what we are hoping to see is whether we can deliver comparable educational outcomes. Obviously, every part of the puzzle makes a difference in the overall outcomes but we, in SDU, have always toyed with the idea of how much of the cost is going into which element of the model and can we explore lower cost. So, we do believe that there is a balance to be found which invests less in brick-and-mortar, more in teachers, and maybe a little more in technology or alternative learning materials and methods. I know it sounds strange that you're hoping to put in less money and get more out of it but that's what innovation is all about. So, while we respect what we've built over time, we necessarily have to reject it to be able to build something even better.

Q. ...isn't 'reject' a strong word?

Zia: Yes, in the sense that there are things we hold very dear about our model. But, for the core model to advance, SDU is also sometimes a laboratory to test those ideas in the field. For instance, we are questioning whether we need as much invested in transportation of teachers—now that those communities have come so far and have a lot more in terms of residents of those communities who are educated. Actually, SDU and the government schools have enabled us to accelerate that process because we know now how we can go about hiring teachers from the localities where those schools are, and we have taken on the aggressive task of reducing the cost of transportation. That would never have been possible, nor would we have been so confident about it had we not tested it. So, we are unafraid of questioning ourselves and our assumptions on how these things work.

Q. Let's move to Marketing and talk about managing and strengthening the TCF brand.

Zia: I think it is important to talk about how we manage the TCF brand and how, over time, it has evolved from the ground up and organically wherever it has been taken up by volunteers, and—not so much from the control angle as from the enabling angle—we need to clearly define these roles. We, in Pakistan, are not used to having multi-national headquarters but we have to find some of that discipline as well as some of that organic finesse of managing a brand which is ultimately owned by supporters and global volunteers. So, you can't drive it top-down and yet we need alignment, we need support, clarity of brand strategy, marketing strategy, and segment selection. In those things, we do need to play a role at the head office as well as at the chapter or overseas leadership level. While there's a volunteer out there, that volunteer needs clarity and support from us. I think that's going to happen much more in years to come.

Q. You alluded to the fact that most of the revenue raised in Pakistan comes from Karachi. What is the plan to make TCF a household name all over Pakistan, and also strengthen the brand globally?

Zia: Two things: the way to do it is really to develop the outreach capability in terms of feet-on-the-street or the physical human-to-human contact as well as the opportunity that digital marketing gives us, and we're investing in both. We've set up a team in Lahore, a much bigger team than we've ever had, and invested in it in terms of seniority and quality of resources as well and it's immediately bringing results. And, as we speak, we're investing in a global digital marketing capability which will serve all support groups and chapters and be able to target folks we haven't been able to get through to, in Pakistan and abroad.

Q. Tell us more about the *Rahbar* mentorship program and *Aagahi*.

Zia: 'Rahbar' is a self-managed program, pretty much directed by the volunteer leadership from within the program and a small steering committee of the *Rahbar* Council, which consists mostly of volunteers and a few TCF staff for coordination.

Aagahi is an alliance with Literate Pakistan Foundation (LPF) and they have an adult literacy program *Jugnu* deployed outside of TCF. The partnership has been mutually beneficial because they have been able to scale up through TCF and we have been able to concentrate purely on administration, execution, and operations and reach into the community, which is our strength. For the program, we rely on LPF and we haven't had to reinvent the wheel. There will be much more work on program as we go into new segments of population, such as adolescents who were left out of school. Perhaps this *Aagahi* trajectory will meet our aspiration program of Learning and Life Skills, because that is also going to be outside the schools. So, we will have to take the lead on the program at that stage. From a pure literacy perspective, the *Jugnu* program from LPF has really helped us.

Q. Occasionally, there have been suggestions to create alliances with health initiatives for screenings or basic medical needs, and some were tried in the early years. Where is TCF on that?

We have not gone beyond the Clean Water Project as an added service to benefit the community. We had paused it, but now we are beginning to expand it again because we've learned much more on the distribution, the revenue, and administration model. Beyond that, we have focused on what we chose to deliver well and that's education. Sometimes it's as important to know what you do well and leave the other projects to other great players who are doing them well. Hardly a month goes by when we don't have meetings with other local non-profits who come here to look at our management model and procedures. We're constantly interacting with Indus Hospital, Hunar Foundation, and others and we have projects where there will be a Hunar Institute next to a TCF school, or Indus Hospital or Sina Health setting up clinics in proximity to one of our schools. You'll find a very similar work ethic and ethos in many of these organizations.

2.6 Area Education Managers (AEMs)

AEMs are the essential gears in the wheels of the TCF quality assurance program. AEMs manage ongoing observation and evaluations of teacher pedagogical skills, content knowledge and overall school performance for academics, intervening to address weaknesses in any area of teaching quality by alerting the training department crew to assist with specific teacher training at the monthly INSET (In-Service Training) sessions. This conversation with AEM's Irum Bano illustrates what they do.

Q. Where did you go to school, Irum?

Irum: I finished my Matric at a private school and went to a government college for Intermediate. Then I did my bachelor's and joined TCF as a teacher in Baldia Town, an outlying area of Karachi.

Q. That's in the Lyari area. Isn't that a tough neighborhood? I understand there's high rate of crime there and drugs and gangs—is that true?

Irum: Yes, all that is true but that's where we live and it's not that bad.

Q. Please tell me about your parents and family.

Irum: Our family comprises my parents, my three siblings, and myself. I am single. My older sister Tabassum is the principal at a TCF school in Hub City. An older brother works at a company and a younger brother is in the army. Of the six members of our family, three of us work at TCF. We are very proud of my father who is a *chowkidar* (gate guard) at my sister's TCF school in Hub.

Q. How long have you worked at TCF?

Irum: My father took the job as gate guard at the newly opened TCF school in our area and he encouraged me to teach there. My sister was teaching at a private school. Two months later, my sister also joined TCF as a teacher. I've completed ten years with TCF, in different capacities, starting as a primary teacher then moving up to become an English Language Teacher in a secondary school, then I was promoted to principal at a primary school and did that for two years. I was then promoted as an AEM and that's what I do now. I did my Matric in 2003 and joined TCF after my Intermediate. I continued college while teaching and I have a Bachelor of Arts degree in Education. When I joined TCF, I wasn't sure what I wanted to do but, as time went on, I liked what I was doing and I'm happy that I stayed with it.

Q. How did you become an English Language Teacher? And how were you selected and trained?

Irum: I had taught in early primary grades for a couple of years and I was interested in being an English Language Teacher, ELT. There is separate training for ELT and specialized subjects. I had observed ELT training and I applied for it but I failed the test at first and I was disappointed. I worked hard, got better and applied again the next year. And I was accepted and assigned as an ELT in a secondary school.

Q. How are English language skills addressed at TCF?—and is it difficult to find ELT's?

Irum: We develop English language skills—listening, reading, writing and speaking—on the principles of activity-based learning. It is difficult to find qualified ELTs but we are seeing many more students come back as teachers. In fact, more than a hundred TCF girls[5] have come back as teachers, just in our area. Hopefully, many more will train and qualify as ELTs.

Q. What challenges have you faced in your roles as teacher, principal and now as AEM?

Irum: As principal, I would get veiled threats demanding that I should admit children from a feudal *vadera* (tribal chief or feudal) family. This was common in Soomar Goth and Baldia Town. Drugs are a big problem there and so is the violent culture. I had to meet with the men and explain that there is a reasonable process we follow for admitting children and there is a limit to what we can do. I would also explain that we could take a small number of children in a remedial program and accelerate their learning to get them into an age-appropriate grade. The people are not aware of how a school system operates but when they're explained in a nice way and given some options, they usually understand and they calm down. We help them by accommodating the child in a remedial program which is customized to the child's needs.

For example, there was a 12-year old boy who came by himself and asked for admission to the school. He was from a Pakhtun family that had moved from KP and he had been to a madrasa but could only speak a little Urdu. His father was a laborer and worked long hours. The child's age was appropriate for 5th grade but he had never been to a school. We asked him to bring a parent so he brought his grandfather who couldn't speak any Urdu but he insisted that we should admit the boy. With the boy interpreting Pashtu-Urdu between us, we agreed to take the child and, between all the teachers, we coached the child in our free time, just enough to groom him and get him started in a combination grade 2-3 classroom. In a few months, he brought two of his younger siblings, 5 and 6 years olds, and we admitted them to KG. I think he had 6 or 7 siblings. I never met his father, who was always working. We admitted the 12-year old for one year and he was moved up to 3rd grade but he was 13 by this time and it was getting very awkward for him to be with younger children who were better learners than him. Realizing that he would have a problem adjusting to the 4th grade, I spoke with the principal of a government school in the neighborhood and they took him in 5th grade. The classrooms in government schools can have wide disparities in ages of the children so it is not difficult for the 13-year old child to adjust over there. Maybe, if he's ready, I'll try to bring him back in a year and admit him in 6th grade in our TCF secondary school. His two younger siblings are both doing well in 2nd grade. If it wasn't for him, his siblings would perhaps not have come to school either. That's an example of how we deal with unique situations.

Q. So, what do you do as an AEM? And what are your personal goals and aspirations?

Irum: The TCF South West region is the largest in terms of students and numbers of school units. We have five areas in the region. I have 56 units and 450 teachers to manage in my area. Sixteen of the units are secondary schools. I guide and support the school principals and teachers, keep them motivated and pumped up, help to resolve their problems, and observe their working as it relates to academics. We have a checklist of items to focus on, key performance indicators for pedagogy and teaching quality, which areas are strong and which ones could use some help and more training. We also sample student learning through observation and random interactions with them. The AEM visits every school on a monthly schedule, checking on whether corrections were made from previously set targets, often giving priority and extra visits to a school that may have weak areas. The Area Manager's focus is on administrative issues, such as the hiring of new teachers. We have an Area Office in one of the schools in Baldia. My day begins with either school visits or meetings or interviews at the Area Office. I schedule school visits to observe and evaluate teaching in the classroom, compile the data, and submit it to the AM and RM. As for the future, in a few years I think I'll be ready to move on to something different, maybe a position in academics at the head office. We'll see. But I'm quite happy doing what I do.

2.7 Conversations in Balochistan

I accompanied the Regional Manager (retired Brigadier) Mansur Aslam on a trip to TCF schools in Balochistan. On the way and in conversations at the school locations, Mansur informed me of the unique cultural and political challenges of Balochistan, the largest of the provinces but the least populated and the least developed, with occasional uprisings for autonomy—perhaps more as a demand for attention than independence or separation. The province is heavily tribal-feudal and also has the poorest education infrastructure at all levels. We drove west through the Lyari area of Karachi and crossed into Balochistan at Hub, arriving at the TCF school in Vinder three hours later. The school visit was pretty routine for me—the usual conversations with the principal and staff—but the special part of the trip was a home visit to meet a student's mother and the fact that this was in a small town of Balochistan. At the Vinder campus (funded by corporate donor Pakistan State Oil, PSO), the first conversation was with school principal Irum Naz.

Q. Where did you complete your schooling and college and how long have you been a principal at this school?

Irum Naz: I joined as a teacher in 2009 and I've been the principal here since 2013. I went to a private school in Sher Shah Colony, completed my B.Ed. from Karachi University and did my master's in Political Science. I had to prepare privately for the master's degree and take classes in the evenings or on weekends. There was a lot of self-study as well.

Q. Tell us about your family and what they are doing.

Irum Naz: My mother is a homemaker, father works at a bank, my brother is an engineer. One of my sisters was teaching at a TCF school and she has recently married so she's undecided about what she will do. Another sister has done her Intermediate and my youngest sister is in 5th grade.

Q. How was your own learning experience as a student?

Irum Naz: Of course, I had taken math in school but the concepts were not well-founded. My teachers couldn't explain the math concepts and it was a matter of memorizing or guessing the right answers. It was learning by repetition, like a parrot, without understanding it. My conceptual knowledge got better as I began to teach math. I often wonder how fortunate these children are in TCF schools who can get the help to learn the proper foundational concepts.

Q. How is the teaching different at TCF?

Irum Naz: It's because our teachers are being trained in the right concepts and proper math pedagogy. That's not the case in most public schools or low-cost private schools.

Q. And please tell me about the Principal's Academy at TCF.

Irum Naz: As principals, we are trained to have a better understanding of how staff and children should be managed, understanding TCF policies, how to deal with conflicts or challenges, how to identify weaknesses in teaching quality and how to correct them, and how to develop good team-work and camaraderie among teaching staff—these are some of the areas covered in training sessions of the Principal's Academy.

Q. Have you faced any unusual challenges in your role as a principal?

The community here does not have many educated parents. The earlier Parent-Teacher meetings had poor participation. Hardly any mothers would show up. The attitude of the parents was that the school and the teachers were totally responsible for the child's development and growth. If the child was not on time or had poor hygiene, they expected us to correct that. With time, parents now understand that, along with the school and teachers, they too have to be involved in the child's development.

Q. Have you experienced any threats?

Irum Naz: Once a retired army major demanded admission of his child and, even though he could afford to pay a reasonable amount as fees, he was asking for his child to be admitted at no cost. And this was after admissions were closed for the year and the classes were full. He brought a small crowd of media reporters with him and it was quite a circus. We had to ask for the Area Manager to intervene, to calm things down and explain that we have rules and policies regarding admissions. We try our best to accommodate all children but we have our limits too. Sometimes we have to decline admission because the child does not pass the test and even then, we try to take the child in a lower grade and help the child catch up for an age-appropriate class.

Q. Are your teachers from the local area or are they transported from distant places?

Irum Naz: About a third of our teachers are local. Others are from Hub City or Baldia or other places. The school has been here for 10 years so we're seeing some of our graduates come back as new teachers. That's good to see. TCF has brought about a change in the community, and parents value what TCF has done for their children. Teachers who move away, either because of marriage or for some other reason, easily find work because of the experience and training they received here at TCF. I have personally benefited a great deal from the work here.

A TCF Mother Speaks

Q. You have two sons at the TCF school here. In terms of quality, what did you look for in a school?

TCF Mother: We feel that education is especially important and we checked out the school. We also looked at a private school and a government school and decided on TCF because we liked their ideals and the way the teachers conduct themselves. Everything is done the right way. I have no girls but I would have no hesitation sending my daughters to the TCF school. I feel that girls should also get the best education and all children should go as far as they can in education.

Q. Why is it necessary to educate girls when they're going to be homemakers?

TCF Mother: They can also go into professions, whatever they wish to do. I have a sister in Punjab who has completed a college education and she works at a bank. A younger sister is in school and I know she'll go far.

Q. What part of Punjab are you from and what brought you to Balochistan?

TCF Mother: We came from Sialkot fourteen years ago. My husband came to work on a construction project and settled here. He now owns a barber shop business, actually three locations, and he is doing well. Both of us have a Matric education but we didn't go any further.

Q. What would you like to say about progress in the country?

TCF Mother: Progress is badly needed in the whole country and it should begin with changes right here in Vinder, Balochistan. We need better schools, better health clinics and hospitals, more job opportunities, and better civic sense among our residents for clean communities and neighborhoods. As families, we must work closely with educators in schools to bring about change for our next generations.

Q. Since Balochistan is very tribal, have you felt any ethnic tensions in the community, being from Punjab?

TCF Mother: Not really. We are comfortable blending in and being part of the community here. There have been some radicals who have made disparaging remarks about us. But my husband and I are down-to-earth people and we get along with everybody. We respect everyone and the minor cultural differences. We are very happy that things have gone well for us and we feel that we are very much a part of the community.

On the way back from Vinder, we made a stop in Hub City and met the school principal Zebunnisa, who spoke with confidence about her role in the system. She is the youngest in her enterprising family; one of her brothers has a construction business and the other is a graphic designer. Of her three sisters, one is a teacher. Zebunnisa has been with TCF for six years, one year as principal. Her own children go to a TCF school, a daughter is in grade 9 and a son in grade 3.

Q. So, what dreams do your own children have?

Zebunnisa: Their dreams change by the day. My son talks about being in the army and my daughter wants to be an aeronautical engineer in the air force but that will probably also change many times.

Q. How much education did your mother receive and did she push for your education?

Zebunnisa: My mother had a 6th grade education but she can read and write basic English and Urdu. Both my parents encouraged and supported our education.

Q. What are your feelings about the new TCF Intermediate College?

Zebunnisa: I think it's a great step and I hope that someday we'll have a TCF college in Hub as well. Most of our school graduates here have to travel long distances to Karachi.

Q. Are the adult literacy program *Aagahi* and the mentorship program *Rahbar* operating in Balochistan?

Zebunnisa: Yes, some of our teachers run the *Aagahi* program out of their homes and it's doing quite well. The *Rahbar* mentorship program is in the secondary schools. Both programs are being run in Balochistan.

Q. Besides education, what are the other needs for a community to prosper and produce good citizens? And, is there an occasional reminder at the school assemblies that speaking the truth is an expectation in society and that it's encouraged by all faiths?

Zebunnisa: Yes, education builds multiple capabilities and influences the child's behavior and broader outlook, but there are also other needs of a community and individual—like food, clothing, shelter, etc. Through education and growth, a child gradually learns awareness of the needs of the family unit and makes the connection between education and her capacity to earn the income for acquiring those necessities of living. And, yes, at the assembly we frequently have a message to focus on personal values, such as the virtues of speaking the truth, personal cleanliness, hygiene, and environmental awareness.

Q. Why is Balochistan known as the least developed province?

Zebunnisa: Some progress has been made in the last two decades but education still remains the biggest need in Balochistan. There's strong tribal influence and provincialism in the local Baluchi mindset and we understand there are political reasons for it. The common slogan we hear is 'Balochistan First', implying that Pakistan has secondary importance. We often have to cautiously debate and very gently soften that view by saying that Balochistan is part of Pakistan and, yes, it does deserve a better share of the development pool. But education at all levels is the greatest need in the province. TCF has been a great boost for our underprivileged children and I feel pride in working here and being a part of this revolution that we are bringing about. Things are changing and we see more and more girls completing secondary school and going on to college and careers. Several of our own school graduates are coming back as TCF teachers, which is good to see.

Another chat was with AEM Qurat-ul-Ain Shaikh at the Hub school. She attended a private school and taught at one before joining TCF. Ms Shaikh has also worked as a news anchor at a TV channel.

Q. What are your duties as an Area Education Manager?

Qurat-ul-Ain: Our role is to focus on quality issues and support the principals and teachers in our area schools. We monitor quality, identify areas of weakness, and focus on improvement in those areas of instruction. Let's suppose I observe math teachers in my area having difficulty in teaching concepts of fractions, I will request intervention by people in our Training Department who conduct the training through our INSET (In-Service Training) Program, held on the last Saturday of the month, and the trainers will address those weaknesses and remedy them—whether its math, history, English or Urdu. That's how we cover various subject areas that require attention and jump on them immediately to rectify any weaknesses that we can identify and not wait for the annual professional development sessions which are only in the summer. My job is also to coordinate and organize the INSET with the RM, the trainers, principals and teachers.

Q. Do you also identify teachers who have potential to become good trainers, and what are the criteria?

Qurat-ul-Ain: When I observe teachers who have strong content knowledge, good pedagogical skills, and a few years of teaching experience, I recommend them to be selected as trainers. The final decision is made by the Area Manager and the Regional Manager.

Q. How has your work experience at TCF helped in your own personal development?

Qurat-ul-Ain: I believe I have learned to speak with confidence because of the work I do at TCF. What I did as a news anchor was scripted for me and all I had to do was read from the prompter and present it. I have given many interviews for airlines and for bank jobs and auditioned for media positions. I have honestly learned a lot about the value of communication in my job as a TCF teacher and trainer— how pedagogical skills are developed and refined, how to understand the unique personalities of the children we work with, and how to communicate with children. TCF trained me to acquire these skills and develop confidence in these areas. My grooming and learning with TCF have helped tremendously to build my confidence and I can speak very comfortably about education related matters.

I live in a reasonably nice, middle-class area of Karachi and I feel sorry for the children attending some private schools there, paying 4,000 or 5,000 rupees in fees and not receiving as good an education as we offer here at TCF for virtually no cost. These TCF children are really fortunate and I often tell them about the amazing systems of the TCF network, the importance and focus we have on quality assurance and the good work being done by the entire organization. I am so fortunate to do what I do for education. I have no desire to do anything else in life because education is a *sadaqah jariyah* (a gift that goes on giving, in perpetuity) and there is no other thing like it, no better reward in life than the satisfaction I feel.

I've been with TCF now for ten years and I have a young son, not quite two years old. My husband has a good job in the media and he often tells me that I don't need to work for the income. Honestly, it is not the income or the salary I make. The intangible reward that I receive is far greater. Yes, I have worked hard to be where I am. I had an Inter (12th grade) diploma when I joined TCF as a teacher. I went to college and university and completed my master's while I was teaching in the early years, along with my media job. My father would advise not to push myself so hard but I love to stay busy and I pursue my goals with determination.

Q. How about your siblings and their education level?

Qurat-ul-Ain: Both my sisters are well educated. One of them is a TCF teacher and the other is in the audit department with a bank.

At this point, I turned to Regional Manager Mansur Aslam for his comments. He thoughtfully added:

Mansur Aslam: Qurat-ul-Ain was being modest. She has a difficult area and has to travel a lot, from North Karachi to her school locations, leaving early in the morning and dropping her son for childcare, and picking him up after a long day. All areas have their challenges but her area has some special ones. A dynamic that comes into play has to do with ethnicity. People can be sensitive to different ethnicities and because Qurat-ul-Ain comes from Karachi and she is ethnically Punjabi, she can sometimes be subject to challenges. For travel, TCF has helped the AEMs by providing them with a car and driver. With dedicated AEMs, we have been able to identify the gaps and challenges in the content knowledge of teachers and quality of our teaching and we have learned how to manage and quickly resolve these issues. We started a concerted effort to improve teacher content knowledge and test it frequently. As a result, our scores for teacher content knowledge have been improving for the Balochistan faculty and we believe our student learning outcomes will also show corresponding improvement. The associated benefit of these efforts is that along with improvement in quality of teaching, enrollment has also gone up. All this coordination, detailed testing and training of teachers takes time and we are doing our very best.'

Returning to Qurat-ul-Ain, I asked her:

> **Q. Good internal communication in a large organization can be very important. When a new policy or program module is introduced by TCF, what is the flow of information from the Education Department or Academics to you and to the schools in your area?**

Qurat-ul-Ain: The process is that orientation to the new program is done through the REMs (Regional Education Managers) and, if needed, the principals are also called to the Head Office for orientation meetings. For example, when the new math curriculum and textbook *Meri Riyazi* (My Math Exercises) was introduced for KG and grades one and two, the principals and teachers were asked to go to HO for the orientation.

> **Q. With the distances you travel, your day must start quite early. Please take us through a typical workday.**

Qurat-ul-Ain: My day usually starts between 6:30 and 7:30 a.m. I have to be at Head Office by 8:15 a.m. Depending on the nature of the meetings for the day and the school locations, I may even leave home at 6 a.m. I usually drop my son at the childcare nursery at Head Office at 8:15 a.m. but if I have an early meeting, I leave my son with my sister for the day. I wind up work by 4:30 or 5 p.m., pick up my son and get home by 7 or 7:30.

> **Q. It sounds like TCF provides day-care services for some mothers working at the HO?**

Qurat-ul-Ain: Yes, childcare is another wonderful service benefit for the mothers who work at the Head Office. The office opens at 8 a.m. and there are two caregivers and they manage up to eight children.

2.8 Fiscal Management and Compliance

Chartered Accountant Khwaja Bakhtiar Ahmed has been the CFO since 2010 and also serves as Secretary of the Corporation. His responsibilities include financial forecasting and reporting, ensuring compliance with regulations, filing reports with the SEC and the Pakistan Center for Philanthropy (PCP), maintaining the records of the board, timely elections of directors and related governance actions. An audit department conducts annual audit of each school to ensure accounting procedures have been followed and an audit committee has internal oversight. The auditors are international accounting firm KPMG and an annual report is available online. Recognitions and awards have been received from the Management Association of Pakistan, the South Asian Federation of Accountants, the Skoll Foundation, the Magsaysay Award, WISE Qatar Foundation, UNDP and the Schwab Foundation.

2.9 The Founders of TCF...the 'A' Team

The initiators of non-profit causes are typically successful individuals driven by a strong personal motivation for social change. The founders are also compassionate and generous individuals, often a story unto themselves, and with interesting insights into social issues. The Citizens Foundation is fortunate to have six brilliant individuals as its originators, who have shaped the organization and given a huge boost to quality education for underprivileged children. Even before starting TCF, these extraordinary men of strong faith have given of their time, energy and resources to several charitable causes for health and education. They are high in the ranks of dedicated Agents of Change and especially recognized for their contribution to solutions for education in Pakistan.

Leading up to its formal birth in 1995, the six co-founders of TCF were Rashid Abdullah, his brother Arshad Abdullah, Haamid Jaffer, Ateed Riaz, Mushtaq Chhapra, and Ahsan Saleem. Aggregating their combined business acumen to organization and management, they made an all-out commitment with no room for failure. Collectively, they were taking perhaps their biggest personal risk with full knowledge that the stakes were high and that TCF would be a long haul. And, with poise, self-assurance, lots of prayers, unwavering belief in the cause, support from their spouses and families, backed by close friends and associates, and banking on their individual credibility and stature in the business and social community, not blinded by their egos or looking for celebrity, they took the plunge and made the momentous decision to launch TCF.

Of the original six, Ateed, Mushtaq, and Ahsan actively serve on the Board of Trustees and the governance leadership rests with these three fine gentlemen. What follows are personal perspectives with signature characteristics which also contribute to the fascination of TCF and its achievements. The often-meandering conversations with these men covered interesting details and history of TCF (not always in chronological order) and posed an interesting editing challenge; but I think I've arranged them in a reasonably sequential order, maybe with a few confusing elements—but that's very Pakistani.

Rashid Abdullah, a businessman, prefers to keep a low-profile despite his valuable contributions in the formative days of TCF. His brother Arshad Abdullah, an architect, was an energetic director on the Board until he succumbed to cancer a few years ago. Arshad was a respected, gentle giant, leading with a quiet and thoughtful demeanor as he steered the organization. Haamid Jaffer, an engineer-business entrepreneur, served on the Board for ten years and continues to support multiple charitable programs, notably health initiatives.

Architect Shahid Abdullah, younger brother of Rashid and Arshad, although not in the circle of co-founders, has been active in the TCF mission since its inception and has contributed immensely to the early design work for schools and architect services to TCF and, to this day, his architecture firm provides TCF with professional services at no cost. Shahid has served on the TCF Board and has been the founder and force behind the vocational training programs of Hunar Foundation, a successful spin-off from TCF.

A Personal Note: Over the years, the opportunity to know and work with the founders, managers, leaders, the amazing staff, volunteer colleagues and supporters of TCF has been a deeply satisfying experience for me. I am blessed to serve with this amazing organization and family of thousands, for the mission to reform Pakistani education. The conversations to follow are informal story-telling conversations with the three co-founders—Mushtaq, Ateed and Ahsan.

Mushtaq Chhapra

A textile business magnate, Mushtaq was my gateway introduction to TCF, on a visit to Karachi in 1999 when I called to ask him about TCF programs. He was three years my junior in school in 1963 and we had not been in touch since, but gregarious Mushtaq has a sense of humor that quickly puts you at ease. With these marvelous tools and his ability to touch heartstrings with stirring stories of the plight of the poor, Mushtaq is comfortable reaching out to the philanthropic and business communities. He is non-stop energy, always on the go, and traveling frequently. He starts most days on the golf greens at the crack of dawn. Like other founders, he is deeply involved with several social causes and supports each one generously. I met up with Mushtaq on a Saturday for lunch at his favorite club hangout and, as always, he was pumped up to talk TCF.

Q. What is the corporate structure of TCF and how does it maintain such efficient transparency?

Mushtaq: TCF is a corporate entity and we are registered with the Pakistan Securities and Exchange Commission as a limited company and we comply with the fiduciary requirements and regulations that all publicly owned business entities are required to follow. As a non-profit and for tax exemption purposes, we are registered with the Pakistan Center for Philanthropy (PCP), an autonomous body that has high standards for certification and compliance. PCP is the registry of non-profits. Its approval and endorsement serve as acceptance for tax-exempt status, which is important to establish long-term credibility and trust with donors locally and internationally. As an expectation of PCP, certified non-profits must function with full transparency, well-established management criteria, high ideals and standards of ethical operations.

Our CFO and VP of Finance is a seasoned chartered accountant with many years of professional history. He is also a stickler for compliance and processes. With his management of financial processes, our annual reports and financials have been recognized by the professional groups for accounting and management, notably the Management Association of Pakistan.

The bottom line measure of our success is that we produce good citizens for Pakistan, well-educated children who will develop into balanced and tolerant adults, so that this country can prosper.

Q. Why was professional management important? Why couldn't TCF have done just as well with volunteers and saved on the cost of management and staff salaries?

Mushtaq: One of our founding principles was that the organization should have professional staffing and management. Volunteers are a major asset and we are fortunate to have a strong cadre of dedicated volunteers at many levels. We have some programs that utilize volunteers almost exclusively, such as our summer school programs, the adult literacy program *Aagahi*, and the mentorship program *Rahbar*. Fundraising and networking with donors is almost all done by volunteer groups and that's a major undertaking. But for consistency and sustainability of the organization, we feel we made the right decision to have professional managers at the executive and staff levels and also in the teaching faculty. We pride ourselves on our professionalism in management functions.

Q. It is remarkable that TCF is a magnet for people who seem to be satisfied doing what they do, getting paid far less than what they would make in the corporate world, yet working with the zeal of missionaries. Your executive and management staff are teams of very capable, idealistic individuals dedicated to the cause of education for nation-building and remedies for social injustice. The work of TCF has become a personal mission for many. How has TCF been able to create such a culture of service?

Mushtaq: That is so true. *Alhamdulillah,* we are blessed with selfless people, starting with our CEO and VPs, the entire office and management staff and their teams, to the teaching faculty and support staff at every level. We could not have planned this any better. The culture of selfless service has evolved and become stronger over time and we see that even at the level of the school van drivers, the gate guards at the schools and the school maids. There is a sense of ownership and pride among all employees when they see the visible results of the programs we have in our schools, the smiles on the faces of the children and the parents, the changes in the families and their communities.

I am convinced that credit for this culture of service at TCF goes to our CEO Asaad and team of department heads, all exceptional individuals who have given up so much, sacrificed lucrative incomes and careers to give of themselves at TCF with incredible zeal and devotion, going out of their way to serve our underprivileged youth and communities. The head teachers and principals at the schools, the young teachers—all of them are amazing and so courageous to be doing what they do, having such strong desire to teach, to change the world. I get choked up thinking about it. We have had such fortunate lives with everything we have wanted. Most of these young teachers come from modest means, yet they have so much to give to others. I really think the teachers are the true Agents of Change.

The top managers have come to TCF from good corporate jobs or after retiring from military service. They made the decision to join TCF with the knowledge that we could not offer them competitive salaries or expensive benefit perks. Yet, here they are, growing with TCF and seeing the fruit of their labor in small tangible ways and in many intangible ways. Their families also deserve credit for willfully giving up the better life of the corporate world.

Q. How has TCF been able to achieve a nearly 50 percent gender ratio in its school system?

Mushtaq: In talking to the communities, we decided that we would employ only female faculty in our schools, and that has been a most remarkable and successful decision because it has given comfort to the parents and we have a near 50-50 gender balance in our schools. We now have more than 600 young ladies, former students at TCF, who have come back as teachers in our system. That means that a job is waiting for young women who graduate from our schools, get some college education, and come back to teach. It is also an encouraging sign that these young women are giving back to their communities as teachers and filling a huge gap in the education system. We feel we are providing an opportunity for good employment for these young women from lower-middle class families who may not have many choices. So, it's a win-win situation for all.

Q. Back in the mid-1990s, you and a group of friends figured out that quality education for the underprivileged masses could be the beginning of a national solution to many of the gaps, inequities and social injustices in the country. And, so the experiment began with a handful of schools and the birth of an organization. The rest is a truly incredible story which we're bringing to light through these conversations and narratives. But, the name 'The Citizens Foundation'—what was the thought behind the genesis of the name?

Mushtaq: Access to quality education was badly needed in under-served areas and urban slums, and that was our focus from day-one. But we did not want the name of the organization to be associated with the underprivileged or 'the poor'. Very sadly, education was a national need then just as it remains a dire need to this day. We began to think of a name that would represent all people of Pakistan and that everyone would be comfortable being a part of the cause of education and feel attached to it as a national solution. Thus, the name 'The Citizens Foundation' was born.

Q. What do you recall of the first five TCF schools and the early management teams?

Mushtaq: We built the first five schools in Karachi with contributions from the co-founders as seed money. No other donor funds were used. We employed Sabeeh Sahib as the best manager we could find at the time. He had just retired as CEO of the Pakistan Steel Mill and he was also a retired army general with great administrative skills; so, luckily, we got off to a very good start with management. Sabeeh Sahib was our CEO for the first five years and still serves on the Board as a trustee.

Now, after the first five schools, our story takes an interesting turn because we began to engage potential donors, inviting them to see our schools and learn what TCF was all about. We had started with primary schools in the worst of slums or *katchi abadis* of Karachi, densely populated areas with no schools or very poor schools. These five TCF schools are still there; in fact, they are all large campuses now with multiple school units in each campus.

Box 2.10 Karachi...and the First Five TCF Schools

In the 1950s, Karachi's population was probably 5 million. For privileged families, the preferred residential areas were Clifton, Bath Island, Parsi Colony, Catholic Colony, Shikarpur Colony, Amil Colony, Garden East, Bahadurabad, PECHS, and the KDA colonies. The middle-class lived in old apartment flats in Saddar, Kharadar, Burns Road, Bunder Road, or in small homes or 'quarters' built for federal workers in Paposhnagar or off Jehangir Road and Lawrence Road. Nazimabad and Lalukhet were recently developed areas. Karimabad and Azizabad were still on the drawing boards. Blue-collar *mazdoor* (laborer) and *muhajir* (refugee, migrant) families were in Sher Shah, Lyari, Patel Para, and further out in Malir, Korangi-Landhi industrial areas, North Nazimabad, or New Karachi. In the 1960s, the newly built Karachi University campus was out in the boonies—in the middle of nowhere!

The city is now home to 23 million, many from far-away regions, here to make a living and plant roots. Housing is expensive but there are industrial and service jobs for everyone. Rapid urbanization goes on, much of it poorly planned and unauthorized. Ultra-expensive houses with modern amenities have come up in Defense and other prestigious areas. High-rise buildings keep going up for middle-class apartments. Yet, areas like Sher Shah Colony and Lyari suggest images of densely populated, poorly built, or dilapidated homes in grossly unhygienic surroundings, with poor roads, illegally connected utilities, absence of clean water, and non-existent sewer systems.

Chances are you've never heard of Goth Dhani Bukhsh, Mengal Goth, Sumar Goth, Yusuf Goth or Machar Colony. That's where the first five TCF schools were built in 1995–96. As of December 2018, there are 200 TCF school units in the greater Karachi area, plus a TCF Intermediate College. – *Author*

Q. Why is education in the schools not totally free?

Mushtaq: From the start, we established that the schools would not be free charity schools. We asked for at least 10 rupees per child as the monthly tuition fee so that parents and family would have a sense of ownership in a child's schooling, that they would feel they were getting something of value. That was the threshold amount we felt that any family could pay but we have a very liberal sliding-scale system by which the school principal can determine how much the family can afford to pay, depending on income, number of dependents and other factors. In many cases, we charged only 10 rupees for all the children in the family and we had some other ground rules—like the girls in the family could not be excluded. Our minimum tuition has gone up to 25 rupees per child for the monthly fees, but again we are relaxed about it. We heavily subsidize the uniforms, books and school supplies. The tuition and other costs we receive from the parents are only about 5 to 10 percent of our revenues, the other 90 to 95 percent is subsidized by TCF donor contributions.

Q. The financial hardships in the communities are shocking. How do families survive on so little?

Mushtaq: To this day, I can't understand how a poor family survives on such a meager income…with the number of children and other dependents in each household, with no food on the table, having just one inadequate meal on most days. And, here we ask them to send their children to school for an additional cost, small as it might be. When we invited our first donors to visit the schools, it was a tremendous culture shock to them, because most people had never been to a *katchi abadi* and it was a learning experience for us as well. Our lives are such that we are restricted to our own comfort zones and these visits were a huge eye-opener for the first-time visitor, many of whom were our close friends and from our own social circles. It was mind-boggling to see the reactions of the affluent families and their children from elite schools. It was a shocking experience especially for the rich children and they started to realize how fortunate they were, how Allah has blessed them with good homes. and that their parents could afford to send them to the best schools and buy them good things and expensive clothes. Here, they were seeing that a majority of the population was deprived of every necessity in life. The donors realized that unless there were radical measures taken to give the underprivileged an equal opportunity with education, that it would be impossible for the poor to come out of the poverty rut.

Q. How did the early public reaction influence your plans and growth for TCF?

Mushtaq: Gradually, the donations began to come in and we added more schools. In the fourth year, the contributions gained momentum and our growth took off. That was also the year that we explored contributions from overseas Pakistanis, and we formed the first overseas group of donors in Dubai. By this time, our history and credibility were established, and Pakistanis abroad were looking for opportunities to give back to the mother country through a reliable organization that operated with transparency and with the right processes in place. Very early, we put into practice good procedures of financial management, including annual audited reports, and all these steps helped a great deal in distinguishing us as a dependable organization. It became evident that our needs to support our programs were growing and there was also growing demand from donors to build more schools.

Q. By the fourth year, it must have dawned on you that secondary schools will be needed.

Mushtaq: Yes, absolutely. When we started the Foundation, we were really quite naïve and inexperienced. We thought we would just build primary schools and that would be our mission. Children would graduate from the 5th grades and they would go on to the government secondary schools. Obviously, that wasn't to be. About the time the children reached 4th grade, the parents, the teachers and the children were very insecure about what was going to happen. The Board met with the management and we came up with a plan to build a secondary school for every three primary schools. These would be large two-unit secondary schools with labs and other amenities. In some cases, we didn't have the land to build the secondary schools. Even today, unfortunately, there are areas where we don't have secondary schools, but children have managed to get into private secondary schools.

With the need for secondary schools, our financial needs both for building and support of schools had to be refocused and we had to create new and novel methods of raising funds. Volunteer groups like 'Supporters of TCF' were started as fundraising arms in the major cities. The founders and directors got busier, meeting with major donors and corporate donors. We also began to look overseas for organized fundraising in the UAE, the UK and USA, connecting with TCF supporters to organize local groups for international outreach and fundraising. That was a big boost to our fundraising efforts and I think we did a good job of that. The awareness we created for TCF programs and generally for the need to support education reforms also produced encouraging results, thanks to the concerted efforts of our Marketing teams and Grants teams, within Pakistan and globally, to inform people and donor agencies. It was all a well-coordinated effort and—our hat's off to our staff and volunteers! Especially because the overseas groups were operating with minimal staffing and a lot of the work was being done by volunteers for several years, which was not sustainable. Finally, the overseas groups hired staff and professional managers.

Q. What proportion of the revenues and budget needs are raised in Pakistan?

Mushtaq: Of course, when we started, all the funds were raised locally in Pakistan. After a few years, as word spread and we became organized with supporters abroad, 30 percent of our revenues were received from the Diaspora donors and 70 percent were raised in Pakistan. A fact that is not public knowledge is that even today, *Alhamdulillah*, 50 percent of our revenues are from Pakistani donors and an equal amount from overseas donors, mostly individual contributions, with some grants and corporate contributions. This ratio has reached a 50-50 balance because our fundraising efforts overseas have increased consistently, especially in the US.

We are fortunate to have a fine-tuned organization in the US. It is managed professionally and staffed by dedicated people. But they could use more hands. There are about 35 established local chapters of TCF-USA and they held over 50 community events in 2017 and nearly 70 events in 2018. Many of these are social outreach events. Our other major groups in the UAE, UK, Canada are also doing a good job. The UAE group oversees activity in other Persian Gulf countries and the Middle East. We have smaller groups of supporters in Australia, Italy, Switzerland, and Norway and we need more TCF champions to take the lead in European countries like Germany, and in Singapore—wherever there is a sizable Diaspora. Without the international contributions, it would not have been possible for us to reach the milestones that we have. It all adds up and helps the education of Pakistan's children.

Q. Please tell us about the Clean Water filtration systems in many TCF schools and how it is benefiting the communities?

Mushtaq: In our wildest dreams, we had never imagined that we would partner with other entities for programs like clean water, mentorship, and adult literacy. But all these programs have done well. At this time, we have about 20 water filtration and supply stations in TCF schools. Our water supply is from ground wells, which we install when the schools are designed and constructed, so we don't depend on a community water supply that may be sporadic. We have reservoir tanks for water storage at all TCF schools. For the filtration systems, we find a man from the community and assign him the water supply operation. He sells the clean and treated water to the community at a nominal cost of one rupee per liter whereas the normal rate is 10 rupees a liter. So, the community gets a good deal and clean drinking water at regular hours. There is a small cost for electricity, which TCF covers. Most homes in the *katchi abadis* don't have plumbed running water supply and people fill up for their daily needs at the local water stations when there is flow or they purchase water from retail vendors.

Q. Any other partnership ventures?

Mushtaq: There's a non-profit in Islamabad that is training our students in sewing garments on an industrial scale to supply well-known retailers. We will be contracting with a non-profit to produce the uniforms for our students. After all, we are a large consumer of school uniforms. Why not give part of the business and jobs to some of our own?

Q. What's happening in alumni development activities?

Mushtaq: We have an active Alumni Development Program that is focused on facilitating admissions to colleges and universities for TCF graduates. We must do more to utilize our alumni in other ways. I would like to see us hold a 'National Alumni Conference' to get the alumni body together, get everyone into our database, and learn what they are doing, how we can help, what their needs are, what they would like to do. We should channelize this resource to fully capitalize on their abilities. We, as the founders and stakeholders, should think about spending our energies on further refinement of the alumni programs. I feel strongly that the next Ateed Riaz, Ahsan Saleem, or Mushtaq Chhapra should come from the alumni, from the future Nadeems and Imrans, Iqras and Sidras—because they have the potential and the abilities to take this movement to the next level. We see about 50 alumni in ADP activities, but we don't know where the other 20,000 graduates are or what they are doing. We must track them down before we lose them forever. Let's get them together, perhaps in two locations, Karachi and Lahore. We'll work on it.

Q. The government school adoption program—where are we headed with this?

Mushtaq: The GSP is still in the early stages and, honestly, we don't know where we are headed. We will need to be patient for a year or two and see how it works out. We don't have answers for all issues and we don't have the last word. I'm sure there's a lot to do and many people and groups are doing a lot in Pakistan. It is not possible that one non-profit or group does it all. That doesn't happen anywhere in the world.

Q. In the last decade, when you were also the Chair of the Board, TCF gained a tremendous amount of recognition with international awards. You have kept in touch with several organizations and leaders from all parts of the world. Are they amazed by what has been achieved by TCF? What is their reaction?

Mushtaq: It is more than amazement—probably astonishment—at what has been achieved by TCF. They can't believe that we have 1,500+ schools and more than 250,000 students and 12,000 teachers in our system. When I've gone to international meetings, the annual Skoll Forum at Oxford, or other award ceremonies, I am surrounded by education non-profits that have 5 or 10 schools, or even 50 schools. They find it hard to believe the scale and impact that TCF has created—and that too in Pakistan. I think we could do a better job of spreading the word about TCF globally.

Q. When you are at international forums, are you asked how you plan to influence solutions for the education problems of Pakistan?

Mushtaq: Yes, we are often asked that question, even at home by our own supporters, and our response is that we will try to do that through engagement with the government. We don't express any position of advocacy. We believe that actions speak louder than words. We hope that our system of management can be adopted by the government and we would be happy to share our learnings and practices with them.

Q. Even if TCF adopts a couple of hundred schools every year, and we have 2,000 adopted government schools—that by itself will have a very tiny impact on the system, won't it?

Mushtaq: You're absolutely right. My feeling is that just as we have adopted schools in Punjab, down the road we may decide to adopt similar numbers in other provinces—and then we showcase these adopted schools as models of how a much-improved set of schools can be created with good management. That's the best we can do.

Q. After that's done, and let's say the government adopts the management practices in the school system, can TCF have a watchdog role, to evaluate the system and ensure that the practices are followed?

Mushtaq: All we can do is show the government how to make the *biryani*[6] and, certainly, if they want us to come back periodically and check on it, we could do that and let them know if it needs more salt or other spices! Seriously, that is a role we should play if we can successfully create conditions for those checks and balances. That would really be great.

Q. It seems the early vision of TCF has been achieved, that of creating a model system of quality education with good management. Small corrections and incremental growth may continue to improve internal TCF systems but the bigger solution for national education will remain a reach away, or maybe out of reach. But, the future should not be left to chance. The deep hole that Pakistan finds itself in because of gross

mismanagement of its education system needs to be addressed very quickly. **Mathematically, Pakistan is not even catching up because it is adding more to the population every year than it is adding to schooling capacity. So, hypothetically, if a coalition comprising World Bank and donor countries could come together and offer a package to address the problematic state of education in Pakistan, to fully fund the reforms and capacity needs as a grand system-changing initiative and rebuild the education system, would TCF welcome and support such an initiative, and would TCF want to be a part of it?**

Mushtaq: I would be positively behind a long-term solution like the one you have described, hypothetically. It will need a strong coalition and a plan to be implemented in 5 to 10 years, with the Pakistan government all-in and totally committed. It's best that we don't ask for a handout. The funds should be a long-term loan and we should be expected to pay it back over a period of time. It's also a question of capacity on our part. Can we develop our human resource, management and infrastructure to meet the challenge? I think we can and that's where TCF could participate and contribute, along with other actors as partners.

Q. Of course, it will need to be precisely defined, planned and executed. If we continue to apply makeshift solutions, we may never catch up or solve the bigger problems. The longer a total solution is put off, the harder the problem will be to solve. So, what's the next recognition and award for TCF?

Mushtaq: (Laughs) Allah is very kind. We do what we can. Our Grants teams keep working at it. Who knows what the next award will be, but we have some discussions going on and I am hopeful we will have a major grant in the pipeline very soon. We have to be patient, but we can't be totally passive either.

ATEED RIAZ

Currently in his rotation as chair of the TCF Board, Ateed leads a group of family business enterprises. He has diverse personal interests, which include deep knowledge of South Asian classical music, Urdu poetry, and literature. He loves to quote from the scriptures and is fondly known as the resident philosopher of TCF. In his youth, Ateed was a junior national table tennis champion. He prefers wholesome food and, over a nourishing lunch at his office, Ateed shared thought-provoking views in his unique, contemplative style.

Q. What was the early vision of the founders and what were the initial meetings like?

Ateed: If we really go back to those days, we talked about the fact that there was a lot going on in Karachi in the early 1990s in terms of random violence and civil unrest and no one was addressing these deep-rooted problems. Quite often, Karachi reflects what happens in the rest of the country, both in good and not-so-good trends. There were shootings in Orangi, for example, where 26 people died. Like many others, we wondered what we could do about it, because something had to be done. There was an earlier phase when people had generally become cynical and critical, but they weren't doing anything about it. There was a sense of hopelessness in the city and the country. It made good social chatter and that is what disturbed us most. As the core group, we were all involved in some form of volunteer work, linked with various charities, and we brought different perspectives to the table. We zeroed in and focused on the need for education as the best long-term solution. All of us were products of good private schools, so we set out to build purpose-built schools and a model system with focus on providing quality education to children from underprivileged communities. Then we started to look for a CEO to manage and lead the organization. It was our good fortune that we found Sabeeh Sahib and we hired good managers to work on his team. We were often tempted to add more programs to education—like clean water and other things. But Ahsan kept us focused on the core program of education.

Q. Why education?

Ateed: We discussed several options among ourselves and with others and concluded that education was the best long-term solution. We were quickly convinced that many other social and governance problems existed because of poor education, inadequate access to schools, the dismal quality of teaching, and the mismanagement of the public school system.

Q. So, the decision was made to start an education non-profit that would have a national footprint and deliver good quality education with professional management. Did you have an experimental model in mind, or did you study other models?

Ateed: No, there was no experimental model. We went with a conservative model that we were familiar with—academic excellence, extra-curricular programs, and professional management.

Q. If you were to do it again, would you start with a virtually paperless, high-tech model?

Ateed: Putting pencil to paper is centuries old and part of the learning culture. Technology can be disturbing and disruptive if not used with discretion. It has given us great tools for efficiency and access to knowledge that was not possible before, but we don't need to totally replace the old-fashioned paper and pencil.

Q. So, TCF got off the ground and there were things that were unpredictable, but you folks were smart enough to adjust and grow with the opportunities. For TCF to have a national impact, what was your thinking about the rate of growth and its scale?

Ateed: You see, some growth is planned, and some of it is thrust upon you by circumstances beyond your control. We had hoped to grow at the best rate to reach our goal of a thousand school units by 2012 but it took us a little longer. We accepted that, but we were on track, more or less. We focused on where the need was greatest and sometimes the growth and new locations were driven by the donor who had a desire to build a school in his ancestral village, for example, and we found a way to please the donor while establishing our footprint—provided that the need was there, and it was a feasible proposition in every way.

Q. What is the TCF exit strategy or ultimate goal? At what point do you say: our job is done, let's move on?

Ateed: We were asked that question just weeks after we started TCF. Our answer today is the same as it was then. If the local and provincial governments are doing the job of running the schools and system in a way that is right, we would gladly give them the keys and let the local leadership run their local schools. That is true ownership. Currently, the environment requires a very disciplined structure and it will probably take fifty years or so to be at the point where local communities can be ready to take over the running and ownership of the education system.

> **Q. Your current style of governance at the Board level is a consensus model between the three co-founders, Ahsan, Mushtaq and yourself. There's good synergy and strong bonds of friendship that make it work. However, the optics of the founder-directors staying on the Board in perpetuity is troublesome. How are you balancing that?**

Ateed: We are bringing in new directors and while we, as the founders, may remain on the Board for continuity and governance, we don't want to remain on the Board for reasons of power or because we have special administrative skills, or anything like that. For example, we have formed committees of the Board, and appointed the new directors to run those committees. That is just one example. We have a genuine desire to transfer ownership and we are working towards that goal. We see TCF as an *amaanat* given to us, an asset that we have been entrusted with. We have never been the owners. We have accepted several awards and recognitions on behalf of the organization, not as individual recipients. We believe in retaining our founding members and honoring them. Even if they are not able to participate actively, they contribute with advice and words of wisdom. That's our culture. It's like a family. You don't ask an elder brother to leave.

> **Q. As a co-founder, what is your message to readers in Pakistan and the world audience?**

Ateed: The world is lacking in tolerance and the test of tolerance is not in peaceful times. The test is when there's a conflict of principles and one has the ability to stand back and take oneself away from the conflict. We hope that through TCF we have engrained those principles of tolerance in the children, with no place for prejudice, hatred, or xenophobia in their hearts, with nothing but love and compassion for their fellow humans. We hope that our teachers—with the kind of curriculum, the values, the training and skills we have imparted to them—will be the agents of change and produce an entire body of students and future citizens who will, in turn, continue to work on these principles of tolerance and compassion. There may be events and circumstances thrust upon us due to no fault of ours, like the Soviet-Afghanistan conflict, but we have to learn to manage them and not be overcome by them.

Q. Do you have any regrets? What would you have done differently?

Ateed: I would like to see greater emphasis on non-academic, extra-curricular programs, although we have probably done the best we could have. I would like to see more learning opportunities through healthy competitive sports and games, cultural growth, literature, poetry, art, and so many other things. That is something that I hope the new leadership and the management are able to drive in a better way than we have. We have a rich heritage of culture, literature, and poetry in our languages that can soften us, internally—make us more tolerant. We have to teach our children how to resolve the personal, internal conflicts that we are all faced with. We have not done enough of that.

Ahsan Saleem

Ahsan is CEO of Crescent Group, a set of publicly held industrial companies. A calm demeanor is his signature trait. His measured, balanced views on all matters are a treat to capture as his thoughts and rationale slowly unfold. As the Sunday-evening conversation progressed over tea in Ahsan's poolside garden and the chirping of the birds entertained me, it became apparent that this was to be an informal, free-flowing exchange and Ahsan's answers would not always match my questions. However, by the end, we had traveled a great length of history, with amusing stories and vital information, in Ahsan's inimitable style.

Q. What were the early ideas and challenges, and what adjustments did you make?

Ahsan: Actually, it's a strange story because even before TCF came to mind, we had been meeting with various groups of people in which three or four of us were the common denominators but there were other people too. As you know, Karachi was burning in the early 1990s so, one of the very audacious ideas was to form a group of vigilantes to counter the violence and crimes. Obviously, that was dropped very quickly. There were many other ideas kicked around before we zeroed in on education. Originally, we began by saying that nothing is solved if we keep criticizing and just talking about the problems. We had to stand apart from those who were not doing anything and come up with some solution. There were also differences of opinion about what should be done because, before setting our focus on education, we toyed with the idea of doing something in health. In fact, there were two plans. One was education, which we arrived at after eliminating health and other things because, and as we've said numerous times, the root cause of health problems was poor hygiene and that was because of poor education.

The other idea was that we should do more for the local artisans and craftspeople to increase their incomes. We had studied cottage industries, starting with the *Banarsi* silk weavers, who were getting paid paltry sums by the two major retail outlets in Karachi. The retailers were making huge profits on the backs of the work done by the exploited weavers. There was a Banares Colony in the slum area of Orangi. The poor weavers had no capital, so the retailers would give the workers just enough money to get the raw material in return for a promise to purchase everything they produced but the weavers were restricted from selling their products to any other outlet.

We had also started a pilot project on that idea, but we dropped it because once we got into education, we realized that we should stick with just one program. At that time, if we had set our sights on 100 schools or 500 schools as a target, that would have been a lot. The credit goes to Rashid Abdullah, who urged us to set a higher target of 1,000 schools. We embraced that target because of Rashid or we may have settled for 500. That's how we arrived at the target of 1,000 schools and it has given us stronger standing and credibility in the community.

Q. So, you put together seed money for the first few schools and TCF got off the ground. What were some of the guiding principles of your charter?

Ahsan: In addition to the goal of 1,000 schools, we set some ground rules for ourselves. One of them was that we would have professional managers run TCF—find the best people, not hire mediocre personnel.

We wanted to have a national footprint with presence in all provinces and uniformly good quality schools in all locations, not just a few islands of excellence. We agreed that we would first build a few schools with the seed money, debug the system, make sure that it operates well before we go out in the community and ask for more money. So, the six co-founders contributed to the seed money and the reserves pool for staff salaries and expenses, enough for two years. Our first office became available thanks to Rashid because their offices were in the NIC building and they had a large room to spare, which they gave to TCF to get started with a staff of six people. Initially, as you may remember, we were on the ninth floor.

Q. You started with five schools in 1996. When did you hire General Sabeeh as the first CEO?

Ahsan: It was a series of amusing coincidences in Islamabad that led to the hiring of Sabeeh Sahib. We had almost decided to start with TCF but two of us made a trip to Islamabad to look at Shifa Hospital as a medical model of the sort we were also studying, just in case we decided to go into the health sector instead of education. And there we ran into our dear Ardeshir Cowasjee[7] at the Marriott. That was in the summer of 1995 and there was a lot of judicial activism going on at the time. Cowasjee, a vocal critic of the government, announced—not surprisingly—that he had to appear in the Supreme Court on contempt charges and asked us to tag along for support, so we went with him to the Supreme Court. At the court, we ran into General Sabeeh who was there also to support Cowasjee!

We had been thinking about possible candidates for the CEO position and we knew that Sabeeh Sahib had recently retired from the Steel Mills and that he was a very capable administrator. So, we asked him to join us for lunch and told him about what we were thinking in terms of TCF but stopped short of making him an offer. Upon returning to Karachi, we conferred with the other founders and then we called Sabeeh Sahib with an offer to be the CEO. His first reaction was that he did not want to work for anyone else but wanted to do something on his own. One of us—it could have been me—literally challenged him by saying that if he had seen any action in the army, it could not have been action like what we had in mind, that this battle for education was a big war! So, if he was up to it, we invited him to join us as the CEO. He accepted the challenge but said he wouldn't take a salary, to which we had to say that we couldn't have a CEO who would not accept a salary. Eventually, he agreed and we started with him as the first CEO. He deserves great credit for some of the good foundational things that happened at TCF.

Q. Among the leaders, who was the visionary for the programs, or running of the schools?

Ahsan: Actually, there was no vision to start with. We were a bunch of stupid people, all of us—seriously! I was probably the youngest, just 40, and none of us were more than 50 years old. So, if we look back and say that we were the visionaries, that wouldn't be true. There were none! We were a bunch of daredevils who had latched on to something that was the need of the time and we didn't know it would get so much empathy from the public. We did our math and projections, but it was a bit scary when we aimed for a thousand schools. And, the projections were also probably not accurate. To mitigate the fears, we did the calculations and, somehow, they stuck and made it easier to work on that target. Now, twenty-plus years later, we've learnt so much that everyone may think we are some kind of great thinkers, but we didn't know much, really. A simple task was set, and I think we made some mistakes and took some chances. But I don't regret that because it gave us an opportunity to learn from our own errors. For example, we broke ground for the first five schools in December of 1995 and the schools opened in May 1996 in five of the poorest locations in Karachi, in distant corners of the city. That added to the difficulty of the project. Later, as we got smarter, we made the adjustment and followed a plan to build in clusters. We also hadn't given much thought to planning for secondary schools. In a few years, we realized how different the needs and dynamics of secondary education were compared to primary schools. In fact, our first secondary school was a single unit in Umar Mengal Goth and we learnt that it would be more efficient and cost-effective to build the secondaries as two-unit schools with three or four primary schools feeding into them. And that's how the cluster concept was born. So much for vision and planning!

But, after two or three years, we began to get the right idea and develop 'vision'. There were nuanced phases, like the first phase was about getting the children off the streets and into schools. I think it was relevant at that time. And, at the same time, there was the realization that we might be catalysts, but the *real* agents of change had to be the teachers, and that we would have to manage them with care and great attention, train them to become true professionals with a passion for teaching, support them, and value them. The next phase would be when the children themselves would become the change agents, followed by the final phase, maybe in fifty years, when the communities would evolve into the role of change agents.

We articulated these dynamic phases of the vision and, very interestingly, a few related things occurred as a result of identifying the final phase, that of the communities being the ultimate change agents. For that to occur, there has to be empathy in the communities to understand what the children of the new generations are achieving through education. And, to achieve that degree of empathy, we had to discover and implement ways of introducing literacy and enlightenment in the communities as well, so that the value of education would be recognized and valued. For community and adult literacy, we introduced a *Jugnu Sabaq* (literally, *The Firefly Lesson*) program which is now the *Aagahi* program. The mentorship *Rahbar* program was added shortly after. Keeping our focus on basic education, we realized that strategic partnerships were needed, and these could be valuable in implementing the ancillary community programs such as *Aagahi* and *Rahbar* and the clean water project. The *Aagahi* program has excellent delivery mechanisms through our strategic partner. We started looking at schools as beacons of light that could be leveraged for the benefit of the communities.

An instinctive, early decision was to build small schools and locate them right in the neighborhood. Later, we discovered what studies have also shown that 600 meters is an arbitrary limit of comfort for most families in poor communities. Any distance beyond that may not feel safe for a girl child to walk by herself.

Q. By the third year, twenty schools were up and running. You had a basic administrative team, a core of teachers and principals, a teacher training system and the infrastructure of an organization poised for growth. What happened after the first three years?

Ahsan: We built five schools in the first year, five more in the second and then ten in the third year, of which one was in Lahore, the first school outside of Karachi. In the period that Sabeeh Sahib was CEO, we were up to 200 schools. In the next phase of three or four years, we grew to 500 schools. As we were nearing the 500 mark, the four of us— Arshad, Ateed, Mushtaq and I—went back to the drawing board, and we made a new organizational chart. Haamid had stepped away from the Board by this time. That is when we also realized that the first 500 schools needed a very regimented, clock-work structure with uniformity for the school system. Branding and identity were very important. By this time, the staff had grown, and we had a mix of civilian and retired military managers. Supporters were asking why we were not adding schools in difficult places like the interior areas of Sindh, or Balochistan, and KP, where the conditions in education were extremely bad. Our answer at that time was—and it was the right answer—that we were relatively small and didn't have the capacity to directly challenge, or take on communities and their leaders, to change their attitudes. We couldn't be confrontational with feudal groups who were resistant to or plainly opposed to modern education, especially for girls, because that would only hurt the cause of promoting education. These were the *vadera*, the feudal lords and tribal leaders. Feudalism is a mindset, not just the cruel, authoritarian practices of the owners of large tracts of land. People with no land ownership can also be highly feudal in their attitudes. So, we had to soften our approach into those communities, be patient and strategic, and wait for the right opportunities.

Our battle is with illiteracy, not with people—and we were determined to address it wherever we had to. But we also had to be realistic and patient. We couldn't force the communities to accept us and our schools and teachers. Eventually, word gets around, community attitudes change, the feudal leaders see that it makes sense to have good education. And there comes a time when they bend a little. Take the example of the Badin and Keti Bandar areas in Sindh, where conditions were terrible until ten or twelve years ago. Through the right connections and strategic work, we got a foothold there with an opportunity to build a few schools, knowing that the need was for many more schools. Once we had some momentum, we asked donors to support the building of schools in these areas and constructed them in rapid succession. Now we have a number of schools in that difficult area, all doing well, and those villages are changing—all because we were patient and waited for the right opportunities. There was no point in aggressively picking a fight with the *vaderas*.

Box 2.11 Feudalism

The culture of feudalism is commonplace in Pakistani society and Vadera, Sardar, Khan, Chowdhury, and other titles of honor are attributed to powerful feudal lords. Feudalism is broadly defined as a way of structuring society around relationships derived from the holding of land in exchange for indentured service or labor. Traditional symbols of a feudal society are the possession of financial or social power and prestige as a result of massive land holdings and wealth. Economist-philosopher Adam Smith described feudalism as a social and economic system defined by social ranks, with social and economic privileges and obligations. Karl Marx defined it as the power of the aristocracy, the ruling class, for control of arable land leading to a class society and based upon the exploitation of the workers. – *Author*

There are still many areas where campaigns like Keti Bandar are needed badly. We hope that the communities themselves will advocate for education for their children and demand it from the government. These are areas where there has been a failure of both, the supply side and the demand side but very clearly a failure of the demand side in great part because of the feudal culture and general backwardness. There is no tradition of education in previous generations, so these were significant changes for these communities and they need to be built upon along with other infrastructure improvements.

Q. What organizational changes took place as TCF grew nationally?

Ahsan: Our first school outside of Sindh was in Lahore. Then we increased our footprint by building in Islamabad and other major cities in other regions. We did that to increase our visibility and presence but also for ease of management controls. Building regional management teams was easier in the major cities than it would be in the smaller locations. We formed management 'Areas' to be administered by Regional Offices. This organizational structure seemed manageable and we went with it.

Q. When were Education Managers appointed?

Ahsan: The positions of Education Managers were created in the first year. As we set up the Operations team, we also set up an Education team with three sub-areas. One was Policy which included curriculum development, design of the syllabus, lesson plans, and teaching guides, etc. The second area was Teacher Training and the third was Monitoring and Evaluation. Our Teacher Trainers conducted the pre-service training and professional development in the summer months when the schools were closed for vacations. The same group of teacher trainers did Monitoring and Evaluation throughout the year, when classes were in session. This group later evolved into the Master Trainers, who trained the teacher trainers as well as the teachers.

Q. When did teacher training get started at TCF?

Ahsan: We had firmly decided that we would not send any untrained teacher into a classroom. So, our first batch of TCF teachers was sent to Teachers' Resource Center (TRC), an independent training institution that had a good program for training of teachers. but their training was primarily for teachers from the English-medium private schools catering to elite and middle-class families, whereas we served a very poor population in our schools and the medium of instruction was Urdu, not English. We observed a TCF teacher who had trained at TRC creating a math problem at one of our first schools in Machar Colony. The problem was something like: 'Ahmed's mother gave him 500 rupees and asked him to go to the supermarket to get 5 kgs of apples...' The teacher said that the problem was exactly what she had learnt at TRC. Now, we thought the problem didn't make sense for a poor child from a Machar Colony slum family—a child who barely had one meal a day and not even enough drinking water because of costs. He had never seen 500 rupees, or ever been to a fancy grocery store, or bought apples—never had any of these luxuries. In that case, we tactfully suggested creating math problems that the child could relate to in his or her own environment—and that's when we decided to do our own teacher training, hire our own trainers, and developed our in-house program of pre-service training and professional development. And, I think that was a good decision.

Q. How did the teacher training program evolve? My understanding was that there would be training centers in the major cities and teachers would be brought to these centers. But that plan changed to taking Master Trainers to various regions to conduct the training of teachers.

Ahsan: You're right. The initial model was to have teacher training centers and the first one was in Karachi behind BVS School in a Cowasjee Trust property. When we got to twenty schools in Karachi in the third year, we had 160 teachers and that was the capacity of that space. So, when we added secondary schools, we started using them as training centers in the summer months, but we still weren't sure what we would do in the future. Currently, all training takes place at secondary schools because they are better furnished and adaptable for adult use. Regional 'hubs' are identified for the purpose of teacher training where one school serves as the training center in a 40 to 50 km radius and teachers in that region are transported to the school. Logistically, it would be a nightmare and a huge challenge to transport and safely lodge 12,000 women in a handful of major cities during training for several weeks. Most of the teachers are young women and their parents or husbands would be very concerned about them being away overnight or even for several weeks. So, the training has to be taken closer to the homes of the teachers. It has to be a day-time activity and teachers must be bussed back to their homes every day.

Q. When did TCF start operating the system of pick-and-drop transportation for teachers?

Ahsan: From day one, and I think it went a long way at that time and it adds value to this day. It's not only a means of transport for convenience, it also brings dignity to the teachers and provides them a sense of security. In most areas where we have our schools, we couldn't find enough teachers locally. So inevitably, we had to import teachers from other communities. We operate in tough conditions and our schools can be difficult to get to by public transport and there is also the issue of promptness. The distances, the heat, rain and security issues all add to the difficulty of the teacher's job and daily routine.

Q. And, are the teachers charged for the transportation provided?

Ahsan: Yes, they are charged a small amount, which is a tiny fraction of the cost. Now that we have the experience of twenty years or more, and we have clusters of school for the most part, we are experimenting with larger vans that can transport teachers to and from more than one school at a time. So, we are constantly trying to optimize our operations with efficiency and cost containment.

Q. There are many one-off schools started by individuals or family foundations as philanthropic initiatives that mean well. Most of these are one-room schools for children from poor families in the neighborhood. Some of the schools take on more capacity but they eventually become unsustainable or difficult to manage by the patron family. What happens to those schools, the children and the community and has TCF taken over such schools?

Ahsan: Yes, there was such a school with 300 children in Rawalpindi and it was run for thirty years by a fine, older couple in a very poor community, a slum mostly for migrant families from the north. Finally, the aging couple couldn't manage it and offered it to TCF. The school structure was old and inadequate, but the community demand for education was obviously well-established. So, we built a new school in the community and there was a happy ending. The tough thing is that sometimes such schools don't fit our model, and, at least on the surface, they cannot be adapted to our system. We must be creative and not so rigid with our strict standards and regimented procedures in adapting such a school to our system. With a little imagination, that can be done.

Q. At one time, when you had roughly 500 schools—halfway to the goal of 1,000 schools—there was a major shuffle in the management style of the organization that took place.

Ahsan: That is the time we decided that we should get a CEO who would be an industry leader with an approach to a management style other than the regimented military approach. That's when we were drawing the organization chart for the next 500 schools. We had done a similar exercise when we reached 100 schools. We had paused and asked ourselves: what kind of organization design do we need to take us to 500 schools? So, at the 500-school milestone, it was time to redesign the organization, to find alignment of all management functions with our mission as well as with our vision. We created the new organization model—a home-grown model drawn up by Mushtaq, Ateed, Arshad and me. We didn't hire McKinsey or any consultants. We saw that the organization has two distinct flanks because, when we think about it, we ask ourselves: who do we work for? There's a strong view that, actually, we work for the donor, because the donor has a need to give and we are the conduit to fulfill his or her need to give. So, in a way, we are working for the donor. The other view is that we are working for the child who is in our school. The hybrid is that we're working for both and we're trying to balance it because, if the donor does not exist, then the student at the other end also does not exist. So, we're working for the donor who is essentially the investor and the return for the investor is what the child actually gets in the end, the learning outcomes. You know, it's very difficult to translate in a non-profit model who you are working for. So, we decided we are working for both, the investor who is making an impact investment as well as for the child in our school.

Essentially, we need sustainability at one end and we need outcomes at the other. Before reaching this phase, we were talking about sustainability but at the other end, as we are programmed to do, we were counting numbers which you could say was 'output' rather than outcomes. By this time, we were a little wiser and we were really thinking of everything in terms of vision, and we changed our thinking from output to outcomes. When you're thinking output, you're thinking of numbers: 500 schools, 3,000 teachers, 150 cities, 70,000 children, and so on. But, when you translate it into outcomes, you still have the first three— the number of schools, the teachers, and children—but, then you ask: okay, what *kind* of children? So, a new area of student development comes in, a new area of community development comes into play because when you convert outputs into outcomes, you have the new qualitative targets as well.

When we designed the organization, we knew that we would need sustainability, both financial and organizational sustainability. Financial sustainability would cover inputs, and the entire value chain right up to learning was input. And that would mean that Resource Mobilization is financial sustainability, and also the programs on which we don't spend any money but receive value for them. The volunteer program and the executive volunteer program, they are also inputs. Then, the learning achievements and the organizational development in terms of human resource are outcomes. We said we would reduce the number of reports to the new CEO who would have a VP of Inputs, and on the other flank, a VP of Outcomes. Then we'll have a person of the same level to keep score. So, a VP of Finance and Control would keep the score and that would be the CFO. We upgraded these managerial positions.

Q. ...and did this reorganization take place in 2009?

Ahsan: Yes. When we had the first 500 schools, we thought it was time to reshape the organization for the next 500 schools and probably beyond. It was almost a defining moment and the paradigm change occurred in the organization.

Q. That's when the team of Asaad Ayub as the new CEO, and the team of Ahson Rabbani and Riaz Kamlani as new VP's was formed, and Bakhtiar Sahib became the VP Finance.

Ahsan: Yes, and it was a good thing that we took the time for this re-thinking and remaking of the management team and the organization.

Q. What's the thinking now that the 1,000-school milestone is in the rearview mirror?

Ahsan: When that milestone was reached in 2015, some chapter leaders raised a good point and asked us what would be our 'rallying cry' now that the 1,000-schools goal was reached. We didn't have one. Facts on the ground were that we had to correct a lot of mistakes that we had made in the early years. We had ended up with a lot of isolated schools, one school with no other TCF school in 20 miles, so that was hardly a cluster. In the meantime, development has taken place and we can't build another school close to it because new homes have come up, land values have gone up, the areas have changed. That was one challenge. The other mistake was that there was a mismatch between the number of primary and secondary schools, and that mismatch had to be filled or corrected. When we reached the 1,000 schools, we worked out the mismatch and determined that we would have to build 375 more schools to complete the clusters and to largely correct the mismatch, realizing that a 100 percent correction was not possible. So, we could sulk about it or accept the fact that it would not be possible in all situations and that we would have to let the children finish primary school with TCF and look for other solutions. Hopefully, new government schools will help to fill the gap. But we accepted that we would build the 375 odd schools we had identified in this exercise. Another thing that happens is that the numbers can change over time, because of organic growth that goes on. But what is our new rallying cry? At the GCC in 2015, we debated 'TCF Next' and set the goal of impacting 1.5 million learners—including the children in core TCF schools, adopted government schools, and others who can be reached through programs for adult literacy, e-learning, through radio programs, etc. But our wallet doesn't support that rallying cry of 1.5 million learners. When the wallet can't support the rallying cry, it's only rhetoric. How long we are going to stay with that rhetoric is a question we must tackle. The board, the organization, the donors, all of us, rallied behind and owned the goal of 1,000 schools. Now, if the organization does not own the goal of 1.5 million learners, it becomes meaningless as a rallying cry. In recent discussions, we have been talking about this, but my rallying cry is to protect what we have, that we can't jeopardize the core programs, that we should draw a red circle around the core programs and do whatever we can outside the core programs but not at the risk of compromising them.

So, I'll say that, currently [2017], our rallying cry[8] is in limbo. But I feel strongly that the TIB program is an effective and sound program. TIB did not get the traction it should have, but we should not be discouraged by that because, sooner or later, its benefits will be recognized. Other ideas have also been kicked around. We, as the Board, are a council of quality control. We're not running the program. The organization runs the program. We have a great burden of protecting what we have because people have trusted us with their money and we can't jeopardize that, so it's a sacred cow. The point is that there are also 'problems' with us, the three remaining co-founders, and it's a good thing that we're not managing the schools. Because, as the founders, we also begin to lose our minds [laughs]. Every one of us is over 60 now and it's important that we don't use TCF as a platform to experiment with our pet projects. That's why I say that we are a council of quality control rather than a group that manages the day-to-day operations. We receive many ideas and we have to apply quality control practices and sift through the proposals and ideas.

Largely, our nature is that we are a collegial group and we have a large number of stake holders. After the founders are gone, our children will not run TCF. The founders have been given the unique privilege of being a little more equal than the others but it's a much larger group that 'owns' TCF. The larger the group, the more ideas are generated, and we only have the privilege to basically quality control those ideas and some people are unhappy when their ideas are not accepted, because they also own the organization like us. Their displeasure is valid, but we think that we are doing quality control, so the idea-giver has a 'lesser' right because he has been thinking one-dimensionally whereas we, the founders, look at proposed ideas along many dimensions. This can happen among the founders as well. For example, one of the founders may propose an idea which is shot down and he can become slightly annoyed, but the nature of the relationship is such that we get over it quickly and without any damage. So, we must realize that it is not the founders who own the organization. The 'owners' of the organization could be in the hundreds and everyone can feel that he or she has the right to influence decisions—and they do have the right—but the challenge we face as the board is that our governance and our succession should be set on solid ground. In our peer group of education non-profits, the founder may be the CEO and also the CFO and the CMO. Whereas, at TCF, we now have the fifth chairperson of the board and we have defined term limits for directors and chairpersons. Another decision was to not pass on directorship as a family legacy, but to select from people who have earned their stripes through service to TCF.

Q. For future leadership, is thought given to grooming of leaders from the TCF alumni, since they are expected to be stronger stakeholders of the future? And what are the special voting privileges of the founders?

Ahsan: I agree that the alumni are the future stakeholders and owners of the organization but I think we are a few years away from seeing the alumni take a leadership role, although we have involved them in the new TCF College Council through the ADP program. We will continue to groom them and support the ADP.

We have an understanding between the founding directors that we would have unanimity in our decisions. In other words, each founder has veto power. And, at every stage, there have been situations where

> ## Box 2.12 TCF Operating Costs: where do they get paid from?
>
> The TCF annual operating budget is roughly $30 million (2018). About half of that is raised in Pakistan. Close to a third or $10 million is raised and contributed by TCF-USA. The balance 15 percent is received from donors in the Middle East, UK, Canada and other parts of the globe. – Author

one of us has disagreed, and we have heated debates and fail to convince a dissenting founder, but we respect the dissenting vote and agree to go along with it. We don't agree on all things, yet there is great deal of harmony when decisions are made, despite each one of us being fiercely independent, which is rare in the Pakistani environment.

At present, we have no limits on the terms of the founders. I think we will probably cap it at thirty years, which I think is valid, so that we can evaluate the performance of the other directors and groom them. We realize that our 'wicket can fly' at any time (a cricket term, same as being 'struck out' in baseball). We are creating Regional Advisory Boards to guide the efforts of TCF in the regions. We're encouraging them to engage with the programs of the organization and its supporters. To add a new dimension to our governance, we have also chosen some overseas supporters as directors on the Board and we will continue to add them to the Governing Body as well.

Q. Looking back, what have you learned from the adjustments made?

Ahsan: At various times, events have defined what direction TCF would take. As I said, one defining moment was when we reached 500 schools and the reorganization that we implemented. There were several good decisions made at that time. Another was the realization that we were seeing a lot of excellent creative energy from the managers and staff who had come from different backgrounds and with diverse perspectives. Fortunately, we recognized that in order to nurture that creative energy and allow our people to think on their own, we did not need to be a regimented organization. As a result, we have experienced tremendous innovation and steady growth.

The 'B' (Best) Team of TCF

In the preceding conversations, we have learned about TCF history, operations, its core leadership and management. The incredible outcomes over the last two decades have been possible, to a great extent, because of the scores of outstanding global and Pakistani volunteer leaders and thousands of supporters who serve tirelessly at many levels. These are the people of the TCF 'B' Team, all distinguished Agents of Change in their own ways, too many to recognize individually but some standouts deserve mention here as leading stalwarts. They are representative of the many, many others who also give selflessly of their resources, their energies and valuable time to serve education.

Top of the list on the 'B' Team are three Karachi leaders—Nilofer Saeed, Bushra Afzal, and Adnan Asdar. In the Diaspora, Ishaque Noor and Shahab Haider of Dubai have led and sustained the efforts in setting up the first overseas group of TCF supporters in the UAE. Imtiaz Dossa and Tariq Hussain of London have been stable presences and leaders in the UK chapter. Danial Noorani of Chicago founded TCF-USA and led the chapter as its president and CEO; Arif Gafur of Houston was the *pro bono* CEO of the US chapter and currently serves as president. Aziz Rakla of Toronto is the founder of TCF's Canada chapter and serves in multiple capacities; and Sajid Salman serves *pro bono* as the current CEO for TCF-Canada. Among the people in the nascent support groups, special mention should be made of Gretchen Romig of Milan, Italy, and Nadia Ahmed of Oslo, Norway, who lead support efforts in their communities.

Collectively, the teams and the people of TCF—every one of its amazingly dedicated thousands of teachers and staff—are all on this unprecedented journey, with the goal to see more Pakistani children receive quality education through effective reforms in the education system. Readers are urged to 'hop on the bus' to serve the cause of education. The personal rewards are great…and guaranteed.

Notes

1. The TCF Community Development Unit (CDU) is a team headed by volunteer executive Amina Khalid, a graduate of Wharton School of Business. Amina also oversees the TCF Grants Team. The CDU manages two major programs for TCF – the Clean Water Project and Aagahi, the Adult & Women's Literacy Program, through alliance with a partner organization.

2. Message From The CEO, Annual Report 2018, TCF, 4 February 2019: https://www.tcf.org.pk/annual-report-2018/message-from-the-ceo/.
3. See Box 2.6: TCF-in-a-Box.
4. See Box 2.9 Public Advocacy in Education.
5. Nationally, in 2019, there are more than 600 teachers who were students in TCF schools.
6. Biryani is a delicious dish of rice, meat, and potatoes.
7. Ardeshir Cowasjee (1940–2005), an outspoken and witty shipping magnate, enjoyed taking jabs at the government in op-ed columns of the daily *Dawn*, often berating the authorities for mismanagement and corruption. He became a major TCF supporter and funded a large flagship TCF 'Cowasjee Campus' in the Lyari slums of Karachi. There are ten school units at the Campus.
8. Since the GCC in early 2019, the new goal and rallying cry is 'Two Million by 2030'. TCF plans to continue expanding its effort for formal education through TCF 'flagship' and partnership (adopted public) schools; also increase its outreach through the literacy and life skills programs, to empower those who have missed their first chance at schooling.

Chapter Three

The Saleem Family of Ibrahim Goth

When money for day-to-day living and saving for a modest and very basic home were the primary concerns, education of the children was still a high priority for Majeedan Bibi and Muhammad Saleem[1] which speaks of their belief that education is the only certain exit from the struggles of perennial poverty and hardships. When the challenge was poor quality public schools and long distances to be traveled, they found solutions. When their neighbors were reluctant to send the daughters to school, they offered support. They didn't pull their children out of school and send them to work. And, each one of their five children (Uzma, Nadeem, Sidra, Iqra, and Yasir), *Masha Allah*, are marvelous success stories on their own because they have ownership of their destinies.

The story of the family begins with the central characters of this fabled narrative, the proud parents. None of this would be possible if these parents didn't have an enlightened outlook despite their own minimal education and simple, rural lifestyle. As migrants universally do, they stepped out of their comfort zone, took enormous risk and moved to the big city to resettle and work for a better future for their family. But, before going any further, we should point out that this is one of many stories of hard-working families finding a way out of poverty by educating their children, not asking for a handout, striving to break the barriers of class and achieving a better life. These families are the outstanding Agents of Change.

3.1 The Parents

Majeedan Bibi and Muhammad Saleem are the finest example of countless parents who give up comforts and many hours of their lives for the benefit of their children. Despite tough times and meager resources, with hard work and the extra effort that only caring parents are capable of, they have accomplished the dream of all parents which is simply to give their children a good start in life. And, defying the odds like many underprivileged families, they have supported the children through university education. This is the composite story of an amazing family.

Majeedan Bibi is the regal queen of the Saleem family household and clearly the heart-and-soul of the clan. Thoughtful, cheerful, hospitable, and gregarious are the images I have of her and, like all mothers, she is full of love and kindness. With her radiant smile and captivating charm, she can carry on animated conversation and confidently offer her opinion. Behind the veil of simplicity is a very smart lady who is the control tower of the home, multi-tasking and tracking everything in her domain at any given time.

Customarily, a visitor respectfully addresses the lady of the house as *Bhabhi* (brother's wife). So, Bhabhi Majeedan Bibi grew up in a village near Sheikhupura, Punjab. Her schooling was up to grade 5 in a village public school and she has great memories of that time. Working in the fields and helping in the home were expected of most girls and that's what she did until she was married at the age of 17 to become part of a multi-family unit with her in-laws and relatives sharing a common household. She spoke Punjabi but her limited schooling was in Urdu. She maintains the ability to read and do basic arithmetic and helped her children with their schoolwork, which they recall fondly. The conversation with Bhabhi took off spontaneously. Before I could set the stage with any leading questions, she launched into a motherly oratory that was worthy of content for the book, so I turned on my recorder and let her keep on rolling.

'I thank Allah and I also give credit to my mother-in-law, the children's *daadi* (paternal grandmother), who would always pray for their prosperity. All people work hard but Allah's blessing is the reason some make it and get ahead. My job was to raise the family, wash their clothes, make the meals. I didn't have much education to help with their schooling and their father worked very hard. Allah has helped us to raise good, successful children. I would sew clothes to supplement the family income, and I would send Nadeem to get threads and materials for me. Sometimes he would buy the threads and stuff but drop some on the way home. I would pull him by the ear and send him back to look for them [laughs heartily]. As I said, our children have done well and now they spoil me and don't want me to do any sewing. They want me to take it easy.'

The strong and emotional opening was followed by formal small talk until I re-directed the conversation to a lighter topic, like match-making for her older son Nadeem. 'So, Bhabhi ji—when Nadeem comes to the US, can we get him married to a pretty *Amriki larki?*' (American girl) I asked, tongue in cheek. With giggles and laughter all around, Bhabhi said, 'Wherever his destiny is, that's fine with me. We humans can't do anything. Whatever is destined will happen. All people are fine. It takes both sides to make a good relationship, a good marriage.' I had taken a chance with that silly suggestion which could have offended her. But I was floored by Bhabhi's quick come back with a mix of humor and pragmatism. The lighter tone was set, and the chit-chat led to a sumptuous Sunday brunch of *saag* (greens) and *paratha* (soft, flaky, roti-bread) that I had especially requested. After the delicious meal and *chai*, we settled into a more serious conversation with Bhabhi and Saleem *Bhai* (brother), the patriarch and backbone of the family. As a parent, he deserves equal admiration for the success of the children as he was the main financier, transporter, and security provider for them, especially for the girls.

Muhammad Saleem moved to Karachi at the age of 20, leaving behind Majeedan Bibi with the first-born baby girl Uzma and his own mother, in the small town of Naushahro Feroze. He found work at a copper wire factory near Ibrahim Goth and lived in shared, temporary housing until he could send for the family. They joined him when Uzma was 6 years old and she had started school in the village. Saleem Sahib retired in 2019 after nearly 40 years of service and, as a senior employee, he has now moved up to a supervisory position at the plant. He has also moved up from a bicycle to a motorbike as his means of transport but, in other ways, he remains grounded. His calm, peaceful demeanor is remarkable. In America, he would be considered very cool and laid-back.

The wage he makes is about 32,000 Pakistani rupees a month (a little more than US$210) and there's no annual raise or bonus. The labor pool may get a salary raise every five or ten years. There's no set minimum wage, no benefits, or pension program. It's an unregulated, unaudited, non-unionized place of work where labor conditions are not monitored and workers' rights are generally not protected. The employees work at the bidding of the owner but they're thankful that they have a job and a steady income.

Q. Bhabi ji, I'm going to ask you a few questions now. What was the level of your education and where did you go to school?

Majeedan Bibi: We lived in a village near Sheikhupura. There was no school in our village, so we walked to a school a half-hour away. I completed 5th grade and it wasn't easy because it wasn't very common for girls to go to school. I had four sisters, one older than me who stayed home to help with chores or help in the fields with our father. The younger sisters went to school, and they also went to secondary school. One of them even went to intermediate college. I have three brothers *Masha Allah*, one has a BA and he recently retired from the [Pakistan] Air Force. My older brother went up to 9th grade and now looks after the family's land for *khaitibari* [farming]. The youngest brother has an FA [Faculty of Arts diploma, two years of Intermediate college] and he's in the army.

Q. Fortunately, you and Saleem Bhai received some education and children usually go further than the parents. So, it's because of your own education that your children have done well. Now, with your prayers, they are going to change the world. But they also have to work hard.

Majeedan Bibi: Yes, everyone has to work hard. We have to support each other and pray for the best. Their father was always helpful in getting the girls to their schools, or to and from the bus stop. He was always concerned about the safety of our girls and went out of his way for their protection.

Q. Saleem Bhai was very helpful in getting the girls to their schools, or to and from the bus stop.

Majeedan Bibi: He was always concerned about the safety of our girls and went out of his way for their protection.

Q. Uzma took the first step, completing her BSc and then her MBA. A few years later, Sidra and Iqra followed and went to college. What were your concerns for their safety when they wanted to go to college?

Majeedan Bibi: We would constantly worry about them. We trusted their judgement, but times were bad. There was violence and rioting at times in the city. The buses would come to a halt and we had to make calls to find out where they were and how to get them back home safely. It all worked out, *Alhamdulillah*. Their father would go on his motorbike and, to our relief, bring them back home safely. The TCF teachers were all very nice and gave us encouragement and support, which helped us to face the challenges. We had faith in Allah but always breathed a sigh of relief when they were home safe and sound.

Q. Once the tradition of education is set in a family, it keeps on going, doesn't it?

Saleem Bhai: We didn't know what it meant that Uzma was doing her BSc. We would ask around for advice, but Nadeem had the right ideas and discussed the best options with Uzma and they would come to a decision and then ask for our approval. Because of Uzma being so determined to go further, the younger ones have also been able to go as far as they have. If Uzma had stopped after Intermediate college or her bachelor's degree, perhaps her younger siblings would not have had the urge to go to university. Uzma also helped with tasks at home and with her mother's sewing projects for extra income. My own earnings were hardly meeting our needs.

Majeedan Bibi: My mother-in-law would often tell me that I was putting too much load on Uzma with the sewing and housework. But Uzma carried her responsibilities very well and never complained. She's a wonderful child, like all my children, *Alhamdulillah*. She loved schoolwork. She would help her younger siblings and every one of them has worked hard to get ahead. I'm especially proud of Uzma for achieving what she has, becoming a civil service officer and being able to stand on her own feet. She has been a wonderful child and a great mentor for her siblings. She would study late into the night after I went to bed and every free minute during the day also.

Q. Then it was Sidra's turn to go to college. Did you have any concerns about her going to medical school, the long hours, or anything else?

Saleem Bhai: She always had a fondness for science and medicine, and she was determined to be a doctor. She did very well in her early years in school and intermediate college. She is the first doctor in our entire family and that's a proud feeling for us. No, we had no worries about anything. Sidra was set in her goals and kept her focus on medical school.

Majeedan Bibi: *Masha Allah*, we are so grateful to Allah.

> **Q. Sidra is in Chicago these days, so I'll speak with her when I get back to California. And did Iqra tell you about her trip to California and the fun we had showing her around?**

Majeedan Bibi: Yes, she speaks fondly of the good time she had and that you showed them the best spots and the big universities in your area.

> **Q. Did she tell you about the sing-song we had in the car? I was getting a bit sleepy on one stretch of the road, so I asked Iqra and her two girlfriends if they could sing to keep me awake and they did, and I joined them, and we all had a great time singing our favorite songs! And what do you think Iqra will want to do after graduating from LUMS and how do you feel about that?**

Majeedan Bibi: No, she hasn't decided or told us what she'd like to do. She'll probably ask Nadeem for guidance before we hear about it. A lot of the credit for being the mentor in the family goes to Nadeem. First and foremost, of course, it's thanks to Allah and His mercy, we are always grateful. But Nadeem has been a godsend to our family. He has a good head on his shoulders and always looks out for his siblings.

Saleem Bhai: Iqra should do whatever she would like to. We have no feelings, one way or the other.

> **Q. And what about Yasir? What do you see in his future?**

Majeedan Bibi: *Insha Allah*, Yasir will make us proud, he's working hard and doing well at Habib University. *Insha Allah*, he will be a very big *afsar* (officer in the civil service).

> **Q. Masha Allah, all your children are wonderful—thanks to your prayers and guidance. What would you like to say about TCF and how it has played a big part in changing your lives?**

Majeedan Bibi: To tell you the truth, Bhai, I am always singing praise of TCF. It is all because of TCF that our children have done well, and they are at good stations in life. We had no school in the area, in Ibrahim Goth, not even a government school close to home and there is none today.

Nadeem (interjecting): That's because this is an unauthorized area—*katchi abadi*, not a legally built area. If you take the TCF schools out, there are no other schools here. There are three TCF primary schools here that run afternoon shifts too, so that's 6 units and there's a 2-unit secondary school running two shifts each. So, we have ten TCF school units but we still need more schools. I think we could easily have 10 more schools in the area.

Saleem Bhai: I've heard that children are turned away from admission in kindergarten at the local TCF schools because they are full to capacity.

Majeedan Bibi: Thanks to TCF and its supporters, the teaching is very good so everyone wants to send their children to TCF. And there is no other option, no other schools. But TCF should think about opening a school in my village near Sheikhupura because there isn't any school there.

Q. **I think the people in Sheikhupura should ask the government to build schools there. TCF is now working with the government, adopting some schools. Would you like to add anything, any suggestions for how the education system in the country can be improved?**

Saleem Bhai: It's a tough challenge. What TCF is doing is very good but the public should put pressure on the government to improve the system, build more schools, and run the schools like TCF does. There was no secondary school close to our home when we wanted Uzma to start in 6th grade. We got the run around at the public school near *Sindhi Hotel* about 2 miles away, but we finally got her in with some help. It was not very convenient, but we had her in that school for two years until the TCF secondary school opened and she transferred there in 8th grade.

Majeedan Bibi: We had to plan with the families of the other girls who were going to the same school, so there was always an adult with them when they walked to school and returned home. But we have seen good changes in our local area because of the TCF schools. Many children have benefited from the schools in Ibrahim Goth. Who knows where our own children would have gone and where they would be today. Thanks to Allah and the TCF schools, they have stability in their lives.

Nadeem: The Ibrahim Goth secondary school was one of the first six TCF secondary schools and Uzma was in the first batch of TCF students to pass the 10th grade Matric exam in 2003.

Q. How are health facilities or clinics in Ibrahim Goth?

Nadeem: There are no hospitals here and no public health clinics. There are a few private clinics, but they don't have qualified doctors. Typically, there is a 'compounder' [a dispensary worker] who will examine patients and dispense medicines at a nominal cost. Their services are not very reliable.

3.2 Uzma Saleem
MBA, Bahria University,
Assistant Accountant General, Sindh,
Pakistan Audit & Accounts Service

The eldest of five children in the family, Uzma is the pioneering trailblazer and the anchor for her entire generation in the family. She has passed on her personal attributes of smart resolve, discipline, and determination to the younger set and also earned the respect of her community as a role model and as one of the first girls in Ibrahim Goth to finish secondary school. Uzma went on to college and Bahria University, graduated with an MBA on a merit scholarship with the highest GPA in class, and passed the Central Superior Services (CSS) exam for the civil service. Remarkably juggling the challenges of her final year at Bahria University, she achieved three major goals in the same year. Uzma works for the Audit & Accounts Service of the federal government and since April 2017, she has been an Assistant Accountant General assigned to Sindh.

Uzma was finishing up an eighteen-month training program for the civil service when I first met her in Lahore. It was unimaginable that a recently-married, young Pakistani woman, from an underprivileged family in Karachi, had convinced her husband and her in-laws that it was important to pursue the civil service professional training in Lahore and that it would pay off in the long run. She is bold, eloquent, witty, and mature beyond her years. Her story is fascinating and confirms the depth of her knowledge and extraordinary ability to think on her feet. Here's a teaser quote from the interview that follows: 'We are not here merely as accountants. We should be good at policy and decision-making too. [...] that is the expectation citizens should have of their public servants, to make good decisions for good policy. And that's why I would like to do a Master's in Public Policy and seek opportunities in that field of study.'

The wide-ranging exchange with Uzma was on a Sunday morning in February 2016 at the LUMS cafeteria. Her sister Iqra, a student at LUMS at the time, was also present. An amusing point of Uzma's early education in a public school is that, by her own admission, she couldn't add 23 plus 33 in 7th grade. But, here she was, an MBA graduate and a passionate civil servant, thanks to the support of her parents. At times, Uzma's smart insights left me in total awe of her remarkable maturity, confidence, and poise. She is now the young mother of a beautiful baby girl, Inaya, born February 2018, and continues to work full-time.

Q. Please tell us about your personal journey. What are your memories of early schooling? I understand there was no school in Ibrahim Goth and that your father would take you to the nearest government school on his bicycle before going to work.

Uzma: Before we came to Ibrahim Goth, we lived in a village near Naushahro Feroze, in upper Sindh, past Nawabshah. Our home was close to farming lands and my mother, my *daadi* (paternal grandmother), and I lived there. My father had found work near Ibrahim Goth, Karachi. Between a few villages, there was a two-room government primary school, where I started my schooling. As my father got settled in his factory job, we moved from Naushahro to Ibrahim Goth. My parents were eager to send me to school, but many families didn't see the need to send their children to school. Most children in our communities would work to add to the family income and the parents would save the expense of their education with the thought that going to school wasn't important, that the children will learn as they grow. In the early days, my parents convinced a few families in our neighborhood to send their children to school. The closest government school was a thirty-minute walk from our home and my father would take me to school on his bicycle or the mothers would take turns walking a group of us children to school. I finished 7th grade at the public school but I didn't learn much. I could not read or write much in Urdu and hardly knew the English alphabet. When a TCF secondary school opened, I started 8th grade over there. The TCF school in our neighborhood has turned out to be a life changer for me and my siblings—and for hundreds of other children in Ibrahim Goth.

Q. Describe the learning you experienced in the government primary school through 7th grade.

Uzma: There were three teachers in the school and they would take turns in the classrooms. I don't think there was a system or curriculum that was being followed. Some days, one of the teachers would be absent or just stay in the staff room and not teach at all. And, the teaching was often like the teacher reading from a book and the children who had picked up some reading skills would read along, but there was no help for the children who couldn't read and they just got left further behind. The teacher would then go over the questions and answers related to the text that was read but there was no thinking required on the part of the children. I realized when I went to a TCF school—later, I also taught at one of the TCF schools—that a child wants to learn something new every day, that not all children are equal in their learning abilities, and that some may need a little extra help to keep up with the class. There was none of that in the government school.

Q. How was it in math?

Uzma: Honestly, I didn't learn any proper math concepts until I started in 8th grade at the TCF school. I could not do double digit addition or subtraction, just very simple arithmetic like 2 plus 2. For example, I couldn't add 23 plus 33 because I had no idea of how to do double digit addition. That's the way it was in all subjects. We had fifty girls in one classroom and we had very few desks or chairs to sit on. The desk and bench were made to seat three students, but we would have five girls on each bench. It was always crowded and uncomfortable, and there weren't enough desks and benches for everyone, so we had to bring our own small pieces of floor mats to sit on. Sometimes we would get a mat piece from the school. That is still quite common in public schools and some schools have sheets or *durees* (cotton rugs) to sit on.

Q. And when was science introduced in the government school?

Uzma: I really began to learn about science, math, and social studies when I moved to the TCF school. At the public school, with no testing of outcomes, the teachers just went through the motions of teaching, if you can call it that. We were never told 'we are now in a science class'—the teacher would just read from the textbook, and we followed what we could. There was no demonstration or physical experiment to observe or perform on our own, hence no learning by experience. In the English class, we would work endlessly on writing the alphabet, or copying a few words from the board. We didn't know how to construct sentences or make sense of what we were reading or writing. I was mixing up capitals (upper case) and small letters (lower case) in the same words. I was in 8th grade at TCF when an English teacher took me under her wing and gave me extra help to teach me the difference and showed me how to construct sentences and use punctuations. I felt helpless at times, but I was determined to overcome my weakness. I worked very hard that first year at the TCF school. My study and homework time were difficult to manage as my mother also needed help with housework and my siblings weren't old enough to help at home. But, somehow, I got it all done because I was so excited to be in a different school and I didn't want to disappoint my teachers.

Q. The Ibrahim Goth community continues to grow. The number of households have probably doubled since you were in the public school. Have classrooms been added to the public school you went to, or have more public schools been added in the area to serve Ibrahim Goth?

Uzma: No, the government school is just the same. To the best of our knowledge, no additional classrooms or schools have been added despite growth in the community. The TCF schools are the only good schools in Ibrahim Goth and they are full to capacity. We need more schools. There are a few low-cost private schools in the area but their quality is questionable.

Q. You work for the federal government. Now, as a public employee, do you have a broader perspective of planning and implementation, why more public schools or other services have not been added in Ibrahim Goth? Is it because the *katchi abadis* are unauthorized or 'temporary' that they present a challenge to the planners and the bureaucracy? Has the government not added to the capacity of public schools because TCF and the low-cost private schools are partially meeting the needs of the community?

Uzma: Yes, I do have a broader perspective now and I can understand the challenges in planning. The people with me in the District Management Group, now called Pakistan Administrative Service (PAS), make the projections and propose the funding for hospitals or schools that should be added in underserved areas. But it is difficult to explain the problems to the bureaucrats at the top because they are so removed from the local conditions. I agree that they also accept the NGO schools as being sufficient for the area and don't work on the need for additional public schools. It's a vicious cycle. Yes, Ibrahim Goth is a community of unauthorized dwellings, but there's no going back. The community is permanently here. The residents are trapped and have no voice because they don't understand the problems. They don't know how to express their needs and demand better public services.

I think a radical shift in town planning and rehabilitation of unauthorized homes is needed for the *katchi abadis*. The government should build a planned community with sanitation, utilities, and public services such as schools and medical facilities, and community spaces, thus creating a *new* Ibrahim Goth, which should be re-built in the same general location in phases, so that people are not displaced but relocated in better homes. It should be done in a way that is financially viable for the community, with easy housing loans, and the families can become legal owners of their properties and have the pride of lawful ownership.

Q. That would be ideal. Going back to your early school days, there is a sharp drop in enrollment between 5th and 6th grades. What was your experience with drop-outs in the public school?

Uzma: Yes, there was a high drop-out rate. Many of the 6th grade girls dropped off because the parents felt the girls had received 'enough' education, that they were older and needed more protection, that they could help the mothers at home either with chores or sewing of garments to supplement the family income. I was the only 6th grader from my group that continued—thanks to my parents and my hat's off to them.

Q. As you were growing up, were you aware of the deficiencies in the public-school education?

Uzma: To be very honest, I had no basis to compare, as I had no exposure to a different system and there was no other option at that time. I was too young to think seriously about the quality of my education. But, when I transferred to the TCF school in 8th grade, I became sharply aware of better teaching and what it is to be in a streamlined school system and what *quality* education feels like. It gave me a new direction in life, both academically and professionally. By the time I was in 10th grade, I had a new sense of confidence, a different outlook, and aspirations for higher achievement through education. I looked for opportunities and started developing personal goals, and what I would like to do in life.

Q. How was the transition to the TCF school?

Uzma: The first time I went into the TCF school, it was an intimidating experience. It was a freshly-painted, shiny, new building, and I wondered if my parents could afford the fees. But the teachers and principal were very encouraging and told us about the sliding scale fee structure. I had to take an admission test and I am embarrassed to say that I left the English, science, and math questions all blank, because I had no idea how to answer the questions. The principal was very accommodating and said I would be fine if I promised to work hard. I am deeply indebted to the math and English teachers who gave me the extra help I needed, correcting my bad habits, and giving me a new foundation to learn everything in a different way. I didn't disappoint them, and I did well through 10th grade. I felt safe and protected, almost pampered, for the three years at TCF. If we needed help with anything, the teachers and principal were always there for us.

Q. And, what after 10th grade? How did the journey continue?

Uzma: The same story was repeated, in a sense, with many different challenges. Karachi has a centralized system for admission to the government's intermediate colleges. I was assigned to Abdullah Government College for Women which was an hour and half away by bus. My mother would wait with me at the bus stop until I got on in the mornings. I would call my father when I got back, and he would pick me up at the bus stop on his motorbike. I took pre-engineering courses at Abdullah College and then taught a kindergarten class at TCF for three months. College expenses for my BSc were partially covered by a TCF scholarship sponsored by Standard Chartered Bank and I made up the balance from sewing and tutoring income.

Q. What were your thoughts after your bachelor's degree and during your teaching days at TCF?

Uzma: I wanted to give back to TCF and to our community, so teaching at TCF seemed to be a good option at that time. After finishing my undergrad studies, I went back to teaching English language for three years at the TCF schools in our *goth*. I taught 1st through 5th grade. From someone who was terrible in math and English as a student, I became a strong math teacher and good in English too. I was selected to become a teacher trainer but at that point I gave more thought to other options, that I didn't need to feel confined, that I could do much more. So, I talked it over with my brother, Nadeem. I was thinking of going for a Master's in math, but he convinced me to consider an MBA in Finance, that there was a demand for this, and it would help me in my personal and professional growth. So that was the decision I made.

Q. How was your study experience in the MBA program?

Uzma: My first trip to Bahria University was embarrassing. I got lost on campus. When I got to the admissions office, I had to fill an online application on a laptop and I didn't know how to use a laptop. At home, my father had set up a used desktop computer for us, but I wasn't used to a laptop, so I asked a lab assistant to help me. He was nice and helped me with the application but said it will be difficult to go through the MBA program if I couldn't use a laptop. How would I do presentations, assignments, and so on? He suggested I should take some easier program I assured him that I was a fast learner and I could do it. Anyway, I passed the test and went through the interview process, and I was accepted.

Q. How would you rate your English proficiency at that time, and how has it improved?

Uzma: I can't say that I was proficient in English, but I felt my comprehension skills were better than other students who came from public schools. In the aptitude test, we were given a paragraph in English and had to answer questions which tested comprehension and expression skills. I found that slightly difficult because my BSc was from a government college where all learning was in Urdu, but my English classes at TCF helped me to get through that. The math and other tests were easy. I feel quite confident in English now and apply it in my work every day, though I mix it with Urdu to make it easier to express myself.

Q. Bahria is a private university. What were the costs and how did you manage that?

Uzma: The admission and first semester costs added up to 92,000 Pakistani rupees and that was paid by TCF. I had the highest GPA in class in the first semester, so I got a 50 percent scholarship from Bahria for the second semester and TCF paid the other 50 percent. Fortunately, I maintained the highest GPA in my class and continued to receive the Bahria and TCF scholarships on merit. My highest GPA was 3.8 on a scale of 4.0.

Q. Then you moved on to your second year at Bahria?

Uzma: Every year, the State Bank [of Pakistan] invites two students from several business schools to a six-week internship at the State Bank. I was selected from Bahria for the prestigious internship and that was a great experience, a life changer for me. After the internship, I was convinced that I wanted to work in the public sector, work for the government, bring about change, do something meaningful—ideally, work at the State Bank.

Q. 'Bring about change'…what does that mean to you?

Uzma: I would have discussions with the department head at the State Bank and he would explain how the Bank was an autonomous institution and a regulatory authority. Because of the 'corporate culture' established by the former governor, Dr Ishrat Husain Sahib. there is transparency, everyone comes to work on time, and it's very different to a typical government department. That was the idealism I had, that I wanted to see more government programs run like the State Bank and hopefully, bring about change through good governance. And that was what drove me to take the CSS exam.

Q. What was the CSS exam like and how did you manage the many things you were doing at the time?

Uzma: The CSS exam consists of twelve subjects, over six days. That was very hectic for me and I've never had a more challenging time. There are no classes for the CSS, it's all by self-preparation so that took a great deal of time. I was in the final semester at Bahria when I took the CSS exam, also working on my master's thesis and tutoring children in the neighborhood ... I still had to make some money for bus fare! They test you on everything under the sun for the CSS test—from English skills and current affairs to your knowledge of geography and sciences. Your political knowledge of world affairs, your approach to possible solutions, your understanding of the subject matter, how you look at the choices before you, how you make decisions in conflicting situations, finding solutions in gray areas because not everything is black and white.

Q. How were technical skills tested in the CSS exam? And, how many people took the exam that year?

Uzma: Technically, I was tested in accounting and audit procedures. About 25,000 persons took the test out of which 439 passed the written test. Then there are psychometrics and the typical personality testing with blotter diagrams asking for your interpretations—that was for two days. Then the technical testing and a panel interview. After the interviews, there were 230 applicants selected and I was one of the lucky ones.

Q. How was your final semester at Bahria and what other challenges did you face?

Uzma: The CSS exam was over, and I had to focus on my master's thesis in the final semester. Then it was a waiting game and I was richly rewarded, *Alhamdulillah*. That was the best year of my life. I passed the MBA finals and I was awarded a gold medal by the university. My thesis was accepted for publication in the European Scientific Journal and I got the news that I had passed the CSS exam. I couldn't have asked for more!

Q. It must have been a tremendous feeling to successfully achieve multiple goals in the same year. How did you start your professional life in the civil service?

Uzma: In the civil service, I opted to join the Pakistan Audit & Accounts Service (PA&AS) because it not only manages the accounts at the local district level in health, education. or other matters of concern, but also works with the provincial and federal governments. Working at the people level appealed to me and that's why PA&AS was my choice. I've been almost a year in this assignment, including the Common Training Program, and now I'm in a Specialized Training Program. My background and interest being finance, audit and accounts, the assignment was suitable for me. As an Assistant Accountant General, my focus will be to ensure that public money is properly utilized and accounted for.

Q. We've been pulling for you for a few years ... could you please allocate a little extra money for education?

Uzma: [Laughs] Yes, we'll do what we can in the budget process. I just want to get done with the training!

Q. Now, Iqra is also studying Finance, and she is at LUMS. So, it's possible that she could become your boss.

Uzma (laughing): Honestly, I'll be very happy. She will avenge all her childhood frustrations with me. But, really, I'll be very happy for her and it will mean a lot for me. She is going to LUMS after all, a more prestigious university than Bahria, so she's already ahead of me!

Iqra (laughing harder): *Insha Allah!* I'll give her dirty looks like she used to give me!

Q. There could be 'corruption' at the hands of the Saleem family mafia—we can't have that! (We continue after a laughing break). So, very soon you will be done with your training. What next?

Uzma: Yes, I have two more months to complete the training then we'll be posted out to our assignments. We will have our preference of cities and I'll ask for Karachi. Then we'll be given the choice to work in one of the accounts departments, either for the Sindh government, or for the Pakistan Navy, Military, or Railways services. Based on availability, we'll be assigned to one of these departments. My position title will be Assistant Accountant General if I go for pre-audit services, or I will have the title of Assistant Director if I work on the post-audit side. I would like to be on the pre-audit side.

Q. Those are tremendous achievements for a young woman who couldn't add 23 plus 33...but, let's fast forward five years. Where do you see yourself, given your recent trajectory?

Uzma: *Insha Allah*, I'd like to study abroad for a couple of years and I'm thinking of applying for scholarships and seriously looking at options.

Q. What do you expect to gain from studying abroad?

Uzma: After having worked in the government sector in Pakistan for a couple of years, I will gain experience in a foreign system, which can be valuable in broadening my perspectives. Coming out of Ibrahim Goth, then going to secondary school in a TCF setting, and moving up to where I am today, I have gained such a wide range of experience that I could never have imagined. The more exposure one gets, the better the personal growth one experiences and the better the analytic and decision-making capabilities. We are not here merely as accountants. We should be good at policy and decision-making too. Going abroad to study will greatly enhance my decision-making because that is the expectation citizens should have of their public servants, to make good decisions for good policy. And, that's why I would like to do a master's in public policy and seek opportunities in that field of study.

Q. As we know, not all universities deliver good education. Some are excellent institutions, but many are money-making factories that churn out degrees. Most graduates from good institutions prefer to go into the private sector, the corporate world. Is that because of the skepticism, possibly a stigma, of working in the public sector?

Uzma: I agree to some extent, but I would argue that it's a common misperception about the public sector. I see healthy changes taking place. For example, most of the folks in our batch are graduates from foreign universities, and there are about 30 graduates of LUMS and IBA and other top-listed universities such as NUST and UET. We also have several physicians from Dow Medical College and engineers from NED in our batch. I estimate more than half the batch are professionals with law, business, or finance degrees from top Pakistani universities or abroad and they have made the choice to work in public service. For those who look strictly for monetary benefits, the corporate salaries are obviously much higher. But the public recognition, the authority, and the opportunities that we have are not there in the corporate sector. Also, your advancement is more predictable. Your trajectory in the private sector is less predictable. So, it's a matter of personal choice. The 25,000 applicants in my batch for the CSS exam preferred to come to the public sector. There are very few openings in the public-sector jobs, so it is highly competitive. You are going up against applicants from the best schools like Beaconhouse and the best universities like IBA and LUMS. The very fact that I made it on merit is evidence that the selection process is transparent.

Q. Is there sincere desire among the new batch of civil service officers to serve for the public good?

Uzma: Do I have to give an honest answer? (Laughs). My motivation is to be of service for the public good. I didn't know much of the 'hidden benefits' of public sector jobs at this level and I probably don't know much even today but I get the sense that among the civil servants that I work with, there is divided interest and motivation. There are a few bad apples who openly say that they are in it for the power of the position and the money that can be made on the side. Some people are looking only for job security and they do it just as a job. Then, there are some who feel that now that they are in public service, they should do a good job and make things better for the country. They understand the responsibility we have as custodians of public money and want to see that the public good is served. So, my observation in my own batch is that it is divided in this way: some people are in public service just for the power and the illicit earnings, and many of them will openly talk about it; and there are some who are in public service to serve the public good. I think that the larger group is of those who want to serve the public good.

Q. It is probably not very difficult to know who the bad apples are?

Uzma: Yes, when you work with a group of people you find out what the group dynamics are very quickly.

Q. In your department and in your position, is there opportunity for personal favors?

Uzma: Yes, quite a bit. For example, as we audit government departments and they want their budget request or expenditure bill to be approved, there can be requests for inter-departmental personal favors. But we must guard against any financial favors or abuse of power. That is always a big challenge.

Q. Looking at countries like South Korea, Singapore, India, China, how have these countries made great progress economically and stabilized their political systems?

Uzma: I think there are several inter-linked factors in the development and economic success of a country. From my personal view and as a public servant, we must look at the governance levels from top to bottom. The policy makers at the top—the secretaries, department heads, the top bureaucrats—need to run the state machinery and ensure that the state functions are working efficiently at all levels. Then, we also have the institutions of the military and the political machineries. All these pillars of governance must work together to run the state. The bureaucracy has a huge role in this as well. For example, if the PM [prime minister] is to receive a summary report, the Section Officer of the Office Management Group, a bureaucrat, is to prepare the report and send it to the PM. If it's an expenditure item, the audit people are involved in the report. If it's a school to be built or not, the Assistant Commissioner of a local district, a bureaucrat, is the one who decides. So, there are multiple layers of bureaucracy that must play their respective roles and each one must do it efficiently, or the whole system suffers. That's the problem. Our bureaucratic machinery is not efficient, and it caves in to the pressure of powerful local interests who have the backing of politicians. We have corruption in many forms—professional dishonesty, incompetence, and no motivation to make the system better. Bribery is prevalent because government salaries are relatively low, and people feel they can rationalize taking bribes routinely, to make up for the low salaries. I think that is totally wrong.

So, bureaucracy has an important role and education is a key factor in every aspect of governance and life in general. If my family and I had not received the education that we did, we would not have been aware of these ills in our system, we would probably not have the sense to make these observations. But, despite these factors, I feel that the bureaucracy, as a system, must work efficiently and if that is achieved, it would prevent vested interests from coercing the bureaucrat to do something which is unethical or improper. Powerful persons can threaten and can force the transfer of a government officer who doesn't go along with an unethical request. If the officer has the courage to stand up for ethical principles and declines the request, he or she will probably get transferred. The replacement officer might also suffer the same consequence. So, how many people can they punish in this way? If the bureaucracy were to unite and run the state machinery in the right way, then things would begin to get better, I'm sure. Take Singapore, for example. They were a colonized country just like ours and they inherited the same system of bureaucracy that we did. The problem is not with the system; I think the problem is with the people who are running the system. We are lacking the checks and balances that are needed in an efficient bureaucracy. The red tape and frustrations that citizens experience with the government should be eliminated—and I believe these problems can be solved by the bureaucrats and the issues of corruption can be mitigated by the bureaucrats themselves. Again, I'd like to cite the example of Singapore. Perhaps we just don't have the strong will to make these corrections. Perhaps we are easily tempted and distracted by personal gains.

**Q. After the CSS exams, departmental appointments are not
always made on merit or based on skill sets. Ideally, we should
have technical experts or technocrats appointed to decision-
making positions for optimal efficiency in the bureaucracy, at
least in the top layers of management. Are you seeing a move
in that direction, where technical experts are given preference?**

Uzma: A new initiative has been announced which will be cluster-based.
The Customs Service, Inland Revenue Service, Audit and Accounts
Service and the Commerce & Trade Group will comprise one such
cluster, since these agencies are finance related, and specialists with
degrees in finance will be assigned to this cluster of agencies. I believe
this is to be implemented in 2022. If a similar pattern emerges in
other cluster assignments, this could be a positive step in the direction
of creating the technocratic teams you refer to. I can relate to the
inefficiencies created by poor assignments. In my specialized training
program for Audit and Accounts, we have two physicians, two from
liberal arts, three engineers, one with a master's in management, two
economists, and three of us from a Finance background. I can't blame
them, but the physicians and liberal arts graduates are having difficulty
understanding accounting terminology, how to read financial statements
or reports, because their backgrounds and specialization are in totally
different fields. With the new cluster-based concept, they will probably
assign management specialists to the Pakistan Administrative Service,
so I think that will be a good thing.

**Q. It is probably difficult to fill all assignments with the right
technical experts, but the non-experts could be trained on-the-
job to become specialists, like the doctors and engineers and
others in your group are being 'technically' trained in accounts
and audit procedures. That should work, don't you think?**

Uzma: Yes, if the technical training is rigorous, it should work.

**Q. Is there any ongoing redesigning or realignment of department
functions?**

Uzma: No, not very much in terms of redesigning functions but there's
a push for automation and digitalization of all processes. They've

introduced newer versions of database software and the departments are struggling to convert from a manual to a computerized system. It will take some time but it's happening and we're seeing more data on-screen. Automation and digitilization will improve accountability and reduce corruption and waste. There's a lot of back log in paperwork. We have huge stacks of paper files in all the offices. Retrieval and relocation of the paper files takes so much time and slows down everything.

Q. Uzma, starting in the early years, how can civic responsibility become part of education at all levels?

Uzma: We should start by making the child responsible with small tasks at a very early age. When I was teaching kindergarten, I felt that in addition to classroom learning the young child needs training through role modeling by adults and teachers. They must be told that the wrappers (packaging) from snacks should be disposed of in the trash cans, not casually dropped on the ground. They must be asked to share things if they don't do that on their own. They must be taught that speaking the truth and honesty are the expected ideal, that courtesy and kindness are to be practiced all the time. Education brings about change in behavior and acceptance of these norms. Good behavior is adopted by the child only if it is frequently reinforced by adults in the child's life. Our own neighborhood in Ibrahim Goth is a good example: it is much cleaner than it used to be because more children are going to school and the families are more aware of their civic responsibility. It was 'normal' for girls to end their education in the 10th grade. Now, that has changed. More and more girls are going on to university. As these girls become educated mothers, they will also be stronger role models for their own children.

The parents of a couple of girls I know from our community were successful in having a new bus route added so that the girls could go to a university which was not accessible before. These parents exercised their civic responsibility and used their voice. And it was all because of education. It always starts with education and good changes follow.

The founders and supporters of TCF are a prime example of civic responsibility. With the movement for education, they have put in motion the changes that my siblings and I have experienced in our own lives. I was among the first students from Ibrahim Goth who completed a university education and, if it wasn't for the TCF school, I don't know where or what I would be doing today. And, that's true for my siblings, too. I see visible signs of change in the youth from our neighborhoods. They are getting into good jobs, going into small businesses, becoming good citizens. I realize we have a long way to go and there are many challenges, but the change is underway, and I feel that it is largely because of the education movement, the realization that young people must be educated in good schools. It is only the beginning and the next generation will do better, I'm sure.

In our own extended family—my uncles and their families who live in the villages of Sheikhupura and Naushahro Feroze districts, where we came from—they don't see this change taking place. Education is poor, their children are growing up in rural conditions with no opportunities and options that are available to us because of the education we received. And, it all started with the education we received at the TCF school.

* * * *

And, that was the conversation with Uzma Salim, an outspoken, bold and brutally honest young woman who will be a beacon for many more Pakistani girls and boys. As this outstanding Agent of Change continues on her life journey, it will be interesting to track her progress and professional trajectory.

* * * *

Update

February 2021: Uzma was promoted to Basic Pay Scale (BPS-18) and is currently a Deputy Director in the Commercial Audit division.

3.3 Sidra Saleem
MD, MBBS – Dow Medical College

The middle of five siblings, Sidra is a medical graduate with an MBBS degree from Dow Medical College in Karachi. She was in the US in 2017 for three months which included a four-week elective in pediatric neurology at the University of Illinois Chicago (UIC) Medical Center and a four-week rotation in general surgery. The trip was sponsored by UIC and helped her gain didactic and clinical experience in the American system of medicine. Sidra returned to Pakistan in May 2017, completed the one-year 'house job' requirement, worked at a hospital for a few months, passed Steps 1 and 2 of the USMLE (Medical Licensing) exams, and applied at nearly two hundred residency programs for physicians in the US, her first choice being adult neurology with internal medicine as an alternate.

Like her sisters, Sidra is a petite young lady with characteristic professionalism which comes from the discipline of intense study and clinical training that physicians must endure. She quickly warms up with confidence, poise and maturity in her mannerisms and communications, expressing herself with economy of words, precisely and thoughtfully. The depth of her knowledge at a young age is striking. Just nine years ago, she was in 9th grade at a TCF school in Ibrahim Goth, struggling to learn English as a language.

As she marches on, Sidra recognizes that she is following in the footsteps of powerful girls before her who have similar stories. Her journey is a testimonial to underprivileged Pakistani girls that 'getting ahead' is possible with perseverance, support from family—and a little help to level the playing field. That's what TCF has done for Sidra and as we discover in this conversation, Sidra is making her own path.

Date of interview: May 2017, Chicago.

Q. So, you are now Doctor Sidra Saleem—congratulations! How did you get this opportunity to be at UIC?

Sidra: Yes, finally a doctor! Five years of medical school is a tough, long road. The opportunity to come to UIC is offered annually to the top ten students at Dow and I was one of them this year.

Q. What challenges did you face at UIC and how did you adjust to the different system?

Sidra: The US system is totally computerized, and every physician has unique access to the records including lab work or other investigations. In Pakistan, we have a paper chart for each patient with paper records and the physician documents everything manually, on paper. It took me about a week to understand the system in the US and get used to it. That was a big challenge. I had heard about it, but I didn't realize how extensive it was. American physicians in my rotation were helpful and gave me good guidance during the adjustment period. It was a great learning experience.

Q. Did you have any difficulty with language in the clinical setting at UIC?

Sidra: Growing up in Karachi, I wasn't listening to American songs or watching western movies, so in the first few days I had a hard time understanding what people were saying. Also, American expressions and styles of speaking are very different, so it took a little time getting used to the common every-day conversations and making myself understood. I had to think about how to phrase my questions and make sure patients understood me and that I was understanding their response, but I got better in time. People from different regions express themselves in interesting ways. But I had no problem with medical terminology because we use the same books and clinical guidelines in Pakistan.

Q. What did you like most about the American system of medicine and the way things are done here? Will you be able to apply some of the learning to your clinical work in Pakistan?

I was very impressed with the doctor-patient interaction, the patient being able to express all her queries and the doctor listening, patiently. The patient flow is smooth, probably because there are fewer patients to be seen, and the hospitals and clinics have well-organized systems and well-trained personnel to help. In that sense, things are very different in Pakistan. In the out-patient department or OPD in a public hospital, we may have three or four doctors and more than a hundred patients to be seen in a few hours. Most patients are very poor, and many are not educated so they are not able to express themselves very well. They may have no idea what is wrong with them or the diagnosis, they don't understand the treatment they are getting, or what their options are. Our examination areas are also very small and crowded and there can be privacy issues, gender issues, and problems with communication. So, when I get back, I will try to implement what I have seen and learned about managing patient flow, try to improve patient care, and also improve communication with the patient and family.

Q. You also participated in a study at Adventist Midwest Hospital in Chicago. Was that a statistical study or part of a clinical research?

Sidra: During my four-week general surgery rotation, I helped with an analytical study of the cases of gall bladder disease seen at the hospital in the last three years. It was a statistical research project.

Q. What is a 'house' job? Is it the same as residency for American physicians?

Sidra: After graduation from medical college, a house job is a mandatory one-year service at an approved hospital, after which you can practice medicine in Pakistan. Residency in the US is the period of clinical training for specialization in a specific branch of medicine.

Q. For your elective, did you select pediatric neurology at UIC or was it because there were no openings in other specializations?

Sidra: I wanted to do rotations in internal medicine or family medicine but there weren't any openings in those areas. So, I took pediatrics and, within that, I selected the sub-specialty of pediatric neurology. That experience was very good, and I fell in love with neurology and, ideally, that's what I'd like to do.

Q. Please share your personal journey, from the early years in school to medical college.

Sidra: I went to a TCF school for eleven years, from kindergarten to 10th grade. What I remember distinctly is that the teachers were very caring and gave individual attention to all students. When I was in 8th grade, I got interested in medicine. As you've seen in Ibrahim Goth, there are no qualified doctors in the whole area. There are a few clinics run by persons who may have some experience working as 'compounders' (making prescription mixtures) and they put up a sign and set up a 'medical practice' dispensing mixed medication, probably placebos, and giving shots to almost everyone. They are not trained physicians but the system is poorly regulated and people don't know the difference. So, I had set my sights on being a doctor, but I was also nervous about not getting admission to medical college because of the stiff competition and so many applicants from elite schools who would have a better chance of getting in. I would often think of back-up plans if I didn't get into medical school—such as pharmacy, or nuclear medicine technology, and other options. But I had my heart set on medicine and when I got my matric results, I was encouraged and thought that I could get into a good Intermediate college for pre-Medical, which I did. I went to PECHS College for Women. The environment in Intermediate college was very different. I would see girls from affluent families being dropped off by their fathers or drivers in nice cars, or a group of girls coming in private vans, when I would have to spend an hour to get there by public transport. But I kept the focus on my studies and I took extra classes and tutoring in pre-med subjects like physics, chemistry and biology. TCF also helped me with the cost of private tutoring.

Q. Being a top student, why the need for extra tutoring?

Sidra: A few reasons. I had come from an Urdu-medium school system at TCF and had switched to an English-based medium of instructions in Intermediate college. That was a huge adjustment and I had to do well in the entrance test for medical school, so it was a good decision to take the extra tutoring or my grades wouldn't have been as good, and I wouldn't have made it. The system and education in the Intermediate colleges is not very good and it is quite common to take tutoring if you're serious about getting into medical school.

Q. So, what were your scores in the Intermediate Board exam?

Sidra: I scored 87.5 percent and I was 24th in the city-wide rankings, so I made the Honor Roll.

Q. Did you apply to medical school after Intermediate? and how many medical colleges are there in Karachi?

Sidra: Yes, I applied right away. There are three government-run medical colleges in Karachi—Dow Medical College, Sindh Medical College and Karachi Medical & Dental College. There are probably ten private medical colleges. Admissions are on aggregate scores of the Intermediate college exam and the entrance tests. I was selected on the merit of my scores.

BOX 3.1 THANK GOODNESS FOR SMALL FAVORS

Quotas: In most provinces, a 'quota system' limits the number of admissions for residents from outside the local area. Another stringent quota restricts the number of admissions from the Cambridge system to professional medical and engineering programs, giving a numerical advantage to student applicants from the public school or government Intermediate college systems. This probably achieves some degree of equity and balance for the student from public/government Intermediate colleges.

Coaching Centers: the ubiquitous tutoring centers cater to cadres of students from the Matric and Cambridge systems. Students from the Matric or public/government Intermediate college systems need the coaching classes because classes in the government schools and colleges are often irregular and the overall quality of instruction is sub-par, giving no other choice to the public system student who is serious about getting into a good university program. The coaching classes help the students from the public school/college systems to pass the Intermediate Board exams with 'average' grades. The Cambridge students often take the coaching to further improve on their better-than-average grades, thus, increasing their chances for admission to expensive, elite universities or improving their Scholastic Assessment Test (SAT) scores for foreign universities.

Q. What were the language issues you faced in medical college and in clinical practice, because the books and lectures were in English, all patient interaction was in Urdu, but documentation in English? How did that work out?

Sidra: That was a major adjustment again. The workload is heavy, with many subjects being covered. At times, it was difficult to quickly comprehend what I was reading in English, so I kept a pocket dictionary with me for quick reference. It got easier with time and, by the second year, I don't think I needed the dictionary at all. So, it *can* be done because we had a reasonably good foundation in English at TCF. But obviously I wasn't fluent because I didn't have much opportunity to speak or practice my English.

Q. Because you were determined to overcome the language issue, you managed to get it done, but with great effort. Do you think it would be helpful to have greater emphasis on English from 4th grade?

Sidra: Yes, as long as colleges teach and test in English, and the aim is to send more children to college, there should be greater emphasis on English starting in 4th grade. English is important to get into the top universities and language disparity discourages students from even thinking about university. Most children from Urdu-speaking or native-language homes are not exposed to any English so I also think there should be more exposure to English starting in 3rd grade, much more than what's at present in TCF schools. Skills need to be developed with more reading and writing exercises on abstract subjects to facilitate thinking in English. I realize it isn't easy to find good English teachers, but better language skills would help students get into university.

Q. When you start your house job, general medicine and general surgery are required rotations, but you will have to select two optional rotations. What will be your two options? And what do you plan to do after the one-year house job rotations?

Sidra: I think I will select neuro-surgery and pediatrics as my two optional rotations. I plan to take one part of the USMLE test while I'm doing my house job and the other part right after I finish my house job. Then I plan to apply for residency programs in the US. There's a 'match' program in the US through which each applicant is given a choice depending on availability of programs, locations, and the applicant's scores.

Q. ... and what after your residency and specialization from the US? Will you return to Pakistan and what do you think you will want to do?

Sidra: Yes, I definitely want to return to Pakistan, and I would like to work as a consultant [specialist] and set up good medical services in Ibrahim Goth.

Q. Has TCF been a major player in your professional education?

Sidra: TCF has been Allah's greatest blessing for me. My siblings and I have never had to worry about financial need for education at any point. In my education journey, even for this trip to Chicago and my study at UIC, Dow had clearly informed us that if I were selected, I'd have to pay $1,500 per month to UIC. I met with Mr Kamlani at the TCF head office and he assured me that financial assistance would be extended to me for this experience. So, TCF paid for my travel and food expenses. I lived in the hospital apartments and boarding charges were waived by UIC after they heard about the great work of TCF.

TCF has been like a mother to me, never turning me down, always encouraging me to go further. Based on our family earnings and where we live, if it wasn't for TCF in the early years of our schooling, I don't think we would have had these opportunities. We would have probably gone to a government school, like Uzma did for a few years, and you know the state of the government schools. There just isn't much education going on there. At the most, we would have gone up to 10th grade and then who knows what we would be doing. It would have been very difficult to get ahead. I consider myself very lucky that there was a TCF school in Ibrahim Goth when I started my schooling. The teachers at TCF were amazing, always concerned about us at a very personal level, asking us about anything that could be concerning us. These are the blessings that we have received from TCF and we are eternally grateful for them.

Q. If your father had said, firmly: 'School up to 5th grade is enough'—what could you have done?

Sidra: Knowing what I do now, I think I would have rebelled [laughs] ... but I don't think my father would have ever said that either. Even though things are generally much better for girls, I feel that 80 percent parents in our area still do not support their daughters going to college after 10th grade because there is no college close to our homes and public transport is the only way to get to colleges and it takes hours. The parents can't make the commitment to take the girls to the bus stops and be there to pick them up, all the extra things that our parents did for me and for my sisters to enable us to go to college.

Q. So, what about the 20 percent of girls who do go to college? Is that because the parents have a better outlook for education and are willing to bear the hardships, make the extra sacrifice—or is it because the girls are more forceful and convince the parents that they should be allowed to go to college?

Sidra: A little of both, I think. The parents have to be somewhat flexible and willing to find solutions. In some cases, my parents have spoken to other parents to try to convince them that the girls should go to college. My parents are not always successful. That's unfortunate but one consolation is that some girls who are forced to stay home can take private tutoring at home and then take the college Board exam. I have also tutored a few girls at home. These girls miss out on the college experience but at least they do move up the ladder in terms of some education beyond secondary school. We can only hope that they are able to use the education later in life and perhaps even go on to university after they get married. I hope that someday in the near future, we will have colleges for girls in places like Ibrahim Goth, so the girls don't have to travel long distances.

Q. For the five years of medical college, you have lived at home and commuted long distances to Dow Medical College by bus. How did you manage that?

Sidra: Fortunately, Dow Medical College provides a bus service for the outlying areas. There's an assigned point for pick-and-drop which was a twenty-minute walk from our home and then it was an hour and fifteen minutes' drive in the bus. The bus service was a huge blessing. It would have taken me twice as long by public bus and that would have been very exhausting.

Q. You and your siblings have been able to get ahead because of the education you received, and you have learned to adapt socially. Did you ever experience discrimination or hear any remarks from your professional peers in medical school or in any other setting?

Sidra: I don't think so. I never heard anyone say 'Oh, she's from a TCF school'. My friends were comfortable and cordial with me. There can be some snide remarks in some situations, but I didn't experience any.

Q. How can children from underprivileged families be prepared to make the social adjustment when they mix with children from affluent families and elite schools?

Sidra: I think the children have to learn how to make the social adjustments on their own. It isn't that hard. Children from underprivileged families who go into a socially mixed environment should remain focused on their studies. Social acceptance also gets easier if you get good grades.

Q. But, there is also the need to have a head-start in making social adjustment. Should children from TCF be counseled to reach out and extend a hand of friendship, regardless of social class?

Sidra: I agree totally. Our TCF children can easily be counselled and made aware that, in the real world, there are varying levels of wealth and that we must accept that and know how to deal with it. Also, cleanliness and personal hygiene are important. Obviously, an affluent person can afford to have cleaner, smarter clothes and be well groomed, because they have running hot water and better soaps and toiletries, and they can use perfumes and other cosmetics. But everyone should practice good hygiene and be clean in their appearance and in their personal habits. I agree that TCF children must be counseled, especially in the 9th and 10th grades before they go to college and come out of the sheltered TCF environment.

Q. Who are your role models among your peers?

Sidra: Without context, I can't think of a strong role model among my peers, but I try to observe and emulate good qualities that I see in my friends and peers. I deeply admire the qualities of humility, kindness, and being down-to-earth. I see these beautiful qualities in my parents. I hope I can always be like them.

Q. What do you think about Uzma Salim? Iqra seems to think that Uzma is her role model.

Sidra: Uzma *baaji* (big sister) has taught me many social etiquettes that I wasn't aware of—how to interact with people at different levels. Yes, she is a great role model and always encourages us to move ahead with confidence and never to think of ourselves as lesser than anyone else… to work hard, to look for opportunities, and participate in everything possible. As you probably know, things were much harder for her when she started her education journey than it has been for Iqra and me. I can imagine how difficult it was for her to get around and how *Abbu* [father] helped her to make sure she got to college and university classes by public transport. Back in those days, there were fewer buses and longer wait times.

Q. Fast forward 10 to 15 years … what will Sidra be doing?

Sidra: At that time, if you visit Ibrahim Goth, you will see an impressive hospital where well-qualified doctors and specialists will be voluntarily treating patients and giving good quality care to our neighbors in the community. That's my dream and *Insha Allah* it will happen.

Q. Are more schools needed in Ibrahim Goth?

Sidra: Yes, I think we need more secondary schools and colleges for girls. Boys can take the bus to get to college, but many parents are very concerned when their daughters have to travel by public buses.

Update

September 2018: Sidra is back in the US for five months. She has passed the ECFMG and is certified as an MD. She has completed the one-year house job in Karachi and worked part-time as a Medical Officer (hospital physician) in North Nazimabad, a twenty-minute drive from home. The private hospital provided pick-and-drop transport. She has passed Step 1 and Step 2 of the USMLE exam and she's cautiously optimistic that she will receive invitations for interviews at neurology residency programs she has applied to. In the meantime, she is lining up opportunities for observership or as a research assistant, which would boost her chances for a residency program in neurology. With remarkable resourcefulness, and thanks to the Internet and the community of TCF supporters in the US, she has been able to make contacts and find opportunities on her own.

February 2019: During her five-month stay in the US, Sidra completed two neurology observerships in Houston and appeared for five interviews at neurology residency programs. She now awaits the outcomes. She has managed her lodging and travel with ease, staying mostly with TCF supporter families or their friends in the US. She has comfortably travelled on her own and knows her way around the local transit and subway systems, airports, South West Airlines and Uber just as well as most Americans do.

I asked Sidra about the social challenges faced by young educated women when there is disparity in education between spouses; the lack of understanding for women's health issues; male attitudes about the role of women and how they can be changed; traditional practices and the possible role of *mullahs* (clerics) in bringing about change. With acknowledgment of slight discomfort on her part, Sidra boldly discussed the sensitive topics of menstruation, family planning, contraception, marital issues, and disparities in education. Here's the last part of my conversations with Sidra:

Q. In an earlier conversation, you were telling me about the difficulties young women have after completing their education and starting their careers, then they get married and start a family. In many cases, they are married to men who are controlling, conservative, and may not approve of women being 'independent' or working outside the home. Could you talk about those issues?

Sidra: Yes, there are girls like me who complete their education and start a professional life and they have to—actually, their parents have to—choose a husband for the girls because marriage is commonly arranged by the parents. Typically, the match is made in the same community or extended family. If she's lucky, the girl may have some say in the decision-making. Boys or young men from conservative, male-dominated families are usually also conservative and authoritarian. They have seen their fathers being rude or inconsiderate with their own wives. So, the young prospective husband who has been raised in such a household will probably be of the same mindset and will not respect women as equals. The prospective husband may be well-educated, maybe equal to the girl's level of education. But, in most conservative families, there is often some friction, even if it isn't openly expressed, because the man will assume that women are responsible for all household chores and care of the children. There is no room for discussion or planning of how the responsibilities are to be divided and the wife has to cope with whatever crisis may occur, such as a sick child or some such thing. If she isn't able to cope with the crisis, she has to make the choice between work and home and, if adjustment is needed, *she* is the one expected to give up her job or career. There is no room for compromise or finding another solution.

You've seen how women in our communities have to work at home, spending a lot of time and energy to do the daily chores. Most homes don't have laundry machines and many women spend almost a whole day doing the laundry every few days, drying the clothes on lines, and then pressing the clothes. I have observed that, in women who live in such harsh conditions, their personalities begin to change over time because of the heavy workload. Their patience diminishes, and it begins to affect their families and it shows in their performance at work as well. I am not optimistic that this will change unless ... honestly, I don't know.

Q. What do you think will make the change in male attitudes?

Sidra: I think that the attitudes and mindset of the man are based on what he learned from his own family. Ideally, a couple should realize that they should have close to equal workload in managing the family and the household. Maybe the woman has a little more to do than the husband if she is a full-time homemaker and he is the sole breadwinner.

Q: So, you're suggesting division of labor ... isn't that a foreign concept in most households?

Sidra: That would be great but if there isn't a clear division of duties, then the wife should not be under pressure to do everything. She should be able to give time to her job and personal activities, have some life with her circle of friends too. I think that would be better all around. If young men were raised in families with equality and respect for women, and if these examples of equality are further reinforced in society—in our TV shows, movies and in other ways—then, as husbands, these young men would realize that maintaining a happy family and managing the household is not the sole responsibility of the woman, that everything should be jointly planned and discussed.

Q. Let's say the husband is 25 and the wife is 24, both have bachelor's degrees, both have jobs, and they have a child. So, there's no disparity of age, education or incomes. You can't change what happened with the generation of the husband's parents. But can male attitudes be changed, and what role can education have in changing male attitudes with respect to a balanced family life and equality for women?

Sidra: You're right. You can't change the past. But, in schools and colleges, there should be discussion on what constitutes a family and how a balanced, happy family life can be maintained. At age 25, it may be too late to change the husband's mindset, that male-domination is normal and equality is not acceptable. I believe that seeds of a balanced and happy family life should be planted much earlier—perhaps at age 15 or 16. In our orthodox society, the woman doesn't have the freedom to ask the husband to do something or bring up to the husband what she thinks should be *his* duties, or what he could be doing even occasionally to share in the household chores. If she gathers enough courage to bring up the subject, the typical dominant husband may react with anger and create a bad situation, behaving like a wild animal, showing his power with a temper tantrum. His family will also come to his support and blame the woman for the fight. The verbal abuse may lead to threats or physical abuse and a worsening family situation.

Author: Intimidation and verbal abuse ...

Sidra: Right, and the men who have an authoritarian mindset know that they can control their wives by loud and angry behavior, so the women would never have the courage to bring it up again.

Q. What happens in cases where the women are bold and strong, and refuse to be intimidated? Does it lead to worsening of the situation? Perhaps separation?

Sidra: Yes, I know of women who courageously speak up or ask for some time to discuss the issues with their husbands. They are immediately told that they don't have any right to bring up these issues or it might

Box 3.2 A Household of Multiple Family Units

For young couples, it is quite common to live as a joint family with the husband's parents, especially while the grandchildren are young. With more than one married son, there may be multiple family units living in the same household. Rarely is this a happy situation for long. The powerful mother-in-law often has a resentful relationship with the daughters-in-law and the dominating patriarch of the family demands respect from everyone around him. While there are economic advantages to the arrangement, loss of privacy and the social and personal cost of this traditional lifestyle is often a heavy price to pay.

The bonds of love, respect and mutual support may be better maintained between the family units if joint-family living can be a short-term arrangement, allowing for independent growth and personal development of the young couples, especially for the young wives who need their own space to make a home and nurture a balanced, happy family. – *Author*

result in separation and she could be going back to live with her parents. There is also the threat that pursuing the argument could result in a separation of the wife from the children. And no mother wants that. The prospect of losing her children is painful. So, she remains quiet and lives in a bad marriage for the sake of her children. Women fear that if the situation gets worse, they will have to move back in with their parents and that might be an additional burden. Women may lose custody of the children because there's no such thing as a shared or joint custody agreement between a divorced couple. Unfortunately, that is the reality.

Author: I agree it takes work and compromise to build equal marriages, and gender equality should be addressed in the earlier school and college years. Equal marriages are important. Boys and young men must learn to respect and treat women as equals. Young women too should learn how to appropriately change the male-domination culture by projecting themselves as equals early in life. Gender equality in education should help women overcome the intimidation and domination that men exercise over them.

Sidra: Yes, I agree totally. Equality in marriage is important and women must work towards that.

Q. Among the young women that you know, have some separations resulted in divorce?

Sidra: I know of a few women who have terminated their marriages in divorce, and quite a few women who are unhappy and going in that direction. I know two sisters who were in school with me and both have business degrees. Their marriages were arranged to two young men who are brothers living in rural Sindh and they seemed quite balanced. One was in the army and the other man was a teacher. The families were of equal economic status. At first, everything was fine and both couples started families. After a few years, problems began to surface, and the problems could not be resolved. The wives were not heard or given any right to suggest a solution. The men continued to have a strange attitude towards their wives, and they were probably having affairs with other women as well which they didn't want to discuss. Unfortunately, having extramarital affairs is considered normal and 'a right' for men so there was no guilt on their part. The situations for both couples kept getting worse and ultimately, both sisters ended up divorced from their husbands.

Q. What happened then? Did they move back with their parents?

Sidra: Yes, one of them has remarried. The other is living with her parents and she is starting a salon business.

Q. So, remarrying is not uncommon for a young woman who has gone through a divorce?

Sidra: It is not uncommon, but it is difficult to find a suitable partner. The common perception is that the divorced woman was probably not capable of handling 'difficult situations' in her previous marriage and that it must have been her fault, that she wasn't keeping her marriage in balance. So, if she re-marries, it is usually arranged with a man who is much older, probably a widower, someone who is not well-educated and of modest means. Her choices may be limited. More divorced women, especially if they are capable of supporting themselves and the children, do not remarry and are content living independently.

Q. Let's move to the subject of planning for a family. What should be the ideal size of a young family?

Sidra: The ideal size can be two or three children.

Q. Is there a difference in attitudes between men and women about family planning and contraception? How comfortable is an average, educated young woman in discussing family planning with the husband?

Sidra: There is usually a difference in attitudes about contraception. If there is no disparity in education or age, there might not be a big difference in the way they think. But there is a huge difference in how each one feels about the methods of contraception. Because the woman has to conceive and carry the baby during pregnancy, she may not want to conceive or start a family very early after marriage. The contraceptive method preferred by women is birth control pills, which can result in side effects, especially if they have not completed the family. Men usually say that they are not very comfortable with male contraceptive methods like condoms, and vasectomies are very rare. So, because men don't fully support family planning, it often results in unwanted pregnancies and I have seen women becoming pregnant even when they are breast-feeding a baby less than a year old. In our own neighborhood, I know of families who have nine or ten children in fifteen years of marriage. That's a huge cost to society and to the family as well.

Q. ... and hard on the woman too! Do you see that changing? Has it changed in the last ten years?

Sidra: I don't think it has changed. Most families I know of have a large number of children. Very few families have less than five children.

Author: ... in spite of being educated.

Sidra: Right. The recently educated are an in-between generation, a mix of the traditional mindset and modern thinking. And they haven't reached a level of maturity that would have them really think of these issues.

Q. **When a young woman pursues education, it probably delays marriage and starting a family. But what education can be given to males in the schools and colleges related to family health and family planning?**

Sidra: I think some discussion of family issues, respect for women, shared responsibilities, and equality, should be introduced in 8th grade and incrementally advanced through the 12th grade.

Author: I think there should also be greater push for the role of women being understood by young boys, that women have equal rights and need to be treated with equal respect.

Sidra: I agree but there should also be a section in the curriculum to teach both girls and boys about how things can be done as a family, and to start thinking about family size. For example, in a classroom activity, we can talk about projected living expenses for rent, groceries, education, transportation, etc.—essentially a hypothetical family budget for a couple with one child. The income of the family comfortably meets the needs of the couple and the child. But a few years later, the same couple with five children would struggle even with a slightly higher income level and they would also have a lesser quality of life, need a larger home, etc. because the income would be divided among more persons in the family. I think students would relate to it if such discussion and activity were to take place in the classroom, and even though they may not understand the importance of a family budget, the idea of family size could be embedded in their minds and, hopefully, they would recall it when they are ready for marriage and start thinking about their own families. I think the economic rationale is probably the most effective in convincing men that family planning is important.

Q. **Excellent points. Can you think of other ways in which boys and young men can be informed of the importance of how women should be treated at all stages in life?**

Sidra: The socialization and academic learning that take place in school and college teaches a young person how to interact with everyone regardless of gender, or social status. But if some relevant religious and cultural values can be included in teaching the importance of respect for women, I think it would help to drive the point home, because faith and cultural values are important to Pakistani people and it may be helpful to remind them that all faiths teach respect, equality, and kindness towards women.

Author: Young men and women should be informed that their own children will learn from observing how they interact as parents. The attitudes of parents are picked up by the children and, in turn, the children will treat their own spouses the same way. So, if the husband is intimidating his wife, the son will learn to do that too. Whereas, if the husband has a respectful relationship with his wife, the children will follow that behavior. And I think women also need to be taught this.

Sidra: You're right, the first thing is to be aware that children are observing and learning from your behavior.

Author: So, we agree that the topics of family relations, family development, family prosperity, and family wellness need to be introduced at an early age, probably by 8th grade, and continuously advanced through college.

Q. But what about non-educational interventions? How else can social change take place?

Sidra: Let me think. Maybe we can have social campaigns through the media, that conflict resolution is in everyone's interest and it begins with mutual respect.

Q. How do you feel about the role of clerics or mullahs in supporting social change within families, as it relates to respect for women?

Sidra: My observation is that the *mullah*'s role is limited to the masjid, leading the prayers, and teaching the Quran. I can't be optimistic, but I think the *mullah* could play a positive role in advising people in the congregation that anger, intimidation, and disrespect towards women is condemned in Islamic teachings and by all social reformers.

Author: I understand your skepticism. But we should experiment by requesting a few Imams (prayer leaders) to include thoughts in the Friday *khutba* (sermon), emphasizing kindness and mutual respect between husband and wife, the sharing of tasks, and family responsibilities. Respect for women should be the point of emphasis.

Sidra: The preacher in our neighborhood is ultra-conservative and restricts his wife from even coming to answer a knock on the door! I don't think I have ever seen her outside the house.

Author: Maybe he should be listening to someone else's 'khutba'! Now, let's talk about women's health. Men grow up and get married. They don't have to deal with the normal physiological changes that a woman goes through with menstruation every month. I don't think men really understand what a woman's body goes through in preparation for motherhood and, ultimately, what changes occur in the woman's body during and after pregnancy.

Q. How can men be made aware of the special needs of women's health?

Sidra: Culturally, it is difficult to talk about these things. Even as a doctor, I wouldn't be comfortable talking about menstruation and reproduction with men, although I suspect they must be aware. Teenage boys and girls get the information from the Internet or from each other and they are probably getting a lot of misinformation too. What they learn satisfies their childish curiosity, but they don't develop a good understanding of these things. I don't know how it can be made a topic for open discussion in schools.

Author: Well, puberty is a point in life which is different for girls and boys. While girls accept and learn about the changes that their bodies are going through, boys have no idea. I think it would be helpful if there was a section within Health Education, probably in 8th grade, addressing something like: 'Just as boys go through normal changes at puberty (facial hair, voice changes), girls also go through normal changes in ultimate preparation for motherhood; that these changes occur in all species; that reproduction is a normal part of life in nature.' Understanding that there are differences in normal male and female physiology would help to educate both girls and boys with a common base of knowledge that changes occur in both genders and that these normal changes should be respected. More detail is not needed but information can be incrementally added each year, so that, by 12th grade, the young student, especially the young male, has a better understanding of the changes a woman goes through in preparation of pregnancy—and that babies don't happen without a mother and a father.

Q. Do you think it would be possible to construct part of the curriculum with such information?

Sidra: Men don't seem to be interested in learning about women's health issues. In biology class in 12th grade, there is sufficient detail about reproduction and the menstrual cycle, but this is in preparation for medical sciences. I would even hear boys in medical school complain of why they had to learn about female physiology if they weren't interested in OB-GYN. Boys will just memorize it to pass the test without a good understanding of the physiology or social aspects of what we are discussing.

Author: But the subject is too important to ignore. My suggestion is to somehow connect it with equality, kindness, and respect for women as a social issue, maybe as part of Social Studies combined with Health Education. A basic understanding of physiology is important as a foundation for normal gender differences and the issues of equality and respect for women can be addressed in Social Studies. But they must be addressed clearly and directly, not in a vague, roundabout way. Kindness, respect, and equality need to be stated well and introduced early. Now, let's talk about pre-natal and post-partum care.

Q. What is the average husband's idea of the changes a woman goes through during a pregnancy?

Sidra: I don't think most husbands understand or care about the changes a woman goes through in pregnancy and that she's carrying another human inside her body. They expect the woman to do all her chores just as before and they usually don't show any concern for the woman's complaints of morning sickness or other changes. Unfortunately, most husbands are not at all supportive during the pregnancy. About pre-natal care, even most women are not aware that anything like that exists. Most women will not even confirm the pregnancy with a test, sometimes until the fourth or fifth month. They may realize that it's a pregnancy but they still don't feel the need to see a doctor. A large number of women see a doctor for the first time when it's time to deliver. Many women will have the delivery at home with a family member helping or with a local *dai* [midwife]. I think all young women must be educated about pre-natal care and the need for essential nutrients during pregnancy, and how nutritional deficiencies can affect the baby's and the mother's health. If the husband is not supportive, it makes it very difficult for the woman to ask for help because, in most cases, she isn't allowed to go out by herself or to the doctor. Money and affordability are another issue. The husband will often ignore the woman's needs and assume nature will somehow take care of it. Most women, especially the uneducated, have no access to information so they can't get answers like many of us do with such ease. It's a different world for a woman in poverty.

Q. After the pregnancy, what special needs should husbands be aware of in the post-partum stage?

Sidra: The husband should be aware that the wife's inappropriate crying or unusual behavior could be a case of post-partum blues which is a common problem. Most husbands have no idea what's going on ...

Q. It's a readjustment of the hormones, isn't it?

Sidra: Right, women can become overwhelmed and sensitive, but husbands may think the wife is unhappy with the baby or something else is wrong. I think if the husband were to realize that the baby's care is the responsibility of both parents, that would help a great deal. The baby's sleep patterns are not regulated in the early months and that can take a toll on the wife's energy because she has been caring for the child all day and it would be a big help if the husband volunteered to help with some of the night feeding or changing and allowing the wife to get some much-needed rest. Many husbands feel it is not a man's job to care for the baby, feed or change the baby. Unfortunately, men can be indifferent to women's needs.

Update

March 2019: Sidra is back in Karachi and has resumed her job at the hospital in North Nazimabad. She has been informed that she wasn't accepted at the residency programs in the US. As she contemplates other options, Sidra is also pursuing neurology research projects in Karachi to improve her chances for acceptance in a neurology residency. Giving up is not in Sidra's DNA.

July 2019: Sidra is back in the US. She has joined the Neurology Department of the University of Toledo, Ohio, as a research assistant. She will be working on data analysis of clinical outcomes of therapeutic approaches in Epilepsy and Stroke. Sidra is hopeful that the research position will help her and that she will be accepted to a neurology residency program in 2020.

March 2020: Sidra is accepted to the adult neurology residency program at University of Toledo, a four-year program.

February 2021: Sidra is eight months into her adult neurology residency program at the University of Toledo, Ohio.

3.4 Iqra Saleem
Bachelor's Degree in Accounting & Finance,
Lahore University of Management Sciences (LUMS)

A sharp listener, an avid reader and clearly an independent thinker, Iqra is the youngest of the girls and the fourth of five beautiful children in the Saleem family. She is charming, petite as a little doll, and as fun-loving as an eight-year old. Yet she can be dead serious about achieving her goals and does not like to place second in any competitive pursuit. Boundaries and barriers don't mean a thing to her. Crowds don't make her nervous and mountains don't scare her. While at Michigan State in Saginaw for a semester, she was invited to speak at TCF-USA events in Houston, Chicago and Seattle. Her eloquence came through loud and clear as she brought the audience to their feet in ovation, with tears of emotion and heartfelt pride. This conversation with Iqra in February 2016 was a continuation of the time in the LUMS cafeteria with her sister Uzma, who hung around and chimed in. Iqra's youthful energy and boundless optimism are promise of her being a leader in the making, another Agent of Change from the illustrious family of Bhabi Majeedan and Saleem Bhai.

Q. Iqra, you are the youngest of three girls in your family and you are in your second year at LUMS (2016). Tell us about your early schooling and how TCF has become such a big part of your life.

Iqra: When I started school, there was just one school in our neighborhood, the TCF school. I started in the kindergarten class and went through eleven years of school at TCF. The fees were affordable for our family. I remember I was very competitive and always expected to be at the top of the class. I would be disappointed if I were ranked second or third. The teachers were loving and courteous and never made a child feel inferior if she didn't know something. Because there had been no school in the area, there were no local teachers so, initially, all teachers had to be transported to the school from a distance.

TCF has become a part of my life in so many ways. My journey started in a slum and here I am, at LUMS—one of the best universities in Pakistan. For me, slum-to-LUMS is not just a play on words. There's a story behind it. Yes, I was born in a slum where life is not as glamorous as the bright cities of Karachi or Lahore. The living conditions of a *katchi abadi* like Ibrahim Goth are unimaginable for most young people in other areas of Karachi. Children in places like Ibrahim Goth have limited options for what they can do in their childhood. When boys reach their teens, they are supposed to work in nearby factories and girls are expected to help their mothers with sewing clothes at home to help with extra income, or to help with household tasks. Most children are *expected* to work as the parents don't have the resources to send them to college. From kindergarten through school and college, TCF has helped me to look ahead, given me the grounding and the ability to go as far as I would like to go, from a slum to LUMS.

But, growing up as a girl in Ibrahim Goth, we never had a chance to go shopping in the Karachi malls, or hang out at KFC or at Dunkin Donuts, or go to the movies. We couldn't walk to the bazaar by ourselves unless one of my parents or one of my brothers was with me. There were no parks or playgrounds where we could just go for a walk. It just wasn't done, and to some extent, it is still the same, the same culture and the same environment, except that we now have eight TCF schools (units)[2] in Ibrahim Goth and that is what we hope will bring about change. It is more common to see girls from the *goth* community going to school and to college now and I firmly believe they will bring about the social change.

> **Q. Wow! That's quite an opening. Your family are community champions for the education of girls. You and your sisters are proof of that. In some communities, girls will go to school for a few years and drop out. Was there a high rate of drop-outs between 5th and 6th grade, especially girls?**

Iqra: A few girls did leave school after 5th grade. Our TCF primary and secondary schools were in the same location so that helped with student retention and I think we had fewer drop-outs. By the time I got to 6th grade, some other TCF schools had come up in neighboring *goths* (villages) and, because our secondary school was the only one in the cluster of TCF schools, we got students from the other primary schools as well. So, our overall student numbers didn't go down. In fact, we had three sections in each class of 6th, 7th, and 8th grade students, which was probably unique. But there was a significant drop in girls' enrollment in 9th grade and even more in 10th grade, probably because the families felt the girls had received 'enough education'. Some boys also dropped out because they had to work in nearby factories and couldn't cope with both the job and school. In those days, girls going to college was not very common. In my batch, just two or three other girls went on to college.

> **Q. After Matric, what were the challenges for you and your parents?**

Iqra: The challenges were mostly related to transportation, as we had to travel long distances by bus. There wasn't a good network of roads from our *goth* to the city, so we didn't have easy bus connections to get to college. It wasn't as easy as walking to the neighborhood TCF school. Parents would have to take the girls to the bus stops, wait with them for the bus, and be there at the bus stop when they got back. Mobile phones have been a blessing for girls' education or parents would be worried and nervous until the girls got back from school. These were the challenges for the parents because the girls had to be protected. It wasn't much easier for boys, either. The long distances and the difficulties with public transport are very exhausting. The biggest challenge for children that went to Intermediate colleges was that the government colleges didn't have the best education and, if you wanted to apply to good universities, you needed good grades for which you needed additional private tutoring, as I did. Again, tutoring was an added expense and required traveling to distant places after college classes and taking long bus rides, changing buses two or three times. It required extra commitment on the part of the parents and students. The parents also had to accept that the child would need time to study and couldn't be expected to do many of the chores. All these factors were challenges for the parents and students.

Q. How does TCF track its alumni after 10th grade? And how does TCF contact you or keep you informed?

Iqra: When I was in 10th grade, the TCF Alumni Department asked us for our phone contacts and we were kept informed by text messages. Very few children have computer access or email, and we don't have continuous wi-fi connectivity in most areas. The tracking of former students is done mostly by phone as most people are used to texting or SMS. Alumni tracking is improving but I agree that more needs to be done. I think the students should also take responsibility for staying in touch with TCF and inform them of any change, where they are in their education or work and in their professional careers. That's important also for networking among the alumni, staying in touch with each other.

Q. If a student remains in touch with TCF and understands how to use its resources, that student can be helped with guidance and financial assistance from the TCF Scholarship Fund. Also, as alumni progress in their education or careers, occasional surveys would also be useful, don't you think?

Iqra: That's very true. Take *Aapi* [Uzma] for example. She's not only a TCF grad but she's a leader in her profession and she could be a valuable mentor. Many alumni who have moved through university education and into careers have been given a hand by TCF. But there are also many alumni who have successfully found scholarship opportunities and they've made it into good careers and professions, entirely on their own. You have to admire their courage and determination. However, most children from underprivileged families do need a hand and their connection with the alumni program must be established early in school, probably in 8th or 9th grade. They become very busy in 10th grade. The networking value of the alumni should be emphasized. For example, there could be special interest groups or 'TCF Alumni Professionals Group' within the alumni network, with sub-groups for engineers, medical graduates, educators, civil servants, business and finance majors, computer science engineers and so on. Career guidance, mentorship and peer counseling are also possible from within the network and that would be a help for young students who can relate to the experiences of a TCF alumnus.

Q. Back to your personal story...where did you go to Intermediate college and then how did you get to LUMS?

Iqra: I went to the PECHS College for Women in Karachi. It's a fairly good government college. Either my father or Nadeem *bhai* would take me to the bus stop and wait with me until the bus arrived. The bus trip took over an hour, each way. As I got closer to home, I would make a missed call to my father because he was not used to reading text messages, and he would take time from his factory job to come to the bus stop and take me home. He has done so much for us ... always gone out of his way to help us in so many ways. [At this point, Iqra was overcome with emotion and fondly recalled Saleem Sahib's kindness]. It wasn't too bad during the college trips as I would be home in daylight. But, for the coaching classes I was taking in the evenings to prepare for LUMS, I would come back at 10 p.m. or later in the night and my father was always there, waiting for me. For admission to LUMS, Nadeem bhai encouraged me and guided me to apply for the LUMS National Outreach Program (NOP). *Alhamdulillah*, my Matric scores were 90 percent and that's what they look at most of all, so that helped in my selection. But I had to take an admission test. TCF paid for the coaching classes to prepare for the tests and that helped a lot, financially.

Q. Do you think the TCF Intermediate College will help more children get into good universities?

Iqra: No question about that. These are the smartest children from TCF schools and they've been selected for the college based on their grades. The college will help to prepare these children for the top-tier universities.

Q. You were at Michigan State University at Saginaw for one semester. How did you find out about the opportunity and how was that experience for you?

Iqra: I found out about a program sponsored by the US State Department, the Global Undergraduate Exchange Program in Pakistan. I applied online and had an interview at the US Embassy in Islamabad. There were around 10,000 applicants and 400 were asked to come for interviews out of which 200 were selected for the program and split into two groups. There were 94 students in my group and we were distributed among various universities in different states. There were two other Pakistani girls with me at Saginaw. I took a semester off from LUMS, so I'll do an extra semester at LUMS, which I don't mind. It was a wonderful academic experience. I learned a great deal but I found it to be easier than our classes at LUMS in terms of class participation and presentations. The only presentation I had to do was a discussion of an article in the *Wall Street Journal* and I found that to be quite easy. I was required to take two classes in my major, so I took a class in financial management and investment. I also had to take classes related to American life, sports, history, and an academic course. I took an exercise class 'Stress Relief with Movement', like Yoga. In US history, we covered the pre-civil war period, which was tough…and quite different, because I had no idea of that period in American history. I was surprised to learn of French domination in parts of America, and that women's voting rights didn't become law until the 1920s.

Q. How was the cultural experience, with the American host family and generally in the US?

Iqra: The two other girls and I were adopted by a family as the three 'Pakistani daughters' and they had us over for meals, took us shopping, and on outings. We had a very generous monthly stipend of $400, so we could save and plan trips together, the three of us. We made weekend trips to Chicago, Orlando, New York City, Salt Lake City, and San Francisco. The high point of our trip was definitely San Francisco and the beautiful campuses of Stanford and Berkeley. I would love to go to one of these universities in California!

Q. Why does the State Department sponsor these trips and experiences for Pakistani youth?

Iqra: These trips are designed to promote people-to-people contact and that was achieved. We had an opportunity to meet and exchange views with fellow students and others. Surprisingly, many Americans don't know much about Pakistan. They know more about China and India. They are generally very friendly and helpful, and it is very easy to adjust culturally. Getting around in America was fun and so easy!

Q. You are in your 3rd year at LUMS and your major is accounting and finance. What's next for you? In another year, you will need to decide: go to work, or further study?

Iqra: I am thinking of taking off a year, get some work experience and then probably do my master's. For a career, I used to think my ideal job would be in the corporate sector but I'm now leaning heavily towards the civil service because of the opportunity to influence social change. I'm undecided. I have some time to think. I've learnt a lot from *Aapi* about the civil service and that does intrigue me.

Q. Selfishly, we would like to see more talented and well-educated young persons like you go into the civil service to create the social change we need. What do you think?

Iqra: I think many people are going into the civil service to try and make the change but they either give up because they get frustrated when they don't see change taking place rapidly, or they become part of the bad system themselves. Going into a civil service career has to be a serious commitment and takes a tremendous amount of patience to see real change.

Q. Very true, it is a serious commitment. Uzma, what do you think?

Uzma: If you make the decision to enter the civil service, then you must stay firm and not waver in your motivation to serve for the public good. It's easy to be tempted by material things like brand-name clothing and fancy restaurants or competing with others for social status. But, if one remains focused on the good that can be achieved in a public service job, even a small act has wider impact. Every person has a choice to make in life. I'm sure Iqra will make the right choice when the time comes. She'll be a LUMS graduate, after all!

There are many unknown factors too. All parents want the best for their children and our family is no exception. Our parents have been great, and Allah has been very kind to us. *Abbu* (father) is such a gentle and sensitive person. Despite hard times and limited resources when we were growing up, I don't think I've ever seen him raise his voice or get upset. He's always calm and soft spoken. He leads the family without being forceful or dominating and sets the example by showing respect for our mother. *Ammi* (mother) had her role to play, taking care of the household and adding to the family income with what she could do at home. Both have always been cheerful with everyone, and respectful and loving with each other. That has such a positive impact on the family environment. We have seen and heard in our own neighborhood when couples are upset and abusive with each other, which creates a stressful and negative situation in the family. The young children can't understand what's going on or why, but they can sense that something is wrong, and they can be affected by the tension in the family. Fortunately, we never experienced such unpleasantness in our home. There were times when *Abbu* would work late or overtime, and *Ammi* would let us know that he's going to be tired when he gets home so we should be quiet and not disturb him.

Q. Iqra, you have spoken at TCF events in Chicago, Seattle and Houston. What were your thoughts and your message to the audience?

Iqra: I said that I didn't have words to express how lucky I felt representing my alma mater, the TCF school in Ibrahim Goth and standing among TCF supporters in the US. I could have been one of the street children who have never seen the inside of a classroom. I could be one of the children who spend their days playing barefoot on trash heaps without any constructive engagement. I could be one of many slum children for whom there isn't much to do all day, except roam the streets. I said that I'm very lucky that I had extremely passionate teachers at TCF, who continuously motivated me and made me realize my true potential. I was the first person in our slum and the first TCF student to go to LUMS on a full scholarship, one of the most expensive universities in Pakistan.

> **Q. What were some of the challenges at LUMS—socially, or in transitioning to English as the language of instruction? And how did you adjust to, or overcome these challenges?**

Iqra: At LUMS, my peers are from some of the best elite private schools in Pakistan. I am probably the only one who comes from a slum. In the beginning, LUMS was challenging because of a huge social difference. There is a good blend of diversity, but I couldn't see anyone like me. I could not make any friends for a few months, even though I did spend time with some people—but they talked about Hollywood, expensive restaurants, stylish hangouts, popular novels, recent movies, celebrities, and stuff like that. At first, none of that made sense to me but eventually I settled down and I've made some good friends who are very supportive. It was academics that was a more serious challenge. All classes were in English and I wasn't used to that. But I do my best to adjust to new situations. I would translate entire lectures into Urdu in my mind for better comprehension. Today, two years later, I am comfortable with English.

For students from socio-economic backgrounds like mine, there can be misconceptions about social barriers and financial hurdles. Students from underprivileged families may believe that they can't afford the fees of the top universities, so they don't even think about preparing for the best universities and applying. I have learned that we must look for opportunities and ask for guidance to learn about scholarships or financial assistance and coaching to prepare for admission tests.

> **Q. So, Iqra, what do you think have been the game-changing, greatest blessings in your life? And how do you think you can pass on the blessings that you have received?**

Iqra: I was fortunate that my parents wanted to send my siblings and me to school, and they had dreams of a bright future for us—both the girls and the boys. Because they believed that education was the best way to get ahead. They made the investment of their time and their limited resources, and I think that their love and support have been the greatest blessing in my life. I could never repay them for this blessing.

And I am inspired by the TCF teachers and the entire TCF organization, from the founders to the staff and all the donors and supporters. As a token of gratitude for all that TCF has done for me and for others like me, and to pass on the blessings I have received, I would like to support education through TCF.

Author: Your parents are exemplary people. Thank you so much, Iqra and Uzma, for sharing these thoughts. And, on that note … let's have some chai and wrap it up.

Update

March 2019: Iqra graduated from LUMS with a bachelor's degree in accounting and finance and she is preparing for the civil service exam, following in the footsteps of her sister Uzma.

December 2019: Iqra accepted a position as an Assistant Director at the State Bank. She has the option to take the CSS exam at any time in the future.

February 2021: Iqra is working at the Strategic & Corporate Affairs Department of the State Bank.

3.5 Yasir Saleem
Bachelor's Degree in Computer Science, Habib University

The youngest in the family, Yasir has a disarming and youthful innocence about him. He is a courteous listener. There's a healthy family dynamic that drives Yasir, as he feeds off the energy and achievements of his siblings. He has learned to channel his energies towards higher goals, striving to live up to the family's high expectations. Coping with the hardships of growing up in the difficult environment of Ibrahim Goth, Yasir has made it to Habib University, a distinguished Tier 1 university, on a full scholarship. He lives at home and commutes on motorbike.

In 2018, Yasir was starting his final fourth year at Habib University with computer science as his major. His earlier schooling was at the TCF school in Ibrahim Goth and two years of Intermediate at DJ Sindh Government Science College. He had recently come back from a seven-week stay in the US at UMass, Amherst, on a program sponsored by the US State Department. Here, he talks about his role model Steve

Jobs, his US experience, and his thoughts on future options after his undergraduate study at Habib.

Q. So, one more year at Habib, then what are your plans? Any thoughts?

Yasir: I've been thinking of public service and it's very likely that I'll take the CSS exam—or I'll go to graduate school. I might decide to take a job for some time, I'm not sure, but most probably I'll take the CSS exam.

Q. What programs are you considering for graduate school? And where do you think you might go?

Yasir: I've looked at some data warehouse programs in Germany that seem interesting, or I might go for Artificial Intelligence which has increasing application in just about everything. I am also looking at Fulbright scholarship opportunities for a master's program at a US university.

Q. Your path was paved by your older siblings. Four of you have had opportunities to go to the US for brief educational experiences. It is also remarkable that all of you have been in the top universities in Pakistan and you are now looking at options that will shape your future career. Where do you think you would have been if there was no TCF school in Ibrahim Goth?

Yasir: I would have gone to a government school, just as my siblings would have. I think our parents would have sent us to school regardless, but it was a good thing that there were TCF schools in Ibrahim Goth which gave us a good foundation. If I had gone to a government school, I don't think I would have had the same drive for a future career. I might have settled for a factory job or an office job and thought that was the best I could do. I think our expectations would have been much lower. TCF schooling prepared me for university and a professional career which probably would not have happened otherwise.

Q. Who is your role model?

Yasir: Because of my interest in technology, I admire Steve Jobs. I've done some reading about him, the ups and downs in his journey. His perseverance is a quality I admire very much, how he co-founded Apple, one of the largest tech companies. It's an amazing story, how he was tossed out of the company and then came back to it. It was unfortunate that his life ended pre-maturely due to health issues.

Q. Tell us about your experience at University of Massachusetts, Amherst. How was it, overall? Where did you travel outside of the Amherst-Boston area?

Yasir: It was a 48-day round trip with thirty days of academics at University of Massachusetts, Amherst, and twelve days of study tour. Our program focus was Public Policy and how it is implemented in the US, also to think of how applicable those concepts would be in Pakistan. We learned how to critically analyze factors in developing public policy. We attended leadership courses and workshops at Amherst and I enjoyed the talks we attended at the University of Virginia and our visit to the Boston State House, which gave us an opportunity to learn how state legislatures work in the US. We traveled to cities near Boston and visited the MIT and Harvard campuses, which were amazing experiences. I particularly enjoyed seeing the labs at MIT. As part of the study tour, we also had four days in New York and saw the famous locations— Manhattan, Times Square, World Trade Center, and a few more sites. We were also in Virginia and in Washington DC.

Q. How many Pakistani students were in your group? And did you have much interaction with American students and students from other countries?

Yasir: There were thirty Pakistani students in our group and there was a group of Iraqi students also at Amherst, and we had some interaction with them. We also had regular interaction with American students at Amherst. Overall, it was just a great experience for me because I had rarely been out of the Karachi area and it was unbelievable that I was on an all-expense-paid trip to the US, including a taste of academics and campus life. I was indeed fortunate to be one of thirty students selected from the 5,000 that applied. People in the US are very helpful and friendly, and I learned a great deal about looking at things critically. The experience has helped me to be more confident. I think I used to be shy but not so much anymore. I'm told I am the first student from Habib University to go on this program.

Q. Did you meet any students from Israel or India and how were those interactions?

Yasir: We met a few Israeli students but didn't have a chance to interact informally. There were two girls from India in one of my classes and we had some good conversations. We talked about the bad policies of our governments and misconceptions among people of both countries because of the political propaganda.

Q. How can India and Pakistan have better relations?

Yasir: I think more people-to-people contact and resolution of the Kashmir problem will help.

Q. You mentioned that you saw the Massachusetts state legislature at work in Boston. That probably gave you some idea of how legislation is debated and how it may shape policy. Did that lead to discussion regarding any thoughts you had and how they may turn into better laws or better practices in Pakistan?

Yasir: Yes, my thoughts were related to the quality of education and how it could be made more equitable for everyone. We had a brief discussion in class and the conclusion was that standardizing the high school system in Pakistan would be the starting point to achieve equality in education. I think that would mean implementing education reforms to have uniform policy and better quality of education, and it would require legislation at some point. It is a complex system and I need to have a better understanding of it.

Q. Based on what you observed in the state legislature in Boston, do you think it would be a good idea to have school and college students visit the provincial and national assemblies to see how

public policy debates take place, how democratic institutions work, how they are built and sustained?

Yasir: Yes, I think it will be very helpful for us to understand how legislative bodies work and how policy is developed, how public participation and demand can be integrated in the process through inputs to the local representatives. I think that's a very good idea.

Q. **After your undergrad study at Habib, let's say you take the CSS exam and pass it. Let's suppose you've also been accepted to a top US university through a Fulbright scholarship, and you've been accepted at a top institute in Germany. If you had these three choices, which one would you choose?**

Yasir: After passing the CSS exam, I can defer the start of a job in the civil service for two years. So, I would choose to do graduate study in the US through the Fulbright program, then join the civil service.

Update

June 2019: Yasir graduated from Habib University. He is planning to gain work experience for a year, then probably take the exam for the civil service. I picked his brains for more thoughts on deeper topics …

Q. **Congratulations on your graduation! So, let's talk about social issues, like relations with minorities. Along ethnic-religious lines, Pakistan is nearly 97 percent Muslim. Our minorities are mostly from the Hindu and Christian communities. How can we have greater tolerance for all faiths and eliminate the feeling of suppression or persecution suffered by religious minorities? Was there discussion on this issue in college?**

Yasir: We had some discussion on minority issues at Habib University as part of our liberal core classes. We talked about unfair treatment of other minorities. I feel there should be more open conversation on these topics. In my education up to 12th grade, there was never any such discussion on other faiths or tolerance. At Habib, I had two colleagues from the Hindu community and they had concerns about intimidation and violent incidents, which is very unfortunate.

Reading Recommended for Yasir and Friends

I asked Yasir a string of loaded questions about tolerance; relations with Israel and India; non-Muslim communities in Pakistan; secularism; agnostics and atheists; the Taliban, jihad, and madrasas. On religious tolerance, Yasir said that all people should have the freedom to practice the faith of their choice without fear of persecution. But I gather that many of these concepts had not been addressed in his education or social environment (certainly not in any depth), and that opportunities were needed for exploring diverse views and having open discussion on these subjects in liberal classroom settings. We discussed the importance of free thought and that freedom of expression should not be curtailed, that thoughts should not be engineered and forced to conform to dogmatic doctrine. We also agreed that well-founded beliefs gain greater recognition when free thinking is encouraged.

Having learned a great deal recently from my own reading and research for the book, my suggestion to Yasir and his college-educated peers is to dive into deeper reading on sociology[3]—the study of development, organization, and functioning of society—and the science of the fundamental laws of social relations and institutions. – *Author*

Q. It is interesting that you might be the third in your family to enter the civil service. If that should happen, what is your motivation to go into the civil service and what branch would you like to serve in?

Yasir: I would like to contribute to social change through the civil service and I may want to serve in the police or law enforcement branch, do my part to improve the working of that branch of public services. I may go into the IT department of the police services to contribute to improvements in the systems, making them more efficient by automation, archiving of records, the information gathering processes, HR records, and other aspects of administration. I may even want to explore some applications of Artificial Intelligence.

Update

January 2020: Yasir started a job at the prestigious United Bank Limited (UBL).

February 2021: Yasir is working with UBL Digital as a Data Analyst.

3.6 Nadeem Hussain
BS in Computer Science, Institute of Business Administration (IBA), Karachi;
World Bank Consultant/Technical Assistant to Government of Sindh

From the early idea stage and through the duration of this book project, Nadeem has been my friend and associate: a treasured thought-partner, sounding board, co-editor, and fact-checker; astute (and respectful) critic; and a valuable resource for most things related to TCF, the Alumni Development Program (ADP), or the TCF College, and for countless other data and details. For good reason, Nadeem is among the many celebrated TCF achievers and poster children but he remains totally grounded with humility in his modest home surroundings of Ibrahim Goth, always ready to help anyone and driven by strong personal values of frugal living, modesty, kindness, and compassion. Over the years and through many hours of contact, I have had an opportunity to get to know Nadeem on a personal level. I am confident that he will be recognized as a champion for social justice, equality, and the rights of the underprivileged. Nadeem and family are extraordinary people and I continue to learn about life in the trenches from each one of them.

With his innate special qualities, his acquired talents, his lofty achievements, and deep desire to never stop learning, Nadeem symbolizes and stands out as an exceptional outcome of good education and how a level playing field in education can be instrumental in broader social change. But I hasten to add that Nadeem is not alone in this respect. His illustrious siblings and thousands of underprivileged student achievers are on the same platform of distinction, for they have all been in a tough battle to overcome the barriers of class and privilege and have proudly earned the right to equity in life, largely because of the right education opportunity at the right time.

As the second child in the family, Nadeem came to Karachi from their ancestral village near Naushahro Feroze when he was a few months old. As he ventured outside the home, he and his friends spent the days in the dirt lanes and open spaces of the neighborhood. At the age of 6 or 7, he would occasionally accompany his friends to a government school. 'I was never enrolled in the school, but I would just go with other children from the area and sometimes attend classes.'

Nadeem, now 27, is a graduate of the Institute of Business Administration (IBA), Karachi, one of the highest-ranked universities in the country. He was the first TCF alum at any top-tier university. In 2013, Nadeem was selected for a summer program at University of Massachusetts, Amherst. In 2015, Nadeem was asked by his mentor Dr Ishrat Husain to co-author a book.[4] For the last five years, he has been a World Bank consultant/technical assistant to the Government of Sindh, making a monthly salary of 120,000 Pakistani rupees.

Nadeem's workdays and weekends are equally busy. He is an energetic activist and community organizer, always in great demand, yet managing to make time for his family. Considering that he was a slum-wandering little boy, Nadeem is an avid reader. His knowledge base and maturity are impressive. In the dialog to follow, I have attempted to draw out Nadeem's own accounts and background stories of the various programs that he is a key part of. He plays down his role in initiating the groundbreaking TCF Alumni Development Program to facilitate university education for children from underprivileged families. Here's the rest of Nadeem's captivating personal story …

Q. What are your childhood memories of Ibrahim Goth?

Nadeem: I was just a few months old when my mother, my grandmother, sister Uzma and I moved to Karachi in 1991 to join my father. In my earliest memories of Ibrahim Goth, it was like a small village and families were moving in to settle here. There was thorny, scrub growth all around that people would use to mark the boundaries of the plots of land with a small room or two on it. Most structures were made of mud walls or straw mats which were gradually replaced with block walls and tin roofs. Many families had a goat for milk, some people also had buffaloes and chickens. It was simple, rural living and most people were migrants from the northern parts of the country, here to find work and resettle. There was a community of pottery artisans who made clay garden pots and ornamental *matkas* (water containers, pitchers), and a small community of wood workers. Out of curiosity, some city folk would come to see what the village artisans made and maybe buy a few items. For entertainment, every Friday evening there would be cock fighting in an improvised arena where men and boys would gather and money was wagered. Occasionally, there would also be organized wrestling matches. Things were very different back then. I grew up in the dirt roads of the village, playing and loitering all day with the children of the neighborhood.

Q. When did you first step into a school?

Nadeem: My parents were struggling to get established and there wasn't much concern for education at that time; so, they didn't send me to the government school, which was about a half-hour away. But I would occasionally go along with some children who went to that school and the teachers would let me join the classes. On average, I would go maybe twice a week and sit in the classes with my friends. To pass the time, we took an hour to get to the school and about the same time to get back. There wasn't much discipline or education going on in the school. My early years were aimless until I was eight, and started at the TCF school. Then my life changed.

My sisters, Uzma and Sidra had started at the new TCF school. In 2000, one of the TCF teachers visited our home and suggested to my mother that I should also be enrolled, so I took the admission test, which was tough for me. My mother had helped me with some Urdu writing and the alphabet—*alif, bay*—and I had also picked up some reading skills at the madrasa in the masjid. But I didn't know the English A-B-C. Anyway, I was admitted to 4th grade, which was age-appropriate for me, and I was fast-tracked with extra help from the teachers. I was at the TCF school for seven years and finished 10th grade in 2007.

Q. When did you start working, to earn income?

Nadeem: My first paid work was at a towel loom factory where child labor is quite common to this day. I was 13 at the time and still in school. Later, when I was 15 and I had finished 10th grade, I worked at the copper wire factory for three months where my father is employed. That was during the summer after my 10th grade.

Q. Then you went to DJ Science College for your Intermediate, right? And what does 'DJ' stand for?

Nadeem: Yes, that's right. 'DJ' stands for the name of a philanthropist Dayaram Jethamal and the institution is a pre-partition gift to Karachi. It is a government-run college now.

Q. And, how did your admission to IBA happen?

Nadeem: Before I applied for IBA, it was just a stroke of luck that I got to know about the National Outreach Program (NOP) at LUMS, a scholarship for children from underprivileged families. I had not even heard of LUMS or IBA but a friend at DJ College had clipped a newspaper announcement about NOP and he suggested I should look into it because I had good grades in Matric and I was from an underprivileged family. I had no idea how to apply. I had no email account nor good computer skills. The smartest thing I did was to take a chance and send a handwritten letter by postal courier to NOP-LUMS, saying that I would like to be considered for the NOP. When I think back, I realize how hard it must be for so many other students who are in the same situation as I was—the difficulties in just *understanding* the application and admission process for a university. Anyway, to my surprise, I received an acknowledgement from NOP, by courier, to my father's factory address, asking me to apply online.

It was just my good fortune that, about the same time, Naima Hasan sahiba, a very kind lady at TCF, had sent a memo to all school principals that the TCF Placement Desk[5] could help students with guidance for college admissions. The Ibrahim Goth school principal contacted me and informed me of this, so I went over to meet with Naima sahiba and told her about NOP. She and others at TCF had not heard of NOP at the time, so it was a learning experience for all of us. I got the help I needed and I was able to get the NOP application completed.

Q. This happened in your first year at DJ College in 2008 and was your application accepted?

Nadeem: Yes, I was invited to Lahore for a summer session in which they prepare students for the LUMS admission test. It was the first time I had travelled by myself by train, reaching Lahore late at night with a friend, and we spent the night at Daata Darbar[6] and took a *tanga* (traditional horse-drawn transport) to LUMS early the next morning. I completed the three-week NOP session and there were many very smart students from good middle-class schools and with excellent grades from all over the country. I didn't make it in the LUMS admissions test.

Q. What did you do then?

Nadeem: In my second year at DJ, I applied again through NOP. But I couldn't pass the admissions test for the second time. By this time, and like all other applicants, I had been thinking of other options if I didn't get into LUMS—like going to NUST or IBA, or other places. IBA was my first choice and that's where I applied.

Q. Did you receive any assistance from TCF for admission to IBA?

Yes, I did. Unaiza Ayub Sahiba at the new Alumni Department at TCF was a dedicated staff person who took me under her wing, counseled me, and helped me to set up an email account and showed me how to complete the online application. She went out of her way and wrote to the IBA admissions office asking for my admission test fees to be waived and that waiver was granted. She's a wonderful person and I have learned a great deal from her that I've been able to apply and help my peers in the ADP process. I passed the admission test for the IBA computer science program—but, interestingly, I didn't know anything about search engines, so she helped me with that as well. She also taught me how to have a JPEG digital photo made and stored on a USB flash drive!

Again, looking back, Unaiza Sahiba made things so much easier for me. People who don't know about the huge gap between the social classes probably can't understand why more underprivileged students don't take the initiative to apply and get into good universities. My experience in the admission process for IBA was a complete awakening for me and, during the process, I would often say to myself 'Oh, so that's how it's done' and I would make a mental note of how, some day, I might help others to learn about the process and, more important, how to prepare for the admissions test. The fact is that children like me had absolutely no exposure to many of the things that are taken for granted—good reading skills, computers, internet access, computer skills, communication skills, ease of transport, and so many other things. These are real challenges for underprivileged children which hold them back. The TCF model is making things better for the students there but, we need higher quality secondary and 11th and 12th grade education for college preparation on a much larger scale. As you've said many times, the ADP program and the TCF College will be the game changers.

Q. When was your first realization that your education had helped to remove the barriers of class? For yourself, when did you feel that a level playing field had been achieved?

Nadeem: For me, I think that was on my first day at IBA when I interacted with students from different social-economic backgrounds. My father was the proudest dad in the world on that day. I remember how he emotionally told my family about the congratulations and hugs he got from his factory-owner boss when he announced that I had started at IBA. Then two years later the factory owner's daughter also started at IBA and we were in a class together! Now, that was personal evidence for my family, and for me, that a level playing field had been achieved. And it was a significant achievement for TCF as an organization. That's when I was deeply moved and I visited Ahsan Saleem sahib at his office to let him know of the experience and life transformation I was feeling through the power of education. I think this realization of a level playing field happens with all underprivileged students who make it to top universities through various scholarship programs. It's a liberating, indescribable feeling. I would surely like to see other children from *katchi abadi*s have similar opportunities.

Q. How was your own transition from the Urdu-medium TCF school environment to the English language environment of DJ College and IBA?

Nadeem: It was difficult but, with hard work, the adjustment can be made because we had a reasonably good foundation in English at TCF. The immersion into English at DJ College and IBA left me no choice but to get better. That said, we do need to have more intensive English learning in the Urdu-medium schools, ideally starting in the 4th grade, and we need more English language teachers.

Q. So, how were you accepted at IBA and when was your first contact with Dr Ishrat Husain Sahib?

Nadeem: I was selected for IBA through its National Talent Hunt Program (NTHP), a scholarship program like the NOP at LUMS, which targets students from underprivileged communities. Most students at IBA are from elite schools. But many students from modest means come to IBA through NTHP and I have seen them totally transformed both in academics as well as their personality development, right before my eyes. The NTHP scholarship provides tuition, boarding, and books at no cost, plus an allowance of 3,000 Pakistani rupees per month. These generous facilities are of great value to the poor student and it made a big difference in my case.

As Dean and Director of IBA, Ishrat Sahib was a great champion of equity in education, very supportive, and personally involved with the NTHP. In 2013, when I was in my third year at IBA, I was selected by the US State Department for a program called 'Study of the US Institutes for Student Leaders on Comparative Public Policy' and I was one of the twenty-five Pakistani students sent to a US university for a six-week summer program. I went to the University of Massachusetts at Amherst and also got an opportunity to visit New York, Boston, and Washington, DC, and some of the great institutions in America. When Ishrat Sahib heard that I was the first NTHP recipient from IBA selected for this program, he called me to his office and congratulated me and asked me about my earlier schooling, my family, and my goals. That was my first contact with him. Since then, he has been a wonderful guide and personal mentor and I look up to him with admiration and great respect.

Q. With another student from IBA, you designed a framework for the innovative Alumni Development Program (ADP). Please talk about the genesis of ADP and how it prepares our TCF alumni for admission to good universities? And how has the program evolved since its inception?

Nadeem: After I returned from the US, I was very pleased to take calls from TCF that Asaad Sahib or Mushtaq Sahib or Riaz Kamlani Sahib wanted to meet with me. They asked why more alumni weren't applying and getting into top universities and what could be done to facilitate admissions to the top universities. Asaad sahib was particularly very detailed in his questions. The discussions helped to identify underlying weaknesses in the process and possible solutions. At TCF, the realization had hit home that our secondary and 11th and 12th grade preparation was not good enough to see our TCF grads get into good universities in significant numbers. The student weaknesses were clearly in math and English, communication and computer skills. The solution had to be better academic preparation.

The conversations about helping to prepare college bound children became more frequent and louder in 2010 and I think that was the genesis of ADP. On advice from Shazia Kamal[7] Sahiba, another wonderful lady and head of the Alumni Department in 2011, I had started to engage with the 9th and 10th graders and the alumni, offering guidance for university preparation. But the counseling and academic preparation was needed on a much larger scale. It also had to be organized into a sustainable system and uniformly reach a majority of our student population nationally. So, we started to think about how to accomplish that economically or at zero cost. And we came up with a proposal to engage volunteers from university undergrad students to coach our alumni in math and English and also prepare them in other ways to apply for admission to university programs. It would require a large number of volunteers as coaches and volunteer coordinators, plus dedicated staff resources at TCF.

The proposed ADP framework was to have coaching classes for 11th and 12th graders, and we call these ADP Level 1 and Level 2. These coaching sessions were initiated at IBA. Additionally, and apart from the coaching classes at IBA, we engaged volunteer students from universities to go to the TCF secondary schools and conduct the 'Foundation Level' ADP classes for 9th and 10th graders during the summer vacation. And now, with the TCF Intermediate College, we are selecting the best of the TCF Matriculates, giving them good 11th to 12th grade education, and also helping with their personality development. The cohorts of graduates from the TCF Intermediate College will be the best candidates we have prepared for top-tier university admissions. The College can take only 200 students every year and we are confident that a high percentage of them will do well in the university entrance tests. But we still need ADP coaching sessions for the students who don't get into the TCF College. In a nutshell, that's the TCF-ADP program.

I am focused on ADP and the TCF College because these programs are close to my heart. Engaging the alumni back with TCF is important. ADP has been one of the most rewarding things I've been a part of and, I must admit, it has pushed my energies to the max. Farheen Ghaffar, my colleague at IBA who was from a private non-TCF school, had great ideas and gave me valuable support to develop the ADP framework and recruit the first team of volunteer TCF Ambassadors to be our math and English coaches. IBA gave us the space to hold the coaching sessions and, thanks to Ishrat Sahib, we are still using the classrooms. Coordination between IBA's National Talent Hunt Program (NTHP) and TCF was important and I was the bridge between NTHP and the TCF Alumni department. The ADP program resonated with IBA's NTHP as their aims were the same, which was to facilitate university education for underprivileged youth.

Many TCF supporters were excited at the prospect of seeing potentially hundreds of TCF grads get into good universities. Through their personal contacts, TCF leaders stepped up to facilitate the waivers of testing and application fees and to enable full scholarships for our students at top universities like Habib, Ghulam Ishaq Khan Institute of Engineering Sciences and Technology (GIKI), and others. But we had to build the infrastructure and framework for ADP, develop a team of volunteers, get staff resources, and have a plan to execute it across all TCF secondary schools in Karachi and then extend it to other parts of the country as much as our resources would allow.

Q. So, ADP got started but how did it become sustainable with volunteer teams of Ambassador-coaches?

Nadeem: In August 2011, we had the first group of TCF graduates apply for the IBA-NTHP and one student qualified for the NTHP but was not accepted for the IBA program. Then, the next year, we had four students accepted for NTHP but, again, none accepted by IBA. That was the time when I asked myself: *why are more TCF grads not making it into IBA?* I was in my final year at IBA and I was determined to see more TCF students get into IBA. I didn't know what I was going to do but I wanted to see at least one TCF alum accepted at IBA every year. I spoke with some of the IBA seniors who had graduated and had started their careers. These were very smart people with great credentials. I asked them to help as coaches, become TCF Ambassadors. I had to request this group to understand that the batch of TCF students they would be coaching may not be able to understand more than a few words of English. So, the Ambassadors had to be very tactful, creative, and resourceful in their coaching.

In the beginning, when we didn't have enough volunteers, we had our friends help as volunteer coaches. Ishrat Sahib took a personal interest in our program, but he wanted to see a concrete plan. We informed him that we thought it should be a year-round program which would run every weekend. He was also concerned that the coaching program would not be sustainable with friends as volunteers who were starting new careers or busy with their own study schedules and social lives. Luckily, with our passion, Farheen and I convinced him to give ADP his blessings and approval and allow us to start the program.

Convincing the TCF alumni-students to come to IBA for the coaching classes was another huge task. I used to make the calls to each and every student and also speak with the parents because I felt that I could connect with both the students and parents. We were making hundreds of calls so we had to pool some money to buy phone cards. We couldn't afford to pay the full-price for copies of handouts for the students, so we appealed to the vendor at IBA to give us a break and he agreed to charge us for the paper only when we could afford it. Even at the discounted price, our bill for the year for copies made was close to 20,000 Pakistani rupees, which my friends took care of.

The first year we had some success was 2014. We had one admission at IBA—the first one to be accepted after me since 2010. That was Imran Shaukat. My sister Iqra was also accepted at IBA that year but she went to LUMS. After Imran's successful admission, ADP began to get some recognition that 'these ADP kids were really getting something done'. But there was also some skepticism at TCF. They were concerned that ADP would not be sustainable after I graduated and started to work. I had to convince the people at TCF and at NTHP that I would devote whatever time it took to stabilize the program. They were concerned that, after I left, ADP might not have the institutional support from TCF or IBA because I was the connection between the two. I would come to IBA for three or four hours every day after office hours and on weekends, to make sure everything was running smoothly, meet with the volunteers, keep them motivated, and then make calls to the TCF students.

The Ambassadors were all very smart individuals from super-elite schools. They had good knowledge of math and English but they did not know how to connect with the TCF alumni. I had to train the coaches to do that. I also had to motivate the TCF alumni, tell them 'You can get in but you'll have to work hard'.

The year 2014–15 was a turning point for us. We made news for TCF and for IBA. That was the time they started taking us seriously and TCF realized that this program should be adopted and they should give us organizational support.

That was the year that Arif Irfanullah Sahib became aware of ADP and he said that AAP's after-school program in two TCF schools was not showing an outcome or impact equal to the personal effort and financial investment that he was putting into it, and he was sold on the ADP concept. He committed his personal involvement to ADP and helped us form the organizational structure for ADP, making AAP[8] a partner in the program. I feel that it was the combined energy and the passion that helped us kick off the program. In 2015, we had five admissions to IBA and those five are now running the program. Every year since, we've had one, two or three admissions and this last year (2018), we had five admissions to IBA from the TCF College and two admissions through ADP.

Some TCF leaders helped us open doors at LUMS and Habib. I met with Dr Anjum Altaf and Dr Wasif Rizvi at Habib. I was meeting several people, but only as a volunteer. I would encounter interesting reactions, not all of them were warm or welcoming. There were some logistical, operational, institutional, or bureaucratic hurdles which I couldn't always understand. Sometimes I got the feeling that people thought of me as '... that boy who lives in the *katchi abadi*, his life problems are different and he must understand that it takes time to change things.' But we got past all that. And we recruited Ambassadors from undergrad students on campus and asked them to serve with ADP for at least a year. That's how ADP got started and how it has become sustainable.

Q. I believe that ADP is the game changer for higher education and employability of underprivileged TCF student-achievers. How was the ADP coaching curriculum developed?

Nadeem: Academic Achievement Plus (AAP) was the initiative run by Arif Irfanullah Sahib and his associates. For six years, AAP had run after-school coaching sessions in math and English at two TCF schools and they had a ready-made curriculum that we were able to adapt for the ADP coaching classes. Farheen Ghaffar also helped with ideas for the curriculum and in getting the coaching classes off the ground. I think the ADP got more serious attention from TCF management because of Arif Sahib's involvement on the ADP Governing Body and it's also because of him that AAP is helping with funds for a dedicated staff position in the Alumni Department at TCF.

Q. So, was 2015 the inflection point for ADP and how can the program be expanded?

Nadeem: Yes, definitely. In that year, we had five admissions to IBA. In the same year, we had five admissions at Habib, two at the NED University of Engineering and Technology, Karachi three at FAST National University of Computer and Emerging Sciences and another twenty-plus going to Tier 2 universities. And this did not include medical colleges, pharmacology, or medical technology programs, because ADP does not offer coaching for those programs. Every year since 2015, we've had a few admissions to IBA and this last year (2018), we had five admissions to IBA from the TCF College and two admissions through ADP, a total of seven at IBA alone.

Nationally, TCF is graduating around 5,000 matriculates in 2019, about 3,500 from Karachi and surroundings. But the TCF College in Karachi can take only 200 students to prepare them for university admission. Of the remaining students, the college-bound students will continue to need ADP coaching classes. There are probably more college admissions from Lahore and other areas but we don't have that data.

Rapid expansion of ADP is needed and we must add other universities where we can have coaching classes as we do at the IBA campus. I think the NED campus could accommodate 500 of our alumni and we should explore that and the feasibility of creating more teams of TCF Ambassadors for other locations. It is imperative that the ADP coaching classes should continue so we can reach out to more alumni and prepare them for university admissions. The challenge is huge and it may take years for the programs started in Karachi to reach a level of maturity and efficiency before we can try to implement them in other areas of the country. But that must be our ultimate goal. It will take more resources too.

Q. Perhaps the ADP and TCF teams need to revisit the strategy for ADP to be scaled in other areas. Signing up university students to help with coaching is a great idea. What is the challenge for ADP to branch out in areas outside of Karachi?

Nadeem: It's a big challenge. We have a total of about 110 secondary schools in Karachi, Lahore and Rawalpindi put together, about 75 in greater Karachi alone. Except for Karachi, where we have done fairly well, we've been struggling since 2015 to advance the ADP and assist with more university enrollments in other areas—mainly because it is very difficult to find volunteer coaches to help TCF students with math and English. Over time, we have successfully institutionalized ADP in almost all 75 secondary schools in the greater Karachi area. The Karachi students know about the TCF College and how ADP can help. But in other areas, for example, in Dadu or Rashidabad—both towns are close to Hyderabad, about 100 miles from Karachi—we haven't been able to help all our students through ADP, primarily because we can't find qualified volunteer coaches to prepare students for a SAT-level exam. And there just aren't enough good Intermediate colleges in all areas where they can be coached to prepare for the university entrance exam. That said, there are also several enterprising students who—*without any help from ADP*—have put in the extra work, explored the right resources, and made their way into good universities.

Q. That is remarkable. But how are we tracking progress of the Intermediate students whether or not they are completing 11th and 12th grades, and where they are ending up?

Nadeem: I'm having this constant conversation with Riaz Sahib that we need to know how many of our Matric graduates end up completing their intermediate 11th and 12th grades. We should start with Karachi and track every graduate. We know that roughly 88 percent of our students go to Intermediate colleges but we don't know if they *finish* Intermediate college. That is the first question. And then: What are they doing after Intermediate? Do they continue in education, go to work, or where do they end up? Over the years, TCF has matriculated over 19,100 students and we don't really know what the majority of them are doing, or where they are. That's a concern and we must work to streamline the alumni tracking system.

ADP is a very quantifiable program. If we are graduating 3,500 matriculates annually in Karachi (2019), we can track their progress through their participation in ADP and see where they end up in two years. We should also track students who may *not* participate in the ADP and evaluate how they are doing in two years.

Q. **Finding alumni after they finish school is a daunting task and obviously, TCF is having a tough time. Perhaps alumni should also take greater responsibility for staying in touch with TCF, informing the staff of any change, where they are in their education or jobs and professional careers. What are the frustrations from your perspective and solutions you can suggest—perhaps engaging the alumni to help in this task?**

Nadeem: I think there should be a high-level discussion on what we would like to see our alumni doing. This year (2019), we will have 3.500 students matriculating nationally. The number will be higher every year. My concern is that if we are not able to manage the current number for tracking, we will not be able to manage the higher numbers. As you and I have discussed, I believe it should be the *alumni* who manage the tracking of the alumni, with intern alums assigned to do alumni relations, alumni placement, etc. There should be an alumnus working with operations, and the teams for RMD, the V&A department, and marketing—to see how the work is done and get an understanding of the TCF systems. If we can get 10 to 15 alumni trained in various aspects of the organization's operations, we will have a good resource of alumni who understand our system from the ground up. Right now, it's a monumental challenge and the staff is having a difficult time coping with it. Some of these alumni interns could even become employable at TCF.

Q. **... and, down the road, wouldn't it be remarkable if, the ADP model of coaching with university students as volunteers could be adopted on a larger scale, outside of the TCF network?**

Nadeem: That would be a truly amazing achievement. For the volunteer coaches, that would be a huge opportunity to serve and have tremendous impact in helping to achieve a level playing field. That would be great!

Q. **So, it seems the TCF College was an off-shoot of ADP with the same goal of preparing students for university education. Was the College a major intervention and turning point for the next phase of ADP?**

Nadeem: Yes, absolutely, the TCF College was a major turning point. An Advisory Committee for the college was formed in 2015 and I was

---

Box 3.3 TCF Intermediate College:
HOW IS IT DIFFERENT?

The co-ed TCF Intermediate College has a unique multi-pronged strategy to prepare students for the most sought-after undergraduate programs. It's the only intermediate college in the country that prepares students academically for university entrance tests and also has a curriculum for Social & Personality Development, including training in personal interaction, public speaking, presentations, music, calligraphy, poetry, recitation, and writing exercises. Students acquire basic proficiency in computer skills. They are shown how to sign up for email accounts, taught the use of search engines for basic research, and how to explore the websites of top-tier universities. There's a computer lab and some tests are taken online.

Students are provided van transport to facilitate on-time attendance. The cost per student per month for the College is about 8,700 rupees. However, all students enrolled are offered a scholarship up to 99 percent of the cost on a case by case basis which is evaluated with each enrollment every year. About 75 percent of the students are on a 90 to 99 percent scholarship. The average fee charged after scholarships is 600 rupees per month.

---

asked to serve on it with Riaz Sahib, Arif Irfanullah Sahib, Unaiza Sahiba, and others. And we started working on a plan for the College. I think ADP had demonstrated its impact and that has made the TCF leadership realize that the impact could be even greater if TCF had its own Intermediate college with control of the education quality, which would substantially increase the chances of more alumni being accepted at top tier universities. So, the TCF College experiment was launched in 2016 and the College opened its doors to the first 200 students.

Q. Almost every college student in the US has a laptop. How many students at the TCF College have laptops?

Nadeem: I think very few students may have a PC or laptop. They are not required to bring one to college and the Board exam does not test computer skills or social skills taught at the TCF College.

Q. The College is co-ed and students are provided van transport. From the four cohorts so far, what is the percentage of girls? Are the girls transported with the boys, and have there been any challenges related to the co-ed environment?

Nadeem: So far, the girls are about 55 percent of the four cohorts, combined. Yes, the girls and boys are in the same vans. There have been a few minor challenges that are typical of any co-ed environment with maturing teenagers but we have male and female faculty at the college for harmony and support. All the TCF students have come from co-ed secondary schools so they behave with a high degree of respect for each other and the co-ed environment is not a new experience for them. We do our best to ensure safety and assure the parents. In a few cases where girls have gained admission, some conservative parents have not allowed their daughters to join the TCF College because of the co-ed environment so we respect their feelings and try to find other solutions. We try to do what we can but we can't always convince concerned parents to see things our way.

Q. Tell me about your first job after graduation at the World Bank project with the Sindh government. How did you find out about the opportunity? And what is it that you do for the project?

Nadeem: I didn't want to work with consumer products in the corporate sector, like selling soap or shampoo. I wanted to do something on a larger scale, do something that would make a difference. I thought of the civil service but the process was too long. I wanted to have some income to help my father and support the family. At the Career Development Center at IBA, I found out about the World Bank project and applied as a Technical Assistant. The program was specifically about education reforms and that was of interest to me. One part of the program was to bring technology into the public sector. My degree in computer science and my experience as a volunteer with TCF and ADP helped me get the job.

One component of my assignment was to streamline the complaint system for the government. Before this World Bank project, there was no mechanism for a complaint to be lodged in a school. There are 45,554 government schools in Sindh. It's a very large provincial system with 29 districts. Every school has different dynamics with a wide variety of issues—including political lobbying, ethnic issues, and sectarian issues. Every district and every *taaluqa* (township) has its own social and economic dynamic. So, I wanted to make a sustainable system that would be there after the World Bank project concludes.

Prior to this reform program, there was no culture of using emails for office communication. A letter could take as long as two weeks to go from the secretariat to a local district office. So, my next assignment was to streamline the digital communication of the education department, which employs 200,000 people and includes 154,000 teachers. I was responsible to conceptualize the IT system, help the government to build the physical IT structure, and create a relevant database of contacts of all employees. So, if the Secretary of Education had to send a text message to all 154,000 teachers, it could be done. Initially, it was interventions like these.

But, realizing that there were huge gaps and deficits in human resources, I started to go beyond my stated job description and show interest in different reform areas and sections within the education department. I felt that if I could contribute by offering advice for the testing that was being done to assess learning outcomes, that could make a big difference. A million students are tested annually and millions of rupees are spent and a majority of the government staff do not have the drive or motivation to change the system. I would sometimes receive suggestions to mind my own business. [Laughs]. Unfortunately, it will take years and years to fix education in Pakistan, especially in Sindh.

In the past, there have been programs like the one that I am a part of and there will be some in the future as well. But these are only sustainable if the government employees have the capacity and the ability to run these programs—and the motivation to sustain these reforms. The World Bank or any donor agency will come with a defined mandate and agenda. They will leave when the time is up and the program ends. Then the government bureaucracy should have the ability and the determination to sustain the programs, otherwise they are of no use.

Q. It appears that the change you were trying to drive was in the technical gaps in the system. Was your expected role also to be involved in policy reforms, or did that evolve over time?

Nadeem: Initially, I was mandated to work on the technical development and concept of the IT infrastructure for the department and it involved policy discussions. So, I was part of the top policy making process. Of course, I was not an active participant but I was asked to give input at times. My involvement rose to a higher level, and because there's such a huge gap, I was even invited to sit in on the Curriculum Council meetings. Although I had no qualifications for this, one of the officers felt that I could be a co-opt (ad hoc) member. At the very first meeting, I suggested that TCF should have representation at these meetings because other civic organizations were represented there. The Council is the highest forum in the department and is mandated to revise the curriculum and the syllabus as well. It was not in my job description to be a co-opt member of the Council, but there I was.

Q. Obviously, you had a wider impact, more than just the technical improvements you were assigned. Are the technical solutions being duplicated in other provinces, or are the gaps just as bad?

Nadeem: Yes, absolutely. I am well aware of the status in Balochistan because the same World Bank program is being executed in Sindh and Balochistan. It's called Global Partnership for Education, with a $100 million grant from a consortium, with the World Bank as the financial guarantor. Out of the $100 million grant, $66 million were given to the Government of Sindh and the remaining $34 million were given to Balochistan. The program that came to Sindh became the Sindh Global Partnership for Education and the other became the Balochistan Global Partnership for Education. But their key performance indicators, targets, and mandates were the same.

I think the technical assistance teams in both provinces have tried to facilitate the governments to the best of their abilities. I feel that 100 percent implementation is not going to happen in either province and that is generally what happens to development projects in Pakistan...and I've heard, also in other countries. But whatever has been implemented must be sustained by the recipient governments.

Q. There is no public oversight. So, how can you ensure that it is being sustained or improved upon?

Nadeem: It is incumbent upon the government to ensure its sustainability. As we know, once the donors are gone and the project is done, there is no external oversight. Currently, there are several major donors or funding agencies working on education reform in Sindh—World Bank, Asian Development Bank, EU, USAID, UNICEF and others. USAID has funded the building and rehabilitation of 120 schools and some of those schools in Sindh have been handed over to TCF to manage and run as an Education Management Organization (EMO).

Q. What's next for you, after the World Bank project job?

Nadeem: I am inspired by Dr Ishrat's career and service. I've learned a lot from him in the course of the book on Sindh. I will need to have some earnings but later I would like to have a solid PhD and see where it lands me professionally. I like to write, and I will probably do that from time to time. I will continue to do what I can for ADP and TCF and generally, for education on a larger scale.

Q. How do you see your support role in the family, with aging parents and the need to financially contribute?

Nadeem: Yes, I have that responsibility. My siblings are doing well academically, *Masha Allah*. I am very conscious of the needs of my parents and I want them to have some pleasures in life. They have worked very hard for us and I would like them to sit back and enjoy life. My father is not ready to retire yet and he wants to continue earning to see every one of us get married and settled. *Alhamdulillah*, my sister Uzma is married and working and her good education helps her not only professionally but also in her outlook on life at home. I will have time later in life to pursue my dream of a PhD, *Insha Allah*. Working in the public sector and policy sphere is of interest to me, so I may consider the civil service as a career. I have a very deep association with my community of Ibrahim Goth where I have lived all my life. There are many problems here but this is home for us. I am very open with my wealthier friends and I am not embarrassed to let them know where we live. I am happy that my siblings also feel no embarrassment saying we live in a *katchi abadi*. There are challenges living here but we are making a difference.

I am confident that, if we have a dozen of my peers from the *goth* getting a university education, we'll be able to make a bigger difference for Ibrahim Goth. We'll be able to fix the roads, fix the electricity situation and the sewer system, and the issues of waste management—

get the *katchi abadi* converted to regular, authorized homes, make permanent residences over here, and receive civic amenities from the municipality as well. This will take time and influence. In our situation, that influence can only be achieved with education because we don't have agriculture, *vaderas* or feudal landlords who can pull strings. We don't have any political affiliations either because that can be divisive, not a solution.

We have discussed among my siblings that, as a family, we should be able to support operating expenses for some TCF schools in our area. We don't know when that will happen but *Insha Allah*, we are determined to do that. That will be the least we can do for the TCF mission and for the children in our community.

> **Q. For a sense of living in Ibrahim Goth and urban slums, I'd like to ask about the usual amenities we expect in middle-class homes. Let's start with a basic necessity: electricity and the Internet.**

Nadeem: Internet connectivity is a continuous issue at home. The Wi-Fi router goes off because of frequent power outages. I use the Internet only at the office or at the IBA library on weekends. I don't spend on expensive data packages for my phone. I think we got hooked up with electricity in Ibrahim Goth in the early 2000s.

> **Q. Water supply, regular plumbing, running water and sewer lines—how did you get water before the pipeline and storage tanks were installed?**

Nadeem: In the early days, we had a well on our small property and drew water from it, one bucket at a time, just like in the villages. The water quality was poor, probably also unhygienic, and it didn't taste good either. Then we had the underground storage tank made and installed the connection to receive water. In the next phase, as the family finances improved and we had some savings, we had the overhead storage tanks and an electric pump and plumbing fixtures installed in the kitchen and bathrooms. We still don't have a 'legal' water connection from Karachi Water Board. The main water line connection from some mysterious point to Ibrahim Goth has been

Box 3.4 Ibrahim Goth:
An Urban Slum — *Katchi Abadi*

It's a typical *katchi abadi* about 16 miles or an hour's drive from central Karachi—double that time for heavy traffic. Once a rural *goth* (village), it is now a bustling slum with a population estimated at 30,000 in about 8,000 households. Jobs in nearby factories draw workers and families of refugee migrants to settle here, making it an eclectic, diverse and tolerant community. Transport to city destinations is by bus services operated by private operators. There is no other mass transit or rail service. Most men travel on the ubiquitous motorbike. Car ownership is rare. Families eke out low middle-class living and will probably live here for generations because of lower cost. They accept the poor quality of life. The wall-to-wall homes are of mediocre quality, brick-and-mortar construction, averaging about 1,500 square feet in area. Roads are narrow, bumpy dirt lanes, 12 feet wide. Small stores and restaurants make up self-styled bazaars around neighborhood mosques.

The make-shift homes have become permanently established over time. Some utilities and municipal services are furnished by local government or by unlawful 'utility providers'. The community suffers from lack of essential services for health, sanitation, education, transportation, basic utilities, waste management, fire, or police protection. Most homes have no piped natural gas for cooking, etc. Some use propane cylinders. Refrigerators are rare. Perishable items such as meat, milk, and eggs are purchased every day. A trip to the bazaar is an essential and enjoyable daily activity.

People remember when living conditions were much worse. The major roads, cleanliness, and utilities have improved in the last decade. The general feeling is that the community is maturing, and education has had a big part in the slow transformation.

installed illegally and distribution lines bring the water to underground tanks in our homes. Then, the water is pumped up to overhead tanks and gravity-fed down to the plumbed water lines and fixtures in the kitchen and bathrooms.

Q. Is there a manual hydraulic pump or electric motor to pump the water up to the overhead tanks?

Nadeem: We have an electric pump. I've never heard of a manual pump.

Author: That's interesting. When we lived in Patel Para, there was a community water station where the water was on for a few hours every day for our slum-dwelling neighbors and there would be a row of buckets, utensils, and *matkas* (red clay pitchers) waiting their turn. I remember days when the power was out for hours or several days at a time and the electric pump couldn't be used to move the water from our ground storage tank up to the roof-top tanks. We would have to get a man to manually pump the water. On occasion, we had a *mashki*[9] deliver water from the community water line up to our flat and pour it into a large *samovar* tank in the bathroom to store for bathing, light washing, and cooking.

Q. And, what about sewer drains and disposal system for waste? How is that managed?

Nadeem: The greater Karachi area and most of Sindh are mostly scrub-desert and there are large, natural drains or branches of nearby river systems that are dry most of the year. Although it is totally wrong and environmentally criminal, it is customary for homes, businesses and factories located near these *nullahs* (the natural drains) to direct all the effluent waste and pollutants into these open drains. There is a large *nullah* in our *goth*, a couple hundred meters from our home. It is open, filthy and a breeding ground for mosquitos and diseases. Our *nullah* connects with other branches of the dry river system and eventually flows into the Arabian Sea, untreated and severely polluted. Occasional rain helps the flow and 'cleans' the drain to some extent, but it is a terribly shameful situation. I am embarrassed to talk about it but this condition exists all over the country, especially in suburban and rural areas where there is no drainage system connected to a central waste treatment plant. Waste management is also poor. The household garbage and trash is collected and taken to an open space for burning, which adds to the pollution.

Q. So, there is no waste treatment plant in Ibrahim Goth or surrounding communities and, I presume, there are no septic tanks either, right?

Nadeem: To my knowledge, no septic tanks exist anywhere. I suspect that more than 80 percent of homes are not connected to waste treatment plants, and not just in Ibrahim Goth but in all of Sindh province and the rest of the country. Sewer backups and clogging are a common problem even in planned housing communities and there are very few functioning waste-treatment plants. Everyone seems to 'push' the waste down the line anyway they can, and I don't think any solution is even talked about. Environmental awareness is extremely poor all over the country and much, much worse in the *katchi abadi* and rural areas where raw sewage is disposed of directly into drains and rivers and eventually into the ocean.

Q. Let's move away from that thought. Tell me about the land your home is built on. Did your father purchase the land and build on it, or was he the first one to claim it and occupy it?

Nadeem: My father bought it from a previous owner. There was no legal transaction and there is still no legal documentation or title to the property. There was a small one-room structure and a bathroom, with corrugated aluminum sheets for the roof. When he was able to save some money, *Abbu* added rooms and improved the structure.

Q. How many rooms do you have now?

Nadeem: We have three rooms and one bathroom on the ground floor. One room is for our parents, one for the girls, where all the bedding, mattresses, and pillows are stacked during the day and spread out at night. The third room is a sparsely furnished sitting room. We have a small kitchen with natural gas and electricity. Later, we added two rooms upstairs, one each for my brother and me, and a few years later we added a bathroom upstairs. The total covered area of the property on the ground level is about 1,200 square feet and includes an open parking area for our small car and the motorbikes. The two rooms and bathroom on the upper floor are about 300 square feet and we have a small terrace area where we can enjoy the evening breeze and coolness... until the mosquitos start biting.

Q. Before propane or gas connections, was cooking done on wood-burning fire or with kerosene stoves?

Nadeem: We had wood-burning stoves for cooking because that is the custom in the villages. Then we got propane cylinders. I don't think we ever had kerosene stoves. In 2003, we got natural gas lines installed and that has helped tremendously. The gas is supplied by the gas utility company and I think it's billed at a flat rate.

Q. Is there a heater for hot water in the kitchen and bathrooms?

Nadeem: Last winter was very cold in Karachi so we had a 'Geyser' gas heater installed for hot water in the bathroom on the ground level. That has made life easier, especially for my parents. Before that, we were used to taking cold baths because the weather is usually quite warm. Occasionally, we would heat a large pot of water and mix it in a bucket of regular cold water but that was a lot of work. We are used to taking baths from a bucket and don't have overhead showers in our bathrooms. There's no hot water connection in the kitchen.

Q. Are there regular ovens in the kitchen for baking, or microwave ovens?

Nadeem: No, just gas stoves. We don't have any appliances like an oven, toaster, coffee maker, or microwave.

Q. How about machines to do laundry?

Nadeem: We got a clothes washer in 2008 but the clothes are hung out to dry on clotheslines. There's an electric iron to press clothes. The laundry is done mostly by my mother.

Q. You have a refrigerator now. When was that acquired?

Nadeem: I think we got the first one in 2004 or 2005. It was a used one. We replaced it with a better one in 2008 with a small freezer to make ice cubes in a tray. But there's no room to freeze any food.

Q. When did Saleem Bhai get his first bicycle?

Nadeem: Probably in the late 1990s. He used to walk to work before that.

Q. Did you have a bicycle to go to school or did you walk?

Nadeem: It was a thirty-minute walk to the public school but the TCF school was only ten minutes away on foot.

Q. When was the first motorcycle purchased?

Nadeem: Abbu got a motorbike in 2003, and that was because Uzma was starting college, so he would take her to the bus stop. You could say our transport needs changed as we progressed in our education. After I was older, I used my father's motorbike to do chores and transport my sisters. Yasir got a motorbike in 2013 to get to college and back. Abbu's work was not far from the bus stop so he would drop and pick up my sisters, sometimes making as many as six trips in a day. Other men in the community would needle him that he was going through all this work of transporting the girls for no benefit, that they will soon get married and go away, but he ignored such talk. He has been an amazing father.

Q. You were in the student dorm at IBA for four years and came home on weekends by bus, changing routes a couple of times. How far is the bus stop from your home? And, have the bus service and frequency improved?

Nadeem: The closest bus stop is about a twenty-minute walk. Actually, the service is the same but the frequency has gone down and that's true for the whole city. About eight years ago, there were 32,000 buses and today there are only 8,000 buses in the city. The services are privately operated and probably not very profitable. There is no regulation of the system and infrastructure is very weak. It has been peaceful for the last three years but when conditions in the city were really bad, with frequent riots and chaos, buses would be burnt in protest and there was no recourse for the owners.

Q. There's a Metro system of mass transit in Islamabad and Lahore, which seems to be working well. Is there a planned mass transit in the works for Karachi?

Nadeem: Yes, there is and it might be launched soon but planners say it will only meet 10 percent of the transportation needs. I hope it will make a difference and the network will be expanded. There has been tremendous increase in motorbikes because bus service is so poor.

Q. The drawback is that women don't drive motorbikes because of cultural taboos. Do you see that changing?

Nadeem: I would like to see women ride motorbikes or scooters as they do in neighboring countries but I doubt it will happen in my lifetime. The cultural taboo is very strong. There is a young girl in Ibrahim Goth, about 14 or 15 years old and she's a TCF student. She is occasionally seen riding a motorbike. I think that's great but it shocks most people. It was big news in the community.

Q. When was the family car purchased and for how much?

Nadeem: We got the car about three years ago. It's a used 2006 Suzuki. We paid 550,000 rupees ($5,000) for it.

Q. Can you call for an Uber or Careem car?

Nadeem: With an average household income of fifteen or twenty thousand rupees a month, no one in Ibrahim Goth can afford an Uber. So, there is no demand. I have not used Careem or Uber cars from Ibrahim Goth.

Q. So, your walk to the bus stop is about twenty minutes. How long is the bus ride to your workplace?

Nadeem: The bus ride takes about two hours and I have to change buses. I avoid using the motorbike because of the distance and it's hard on my back.

Q. The homes are not numbered and the streets don't have names or numbers. How is the property identified for the utilities that you receive? Are electricity, gas, and water metered or monitored through a central system, or does a meter-reader person come around to take a reading and do you receive a monthly bill for the power and gas consumed?

Nadeem: We receive power and gas through the utility companies and we get a flat-rate bill each month from the gas company and pay it regularly. Most people don't pay the electric bill and get away with it because the system isn't perfect. Half the homes in the area don't have electric meters or legal power connections. I'm not sure how the meters are read or how the charges are determined. It's still quite new. But at least we do have power and gas.

Q. In case of emergency, how can someone call for police, fire, or ambulance services?

Nadeem: There is no land line phone service in our *goth*. For police assistance or ambulance, they could be called by mobile phone and asked to meet at some landmark and brought to where they are needed. Without the street and house numbers, it is not possible for them to find the home location.

Q. Is your car used very much or just occasionally? And are your sisters learning to drive?

Nadeem: I would say it's a luxury and we use it occasionally when my mother or sisters need to be taken somewhere. I think it's a good thing that my sisters are interested in driving. Yasir is the driver in the family.

Q. When did the family get the first TV and do you have more than one? Do most homes have TVs?

Nadeem: We have a TV and we got it in 2003. I think most of the homes in Ibrahim Goth have a television.

Q. Do you have any public libraries in the area?

Nadeem: Not a free-standing public library in the usual sense but in December 2017, we set up a community library in a local mosque. A few of us TCF alumni boys asked the *masjid* management for use of space in the two upper floors, one floor as a reading room and library, and the top floor for recreation such as table tennis or programs of invited speakers, discussions, or similar activity. The reading room is also used as a place for tutoring school children. The library is run by volunteers who are TCF alumni and we have Urdu and English books. We are adding books and hope to make it a diverse place with books in all local languages and on all topics. In the future, we may be able to use the space for girls at special times or build a separate space for them. These ideas will take some time.

Q. Would you have biographies or writings by controversial political figures, books on literature and poetry?

Nadeem: Yes, absolutely. We've had to respond to some critical questions and so far, we've been able to satisfy the masjid management that this is a community endeavor and we respect the space. We get the English daily *Dawn* paper and we also had a team of local children participate in a spelling bee competition.

Q. Whose initiative and brainchild is this project?

Nadeem: Several TCF alumni came together and thought of it because we were seeing declining interest in books and reading. We were also concerned that the usual places for the young boys to hang out were not promoting healthy ideas, so we want this to be a positive environment for the youth.

Q. Is this a lending library as well?

Nadeem: Yes, we have a simple lending system and books can be checked out at no cost.

Q. Related to the homes and streets not being numbered, how are you registered to vote and were you and the family included in the last census?

Nadeem: We have CNICs (Computerized National Identity Cards) and we registered in the last census so we can vote. The gas and electric utility companies have identified the houses in their own ways, probably by the meter number. When people have their CNICs made, they give a fictitious house number which goes on the CNIC but the number has no legal standing because the area is a *katchi abadi*. The census workers have their unique lists to go by but I don't think the lists are accurate. The utility companies have a better system of home identification for monitoring consumption and for billing. It's all very confusing, not a standardized system.

Q. So, what is your home number, did you 'select' that number yourself and how can you be sure that the same number is not being used by another home a few blocks away?

Nadeem: We can't be certain that there's no duplication but our home number is 119 and that's the address given on our CNICs. There must be people who don't have house numbers and don't feel the need for it. It's a haphazard system. Very few homes have the house numbers on the outside. There is no postal service or courier service in the area, so there's no need to have the houses numbered. When we've had the need to receive any important papers by courier, we receive the package at my father's factory address. People who live in the *katchi abadis*—especially if they are going to university or applying for jobs and expecting important documents—they make arrangements to receive their documents at some other location in the city. We have no postal addresses, hence no postal delivery service.

Q. Do you and your father and siblings pay income tax and is there withholding from your earnings?

Nadeem: My father's income is below the taxable amount so he doesn't have to pay any income tax. Uzma, Sidra, and I are subject to withholding, so yes, we file income tax returns.

* * * * *

The brilliant stories of the Saleem Family of Ibrahim Goth are the cosmic fairytale of this remarkable set of five shining stars. Tenaciously, they keep going and advance their career paths. Money or prestige are not the drivers. In each of them, there is a yearning to do good, to fight for social justice and to contribute to progressive changes in the community. These stories represent many more amazing boys and girls who are on similar transformative journeys with their equally amazing parents and families. Together, these are the frontline, vanguard armies of our 'Agents of Change'. Here are stellar examples of a few more TCF achievers, what they are doing, and their dreams for the future....

- **Ghulam Waris** is from Orangi Town and graduated in 2019 from an IBA computer science program. He is currently working at the A.P. Moller MAERSK company as a Supply Chain Associate. His father is a laborer.
- **Hasan Akhtar Siddiqui** is from Korangi and plans to graduate from the Institute of Business Management (IoBM) in 2021. He would like to be an economist, an entrepreneur, and social activist. He's a finance and audit intern at a consultancy company. His mother is a social worker and a newspaper columnist and father an interior decorator.
- **Ahsan Riaz** from Quaidabad, and currently at IBA; expects to graduate in economics in 2021. He aspires to be a research analyst. His father is a laborer and mother a home-maker.
- **Najaf Baig** is from Surjani Town. He expects to graduate in civil engineering in 2021 from the NED University of Engineering and Technology, Karachi and plans to do post-graduate study. He is doing his Final Year Project on seismic evaluation of heritage buildings in Karachi. He teaches part-time at an institute and also home tutors. His sister is a teacher at TCF; his father is a service worker and his mother a home-maker.
- **Saba Pervez** is from Bhittaiabad, Gulistan-e-Johar. She expects to graduate from FAST University in 2021 from the computer science program and plans to be a web developer and graphic designer. She tutors for income. Her mother is a home-maker.
- **Muhammad Amir Jamil** from Saifal-Choro Goth expects to graduate from IoBM in 2021 from the media program. He aspires to be a photo-journalist and social media handler. He presently works pro bono as a photographer 'just for the experience'.

- **Moiz Ahmed** is from Taiser Town and expects to graduate from IoBM in 2021 with dual majors in math and economics. He would like to be an economist. His father is a carpenter and mother a home-maker.
- **Muhammad Waqar Ahmed** from Korangi graduated from the NED University of Engineering and Technology, Karachi in 2019 from the electronic engineering program. He is currently working as an Assistant Systems Engineer. He has a sister in medical college and another sister at TCF College. His father is a tailor and mother is a teacher.
- **Muskan Amjad** from Korangi expects to graduate from IBA in 2021 from the computer science program. She would like to do a master's in computer science. She works as content writer for a website to support the family income. Her father is an auto-driver and mother a home-maker.
- **Moiza Naveed** is from Jumma Himayati Goth and expects to graduate from Habib University in 2022 from the social development and policy program. She would like to work in journalism and teaching. Her father works in administration and mother is a home-maker.
- **Ayesha Rahman** from Baldia Town expects to graduate from Habib from the communication and design program, she would like to work in sound and film design. Her father is a laborer and mother a home-maker.

* * * * *

Zafar Ali deserves a little extra space because his story is special. Zafar went to a TCF school in Baldia Town, Karachi. He is one of ten children in a Pakhtun family from a village in the (former) FATA, where he went to a government school up to 7th grade and could only speak Pashtu. In 2017, his father was a truck driver and hauled oil or goods from Karachi to the northern cities for onward transit into Afghanistan. His dad is now driving a taxi in Karachi (2019). Two sisters are married; five younger sisters and two brothers are in school. Zafar has a campus job at Lewis & Clark College in Oregon; he sends some money home for support.

Zafar: When my family moved to Karachi in 2010, I couldn't speak Urdu or English. My first interaction in Urdu was when I went to a store to buy something, or I asked a kid to kick the ball to me. We were staying with relatives because we didn't have a place of our own. Everything was so new, I was totally lost. I had no idea why we had moved from our village. My father wasn't at home, and I didn't know if I was going to continue school or just wander in the streets. It was after a few months that a friend told me about the TCF school in the neighborhood. I would see the teachers coming in TCF vans and the children walking to the school in their neat uniforms, but I thought this was such a fancy school and that I would never be able to go there. But my friend told me that I could, and that education was almost free, or whatever you could afford. So, I went to the school and asked for admission…without a parent.

Q. Was it the kind of school that you had imagined?

Zafar: In my village school, there would be fifty children on the floor in a small classroom. The teacher didn't know our names. I had seen a picture of a classroom with children sitting on furniture and pictures on the walls and I wondered if such schools really existed. When I went to the TCF school to take the admission test, the principal asked me to sit at a desk in a classroom, just like the modern classroom I had seen in the picture. I wondered if I would be studying in this classroom and I said to myself 'Wow, this is a real classroom!'.

Q. So, when did you graduate from the TCF school and what has happened since then?

Zafar: I started in 8th grade at TCF and finished 10th grade in 2013. In early 2014, my school principal called me and told me about a college scholarship and that TCF could help me apply for it. TCF staff took me to a presentation about this college system, the United World Colleges. There were children from many other schools, and they were going to choose only five from Karachi. I felt like one of the least likely to be selected. Anyway, I was given the application and I started the process. I went through with my interview and went home and waited. Then one day the phone rings and Sarah from UWC says 'Congratulations, you've been accepted to UWC in Singapore…' and I just couldn't believe it!

Q. So, did you go to Singapore?

Zafar: I applied for a visa. They required many documents and a lot of information and I struggled to get everything together. In the end, my visa application was rejected but they transferred my application to UWC in Bosnia, and I went there and joined in the second semester.

Q. Did that hamper your progress?

Zafar: Again, I was worried about the competition I would face. I was intimidated by all these children from the best schools in the world. But I worked very hard and figured out what I had to do, and it went smoothly.

Q. Did you know what you wanted to do when you were at UWC in Bosnia?

Zafar: I was thinking I'd like to be a doctor. So, I took chemistry and biology, but I changed my mind in the second year. I began to think about social change and leadership and I decided to do something in that direction.

Q. So, what will you do?

Zafar: I'm studying political science and economics, on a full scholarship here at Lewis & Clark College in Portland, Oregon. I expect to graduate in 2020.

Q. Did you think you would ever get this far? And where do you go from here?

Zafar: I often wonder at how far I have come. But I will go back to Pakistan. I don't exactly know what I will do but I will go back. I will not forget where I come from.

Update

May 2019: Zafar is hoping to go to graduate school and do his doctorate. In the long term, he plans to go into politics as an elected public representative and policy maker. 'I see a good politician as a teacher who informs people of the best options, one who can direct public opinion and construct the best policies with grassroots support. I'll do the best I can.'

February 2021: Zafar is starting his second semester at Syracuse University in New York. It is a five-year PhD program.

Notes

1. Saleem or Salim are interchangeable spelling of the same name.
2. Each school 'unit' is a complete cohort with its unique student population, teachers, and staff.
3. *The Stanford Encyclopedia of Philosophy* is an excellent resource, https://plato.stanford. edu/.
4. *The Economy of Modern Sindh* (Karachi: Oxford University Press, 2019) highlights the socioeconomic problems that have beset Sindh and proposes a multi-pronged strategy to address the challenges.
5. The Volunteer & Alumni Department has replaced the Placement Desk at TCF.
6. Daata Darbar: a masjid and Sufi place of congregating that allowed travelers to stay for the night.
7. Shazia Kamal later headed the Education Department and led the development of TCF textbooks and other curriculum and pedagogical standards at TCF.
8. Academic Achievement Plus was an after-school initiative. It's valuable contribution to education and Arif Irfanullah's leadership and support for ADP are discussed in Chapter 4.
9. A *mashk* was a large leather pouch with a shoulder strap, big enough to carry about 5 gallons of water. *Mashki* was the man who delivered a *mashk* of water for a modest price.

Chapter Four

Agents of Change

The preceding chapters were a task of compiling personal insights, historical information, some suggestions for change in the systems, stories of the incredible people and work of TCF, and brief accounts of the student achievers of TCF. This chapter is about a short list of admirable change agents, a diverse but select group of persons who have demonstrated their dedication to transforming education. As innovative thinkers, policy influencers, and advocates of solutions for education, their contributions are both frontline and behind-the-scenes. We begin with economist Dr Ishrat Husain who has been a leading proponent for equal opportunity in education.

4.1 Dr Ishrat Husain

Ishrat Husain is best known for his career as an economist and banker which spans over twenty years with World Bank in Washington, D.C., and Nigeria, followed by six years as Governor of State Bank of Pakistan, the country's central bank. Post-retirement from the banking sector, Dr Husain accepted the Dean's position at Institute of Business Administration (IBA), a prestigious Karachi institution, originally established by the USAID program in the mid-1950s. He has authored several books and monographs. Among his notable publications are *Economic Management in Pakistan, 1999–2002* (OUP, 2003); *Pakistan: The Economy of an Elitist State* (OUP, 1999; Second edition, 2019); *Governing the Ungovernable* (OUP, 2018); and *The Economy of Modern Sindh* (OUP, 2019).

In his writings and on several occasions, Dr Husain has expressed the critical importance of a robust education system as a prerequisite for national development and this conversation with Dr Husain covers multiple aspects of education: the IBA example of institution building, utilizing USAID resources and local philanthropy; organizational

re-structuring and suggestions for further decentralization of the
system from provinces to local districts; and insights on how TCF should
leverage its management expertise to partner with public education.
He suggests the future role of TCF as a provider of education delivery
services with focus on improvement of the quality of teaching and
management of education systems.

Q. After your professional career with World Bank, and later as Governor of the State Bank, what took you in the direction of education?

Dr Ishrat Husain: Well, with the banks that was a job, and I think by
the grace of Allah I delivered what I was expected to. But I realized that
investing in education was my passion because that is the future of the
country. The knowledge economy is driving the global economy and
if we don't go in that direction, I think we will be left behind because,
in these times, the natural resources—oil, minerals, financial capital—
these are not the big players or drivers of the economy anymore. It is all
about new inventions, innovations, imitations, and application of new
technology to goods and services. These are the forces that will move us
forward. We must strengthen our human resources, and it's good that
we have a much younger population. Our median age is 22 or 23 and
there are demographic changes taking place in the rest of the world.
In Europe, America, Japan, the aging population is increasing. Our
population is young, so we can not only do well for our country but also
become the workforce for the rest of the world, if we provide the right
skills training to our younger people. So, that is the premise on which I
decided to contribute to higher education in Pakistan.

Q. As the former Dean and Director of IBA, what were your most satisfying accomplishments?

Dr Ishrat Husain: I am pleased that I had a hand in transforming the
business school into a comprehensive institution of higher education,
which offers undergraduate programs in computer science and IT
services, as well as master's and doctoral programs in these fields,
plus undergraduate programs in liberal arts and social sciences and
humanities, and undergraduate and graduate programs in economics
and mathematics. We also set up Centers of Excellence in journalism,

Islamic finance, entrepreneurial development, and executive education. These were some of the initiatives which I took in my eight years of service at IBA; so, it is now a broad-based, multidisciplinary institution, much more than a business school.

Q. **Please share how IBA was established in 1955 as a USAID program and its impact on the education system of university education in Pakistan.**

Dr Ishrat Husain: Yes, that is correct. It was initially managed by Wharton Business School of Pennsylvania, followed by University of Southern California until 1962. The original faculty and the Dean and Director of IBA were from Wharton or USC. Pakistani faculty members were also sent to these schools and other American universities for graduate and doctoral studies, to be trained for faculty positions at IBA. So, this was the first business school established outside north America. Even in Europe, they didn't have any American business schools and Pakistan had followed the colonial British system. IBA brought about a qualitative change in Pakistan by switching over to the US education system, which is now well established all over the country. IBA was the pioneer in making the shift from the British system, in which you had annual examinations and there were no mid-terms or semester exams, no assignments, and rote learning was the pedagogic rule. In the US system, it was more problem solving and critical thinking, and that was a big shift in the whole pattern of education in Pakistan. Most of the universities follow the semester system now, not the annual board exam system.

Q. **That is good information on IBA, its connection to the US and its role in bringing about changes in the broader system. It sounds like IBA was one of the better successes of the USAID programs.**

Dr Ishrat Husain: Yes, I agree totally. I think USAID was very generous and several Pakistani institutions received assistance from outside agencies, but they collapsed soon as the agencies dropped off the scene. There are few institutions that have been sustained and further enhanced. Yes, the IBA seeds were sown by USAID but its sustenance was by Pakistani academics and policy makers.

Author: ...thanks to good stewardship at IBA.

Dr Ishrat Husain: Well, even before I joined IBA, it was well established as a business school. I was able to see its transformation into a quality institution of higher education by raising 50 million rupees from the private sector for IT and other departments because the government was not able to provide any funding for the physical infrastructure. The structures were built around 1962 when USAID left. There had been no additions to the physical space or the recreational facilities, and the student population had gone up from 200 in the Sixties to nearly 3,000 and we had to build new classrooms, labs and dormitories for the boys and girls, and new specialty centers. So, we constructed about thirty new buildings and facilities inside the Karachi University campus to cater to the needs of the future and no more money has to be spent on that because IBA can accommodate additional student enrollment for ten years without difficulty.

Q. So, when did IBA become independent from Karachi University?

Dr Ishrat Husain: IBA was part of Karachi University until 1994, when it became an autonomous degree-awarding institution. At present, there are no linkages between Karachi University and IBA. The land title has been transferred to IBA for the space that IBA occupies on the university campus. IBA has its own Board of Governors and the Chancellor or Patron of the Board is the governor of Sindh. Most IBA governors are from the private sector and business community so it has a lot of independence for governance. Unlike other universities, IBA is not dependent on the government for financial resources. We have autonomy in determining our salary structure and attract high quality faculty from all over the world, and our fee structure is also much higher than Karachi University which charges a few thousand rupees per year, and we charge Rs 300,000 per semester. So, we are quite independent and self-financing. That's why there is no interference from the government and why IBA has done so well as far as admissions and appointments are concerned, both based on merit.

Q. **For the longest time, you've been a champion for creating a level playing field for education, especially as it relates to preparing for and taking the entrance exams for top tier universities like IBA. How does IBA support that objective? And how are the volunteer TCF Alumni and TCF Ambassadors helping to prepare TCF students for university admission?**

Dr Ishrat Husain: IBA has a 'needs blind' admissions policy. Any student who passes the rigorous entrance exam is assured of complete financial support if the student's family does not have the resources. We have scholarship programs, stipends, grants—many ways in which we provide financial support. In addition, we have a National Talent Hunt Program (NTHP), through which we bring these children from Intermediate colleges to IBA. We coach them in math and English and we train them in social skills, teach them how to dress, how to answer questions, provide them with general knowledge, teach them computer skills, and for those who are selected on merit through our entrance exam, we take care of all their expenses—living and all instructional expenses. And we even give them Rs 3,000 as 'pocket money' allowance so they don't feel at a disadvantage compared to their well-off colleagues. If the students are selected for any of the IBA programs, we give them a full scholarship. We take 30 to 40 students every year through these programs and the number is increasing. That's how IBA helps to level the playing field for children who have not been to an elite private school.

There is a huge academic gap between applicants from elite private schools and TCF schools, especially in math and English. And the gap needs to be filled with extra coaching in these areas. So, there's a standing partnership with TCF, through which the TCF Alumni Development Program (ADP) and TCF Ambassadors [university student-volunteers] run a coaching program at IBA to prepare TCF students for the entrance exam and offer guidance to apply to various universities in the country. The ADP-managed coaching classes at IBA are year-round, with several groups or batches of students attending three times weekly. During summer, the coaching classes are more rigorous and more frequent, seven days a week, for all students, and we have longer, all-day sessions, because the students are on vacation from their Intermediate colleges and tutoring programs.

Box 4.1 IBA, TCF and ADP Facilitate Admission of TCF Students to Top Universities

A partnership with IBA was the first collaboration between TCF and a major Pakistani university, spurring the birth of the TCF Alumni Development Program (ADP) to facilitate admissions of underprivileged TCF students to top tier universities. The IBA-TCF arrangement led to other universities, such as Habib, GIKI, NED and others to follow suit, paving the way for TCF alumni to prepare for the entrance exam, take the tests, and qualify for admission and scholarship. This has been made possible with Dr Husain's support in promoting a level playing field for underprivileged students to have an opportunity for education in the top universities. Dr Husain has been a valuable 'Agent of Change' and his contributions to national education reforms and governance reforms are commendable. TCF alumnus Nadeem Hussain's enrollment at IBA in 2010 and his presence there as a student for four years played a key role in establishing the connections between TCF, IBA and the TCF Alumni Development Program. – *Author*

Q. Legislation has been enacted but is there any serious activity to achieve universal education? What are your views on the challenge of insufficient access to schools, the poor quality of education, and management of the system? And do you think devolution has been a step in the right direction?

Dr Ishrat Husain: I think some good initiatives have been introduced, particularly in Punjab, where private schools have come up in the rural areas and these schools provide about 40 percent of primary enrollment. Punjab has also outsourced a number of public schools to organizations like TCF to improve quality of education and to increase enrollment. The problem has been the politically inspired recruitment of teachers in public schools who would not otherwise qualify to teach. Many of them are not interested in teaching but they were appointed for political reasons. In the last few years, I have seen that this trend is being reversed and, even in Sindh which was most notorious for this practice of political appointments, teachers are now being hired on merit. They have introduced a biometric system and teacher absenteeism has been checked through that; otherwise, there were teachers drawing salaries and not showing up for work. So, it will take some time to find a total solution.

In my article, *Reforming the Government in Pakistan*,[1] I recommend that we should decentralize and further devolve primary and secondary education to the local district governments, much like in the US, where the counties (districts, in Pakistan) collect the property taxes and most of the tax revenue is used to finance the public-school system. Unless you do that, a highly centralized system controlled by the provincial governments will not have good governance, supervision, or inspection and quality control. My difficulty with the present system is that it is still highly centralized at the provincial level. It needs to be further devolved and financial resources given to the local governments, the districts. There are many capable retired educators, civil servants, army officers, and others who could serve on district education boards, and these boards would oversee the management and supervision of public and private schools in the districts; hopefully, they could also work towards improvement in the quality of education. Local education boards should be making decisions that are now made by bureaucrats in the provincial capitals. This would solve the governance and management issues of primary and secondary education. I think college education should remain with the provincial governments and university and higher education should be the responsibility of the federal government. The division of labor between these three branches of education would result in better focus and efficiency. That is the essence of my education reform package.

Q. And, what are your thoughts on the TCF model of schools, and its programs?

Dr Ishrat Husain: I have suggested that TCF should market a package of education services which will make a difference in the delivery of education. TCF has successfully developed a good model of trained female teachers, pedagogical tools, curriculum content, assessment methods, quality control and management processes. These elements should be packaged as a service delivery model and sold to other schools who could greatly benefit from it. Even the government could purchase the TCF package, with TCF to provide technical assistance and training. The multiplier effect and impact will be much higher than the present

TCF model in which you have to rely on donors to fund the schools and operating costs for the programs. That way, you will be saved from the uncertainties and the numbers game of the current model, which will have a miniscule impact on a national scale. The real value and assets of TCF are the curriculum content, the pedagogical tools that have been developed, the assessment methods, the management expertise—these can be leveraged and, as I said, TCF can provide the technical assistance.

Author: I believe your suggestions are in line with what is being developed by the TCF Strategic Development Unit to package and market its intellectual property for greater national impact. I agree that the 'service delivery package' product should be marketed for a price where there is genuine provider demand, so the purchaser has a financial stake in improving the quality of education and in the successful application of the services. The package should not be free of cost because, as a free service, it has little or no value.

Dr Ishrat Husain: Any offer of 'free' goods or services just does not create the same kind of commitment, which is why I am not a fan of DFID or USAID grants. In many cases, recipients accept the grant money but, after a short time, they lose interest in the program or project. Many of the grant-funded programs are not sustainable because the recipients have nothing to lose. They didn't reach into their own pockets and use their own money to invest in it or, as Americans say, they 'don't have skin in the game'. Aid programs only work if the owners and recipients have a financial stake in it.

4.2 Shashi Buluswar
PhD, University of California, Berkeley

Shashi Buluswar is originally from Mumbai, India, which makes it interesting that he would say glowing things about Pakistan and TCF, but he's just that kind of an upright person. As a visionary and pragmatic champion for global development, Shashi lets his work affirm what he believes in. I am amazed by the wide range of Shashi's experiences and the impressive projects he leads. When I first met him, Shashi was a partner at Dalberg Global Development Advisors, a strategy consulting firm that served clients in international development. At Dalberg, Shashi helped the UN Peacekeeping Department in restructuring its global operations, the Gates Foundation on large-scale agricultural development programs in Africa and Asia, the US government's efforts in post-conflict development in Afghanistan, several multinational corporations in their social responsibility agendas, and dozens of NGOs in fighting for human rights, health, education, and economic empowerment. Before Dalberg, he was an Associate Partner at McKinsey & Company, and a Visiting Professor at Northwestern University. Shashi teaches international development at the University of California Berkeley and frequently cites TCF as an exemplary NGO. He is a popular speaker at TCF events in the US and addresses '*How to Scale Social Impact*' and the importance of education.

Shashi is CEO and founder of the Institute for Transformative Technologies at the Lawrence Berkeley National Lab. He is lead author of a groundbreaking study, *50 Breakthroughs: Critical Scientific and Technological Advances Needed for Sustainable Global Development.*[2] He has an MS and PhD in Artificial Intelligence, and an MBA from Northwestern University. He has made several trips to Pakistan on collaborative projects. Along with his family, Shashi is an avid supporter of TCF. In 2013, Shashi nominated TCF for the Skoll Foundation's Award for Social Entrepreneurship, the highest recognition received by TCF. Below is the conversation I had with Shashi at UC Berkeley.

Q. There is recognition that Pakistan's problems can be addressed by Pakistanis without dependence on foreign aid, or foreign experts to come and tell us what to do and how to do it. What are your thoughts on that?

Shashi Buluswar: I am an absolute believer in this notion that only Pakistanis are going to solve Pakistan's problems. On one hand, we are all global citizens and one of the things I keep saying is that—whether it's global poverty or global health issues—as global citizens, each of us has the right and responsibility to work on them anywhere in the world. But the only way any country's or community's problems get solved is that the people from the country take the lead. Again, whether it's TCF or Indus Hospitals, these are not just examples of local leadership but off-the-chart, exceptional examples. About TCF, here's what's extraordinary: there are many organizations that are built on passion and real commitment, many organizations that have good strategic vision of real game-changing scales; organizations with good processes and good leadership in place; and there are organizations that really understand how to work at the community level—knowing that two communities, even if they are a few miles apart, are very different communities. I've never seen any organization be able to pull off all of that so well. In my opinion, of all the NGOs and social change organizations in the world that I have come across, I have never come across one that does such an extraordinary job of both enabling each one of these and at the same time integrating all of them into something successful. The value of such incredible organizations cannot be overstated. I have come across very few that are capable of executing as well as TCF does.

Q. That's very flattering for TCF. For those reasons, I suppose, you were very kind to recommend TCF for the Skoll Award for Social Entrepreneurship in 2013, one of the most prestigious recognitions that TCF has received.

Shashi Buluswar: Well, recommendations are easy. It's the other side that is hard, which is earning the award and delivering great programs.

Q. Tell us a little bit about the process, the behind-the-scenes conversations that take place in foundations that award grants.

Shashi Buluswar: In my old job at Dalberg, I often served as an adviser to several foundations. As a result of that, I am able to do a little bit of match-making. But, again, the organizations have to earn it. It's one of the privileges I enjoy but personally I have very little influence beyond saying, 'Hey, check out this organization', a bit beyond nominating. Behind any success story, there's a whole lot of stuff, some of which is positive and some of it is not positive, and we've seen great examples of celebrated success stories and then something comes out later. You can have extraordinary people do things that are troubling. So, behind the scenes, one of the conversations that happens is: do we know everything we need to know. I often know many of these individuals at the donor foundations who will say 'Okay, thanks for the official recommendation. Now tell us what we need to worry about.' Of all the organizations, the hundreds I have worked with at Dalberg and beyond, I have never had any reservations about TCF. From my lens, which is the same lens I apply to plenty of other organizations, there are only positives.

Q. When an organization is being considered for awards and recognitions, how much weight is given to leadership, the individuals behind the organization? And how did that play out in the case of TCF?

Shashi Buluswar: That's a great question. The social sector loves to worship individual heroes, because they love the narrative of the individual conquering odds and doing great things in changing the world and saving the world. Personally, I find that aspect of things troubling because it shouldn't be about an individual saving the world. Unfortunately, there is too much of that. It should be about a process and system. On the other hand, things don't happen without individual leaders, but I wish that there were more emphases on systems and processes than on individuals, because individuals themselves—even extraordinary individuals—can be flawed. And what you don't want is the whole cause suffering because of a flawed leader. Similarly, that individual can go off and do something else, something could happen to them, and we don't want a large system depending on, and so vulnerable to, the presence and strengths of one individual or a small group of individuals. Having said that, you do need leaders and, ultimately, when the right donor organizations use the right lenses to give these awards, they look at how resilient the system is. So, in my opinion, they do their best to balance the narrative of an individual leader with the resilience of an organization, and to the absence of a leader like that. In the context of organizations like TCF, they look at what processes are in place, how replicable are these processes, how dependent are they on individuals, what if we swap these individuals out, would the systems still continue. And my understanding is that Skoll Foundation found that TCF today is not dependent on individuals because the processes are so well thought-through, well-documented and systematized, that every time a new school comes on board, it's this whole idea of 'TCF-in-a-Box' that can be replicated.

Q. What is your broader perspective on Pakistan's development? How do you see Pakistan breaking through on the world stage?

Shashi Buluswar: The optimistic scenario is that, given the amount of technical talent and the strength of the private sector in Pakistan, it joins the broader conversation of global trade and really figures out a few niches, whatever they are. For instance, in India, the outsourcing and IT thing was big. There's simply no reason why Pakistan can't have the same thing because it's the same DNA, it has a number of really good technical institutions, the private sector is almost equally strong. Obviously, a lot depends on broader context and this optimistic scenario would require a lot of things coming together as well—and education is again, fundamental to that. There are external and political influences that haven't positively contributed to Pakistan but all those things being what they are, outside of its control, really good investment in solid education and entrepreneurship training will be the way to get there.

Reflecting on India, for all its current problems, it was able to capitalize on that particular wave. It had a lot of people with technical talent and entrepreneurial zeal, and access to finance, so the system came together. All of this happened in the Nineties when the Indian government did a fundamental shift in a large number of policies—trade, stock market, access to capital, regulatory reform. It was comprehensive and perfectly timed. If it had happened ten years later, India would have missed the IT boom. The question for Pakistan is, given that there are extractives in parts of the country, there is technical talent for IT, so what's the systemic approach? Broad-based growth doesn't come from only one sector, which is the problem India is facing in that we see massive growth in the high-end consumer sector, in the IT sector, but disparity is still pretty bad. One thing India has probably not done a good job of is broad-based growth because I think there's been too much attention on the narrow successes, number of billionaires, etc., to the point where the deeper problems have been ignored around the systemic exclusion of communities and around the growing disparity. That's the challenge Pakistan faces: can it learn from the mistakes of other countries as well as from things that have gone well, and actually make it broad-based for parts of the country that have not been part of the Karachi-Lahore-Islamabad conversation? Can these be brought into the growth?

Author's note: that conversation was in Berkeley. A few more quotes from Shashi are added here...

• 'Fighting global poverty is not about charity. The moment you put on a 'charity' hat, you're missing the point. I think far too many organizations have used the charity model... *'Oh, we'll save those poor people'*. It's not about that. These are phenomenally important problems of huge global significance that have to be solved... [and] we have to bring the best minds to the problems.' (Source: From video, 'How to Fight Global Poverty').

- Effective organizations are a catalyst for change on a large scale. TCF is one of those unique organizations. Through my work and my travels, I have come to know hundreds of NGOs. I've always believed that well-run local NGOs are often much more efficient and effective than international NGOs, and TCF is an example of that. I would rate TCF among the three best NGOs I've seen anywhere in the world—and certainly the best education NGO, by far. TCF has strong governance; they really understand the needs and challenges of the communities they serve; they design creative and thoughtful programs; they know where to invest and where to stay lean; and they produce exceptional results. (Source: Speaking in Palo Alto, California, May 20, 2017).

4.3 Tooba Akhtar
Teach for Pakistan

"Children are our future. Teach them well and let them lead the way."
Linda Creed and Max Masser, song writers

Meet and applaud Tooba Akhtar, for her devotion and enthusiasm for education of the underprivileged child. Tooba a remarkably sensitive and 'privileged' young woman (privileged, by her own definition), exemplifies the best of human spirit and compassion to transform lives through education. Here, she candidly reveals her emotions and offers glimpses of her own journey as she seeks solutions for social injustice through her class-awakening experience with Teach for Pakistan (TFP). She currently heads the Leadership and Training team at TFP.

Tooba is a 2011 graduate of LUMS and, like most fresh grads, she 'applied everywhere' for a job but also explored TFP, which was just getting off the ground. She met with the TFP team, coming away with a feeling that education just might be her calling. 'The team seemed like very nice people, but I wasn't seriously considering doing anything with them. Then I received an offer from TFP and signed up for training as a Fellow, thinking I would give it a shot and see what happens.' Part of the six-week training and teaching assignment was at a public school—planning of lessons, teaching, observing, the typical day starting at 7 a.m. and ending at 11 p.m. after debriefing meetings at TFP.

Box 4.2 Teach for Pakistan

Teach for Pakistan is a network partner of 'Teach for All', a global organization with a mission to expand educational opportunity and increase the impact of local organizations. It works through trained college graduates and young professionals called Fellows who commit to teach for two years at schools in underserved areas. Upon completing the two-year fellowship, most Fellows continue to work in education in some capacity, either teaching at schools in underserved communities or contributing in other ways to improvement of education and policy. The nascent TFP program was incubated by funding assistance from Aman Foundation and holds great promise for improvement of pedagogical quality in the under-resourced system of public schools and low-cost private schools.

TFP is now independently headquartered in Islamabad and offers opportunity for college graduates and young professionals to perform national community service in a structured partnership between school systems and civic organizations, for the benefit of Pakistani children mostly in the public schools.

Source: https://www.iteachforpakistan.org

Tooba Akhtar: It felt like boot camp, but those six weeks changed everything for me. There were some significant revelations. I remember, in the first week, I would come home in tears. I was teaching English in grades 6 through 8 at a government school for girls in Karachi. These girls were incredible. They were smart, bright, happy. They *wanted* to come to school; they had light in their eyes and worked so very hard as if their life paths would be determined by all of this, the education they were receiving. It made me think: when I was 13, what was I doing? Not much, you know. These girls had responsibilities in their families. It was a stark realization for me that our life paths were decided by where we were born. It kept nagging at me, unsettling me. The other thing that unsettled me was that the school where I was teaching was only fifteen minutes from my home, but I had never engaged with people who were 'different' from me. Of course, there is abject poverty in Pakistan, you see it everywhere, but I had never thought about *who* 'these people' are, and what their lives were like. What do they like or dislike? Who *are* they? They look just like me but our lives are so different, yet our lives are so connected. I think I had a deep, deep unsettling sense of how ignorant, and privileged, and naïve I had been. I had never thought about this, or done anything about it, because of the power structures that continue to exist and the number of people that won't do anything about it. I belong to the privileged class in Pakistan, a privileged family. We are the kind of people who just turn away and never do anything about it, or anything that would affect us greatly. These were the stark realizations that I couldn't shake off. That's how my work with TFP began, as I was rediscovering myself, asking myself what it is that I cared about and what I wanted to do. So, I signed up to teach, and I joined the two-year TFP fellowship program. I have learned and gained so much in that experience. Even then, I remember thinking 'I'll do this two-year fellowship and then go back to a corporate career'. I did a corporate internship one summer during a break from TFP and soon realized that corporate life wasn't for me.'

Author: That's how my phone conversation began with Tooba. Here's the rest of it…

Q. Is it a fair assumption that you went to elite private schools in your early years? And to the best universities as well?

Tooba Akhtar: Yes, my parents moved me around to the best private schools. I went to PECHS School for girls, to St. Joseph's Convent School, to Beaconhouse for my 'O' Levels, and to Lyceum for 'A' Levels. I did my bachelor's from LUMS and later a master's in Education from Harvard.

Q. So, what's next for you? Do you aspire to be in the corporate world or in a consultant's role?

Tooba Akhtar: Neither, not at all. I did some consulting work for a year with World Bank but realized that it wasn't for me. If the work is not meaningful, I find myself not being motivated. I'm quite happy doing what I do, and I'd like to continue in education, stay with TFP as long as they will have me. I see myself working in education.

Q. The interventions by Teach for Pakistan—are they only in public schools or also in low-fee private schools?

Tooba Akhtar: TFP has a mix of government and low-fee private schools but we work mainly in public schools.

Q. In the public schools, you work with teachers employed by the government. What are the challenges when you initiate the program in public schools? Do the teachers resist, or feel threatened by you?

Tooba Akhtar: It's a complex situation but the solution depends on how it is approached. The TFP program is designed to develop a relationship with the faculty, letting them know that the TFP Fellows are not there to check on them or replace them, or change their practices in the school, or tell them what's right or what's wrong. We are simply there for the children, to do our work, and our Fellows show respect to the teachers and defer to their authority. At first, the teachers were cautious around us. It took a lot of conscious relationship-building on our part to earn their confidence and respect. We participate in their activities and spend time in the community with them. They see us working very hard and putting in extra time. Soon, we see that they come around and ask us for help and for suggestions with better teaching techniques because they too are struggling and want the best for the children. We place at least two Fellows in each school and they are with the school for two years, so developing the relationship with teachers is important. Across the board, we have a good relationship established in a couple of months.

Q. In the public schools that you identify for intervention, does the TFP team focus mainly on deficiencies in the curriculum, where help is needed most? I imagine English, science and math would be those areas.

Tooba Akhtar: Yes, that is a central question. We place our Fellows in grades 3 to 8, historically mostly in grade 6, but this year, all our placements are in grades 3 through 5. The first year for a Fellow is setting up the groundwork because we're teaching in a completely different way than what the children are used to. It also takes time for the Fellows to learn about the community of the school. In the second year, we see rapid growth and impact. The subjects we focus on are English, math, science and social studies. We follow the national curriculum but, in our experience, most children in public school are four years behind the appropriate grade level—some children don't know more than just the alphabet in grade 6. So, we bring in supplemental resources and tools from Oxford University Press, Khan Academy, whatever we feel the children need. We follow the curriculum in terms of the learning outcomes and we train the teachers in pedagogical skills, develop their capacity for teaching within a specific framework and scaffolding, how to teach with leadership and how to create learning mechanisms.

Our Fellows decide what the children need, evaluate how far behind others they are, and how much remedial teaching will be required. I think the aim is to increase the capacity of the students to learn on their own, change the way they learn. It is not acceptable that they go back to the old system, the way things were before. We ask ourselves what we must do so that the children continue to do well even after we've left the classroom. It's going to take a few years to become a stronger program, but we have seen good results in schools where we have intervened. As an example, we also know of a village outside Lahore where, for the first time, eight girls are now going to Intermediate college and hopefully, for higher education. These girls are from a school where TFP Fellows were their teachers and we believe that made a difference.

Q. Your Fellows have also worked at a couple of TCF schools. How was the experience at TCF compared to public schools?

Tooba Akhtar: Big difference. The TCF school system is more structured and the teachers are well-trained and courteous. The staff were welcoming from the start and our Fellows were able to advance at a much faster pace because the students were better prepared. We've had great cooperation with TCF.

Q. Please tell us how you personally became involved with the TCF Intermediate College.

Tooba Akhtar: I met Riaz Kamlani Sahib in 2015, when they were setting up the TCF Intermediate college in Karachi and what got me interested was the way TCF was approaching what children needed at that level. We agreed that they needed more than just academic knowledge. They needed development of skills for communications and building of values, because these attributes have a strong correlation with how they achieve in life. We also agreed that the college could be different, that it could have a very conscious curriculum to build social skills, because that directly affects how they perform academically. Shortly after that, we worked out an arrangement for me to join the team and I led the Curriculum and Student Development program for the TCF college. We thought about how we would select children for the college. Since we were not going to teach them traditionally, we shouldn't select them on traditional test-based metrics. So, I designed a system to assess multiple intelligences as opposed to a system that would check their scores in math, science and English. This way we could harness various strengths of the student applicant and not exclude someone who could not speak English very well because we can always teach them how to do that.

Author's note: The children and the schools of Pakistan are 'privileged' to have young leaders like Tooba who are making a difference in the fight for social justice and equity in education. Tooba and TFP are remarkable and much valued Agents of Change in Pakistan.

4.4 Math and English: The Major Weakness

This section is linked with the next one (4.5 Arif Irfanullah) and discusses how the disparity in learning math and English affects the equity balance in Pakistani schools.

Pakistan has a complex, mixed bag of education systems and language issues—remnants of our colonized legacy, which adversely impact the equity balance in education by suppressing and constraining the flow of Urdu-medium grade 10 school graduates into college and university education. Only about 20 percent of the schools teach and test in English. These are the expensive, elite private schools, which cater to the middle-class and affluent, where all conversation and instruction are in English and where Urdu is taught as a second language. The other 80 percent are Urdu-medium schools, comprising the entire system of public schools and low-cost private schools, including the TCF system. Virtually the entire student population in these schools is from underprivileged or low-income families that do not speak English at home.

English is taught as a second language in Urdu-medium schools, and not very well. English proficiency and comprehension can be extremely poor. And, why should this be important? Because, for the student from an Urdu-medium environment, the abrupt switch to English in grade 11 is a huge disadvantage if one is dreaming of a university education. The admission test scores clearly point to math and English as the vulnerable Achilles heel[3] (area of weakness) for children coming out of the Urdu-medium system because the SAT-equivalent test is in English. The children from Urdu-medium schools start with a major disadvantage and relatively few successfully make the transition to university, and not without tutoring or extra help.

This also makes me wonder about math competency and its relationship to English proficiency, as I find it interesting that students from the Urdu systems have deficiency in math and English, both key elements of the admission tests for science and engineering programs. A question then is whether the deficiency in math is because the terminology and concepts are designed to be taught in English, from math books and materials in English. But, if basic math concepts are taught well in an Urdu environment, then, theoretically, it should not be making a difference.

Solutions are being employed to prepare students from Urdu-medium schools to get into top universities and colleges by supplementing the knowledge base in math and English and increasing their chances of passing the university entrance tests. TCF is doing this through its Alumni Development Program and by coaching its alumni in preparation for university admission tests.

4.5 Arif Irfanullah
Advanced Academics Plus (AAP)

I'm fascinated by Arif Irfanullah, the founder of AAP. Arif teaches finance at IBA and, through his online business, prepares candidates worldwide for the Chartered Financial Analyst (CFA) exam. He has an MBA from the University of Chicago and has worked in management positions with international businesses, including Oracle. His thoughts for social change and his service to the cause of facilitating higher education for underprivileged youth are admirable and, in my book, Arif makes the list of Agents of Change. As an education activist, Arif is a deep thinker. We had a good discussion on language issues and I like his innovative suggestions of integrating science and English into one subject area, helping students to acquire English language skills as they learn about science. Perhaps that could be flipped in English-medium schools, with science taught in Urdu? The idea deserves to be thought through and tested.

In 2009, AAP began offering after-school classes in math and English skills for students from low-income families, to improve their chances of acceptance to top colleges and universities. For the first few years, AAP struggled with the model at two TCF campuses, conducting after-school classes for 6th to 8th graders. More recently, AAP joined hands with the TCF-ADP program and is supporting its program of coaching students to prepare for university admission tests.

Q. Okay, Arif, tell us what we should know about AAP, your Advanced Academics Plus program.

Arif Irfanullah: The fundamental objective of AAP is to help children from underprivileged communities get into good universities by supplementing their English and math skills. In our earlier after-school model, we ran classes for 6th through 8th grades in the afternoon. It was a challenge to keep the children motivated and to get qualified teachers. At times, their regular schoolwork took precedence over what we were trying to teach them. For 6th, 7th or 8th graders, it is too abstract to understand that doing better in English and math will help them get into a top university. Other than a few students who were accepted at good universities, we did not see much success—not enough, given the time and money that we had put in.

Q. Please explain why the focus is on giving extra help only in English and math.

Arif Irfanullah: We feel that, if those two subjects can be fixed, the student has a better chance at passing the entrance exams for most universities, certainly for business and engineering programs, and for other programs as well. English and math are clearly the two weak areas across the country for children coming out of the Urdu-medium public school system or the low-cost private schools—including the TCF schools—and that's because good teachers for English and math are difficult to find and all instruction is in Urdu.

Q. So, what is your current model and how is it being implemented?

Arif Irfanullah: Realizing that the original after-school model was not working, and that we were not effective in expanding it across the TCF system or to other schools, we joined hands with TCF-ADP and Nadeem Hussain's efforts to better prepare TCF grads for university admissions through extra help in math and English. AAP and TCF share the same mission and AAP is now fully involved with the ADP program, with funding and support for ADP. We believe that the intervention to help with university admissions should be after the 10th grade, at the intermediate college level. And we are seeing greater success because these students have elected to go to college and they're committed to doing well in the entrance tests.

The difference for AAP is that, in a way, we've moved from the after-school model to a point closer to the end of the education chain, providing a more progressive curriculum in math and English at the Intermediate college level. So, AAP is now involved totally with the TCF Intermediate College, which caters to the top Matric graduates from TCF. My services are in a governance and an advisory capacity for the TCF College which also runs the Student Development Classes in math and English. TCF employs five full-time teachers specifically for these classes. AAP is supporting this through funding and with my time. Riaz Kamlani is also totally in sync with this but anything that we build upon this curriculum could be utilized in future at any government school and low-cost private school.

Q. What is your near-term focus and long-term vision?

Arif Irfanullah: The focus for me in the near term is with ADP and I see this as a continuum for the long-term, to perpetuity. Then, from this, I see two or three things emerging. One is to replicate this program in other schools outside of the TCF system and getting people like Adnan Lawai and Ameen Jan and others involved and see how we can digitize the curriculum we have developed. Once that is set, we can create apps and put them on phones, and so on. That's one offshoot of what we're doing.

Another offshoot would be to develop a school system where we focus on what matters most. I have a feeling that at some point I'll start doing that, once I have more time to develop this idea because this is what interests me most. Right now, I'm seeing that there's too much clutter and we should simplify the teaching by creating a curriculum with fewer subjects and focus on the student being good at math, English, and Urdu, perhaps also adding a regional language, with the subject areas of sciences and social studies woven into or integrated with the language classes. I feel that it can be a huge shift. Obviously, we won't see it happen overnight and I have to work on refining the idea. I would like to see if this idea can be tried at TCF and we can pilot the integrated classes at select schools. I'll be eager to see what can be done and what is achieved. So, my view is to create a much simpler system where a student can do at least what you expect an educated person to be able to do—which is to read, write, and do basic math.

Author: So, sciences and social studies would be integrated into the language classes.

Arif Irfanullah: Yes, I think we could integrate them into the English and Urdu classes. So, part of the English curriculum can be on what plants are all about, and what the human body is all about.

Author: And, in Urdu-medium schools, social studies and science would be taught in English and you're learning about human anatomy and plants in English...gaining knowledge along with language skills.

Arif Irfanullah: Absolutely. Hopefully, the K-10 public education system can be overhauled and reformed, because that needs to happen, but until that happens—if we can successfully bring our 8th graders to a good foundation in math, English, Urdu and one other language, which could be the regional language or the mother tongue—then these children would excel in grades 9 and 10 and be much better prepared for college. Obviously, for that to happen, the teachers need to be trained and available.

Author: The language spoken at home—the mother tongue—could be Punjabi, Sindhi, Pashto, Brahui, or another regional language. But Urdu is the language of the environment and, largely, the cultural identity of the country. I think fluency in Urdu should be required in all schools across the country, in all the various systems. What's your feeling on that?

Arif Irfanullah: I agree, partially. Urdu is commonly spoken but my own children are not that good in Urdu, yet they'll be successful. The language of business and government is English whereas Urdu is used to communicate. Nobody writes stuff in Urdu, unfortunately.

Author: You and I don't write in Urdu because our education was in English and we learned very basic Urdu as a second language, so our comfort level is in English. But the massive public school system and low-cost school system—with nearly 80 percent of the school-going population—generally use Urdu as the primary language and teach English as the second language, because English is the language in college and in business. It's a mixed up, dual-language system which is part of our colonized legacy. We did not correct that in the early years because we were obsessed with the English language as the single measure of 'good education' in the better private schools, colleges, and universities and we also adopted the British-English processes and language in business and government. Unfortunately, we were made to think of Urdu as 'the language of the poor' with the result that public education for the poor was developed in Urdu with only a modicum of English, which has been taught poorly in the public system and low-cost private schools.

Arif Irfanullah: Agreed, the public system is in Urdu, but you take the top universities—everything is in English. This is a big debate with many angles. I'm arguing it from the point of view of a student who has fluency and proficiency in English with better job prospects and better chances of success. It's very unfortunate, but that is the system. Unless we move all tertiary education, business, and government processes to Urdu, we have to live with what we have.

Author: I feel the language apartheid will continue unless Urdu as a medium of instruction is strengthened in all schools, including the private English-medium systems – and English is improved in the public system and the low-cost schools.

Arif Irfanullah: True, I think that would be ideal. Going back to my vision for schools, I would like to see four main subject areas: math, Urdu, English, and perhaps a regional language. It is relevant to the TCF system because we see students struggling. They have so many subjects—and, on top of that, because their math and English are not very good, we are asking them to do even more math and English. The struggle with TCF is that they are trying to do so much and ending up with students who know very little.

> ## BOX 4.3 INTEGRATING LANGUAGE AND SCIENCE
>
> Arif's ideas of integrating subject areas deserves more thought. There's a model of schools in the US that offers a language-immersion program. My granddaughter Aziza (8) is in second grade in a public school that offers a Spanish language-immersion program where she started with a 30-70 Spanish-English ratio in the first grade. The language ratio is 40-60 in the second grade, 50-50 by the third grade and maintained through the 5th grade. Aziza is learning math in Spanish in the second grade—and she speaks Urdu (as L3) with her parents and family.
>
> Arif may also look at home-schooling models where the parent teaches multiple things with an inquiry-based, integrated approach. In one Skype module that I taught my granddaughters Aysha (9), Zenaya (6), and Aziza (8), we combined science and language in a home study session, learning basic concepts of heat, energy, physical states of matter, molecules, transfer of heat, conduction, convection, etc. In the next session, we discussed volcanoes (magna, lava, etc.), where volcanoes are found, and how mountain ranges are formed. The relevant English vocabulary and applicable language skills were integrated. This could easily be done in Urdu or any language.
> – *Author*

Q. The debate about educating our children but not having enough jobs for them—how do you feel about that? Do you think we have enough jobs?

Arif Irfanullah: I feel strongly about this. I used to work for an Indian tech solutions company in the US and in Dubai. I was supporting customers all over the world with people in India doing the coding and other work and I also recruited engineers, mostly from India, because they were well trained and could deliver at a high level. I tried to recruit from Pakistan too, but it was difficult to find qualified engineers and technicians who could meet our requirements. So, if the education and training level of our human resource goes up and meets international standards, the jobs are there. The IT industry demand is there, it can't find enough qualified people. If our students and IT trainees are better educated, they will find the jobs—either in Pakistan or other parts of the world.

Q. Is there a high level of unemployment at this time for college graduates in Pakistan?

Arif Irfanullah: If you look at graduates from a computer science program, it is quite easy for them to find work. Ask any IT executive and you'll find that their biggest challenge is to retain good people. Most of the grads from computer science programs are joining IT companies and become part of the global IT workforce or go into sales and marketing jobs. I encourage students to think about technology related fields because that's where the larger number of jobs are.

Author: A survey by Nadeem (in 2017) found 58 TCF graduates who had gone through college were employed in good jobs. Granted, 58 is not a huge number. But Nadeem feels that college education has paid off for most students and there are jobs to be found, that unemployment among college educated youth is minimal. Nadeem also feels that vocational training is a good option for students who don't want to pursue college but that all students in TCF schools should be encouraged to aspire for university education. I also hear that it's easier to find work in blue-collar trades if you're trained and certified. What are your thoughts?

Arif Irfanullah: I don't agree with that entirely but I feel that more children should go into vocational training and those who have the capacity to go to a good college should follow that course, because I think the jobs will be there for them. Again, this stems from my own experience of seeing people from low-income families in India entering technology-oriented careers. They won't always move up to upper management levels or positions that require highly polished communication skills, but they are technically sound workers who are tougher and more resilient than the children from elite families. So, I would push TCF children in the direction of accounting oriented or audit jobs—things that require hard work and technical understanding. And, in the next generation, their children can do better. One has to move in stages. I feel that if people are well trained, the global marketplace offers plenty of work.

In my business, I hire technical people from all over the world and when I open it up, invariably I find more skilled people from India. Unfortunately, I find that most Pakistani applicants don't meet my requirements for adequate knowledge in finance and good writing skills. So, if I'm looking out for my business interest, I will hire someone from India because there aren't enough well-qualified Pakistani workers.

Author: To be globally competitive, they need both the language skills as well as the technical know-how.

Arif Irfanullah: Agree, totally.

Q. What is AAP's source of funding and how are you supporting TCF with resources?

Arif Irfanullah: The AAP funding is contributed by Umair Khan[4] and his father Azeem Khan Sahib, Adnan Lawai, and me. At this stage, working closely with ADP and TCF College is giving us an opportunity to develop our processes and accomplish the AAP mission, which is simply to help with the admission of underprivileged children into universities. TCF is a tremendous network and the wonderful people there make it a pleasure to do the work we do. Everyone at TCF that I have worked with—CEO Asaad, VP Riaz Kamlani, and others—are all highly professional and immensely sincere. It's taken a while, but I do feel very comfortable with TCF. In fact, the more time I spend with TCF, I recognize the challenges involved in what they do and the scale they have grown to. It's impressive.

4.6 Murali Vullaganti
Helping employability in rural locations in India (and in Silicon Valley)

This brief section highlights an unassuming social entrepreneur from Silicon Valley who hails from India. In his operational success, I see potential of a similar self-sustaining initiative that provides training and paid work for 12th grade educated young men and women in rural locations.

At 1.3 billion, India is the second largest population in the world—and much of it in the rural areas. Dearth of suitable jobs forces rural migration to urban centers, compelling workers to settle in the cities which further weakens the rural economies. With secondary education and job skills, the rural youth set their sights on commensurate employment opportunities, eager to leave the villages and rural townships for the urban excitement of Indian cities. Few make it to upper management positions. But almost all do improve their financial situation and are able to send money home to families. Sadly, the elderly are often left behind without the social support of younger family members. A similar mini-exodus is seen for lucrative jobs abroad in the

Middle East or other regions. Pakistan experiences the same phenomena of migration from rural to urban locations along with departures for overseas work destinations.

For more than a decade, Murali and his team have successfully operated a scalable solution to stem the tide of rural-to-city migration with RuralShores[5] (RS), a self-sustaining social enterprise initiative that is showing steady growth. The cornerstone of its ecosystem is the training and employment of 12th grade educated youth with basic IT and communication skills. The training is in processes and techniques to service the back-office needs of service providers, such as the telecom, banking, financial, insurance, accounting, medical, and pharmaceutical industries. The list of service offerings is not limited, and neither are the potential clients. The youth trainees employed at the RS centers work under supervision of seasoned managers and trainers. For corporate clients, partnering with RS delivers quality operational support and provides an opportunity to contribute to the building of rural communities through Corporate Social Responsibility programs, while local employment of the young rural workforce deters migration to cities. There's also ongoing professional development of the workers and many may continue higher education along with work at RS. Their success encourages fellow villagers to educate their children, including the daughters. The parallels in Pakistan are apparent.

Murali is the enterprising founder and energetic engine behind RuralShores and its counterpart expansion PeopleShores[6] in the heart of Silicon Valley. As a gentle Agent of Change, Murali is available to help with ideas for setup and implementation of similar models in Pakistan or elsewhere.

4.7 Shehzad Roy
A Passionate Celebrity for Education Reform

I was introduced to Pakistani rock star Shehzad Roy by Khalid Mahmood, MD and CEO of Getz Pharma, a generous entrepreneur. Khalid has a Corporate Social Responsibility program that supports education and vocational training, cultural activities, environmental programs, and health services in Pakistan. An avid long-distance sailor (Dubai to Karachi) and an achiever in multiple ways, Khalid serves on the leadership boards of several civic organizations, including Zindagi Trust (ZT), the non-profit led by Shehzad Roy.

I met Shehzad on a Sunday morning in Karachi at the Garden Area government school campus adopted by ZT (the other one is the Fatima Jinnah campus). The school was spacious, neat, and well-furnished with visible signs of caring support and generous patronage from ZT. Shehzad had performed the night before in Dubai at the opening extravaganza for a cricket series and returned to Karachi in the early hours. In the exciting life of a celebrity, he had an hour with me before rushing off for a recording session. But he didn't miss a beat as he proudly showed me the school, and the chess program set up in a multi-purpose room where dozens of chess boards were neatly arranged.

It took me no time to realize that the energetic young man was a rock star both on and off the stage. He was going to do the show-and-tell in his own style and on his terms. So, I gave up and let him tell me about his vision for Zindagi Trust and what he was hoping to accomplish. His rapid-fire narrative was informative and I was impressed by his knowledge of the education system, its politics and realities. There were no eccentric claims of achievements, nor unrealistic assertions that he was out to single-handedly change the system. His desire to serve education was genuine and he struck me as a sensitive, sincere person who deserves appreciation for his dedicated efforts to contribute to education reform in a meaningful way.

Shehzad's earlier experiment in education reform focused on underprivileged children who were missing out on school because they had to work and supplement the family income. He started the 'I Am Paid To Learn' (IMPTL) program, enrolling working children into schools and compensating them through stipends for the lost opportunity. On the ZT website, Shehzad states that they have some 3,000 students enrolled in schools through IMPTL. Realizing that the stipend program was helping with enrollment but had no impact on the quality of the schools or broader reforms to the system, Shehzad ventured into adoption of a couple of government schools to address management and quality issues by supplementing teacher and management resources, providing better learning materials and tweaking the curriculum in the schools. 'The objective was not only to reform one or two government schools but to convert the schools into catalysts which could impact the education system in Pakistan', said Shehzad, adding that the idea of public-private partnership can be made stronger through such pilot efforts and also create an enabling environment to start dialog for reform.

> ## Box 4.4 Chess in Pakistan's Public Schools?
>
> Among the extra-curricular programs Shehzad has introduced at the Zindagi Trust campuses, chess is the most unique activity on the list. Others are art, pottery, taekwondo, football (soccer), and a variety of other sports—all for Pakistani girls and boys in the public schools adopted by ZT. Through chess competition, students learn problem-solving life skills and develop the art of focus, mindfulness, patience and non-aggressive struggle. – *Author*

Q. It seems you have a good understanding of the political environment in the education system and you enjoy strategically rolling the dice. How do you see your efforts contributing to education reform at the state level? Is your vision to create a model that can be replicated and scaled?

Shehzad Roy: I think we achieve replication across-the-board when we successfully influence policy and practices. As you can imagine, reform is going to be a series of small steps. As an example, the textbooks used in government schools are of very poor quality. So, we added high quality textbooks from good publishers and demonstrated that supplementary books should be allowed for use in government schools. We formally introduced that idea with the Sindh government and successfully had it adopted as policy in the province. That's a small example of how innovative ideas can be leveraged: first, by demonstration in pilot environments in our adopted schools, then by fighting for their inclusion in practice and policy. Our policy makers and political leaders are not really aware of conditions on the ground, in each school. And, they shouldn't be expected to know that. It should be the school principal's job to run the school in the best way possible, without the need to get every little thing approved by a superior in the bureaucracy. We must give principals more authority. Devolution must reach all the way down to the school principal. Administratively, it isn't possible for the Secretary of Education to control each school.

Our plan is not to physically replicate the schools we have adopted. That is not possible. But, because we are deeply involved with the schools and the system on a day-to-day basis, we understand how they operate, and we can propose improvements that are cost-effective and feasible, even with some improvements which don't require additional money.

As another example, we suggested management consolidation of several campuses which are in close proximity. Our political leaders don't know that there are as many as *eight* school units running out of one campus, with *eight* principals sitting there. You can't bring about systemic change unless the politicians are made to realize the surplus and waste that exists in the system. That realization will be made easier when you take a school and change it with better systems within that school—the management, the curriculum, teacher training programs, etc.—and then start a dialog with the system managers and policy makers at a high level.

The system cannot improve unless it is devolved down to the local level. In theory, the present system has been devolved to the provinces and lower levels, but in effect it is not working at the local level. Administratively, the Secretary of Education and the politicians should not control all the schools—that just isn't possible. They will have to let go of their controlling powers. This political system of 'gifting' jobs by patronage has to stop. The principals should have the ultimate power to run the schools and, by their own examples, develop squads of good teachers in their faculty teams. The focus should always be the child and schools should be independently functioning units within the larger system, able to build their own curriculum and administer their own testing for learning outcomes. Of course, the students need to take the board exams in 9th and 10th grades but testing in the lower grades should be left up to the school.

At a parent-teacher meeting, a father of two children came up to me and said he appreciated the good learning experiences his children were getting through our innovative programs but, being an hourly-wage worker, he was losing income every time he had to come to these meetings. He said he had confidence in what we were doing and asked to be excused from future meetings. I was stunned by what I had just heard! This was an uneducated laborer giving me a lesson in reality—that, like most parents, he wanted quality education for his children, and he wanted to be involved with the school. The point is that when communities see the change in their schools, they do become involved and I feel strongly that they will soon be ready to oversee the management and ask for better quality of education the children receive, because the new paradigm has been set. It is a myth that poor parents don't expect quality education in public schools, that's not true.

But people are not asking the right questions. We are not asking why, for example, is the child not developing the ability to inquire, or the ability to think critically. I get annoyed when visitors to our schools ask me what grades the children are getting in the board exams. I feel the question is misdirected and my response is that the whole school environment and extracurricular programs should be considered in judging the quality of a school, not just the grades. Of course, learning outcomes are important but our mission is not to improve the grades at just a few schools. The objective is to improve the whole system. Our battle is with the poor system of education. What gives us more satisfaction are the successes of our children in city-wide competitions in science projects, math, chess and sports when they are up against the best from the elite schools, and that goes to show that we are producing confident future citizens.

Q. How are you testing the content knowledge of teachers, and how are teachers and principals given support or additional training?

Shehzad Roy: We are a small system, but we are very conscious of quality education. At our schools, we do our teacher training in the classroom, instruct the teacher on how to teach a class using a particular textbook. We also have government trainers conduct teacher workshops for pedagogical skills; but we could certainly do more. We have subject coordinators who specialize in math and science and give the teachers the extra support and training they might need in those subjects and also for tips on classroom management. ZT has Project Managers at both our campuses to give management assistance to the principals.

I believe that credentialing of teachers is very important. Quality of our teachers will improve with a four-year degree in education as a minimum requirement for credentialing of all teachers. Until that happens, we will just be putting out fires. My thinking is that a new teacher must have the basic qualifications, then she must take and pass the national teacher's test, and then work on the four-year degree to be a credentialed teacher.

Q. In your opinion, what are the two essentials to build and sustain a sound education system?

Shehzad Roy: I would say it has to be a combination of good leadership and persistent engagement of the citizens to demand quality education. We hope that our leaders will show stronger political will to address education reform and that our efforts are creating a good base to work from.

4.9 Education Technology: Ameen Jan
Ed-tech pioneer in Pakistan

EDeQUAL is probably the most viable ed-tech enterprise in Pakistan. Implementation of technology-enabled education has to be an essential component of reform in Pakistan's education system. Adoption of technology solutions can bridge the gap between teaching quality and student needs, providing students with high quality instructional resources to understand concepts and develop analytical and problem-solving skills. Any blended learning effort must also track student performance, to demonstrate that it delivers results.

Ameen Jan is a business graduate from Stanford. As founder and CEO of EDeQUAL, he strives to engage with the larger education systems and providers to deploy technology-based blended learning in math, science, and English. In an op-ed column in *Dawn.com* (September 5, 2018), Ameen said, 'The low quality of public education in Pakistan, corruption in exam boards, and widespread cheating have contributed greatly to our nation's decline'. He added that while getting the millions of out-of-school children into the formal education system must be a high priority, a greater priority is ensuring that the children who attend school get a quality education, with outcomes measured by what students can demonstrate as knowledge acquired from the learning against what they are expected to know at the grade level. The challenge is in accomplishing these outcomes in the shortest time, in an affordable manner and at scale. Ameen holds that the solution to improving education quality rapidly and at scale must involve technology because it can offer access to educational content and assessment tools that are otherwise out of reach.

Ameen cites a (2007) World Bank study as evidence that education *quality* is what drives economic growth and equity, not the years spent in school. Through objective baseline testing conducted by EDeQUAL, his concern is that a 6th grade student in public schools and LCPS has a four-year achievement gap in math, that delivering quality education in science, technology, engineering and math (STEM) must be the focus of education reform, and that without quality improvement, we will not produce educated youth, who think critically, solve problems, read and write well, and work effectively with numbers.

In one EDeQUAL partner school that has implemented a blended learning program, delivered in both English and Urdu, most students gained one year of math competency in four months. The results point to the transformational change that is possible when education technology is thoughtfully implemented and blended to various degrees. 'While technology won't replace teachers, the teachers who use technology will eventually replace the teachers who do not [utilize technology],' says Ameen. He also acknowledges that technology is not a panacea and it should be piloted before it is rolled out at large scale. He suggests a one-year pilot carefully conducted in thirty primary schools to study evidence of key learnings for implementing reform and that this group of 'smart schools' should be selected in a mix of urban and rural areas. The experimental and lean startup would be at very low cost and helpful in defining a model for successful technology-based learning to be implemented on a larger scale. I met with Ameen in 2016 at a popular coffee-hangout in Karachi when he brought me up to speed on the progress of his work.

Q. So, what solutions have you and your teams created for the Urdu-medium schools?

Ameen Jan: The earlier product we had was difficult to implement in the lower-cost segment of Urdu-medium schools for two reasons: one was language and the other was cost, which made it inaccessible for most of the users in that segment. It was English based and used third-party, licensed content which made the price point higher. So, we kept that product for the top-tier market.

We embarked on building a product that was suitable for the Urdu-medium school environment but with the same functionality as the earlier English-medium products, with content that was localized in terms of curricular progression, language, and feasibility. The product was designed for grades 3, 4, and 5—the core primary school years—

using what we had learned in the higher-cost, English-medium schools. To start with, we built a fairly sophisticated math product which is bilingual. Everything on the platform is in Urdu and in English. The delivery of the content is primarily in Urdu but we inject terminology and add sentences in English. So, as the learner goes through it, she begins to acquire English language skills as well, more in an osmotic way. The content is also heavily scaffolded in terms of provincial curricula, whether in Sindh or in KP or other provinces. So, we are textbook-agnostic but curriculum-specific. And we implemented it in our partner schools, the Zindagi Trust adopted public schools. We started with their 6th grade students, assessed them and, as expected, they were not at grade 6 level. They were at grade 2 or grade 3 level and that finding is consistent whether it's in adopted government schools or in low-fee schools. In four months, we were able to bring the scores up from an average of 24 percent to an average of 72 percent, the equivalent of advancing one grade level in four months.

A couple of interesting things began to happen. We said we wanted the teacher to have an important role and we asked the teachers to not use the program to 'supplement' their teaching methods because, frankly, those methods had not produced desired results. We asked them to accept the change [to technology] and we trained and supported the teachers and observed them during the first month. There were the expected hiccups but then the teachers and the students began to feel more comfortable and by the second month, the students became more independent and the role of the teachers began to change as well. The teachers became facilitators for the students who needed help, while they also kept an eye on the more advanced, independent students. In four months, most of the children brought up the learning curve and rapidly became independent. And the pilot with a hundred children in two ZT schools was deemed successful, at no cost to them. We then helped the ZT schools to assess the needs of their infrastructure, advised them to acquire tablets and local servers, and signed them up to pay 100 rupees per month, per child. So, they pay us 10,000 rupees a month, which is affordable for them. And that's one of the models.

We started to talk with other providers like Aga Khan Education Service (AKES) which operates 158 schools, mostly in the Chitral and Gilgit-Baltistan areas, very rural and remote. They also have eight schools in Sindh. Our engagement with them is advancing well [in 2016] and we hope to have agreement very soon. There are some other players like the Education Management Organizations in Sindh, one of them is Charter for Compassion with four adopted schools in the Sukkur area. The other is Beaconhouse which has adopted 50 public schools in Punjab, and there is IBA-Sukkur which has also adopted a few schools. We're making progress but the road has yet to be travelled, recognizing what was or wasn't working, and investing in making the change. There are a few other initiatives in the works at different stages of discussion.

Q. How is your work going with the elite-private Karachi Grammar School (KGS)?

Ameen Jan: Overall, that has gone very well. KGS initially utilized us as a solution for their remedial-need students as an after-school program and that didn't work out too well. We have recently moved to an agreement with KGS to train their entire cadre of teachers in improving their math competency. And we'll move to the next phase very shortly after that.

Q. It takes a forward-thinking and nimble organization to fully adopt technology in a large network of schools. TCF is slowly moving in that direction. What words of advice do you have for TCF?

Ameen Jan: Of the philanthropy-supported schools, AKES is the top of the heap with the drive and desire to innovate for change. The reality is that the vanguard of that change is going to be a very small minority of the total segment. I see a player like AKES being a part of that vanguard because they recognize that they're not getting the quality of outcomes that they should be getting. There has to be a hunger to do better, to innovate and improve. AKES is certainly better funded and more nimble than TCF. The underlying issue, which is far more fundamental, is the willingness to subject ourselves to vigorous, independent, and objective assessment of how we are actually performing. If that is not taken seriously by the leadership and management of the organization, then we don't have the impetus to drive any kind of change.

4.10 Bilal Musharraf
Thoughts on 'Micro Education'

Bilal has a Bachelor's in actuarial science and completed his master's in business and in education from Stanford. Irum and Bilal are a delightful, free-thinking, socially conscious couple. 'The plight of the developing world is close to our hearts. We care about Urdu and we care about Pakistan. It's a no-brainer that nation-states should have delivered on free public education up to high school by now. It's a travesty that it hasn't happened. I would love to expedite free quality education in Pakistan,' says Bilal, who loves to 'noodle' his thoughts and 'pressure test' them. This conversation in late December 2016 is sprinkled with contemporary insights and unconventional ideas which must be considered with an open mind.

Q. **Let's begin with some personal background and how will 'Micro Education' work in Pakistan?**

Bilal Musharraf: I have a graduate degree in education but I really was interested in venture capital and how applied research at the higher education level gets commercialized, because that is the backbone of venture capital. I've been in venture capital but I wasn't interested at that point in K-12 education. I was more interested in higher education and how it ties in with the business sector. Then an opportunity came up. An international school network wanted to expand its presence in North America. So, I joined them. It was a for-profit network of premier schools which followed the International Baccalaureate system and I was in a business development role. That was in 2008–2009.

Then, because I was not feeling satisfied with my day job, I started translating Khan Academy (KA) videos into Urdu as a volunteer. Initially, it was a whimsical thought and then it kept growing and made me feel good. In 2010, I met Salman Khan, founder of Khan Academy, and told him I would love to participate in the work. A grant from Google came through in September 2010 and I was the second guy Sal Khan hired. I was there for four solid years. We internationalized the Khan Academy content, making the site available in multiple languages. The content had moved beyond just videos. The portal also developed exercise platform and analytics, and the rise of Khan Academy is a global phenomenon.

The common MOOC[7] platforms are addressing higher education and I think we're at the point of making that connectivity useful. As education is now reforming, educators are openly questioning what the best way is to teach and to learn, right from the early stage to higher education. It requires collaboration and nurturing of new ideas. So, I think platforms like Edmodo have an important role to play. In the K-12 space, Edmodo has 73 million users in most countries of the world. Pakistan is one of those countries that has a lot of traffic—just as much traffic as India, surprisingly, which speaks well of Pakistan's infrastructure. These are the kinds of platforms that we can leverage. What can be used from a MOOC platform like Edmodo is a fellowship program that can really unleash micro education. Because we don't have enough schools and we don't have enough teachers, the model is one of making teachers social entrepreneurs who would then go out there and provide micro education in any community.

One of the [good] things that has happened in Pakistan is that the National Testing Service (NTS) has become the standard. Those standards must not be compromised and the exit points must be robust. Most higher education institutions will accept the NTS scores. So, it's good to have a universal testing service in place because it levels the playing field, just as the Scholastic Aptitude Test (SAT) has done in the US. Some of the higher education institutes that were exclusively for the elites, had to open up their doors for the other socio-economic classes.

Q. **For the micro education model that you're proposing, it would take a trained teacher-entrepreneur to go out and teach a group of children of school age, each child at his or her individual level—right?**

Bilal Musharraf: We need to unleash our people for learning and people for teaching. If the teaching incentives are there, the learning incentives are clear because the exit points are clear: if you know the content and you clear the exam, you will be pulled into either higher education or vocational training. In the ideal case, you have a well-functioning classroom and teachers who know how to leverage technology and they can directly pull in resources—global, online resources, which are enormous—and raise the bar of what is being discussed and collaborate with their colleagues and peers and children elsewhere in the world so you are not trapped in this ecosystem. All it takes is Internet connectivity to make that happen. At one end of the spectrum is the classroom that has enabled that technology from an infrastructure standpoint as well as educators who are experienced and trained in the ability to leverage technology—they can really take those children to another level. But at the lower end of the spectrum, there are children who do not have access to any schools, any learning material, nothing—basically 'gypsy' children on the streets: they can be engaged through a marketplace of these micro education teachers. We have the National Testing Service and it wouldn't take much to introduce an element that every time a child is taking the exam in any subject, they indicate the NIC (national ID) card of the teacher....

Q. ...and what would that validate?

Bilal Musharraf: Then you would have a database of folks who are good teachers. You have their information and it would serve almost like reviews or skill-based rankings in the marketplace. So, if a teacher goes out and says, 'I'll teach you math for the next year, for a higher education class and I'm going to charge you 100 rupees a day'—what information do you need to decide that you should engage this teacher, or not? If you have the database, anyone can check on their credibility and verify the facts. Because you know that people are getting that desperate, they—even from the lower income segments—are choosing to spend money on private education and getting poor education in the process. So, they will get private education, as long as there is a reliable exit point.

Q. Can the delivery system, as you describe it, be sustainable in the poverty-ridden markets? Or will it only deepen the disparities between the classes?

Bilal Musharraf: Unfortunately, technology is empowering the empowered [chuckles]. These are challenging times and economics and technology are tied together. What it can buy you is not just better life but life itself. So, we are not prepared for those kinds of ethical questions. But whether we can be successful in leveraging technology and convincing underdeveloped ecosystems, that is in the realm of possibility. For that, we must have proof of concepts, start small, think through and hard, and build on that.

Q. Again, please describe the 'micro education' model one more time in simpler language....

Bilal Musharraf: I look at the model of a teacher who has gone through a training program, has an intermediate college or 12th grade education, knows how to teach, and is given a loan of say $5,000 or about 500,000 rupees. The teacher shows the students how they can learn using online resources. It doesn't matter what kind of cohort she inherits. She can figure out the level of this cohort and engage them. Tablets can be purchased for the students, a laptop for the teacher and a connection device. Teacher puts it all in her backpack and she's on her way to teach. No school building is needed. The group meets either in a city structure or union council office, or in the courtyard of a designated home in the community. The investment is a hundred per cent in education, nothing else. Actually, it's a loan to the teacher. Once the devices are paid off, it's a core business source of revenue for the teacher who should have the ability to authoritatively conduct blended learning for a group of students at various levels. If the teacher can have 20 students and charge 100 rupees per child, that's 2,000 rupees a day in earnings, potentially a decent 40,000 rupees a month.

I feel like trying that experiment and seeing how successful that can be. If it is, then it's very scalable as opposed to models in which there are sustainability issues. That's where technology is amazing and easily scalable at very affordable cost. Telenor, a telecom company in Pakistan, is very keen to support education and they may be able to provide a subsidized wi-fi hot spot anywhere. But these are untested ideas, I must confess. They have been on slow-burning fires and incubating. I keep noodling ideas and I'm looking for evidence that will support them. But, if Donald Trump makes our lives unbearable, I'm packing up and going home to test these ideas! Because I really find them in the realm of possibility.

Q. The model sounds like home-schooling. For a gathering place, can the *masjid* be a possibility?

Bilal Musharraf: That's right—why didn't I think of the masjid as a viable location? The standard school model is being questioned now: what value does a school really give you? In the micro education model, the child can be with other children from the neighborhood, or with the family. In school, the child is indoctrinated to behave and learn in a certain way, in silos. These forms of schools developed after the industrial revolution. Humans do not learn or live like that. We absolutely kill love of learning and out-of-the-box thinking in children with regimented schools. Getting away from a 'one-to-many' classroom and creating a 'many-to-many' environment of learning is an art. In schools oriented to discovery learning, you don't teach by telling the child. You teach by letting the child discover and learn. There's a prevailing movement in the San Francisco Bay Area to put children into such schools. Our area is often a trend setter for the rest of the country. I suggest exploring an initiative called Breakthrough Collaborative[8] which offers a unique program for children from underprivileged families with an end game of the children coming back as educators in their neighborhood communities. A large part of the TCF community becoming teachers of the future would be a great goal to have.

Author's note: TCF has nearly six hundred former students who have come back as teachers.

Q. Your optimism for Pakistan—what is it based on?

Bilal Musharraf: I am optimistic when I look at the entire emerging markets landscape. In the last two years, when I was with a hedge fund, it gave me a lot of time to think about that relative to other underdeveloped countries. The institutional equilibrium between the executive, legislative, judiciary branches, and the role of civil society—all those things are benchmarks that are settling down. Apart from that, it's a big country with more than 200 million people. I've travelled extensively through much of the world and I can say that Pakistan has decent infrastructure. The other thing is it didn't matter what was happening in the country, Pakistan always remained connected with the outside world. So, it has all these strands of ideas along with strengthening of the ballot box as the instrument for smooth transition of power, with education and economics taking precedence over strategic defense-related considerations which have trumped things in the past. It has a very large young demographic. The education level may not be very high but the awareness level is high. If ideas catch on, they can go viral very quickly. It's just a matter of getting proof of concepts now and getting the word out.

Q. Do you think Pakistan has reached an inflection point?

Bilal Musharraf: I do think it has bottomed out. A couple of things have happened that are indicative of that. These may not be the best indicators, but the number of movies that have come out of Pakistan in the last two years are more than in the last thirty years. Music is another thing on the upswing. You can look at foreign direct investment that is planned. You can look at the stock exchange.

Q. What segment of education should be the responsibility of the public sector?

Bilal Musharraf: My feeling is that higher education should not be in the domain of the public sector. Higher education should be either private for-profit, or private non-profit. We should have centers of excellence funded by the for-profit sector that are very much aligned to where the economy is going. And we should have private non-profit institutions as islands of excellence. The public sector should really focus on improving K-12. We cannot allow the public sector to renege on its responsibility. So, for a non-profit that is focused on the K-12 sector, in this time when the public system continues to renege on its obligation, our best case is to endeavor to establish schools, to be a lab, to show proof of concept, to showcase as a benchmark of excellence in that ecosystem. And what is the exit point? I give you that education globally is changing so rapidly that higher education is very cost-efficient. So, the exit point is really up to us. If you have thinking individuals who have command over language and understand logical inference, they will be good at anything. And, with soft skills of entrepreneurship, they will be at the peak of the ecosystem. There's so much to do. As long as they can make a living, they will always be able to survive. If vocational training picks up, they can do that. In the meantime, they will not depend on anyone for anything. Herding people into a system of higher education which is an edifice, a house of cards, may not be the best thing. In the entire ecosystem, the decision makers at the top themselves don't know exactly what's going on. They are themselves beholden to vested interests and they're not pushing people in one direction or another and don't care where the world is heading. Maybe they don't know, or they're not capable of knowing, or they don't care.

I think the better bet is to prepare people for being self-employed. They should have the realization that things are going in this direction. The time of a *pukki naukri* (lifetime employment) is over. You will have multiple careers in your lifetime. If you have passion for something, by all means acquire those skills. But, to make a living, you will have to be a master. If you get tired of it, you will have to take a sabbatical for a while, learn a new trade and start afresh and become a master all over again. That's how life will be.

Q. Where does education rank as a priority in the institutional balance?

Bilal Musharraf: We have to move on multiple fronts at the same time. We don't have the luxury of time and we have to prioritize. Resource allocation is the hardest question and there are techniques to figure out what the optimum resource allocation needs to be at each stage. But I would point to institutional balance between for-profit business, the government-funded sector, and the private non-profit sector. And we need that balance in education, healthcare, in media, and we need it in culture. We need that balance not just at the national level—we need it also in our major metropolises. So, you give me that inventory and I will tell you what that resource allocation needs to be. Take the GDP and ask yourself how we are carved up right now. There is no bad or good, it's just that our balance is not right. Because each sector is delivering something different to the ecosystem. The for-profit system is most efficient because it is incentivized to raise revenue and reduce cost, so it's going to deliver on that because investors hold the management accountable. Time horizons are generally shorter in the for-profit sector. In the government-funded sector, the time horizons are longer than the for-profit sector but tighter election cycles. If you can prove that you did something within your elected term in office, well and good. But if you're not getting results, you can be out. That's why education has been a tough-sell for politicians. But that's an argument in favor of education technologies. It's only a matter of time before the proof of concept gets established for technology and the politicians realize that, within their term in office, they will be able to execute and reap the benefits of micro education. And the cost will be a paltry portion of their education budget.

The third, the private non-profit sector, is agnostic of government-funded populism and by its very nature, it is agnostic of the bottom-line. So, if the question is what do we need? And there's an entrepreneur who, as his dying legacy, creates a dance school and it's his choice to do that. But he has created something beautiful in the ecosystem.

Over time, I've gravitated away from looking at the turbulent sea and wanting to create a sea change. You've got to forget about the sea and create islands of excellence, because the sea is beyond our individual capacities and our lifetimes. You have to focus on islands. Of course, I'm thinking of institutions or organizations. Create more and more islands of beauty or excellence, and there's no doubt that once we have that critical mass, the ecosystem becomes sophisticated and calm. Whether or when you get there is anyone's guess.

The Super-Wealthy, Global Agents of Change

Giving a significant amount of personal wealth to worthy causes is commendable and the best way to impact social change. However, it is not everyone's cup of tea, regardless of a mega-billion net worth or high liquidity. Charitable giving is also part of a prudent fiscal and tax strategy and I am convinced that most super-wealthy philanthropists consciously give large amounts of their assets because they believe in the causes they support. It is fascinating to think of generous persons who invest in the work of organizations to pursue specific philanthropic goals on a scale that yields massive impact. To me, the scale of national economies of the super-rich countries is mind-boggling and charitable giving too is in unimaginable numbers. In the US, for example, more than 400 *billion* dollars are donated annually, according to the IRS.

Warren Buffet, along with Bill and Melinda Gates, initiated The Giving Pledge, a campaign to encourage wealthy people to contribute or pledge most of their wealth to philanthropic causes. The pledge has more than 200 signatories, most of them billionaires, and their pledges total over $500 billion! Mark Zuckerberg and wife Priscilla Chan, George Soros, Marc Benioff, Jeff Skoll, and Laurene Powell-Jobs (widow of Steve Jobs) are notable billionaire philanthropists. Benioff has said that he didn't have to make a choice between doing business and doing good, that he could easily align these two values and strive to succeed at both simultaneously. Jeff Skoll's foundation has awarded seven-figure grants to Pakistani non-profits, including TCF.

These are examples of a few American philanthropists who give to major causes. Pakistan too has a long list of generous philanthropists and a strong culture of charitable giving. But we must encourage more mindful giving to education, especially for education reform efforts.

Notes

1. Ishrat Husain, 'Reforming the Government in Pakistan: Rationale, Principles and Proposed Approach,' Lahore Journal of Economics, Department of Economics, The Lahore School of Economics, vol. 12 (Special E), pp. 1-15, September 2007.
2. LIGTT: https://ligtt.org/files/50BTs-Consolidated.pdf.
3. Greek mythology: metaphoric weakness (in the calf tendon) which leads to failure, despite overall strength.
4. Umair Khan—Silicon Valley entrepreneur and MIT alumnus—started Academic Achievement Plus with Arif Irfanullah along with support of his father Azeem Khan Sahib and his business partner Adnan Lawai.
5. RuralShores: http://ruralshores.com/index.html.
6. PeopleShores is a for-profit social enterprise initiative achieving multiple objectives with a charter to bring technology driven jobs to economically challenged communities in the US. https://www.peopleshores.com/.
7. MOOCs, massive open online courses, are online learning platforms.
8. Breakthrough Collaborative https://www.breakthroughcollaborative.org.

Chapter Five

The Right to Education

THE CASE FOR EDUCATION: A HUMAN RIGHT

A rational premise is that education is a vital component in the building of an enriched and sustainable civil society, with multiple benefits accruing to all. So, it can be argued that education improves the opportunity chances for a better quality of life. But, what is civil society? It is the catch-all for organized groups, institutions, and movements outside of government, military, or business. Civil society is the essential driver of most things that citizens may want to have—such as institutions of learning, schools, universities, health institutions, activism and advocacy groups, charitable organizations, social and sports clubs, community foundations, non-profits to support worthy causes, political organizations, professional groups, cultural organizations, and a host of others. In short, just about everything civilian and non-governmental. The components and assets of a civil society are its people and the civic organizations that operate without a profit motive.

The dictionary defines civil or civilian as '…relating to ordinary citizens as distinct from military or religious matters.' A better synonym for civil may simply be 'public', or to do with people. And there are more offshoots of 'civil'—for example, civil rights, and civil liberties, which ensure a citizen's personal freedoms that the government cannot diminish or take away without due process. Civil liberties include the freedom of conscience, freedom of the press, of religious faith, speech and expression, of assembly, and much more. Civil liberties also entitle citizens to certain rights under the constitution—such as the right to security, to privacy, to equal treatment under the law, to due process and a fair trial, the right to own property, the right to life, and protection from social injustice. These undisputed, universal civil liberties and rights—also considered human rights—are generally accepted as absolute, irreversible and inalienable fundamental rights that all human beings are entitled to. By implication, rights also impose an obligation

283

to respect and protect the human rights of others. As expected by all citizens, human rights must have highest priority in cultural and institutional values and should be incorporated into law.

Accepted ideals of civil liberties and human rights, coupled with the Universal Declaration of Human Rights, plus the 18th Amendment to Pakistan's Constitution (Article 25-A) which guarantees universal education to age 16, have laid the foundation and framework of principles for education as a right.

The case made here is that the right to education has roots in well-established and universally accepted interpretations of civil and human rights. With the 18th Constitutional Amendment, the state has unequivocally accepted its obligation to provide education up to age 16. But do citizens have any option when the state does not comply as mandated by the constitution? Ethicists, philosophers, scholars, and jurists have stated that there should be access to just and compassionate remedy if there is denial or violation of a constitutional right. This leads us to the question: What is the good in having a right when no remedy exists for its denial or violation? What legal recourse is available to citizens who are deprived of the right to education? What action can be taken, where does it start, and can it lead to a solution? Can citizens demand reparations? That is the million-dollar question.

The preceding summarized notes on civil liberties and human rights are gleaned from sources of history and philosophy, primarily the *Stanford Encyclopedia of Philosophy*.[1] The universal principles of civil rights and human rights are incorporated in writings dating back to the Magna Carta (1215) and, more recently, in the UN's Universal Declaration of Human Rights[2] (UDHR, December 10, 1948)—the cornerstones of international human rights law.

5.1 Poverty to Prosperity

'The deprived people tend to come to terms with their deprivation because of the sheer necessity of survival, and they may, as a result, lack the courage to demand any radical change, and may even adjust their desires and expectations to what they unambitiously see as feasible.'[3]

Amartya Sen

For many of our fellow citizens, day-to-day life is a struggle. Not everyone dreams of wealth, luxury and opulence. But, in terms of relative improvement of living conditions, a path to prosperity is the

> ## Box 5.1 Article 26 of the Universal Declaration of Human Rights, 1948
>
> 1. Everyone has the right to education. Education shall be free, at least in the elementary and fundamental stages. Elementary education shall be compulsory. Technical and professional education shall be made generally available and higher education shall be equally accessible to all on the basis of merit.
>
> 2. Education shall be directed to the full development of the human personality and to the strengthening of respect for human rights and fundamental freedoms. It shall promote understanding, tolerance and friendship among all nations, racial or religious groups, and shall further the activities of the United Nations for the maintenance of peace.
>
> 3. Parents have a prior right to choose the kind of education that shall be given to their children.

rightful aspiration of every person and not just the privileged few. Beginning with a concerted, all-embracing effort for steady removal of the obvious hindrances to prosperity—such as wars, conflicts, violence, crime, military tensions—and a serious commitment to curb the menace of corruption, the state must take stock of its resources and strategic options for transforming poverty-stricken communities and regions into social units of economic growth and incrementally improving living conditions. Elimination of poverty is a huge task with multi-faceted challenges. But, on a global level, there have been gains in poverty reduction, infant mortality and literacy. More than half the countries in the world have either succeeded in largely eliminating poverty or are making progress in that direction in the face of immense challenges.

Why are some nations more prosperous than others and how do some poor communities transition from poverty to increasing prosperity? Generations of stark illiteracy and poverty coupled with poor education systems and rare opportunity for equitably supplied education: these are the most probable reasons why prosperity remains an out-of-reach aspiration for many Pakistanis living in poverty.

5.2 The Legatum Prosperity Index™

The Legatum Institute[4] (Legatum, meaning 'legacy' or 'gift') is a London-based think tank with a noble vision: to see people lifted out of poverty. Their mission is to create the pathways from poverty to prosperity, enabling individuals and communities and nations to fulfil their potential. The Institute researches and ranks countries based on the criteria of sub-indices—the 'Nine Pillars'—to produce the annual Legatum Prosperity Index™ which tracks the journey of nearly 149 countries. The results explain how and why nations with similar resources do better or worse than their peers and what drives or limits the creation of a more prosperous society.

The goal of the Prosperity Index™ is to illustrate how countries have moved toward or away from prosperity, and to help identify the course that leads from poverty to prosperity.[5] The Institute does this by creating datasets to measure and explain how poverty and prosperity are changing, by conducting research programs which analyze the complex drivers of poverty and prosperity, and by suggesting programs which identify the actions required to enable transformative change.

The Prosperity Index™ has been published since 2007 and goes beyond wealth as the sole measure of prosperity. Instead, it looks at a full range of indicators. One of its fortes is that it is not merely a snapshot in time. Based on years of research data, it tracks and analyses long-standing changes in prosperity and highlights the countries that have made the greatest strides in turning their wealth into greater prosperity. It is not surprising then, to find that the bottom of the rankings is occupied largely by the world's poorest countries and the top ranks are dominated by the world's richest. However, this is not the complete story because, in terms of prosperity, there are numerous factors that determine the life chances and opportunities which are equitably available to all citizens of a country. The Prosperity Index™ considers many of these variables and reasons in arriving at the annual rankings.

In 2018, Pakistan was ranked 136th overall out of 149 countries.[6] In recent times, the three best years for Pakistan were from 2009 to 2011 (highest rank 107th), then dropping drastically to 132nd in 2012. The trend in the last six years from 2013 to 2018 has been virtually flat, hovering close to the lowest ranked countries in all categories and dropping further from overall 130th (in 2015) to 139th in 2016, recovering slightly by two rankings to 137th in 2017 and improving just one rank to 136th in 2018.[7]

Pakistan: Overall Rankings, 12-year trend (2007–2018)	
2007	142nd
2008	140th
2009	107th
2010	109th
2011	107th
2012	132nd
2013	132nd
2014	127th
2015	130th
2016	139th
2017	137th
2018*	136th

* 2018, total 149 countries in the Legatum Index

Source: The Legatum Prosperity Index™ (www.prosperity.com)

Pakistan: Overall Rankings and by Sub-Indexes, 2015-2018				
Legatum Prosperity Index™	2015	2016	2017	2018
Overall Ranking, Pakistan	130	139	137	136
Total countries in Index	142	149	149	149
Sub-Indexes/Nine Pillars	–	–	–	–
1. Economic Quality	101	98	105	104
2. Business Environment	109	117	108*	117
3. Governance	119	100	103	92*
4. Personal Freedom	129	132	132	124*
5. Social Capital	135	137	113*	122***
6. Safety & Security	138	143	143	136*
7. Education	124	125	125	122
8. Health	127	121	115*	107*
9. Natural Environment**	N/A	149**	149**	148

* notable improvements; **ranked last; ***regressing

Source: The Legatum Prosperity Index™ (www.prosperity.com)

Natural Environment Awareness: The most glaring and embarrassing statistic is that Pakistan was ranked at the very bottom of the list of

149 countries in this category for two consecutive years, 2016 and 2017, moving up by just one rank to 148th in 2018. Acute lack of awareness for good environmental practices, poor sanitation and waste management, and endemic industrial pollution are conspicuous reasons for this stark and alarming revelation of environmental insensitivity, which may be explained quite possibly by the high rate of illiteracy, corruption, and governmental mismanagement. It probably has strong correlation also to why Pakistan ranks in the lowest quintile (the bottom 20 percent), 122nd out of 149 for Education and 107th for Health in the 2018 Index.

Education is a key pillar and important sub-index in the Prosperity Index™ and an essential building block in the prosperity of all societies. Greater opportunity for education allows people to lead more fulfilling lives and a better-educated workforce is able to contribute to national economic growth through rising levels of personal income and better living standards. There has been modest improvement in worldwide education, mostly due to gains in adult literacy, which has increased by 3 percent since 2007. Pakistan too has made small gains but the severe gaps in sustainable public education programs loom menacingly large because of the enormous problems of mismanagement, extremely high illiteracy rates, insufficient access to schools, and the dismal quality of education.

Quality of Education should be paramount to all stakeholders in education, indeed most important for the goal of incremental, sustainable prosperity. High level outcomes in education can only be achieved by watchful development and monitoring of a balanced and modern curriculum, and by inserting several high quality inputs, including quality teacher training, and pedagogical skills in an orderly, professional development program; quality books and teaching materials; ongoing, incremental reforms, policy update and appropriate budgeting; and building the capacity for efficient administration and management. Enrolling all Pakistani children in schools will be a magnificent feat, but parents and all citizens must have easy access to determine *what* is taught, *how* it is taught and *why* it is taught—with full transparency and easy access to the information. Building a reliable and transparent rating system for quality, with effective oversight by civil society organizations, would ensure that quality in education is to be expected by all, and not an option reserved only for the wealthy who can afford to pay the extra cost for better education.

The Social Capital of a country is its skilled and educated workforce, essentially the engine that will support its economic growth and prosperity into the future. The creation of a productive, high-value workforce begins at secondary and tertiary levels of education. It cannot be built nor sustained without world-class education systems and institutions for certifiable vocational training. Except for a few outstanding initiatives, Pakistan seriously lags behind in both areas and considerably more needs to be done to build high quality university programs and R&D institutions of distinction. It will require greater investment and far better quality control of the tertiary institutions. With unrestrained proliferation of commercially profitable private universities, the unsuspecting market of students and well-meaning parents as their financiers are probably not the best judge of quality. Regulatory policy along with monitoring and enforcement mechanisms for quality assurance in university education must be put in place. Institutions that deliver poor quality and only make the investors rich should be weeded out, given probationary status, and time to demonstrate improved performance, or closed down by legal statute. As foundational institutions, the primary and secondary schooling systems need most urgent attention, but development of top-notch universities and technical-vocational institutes must not be delayed either.

Global Prosperity in 2018 was at a record high. While prosperity as a whole is increasing, not all countries are gaining ground equally. Prosperity can grow and flourish when its foundations are well established with Personal Freedom, solid progress in Governance, and rapidly strengthening Social Capital. Consider the prosperity of **Indonesia** in 2016, gaining 19 ranks over the previous decade to overall 61st on the Index rankings. Improvement in Personal Freedom (up six-ranks), sound progress in Governance (up 14 ranks), and a rapidly strengthening Social Capital (up 51 ranks) has laid stable foundations on which Indonesian prosperity has flourished and continues to climb. Moreover, in 2018, Indonesia has improved its overall ranking to 49th, an impressive ten-point jump from 2017. But prosperity can also be easily squandered by poor choices leading to bad consequences. **Venezuela**, with its huge oil reserves, has experienced the biggest decline in prosperity over the past decade as millions of once prosperous citizens have fallen back into poverty. Venezuela's experience offers every nation an important warning that each country must continuously protect its hard-earned prosperity for its people.

Regional Rankings, 2018: In the South Asia region, Sri Lanka ranks 67th and India is 94th overall. Bangladesh ranks 109th and has improved its Education score more than any other Asian country in the last five years following significant growth in adult literacy. For a more relevant overview from Pakistan's perspective, the table below lists Countries of Interest to Pakistanis and their overall rankings for 2017 and 2018, in no particular order:

Overall Rankings for Countries of Interest	2017	2018
Pakistan	137	136
Bangladesh	111	109
Iran	117	108
India	100	94
Turkey	88	93
Afghanistan	146	149
Egypt	120	122
UAE	39	39
Tajikistan	102	101
Nepal	89	90
Saudi Arabia	78	86
China	98	82
Sri Lanka	53	67
Indonesia	59	49
Oman	73	69
Bahrain	62	51
Qatar	47	46
Israel	38	37
Singapore	17	21
Kuwait	80	66
Malaysia	42	44
Source: The Legatum Prosperity Index™ (www.prosperity.com)		

Obstacles to Prosperity: A country's wealth does not automatically equate to general prosperity for all citizens, as seen quite clearly in those countries that have large oil reserves or other resources. Among the barriers to prosperity are internal struggles, including sectarian intolerance, civil wars, territorial conflicts, random violence, rampant crime, or border skirmishes leading to constant military tensions and huge procurements of arms, expensive weapons, and disproportionately large defense forces with lavish entitlement programs. Another obstacle to prosperity and a major drain on Pakistan's economy is widespread corruption, which has destructive and damaging long-term results as it creates a culture of tacit acceptance of unethical, shady, and unscrupulous practices at all levels of society. These negatives insidiously drain valuable resources away from constructive actions to build a sound infrastructure and gravely damage the momentum of any planned development effort.

A Measure of Transformation: In measuring prosperity, the goal of the Prosperity Index™ is the transformation of people and the desire to know what their lives are really like, identify what is preventing the lives from being better and how obstacles can be removed. True prosperity should be for everyone, not just for a privileged few. No person should suffer in poverty and social isolation as the result of widespread illiteracy, glaring inequities and blatant social injustice. Given the opportunity, every person should be able to discover, develop and realize the full potential of her capability. Through the insights generated by years of research and data, the Prosperity Index™ is proof that transformation is possible. The research and data also provide the tools and knowledge to help bring about that transformation.

The Message: The Legatum Institute urges everyone—all readers, including you and me—to explore its online sites, study its reports and the well-researched Prosperity Index™ for interesting details and valuable analyses of data—such as why, for example, Norway has dominated and held the number one ranking in most years from 2009 to 2018 except 2016, when it 'dropped' behind New Zealand to the number two spot; why, in the four-year period (2015–2018), the top five rankings have been shared between Norway, New Zealand, Finland, Switzerland, Sweden, Canada and Denmark; why the Nordic countries are in the top quintile of rankings year after year. The answer: good governance and model social democracies; an economic model that nurtures private ownership and egalitarian, democratic, and classless societies; freedom to make life choices; and absence of corruption. Why is it that nations in the fourth quintile of countries, ranked 91–120, generally underperform in Personal Freedom and Governance? Answer: poor basic legal rights, weak rule of law, poor participation in the political process—and, my pet peeve and greatest annoyance—poor quality of education.

In 2018, Legatum observes 'Prosperity is growing, but not equally'. Readers are once again encouraged to mindfully study the online data from Legatum and other sources; use it to inform your vote and to hold leaders to account; utilize it to make better choices; to keep media honest and challenge political interests; use it to educate children, to inspire your family, your friends, and help your communities understand the issues. Most important, use it in ways that will make lives positively better for the poor.

5.3 How Poverty is Measured

The straightforward, traditional method of measuring poverty is to set a poverty line, count the number of people living with income or consumption levels below that poverty line, and divide the number of poor people by the estimated population. This is the poverty headcount ratio which provides information that is easy to interpret. It tells us the share of the population living with incomes or consumption levels below the poverty line. But measuring poverty through headcount ratios fails to capture the *severity* of poverty because individuals with consumption levels marginally below the poverty line are counted as being poor, the same as individuals with consumption levels much further below the poverty line.

The 'Poverty Gap Index': An alternative way of measuring the intensity of deprivation is to calculate the amount of money required by a poor person to just reach the poverty line. In other words, calculate the income or consumption shortfall from the poverty line. To aggregate statistics, the sum of all such shortfalls across the entire population (counting the non-poor as having zero shortfall) is expressed in per capita terms as the mean shortfall from the poverty line. The 'poverty gap index' takes the mean shortfall from the poverty line and divides it by the value of the poverty line. It gives the fraction of the poverty line that people are missing, on average, to escape poverty. The poverty gap index should be used in policy discussions because its unit (percent mean shortfall) allows for meaningful comparisons of the relative intensity of poverty.

The 2018 Prosperity Index: Not Good News for All. National prosperity depends on sound leadership for domestic priorities with a clear and determined agenda for development. The 2018 Prosperity

Index™ presents evidence that global prosperity is at its highest level in the twelve-year history of the Index, but the gap is widening between countries with the highest and lowest prosperity scores. Driven by conflict, war, terrorism, oppressive regimes, and the declining availability of food and shelter, **Safety and Security** is worse in recent years with significant deterioration in the Middle East–North Africa (MENA) region and sub-Saharan Africa. In the Central American and Latin American countries and the MENA region, the severe social dislocation caused by forced migrations due to insecurity and conflicts has resulted not only in the loss of assets, but it has also severely affected personal wellbeing, family incomes, economic growth, education, and all social systems for millions of uprooted families. The emotional upheavals are on top of the material losses and hardships endured for survival. A new beginning for the refugees, when it finally occurs, takes years for resettlement and adjustment in the host countries.

For Pakistan, it is imperative first that peace prevails and that the barriers to prosperity—sectarian intolerance, territorial and border conflicts, military tensions, random violence, lawlessness—are minimized and rapidly removed. We must learn from the examples of conflict-free countries ranked at the top of the Index™ and the other countries clamoring to gain higher ranking. Their prosperity, social programs and peaceful existence are not by accident, but have been earned by good **Governance** and model institutions that develop and sustain classless, democratic societies with freedom and fairness in all aspects of life.

5.4 Pakistan's Spot on the 2018 Prosperity Index™

Pakistan's Spot on the 2018 Prosperity Index™ is overall 136th out of 149 listed countries, far from flattering and a rude wakeup call that tremendous work is needed in all the component sub-indices. A positive consolation and notable improvement for Pakistan in recent years is the all-important pillar of **Governance** (table below) which has jumped an impressive 27 ranks in the last four years. This is an optimistic sign that sustained improvement in Governance will drive other sector indicators and sub-indexes to higher levels as well. We will hope that the Prosperity Index™ serves as an annual report card on where we stand in the comity of nations.

Pakistan: Governance Sub-Index (2015-2018)	2015	2016	2017	2018
Governance	119	100	103	92*
*Out of 149 countries				

Pakistan: How can poverty be measured (and reduced)? In an unregulated, largely non-taxed, and mostly cash economy like Pakistan, it is daunting to project reliable metrics of income disparity and the true nature of poverty. There is probably no official measure of poverty or prosperity except perhaps the GDP per capita, but the census numbers may not be reliable enough to estimate the sector demographics. Without the right data, policymakers cannot possibly tackle the causes of poverty or track progress to effectively improve the lives of those in poverty. What the state can do is provide essential infrastructure of development—housing, roads and bridges, railways and public transportation systems; health services; clean energy with regulated utilities; environmental and waste management; and essential, quality education (schools, colleges) for all children and adults—by which the poor and all citizens can have a better chance to work for economic opportunities and advancement toward prosperity.

Poverty is not limited to Pakistan or to countries at the bottom of the Prosperity Index™. The major developed countries, including the USA and UK, also struggle with poverty and with defining its metrics. Reliable statistical data for poverty in Pakistan is easily a few years off in the future. However, the building of essential infrastructure components is just common sense and important for national development. Without a sound infrastructure—and *quality education*—a majority of the poor may remain isolated in poverty, deprived of the opportunity to find a way out of the vicious cycle.

A New Measure of Poverty: In rural or in urban life, there are certain costs of living such as food, health, transport, housing, etc. which are essential to maintain a decent middle-class life. For people living in poverty (the masses in Pakistan), the family is often the only safety net. The social demographic of the rural family is changing as educated and skilled young men and women of the millennial generations move to urbanized, independent living. There are no state programs of social support for the elderly, the infirm or children; no pension or social security income; no national health programs and typically, no savings to fall back on. Measuring poverty and identifying its cause is essential if action is to be taken to improve the lives of those barely surviving in poverty. Lumping or aggregating the various types of poverty into a single category does not give a true picture of the problem or a path to effective social solutions.

In the UK, a Social Metrics Commission[8] has been established with the aim of developing new metrics of poverty. It is shocking to learn that more than 14 million people in the UK live in poverty. While there are several measures of income inequality and poverty, there are no standard metrics of segmented populations within those poverty statistics for children or adults, or those living on pension sources. Thus, social agencies and policy makers are unable to track progress of programs aimed at particular population segments, leaving a gap in efforts to confront the deeper causes of poverty and for improving the lives of those existing in poverty. Other governments may want to study the practices and outcomes of the Social Metrics Commission and learn from its model and findings.

Pakistan's Multi-Dimensional Poverty Index (MDPI). The MDPI Report[9] of June 2016 is a collaboration of Oxford Poverty and Human Development Initiative, the UNDP and Pakistan's Ministry of Planning, Development and Reform. For this book, I found the data overly technical and better suited for development professionals. I hope that simpler data with reliable baselines and trends will be developed and made available for public education and for use by policy makers.

Poverty and Shared Prosperity: World Bank Report. Is national prosperity equitably shared? Are the relatively poor able to participate in and benefit from economic progress within each country? A World Bank report[10] 'Poverty and Shared Prosperity 2018' monitors indicators that measure the annualized growth rates in average income (or consumption) among 'the bottom 40%' poorest of the population in each country. Because of uneven growth at the bottom and the top, this measure is meaningful as a gauge of how well prosperity is shared within each country.

5.5 Effects of Poverty and Education Level of Parents...on the Child's Brain and Development*

The common characterization of poverty is the scarcity of certain material possessions, property, money, or other resources. Poverty is also relatable to the inability of an individual or family to consistently produce sufficient income for subsistence, savings, and emergency needs. It is a complex concept and degrees of poverty vary by the benchmark and the context in which it is discussed. It is obvious that Pakistan is a relatively poor country with a large population, over 200 million. A huge number of families and whole communities have been living in poverty for generations, with no end in sight.

Studies support the view that poverty and illiteracy are associated with delayed child development and structural changes in specific brain regions involved in memory processing, language functions, planning, decision making, organizational skills, and emotional regulation. These relationships are most evident in the lowest income group. Studies quoted in a post by Eugene Rubin and Charles Zorumski in *Psychology Today** (June 2017), report the influence of poverty on the physical development of the brain, the child's learning ability and development. More recently, research on the relationship of parents' income and educational level on the brain development of children have been reported by Kimberly Noble and colleagues in *Nature Neuroscience*— and by Nicole Hair and colleagues in *JAMA Pediatrics*.

The relationship of educational level of the parents on the brain development in children persists, even after adjusting for income level. Consequently, at-risk children continue to have deficits in school-readiness skills. One of the studies estimates that 15 to 20 percent of the deficits (in school-readiness) directly involve structural brain differences. The studies state that improving the parenting and nurturing skills of caregivers early in children's lives can decrease the effects of poverty on structural brain development. Additionally, the studies suggest '... it is possible that [even] modest improvements in income and educational achievement of caregivers might influence children's brain development and cognitive and emotional functioning.' The post concludes with a disclaimer emphasizing the need for well-designed, specific and carefully controlled research studies.

* Source: *Psychology Today* (7 June 2017) 'Income, Education, Social Support, and Brain Development: Environmental factors can powerfully influence brain growth

in children' by Eugene Rubin MD, PhD and Charles Zorumski MD. https://www.
psychologytoday.com/us/blog/demystifying-psychiatry/201706/income-education-
social-support-and-brain-development

References: JAMA is the Journal of the American Medical Association

1. 'Effects of poverty on childhood brain development: the mediating
    effect of caregiving and stressful life events,' JAMA Pediatrics, 2013.
2. 'Family income, parental education, and brain structure in children
    and adolescents,' Nature Neuroscience, 2015.
3. 'Association of child poverty, brain development, and academic
    achievement,' JAMA Pediatrics, 2015.
4. 'Poverty's most insidious damage: the developing brain,' JAMA
    Pediatrics. 2015.

5.6 Poverty, Malnutrition and Stunting

Contrary to the stark reality, many of us take comfort and consolation
in the false belief that 'no one is really starving in Pakistan'. That may
be true because hardy humans have innate ability to survive under
adverse conditions, getting by on far less food and the essential nutrients
required for healthy immunity and normal growth. But, if subjected to
prolonged 'survival-feeding' at close to starvation levels, a child may
suffer irreversible effects of stunting during the early growth years.
It is in the critical early years of life that learning and socialization
must take place for healthy, balanced development. Unfortunately, the
severely undernourished child becomes a victim of poverty, nutrition
deficiencies, and stunting that can affect physical as well as cognitive
development.

UNICEF estimates that nearly 40 percent children in the developing
world are stunted to varying degrees. Oblivious to many of us who live
well and eat well, almost 10 million Pakistani children under the age
of five are stunted. That's an appalling 45 percent of Pakistan's child
population and this number ranks among the top three in the world,
according to a 2016 study[11] by WaterAid. Around 39 percent of Pakistan's
population have no sanitary toilets in the homes and 9 percent have no
access to clean water.

Stunting is defined[12] as height for age below the fifth percentile on
a reference growth curve and it is an important indicator of nutrition
related disorders. Causes of childhood stunting include chronic or

recurrent infections, intestinal parasites, and low birth weight. Major contributing factors are poor maternal health and nutrition during and after pregnancy. Many of these factors are inter-related. For example, low birth weight is correlated with nutritional deficiencies, and inadequate nutrition leads to chronic or recurrent infections. The vicious cycle is a result of poverty and the inability to adequately care for children because of lack of clean water, absence of sanitation (toilets), and long distances between home and any form of health services.

One of the grim consequences of stunting is impaired cognitive development. When a child receives inadequate quantity of food, the body conserves energy by limiting social activity and cognitive development. Unlike normal children, the affected child is often apathetic and incurious and may not develop the capacity to adequately learn or play. The child's body will also limit the energy available for growth. Studies show that improvement in diet after age two can restore the child to near-normal mental development. Conversely, persistent malnutrition after age two can be just as damaging as it is before age two. It is important to note also that, once stunting is established, it is typically irreversible beyond the age of 3 or 4.

The longer-term solutions are in the challenging all-out alleviation of poverty: planned housing, clean water supply, sanitation, waste management, and other aspects of infrastructure building and economic development. Simultaneously needed is quality education as the change factor and paradigm, the catalyst that would bring about social change. But, immediate solutions must be put into effect to save the unfortunate children.

On an average day in Pakistan, millions are spent by us, the affluent, just on eating out. The same is true for those in the Pakistani Diaspora, and others, wherever we are. So, lack of money is not the issue and essential food is not an expensive commodity. We could easily do our part to save the presently affected children from this endemic malnutrition and distribute essential food and health supplements on a national scale. The nutritious food packages could contain dates, dry fruits, nuts, powdered milk, vitamin supplements, and anti-diarrhea pills. A ten-year campaign should be designed initially with 60 percent funding from a federally budgeted 'Save the Children' program and the balance from a civil society-funded campaign for child nutrition. These are merely off-the-top suggestions; the details and logistics can be left to experts.

Unless there is concerted effort to deal with this scourge, the enormous number of 10 million stunted children will almost certainly add to the existing huge numbers of out-of-school children. It's a scary thought and represents an even bleaker future for the country in the absence of solutions for poverty relief, public-environmental health, and infrastructure building. But we must marshal the courage to face the challenge and get past this troublesome morass to rebuild Pakistan. Just as we mobilized after the massive earthquake of 2005 and the ravaging floods of 2010, we must act as advocates to save the malnourished children. The solution to stunting is another cross to bear for Pakistanis, the Diaspora, and world citizens.[13]

To reiterate, the longer-term solution is alleviation of poverty (planned housing, clean water supply, sanitation, waste management, infrastructure building and economic development) and the importance of education must be re-emphasized. Stunting is not just another minor public health issue. Among many others, it is an egregious and flagrant social injustice being perpetrated upon child victims trapped in poverty. Is our civil society going to be a bystander and wait for 'the government to do something'? Or, will we step up and act as Agents of Change?

5.7 Inclusive Education

'For the young child, there is no second chance. There's a window of opportunity when education either takes place, or it does not.'
Anonymous

The above truism is particularly applicable to the plight of the underprivileged and challenged child. An astonishing number of children are excluded from schools because of congenital or acquired disability, or other discriminatory reasons like race, language, faith, gender, or poverty. The essence of inclusive education is a system that facilitates and welcomes a diverse population of students, learning together regardless of abilities, with equal opportunity to enjoy all activities as friends and peers. Exclusion of a disabled child from education and normal growth opportunities amounts to denial of the child's rights and must not be acceptable in an empathetic society. Everyone benefits when all children are educated together without any distinction—and this must be the cornerstone of inclusive education in Pakistan.

A society as a whole, and its individual members, may be judged by many different standards, some more righteous than others. It is not our place or purpose to judge others. But we must ask ourselves if we possess the conscientious and thoughtful, humane concern for fellow citizens when it comes to how we—as individuals and as a just society—care for the human rights of the most unfortunate citizens among us, the disabled underprivileged child.

Almas Akhtar, a research writer, cautions that education policy can be divisive. Ms Akhtar says, 'Pakistan has blatantly ignored citizenship education... [and the teaching of] coexistence, respect, tolerance, and peace are absent [in our education] ... having a very negligible focus on the idea of inclusive citizenship.'[14] She adds that these factors promote '...apartheid-like arrangements and an exclusionary, passive form of citizenship.' I believe these words resonate strongly within the context of inclusive education.

In 1991, the UN Convention on the Rights of the Child (UNCRC) asked signatory countries to protect the rights of all children through inclusion in mainstream schools, employment, culture, and recreation. Article 28 of the UNCRC[15] states that signatories recognize the right of the child to education on the basis of equal opportunity, encourage the development of secondary education including general and vocational education, and higher education for all.

For Pakistan, a country struggling to provide quality schooling, inclusive education for children with special needs adds to the challenges—but we must not skirt around the issue. Instead of attempting to have the challenged child adapt to fit the capacity of the schools (and society at large), the objective of inclusive education should be to make changes in the school system to meet essential requirements for children with special needs. The most efficient means to achieve truly inclusive education is to ensure that children with special needs shall be provided the opportunity in mainstream schools to develop like all children.

In 1994, the World Conference on Special Needs Education called for inclusion as the guiding principle for integration of children in society regardless of their physical, intellectual, social, emotional, linguistic, or other conditions. Later, the Millennium Framework for Action passed a Resolution in 2002 for an inclusive, barrier-free, and rights-based society for persons with disabilities.

Peter Mittler, renowned Austrian-British educationist and writer on inclusive education, suggests that inclusion should be at the heart of both education and social policy:

In the past, obstacles to participation were defined in terms of physical access to buildings or public transport. They are now conceptualized more broadly to include legislation, policies, public attitudes, or professional practices which restrict access to education, employment, health, housing, and leisure facilities on the same basis as [for] other citizens. However, access alone is only the first step to participation. Thus inclusive education involves much more than mere presence in the classroom: it requires an accessible curriculum, as well as teachers whose professional training has equipped them to meet the needs of the whole range of children in the community.[16]

In a brief conversation with Talat Azad, a friend and UK-based educator with focus on inclusive education and children with special needs, I recorded her unassuming statements:

Every child has varying needs and the teacher has to utilize strategies that work for the child. The teacher can make or break any program. A good understanding of inclusive education and the right mindset are important. Sometimes, there's also the problem of dealing with the parent of a 'normal' child without disabilities, who objects to a disabled child being in the same classroom with her 'normal' child, expecting the disabled child to be sent to a school for children with special needs. The attitude towards disabled persons and children is a societal problem. Change is coming but it won't be overnight.

Pakistan's mainstream schools generally are ill equipped to accommodate children with special needs such as autism, visual impairment, physical limitations, learning disabilities (which often remain unidentified), hearing impairment, speech disorders, and others. Some children with special needs can be considered disruptive to the flow of the classroom environment and may require special assistance by trained personnel. The system of special education schools is even more deplorable and heartbreaking. The number of schools for special needs is inadequate and most children from rural areas do not have access to them. The teachers and district administrators for these public schools are often absent. There are hardly any special training programs for the teachers and support staff. And there are also groups with vested interest that support the segregated system of special education which separates the children with special needs.

As a matter of principle and policy, every effort must be made to include the children with special needs into mainstream schools to avoid segregation. Inclusive education and the participation of children with special needs in all schools does present a situation that requires a policy shift away from a category-based approach toward a more unified set of guidelines, which should include how resources shall be allocated towards improving teaching capacity and accessibility of schools, as well as the provision of reasonable accommodation in competency testing for students with special needs.

Inclusive education must be embraced as the best policy approach for delivering quality education to all children. Through comparative research on inclusive practices in other countries, Pakistani grassroots groups for disability rights, education NGOs, activists, advocates, parents, and educators must challenge the narrative that inclusive education is expensive and difficult to implement. Advocacy groups must engage with policy makers to propose legislation and practices needed to promote genuine inclusion on a national scale.

Poor understanding of inclusion rights and shortage of trained teachers can lead to obstacles which must be resolved. Teaching in inclusive settings must begin with special training for teachers and support staff. Key to institutionalizing inclusive education policies is to begin with better awareness and changing how teachers and school administrators engage with all their students, particularly the students with special needs.

Transformative change in this area will require much more than the reformation of laws and policies. It will require parents, teachers and administrators to understand the rights-based goals and philosophies that are the basis for inclusive education. New cultural beliefs must replace deeply ingrained discriminatory stereotypes about persons with disabilities. Along with compassion and a pragmatic approach, there should be no reluctance to invest in the work of changing how social inclusion is conceived and the value of good education with equality for all students.

National planners must acknowledge that an inclusive education system benefits children from all groups in society—and not just children with special needs—by inculcating empathy, understanding, acceptance, and appreciation of diversity. It is also less costly to transform mainstream schools to inclusive ones through additions of enabling infrastructure and teacher training, than to create segregated special education centers that are poorly managed, divisive, and against the spirit of equality laid down in the Constitution as well as by international conventions. As a measure of reform, Pakistan's planners must review and reinforce legislation for inclusive education, setting a target of two years to complete the process. Only then will the public-sector and private schools take the necessary steps to develop an integrated and inclusive education system for all. The government should assist the schools in developing infrastructure, resource rooms, and teacher training for inclusive programs. There is a fair number of organizations representing persons with special needs that can facilitate this, including setting up assessment protocols, curriculum adaptations and evaluation procedures. A fundamental change in approach and underlying assumptions in policy as well as education administration is needed to restructure the prevalent culture, attitudes, and practices with regard to inclusive education.

The following sections are extracted from Open Society Foundations,[17] a philanthropic organization that supports inclusive education globally.

The Value of Inclusive Education. Systems of inclusive education provide a better quality education experience for all children and help in changing attitudes of discrimination. Schools are the child's first window to the world outside the home and enable the development of social relationships. Respect and understanding grow when students of diverse abilities and backgrounds play, socialize, and learn together with the unique contributions that each student brings to the classroom. Inclusive education reinforces concepts of equal civic participation and life in the community. On the other hand, an education system that segregates children on the basis of disability promotes discrimination against marginalized groups.

By right, every child should be supported by the parents and community to grow, learn, and develop in the early years and, upon reaching school age, go to school and be welcomed and included by teachers and peers alike. In a truly inclusive setting, students and parents participate in establishing learning goals and take part in decisions that affect them. And school staff must have the training, support, and resources to nurture, encourage and respond to the needs of all students.

Segregation of Children. Should the system separate children who need special education? Separation does not guarantee success for children who need special attention. Better outcomes are demonstrated by inclusive schools that provide supportive conditions for learning. Extracurricular activities, peer support, or specialized interventions (for example, training for the visually impaired or hearing-impaired child), should involve the entire school community working as a team.

Elements of Inclusive Education

Teaching assistants or specialists: Staff members can be assets for inclusion or potentially divisive for the program. An ideal assistant or specialist helps teachers address the needs of all students. Conversely, an assistant who pulls students out of class to work with them individually on a regular basis is not inclusive.

Curriculum: An inclusive curriculum has locally relevant themes and contributions to the curriculum by marginalized minority groups. It should allow for adaptation to the learning styles of children with special needs.

Parental involvement: In addition to communications and parent-teacher conferences, inclusion means reaching out for involvement of parents on their own terms.

Moving Forward with Inclusive Education. To make inclusive education a reality, we need to:

1. ensure that educators have the training, flexibility, and resources to teach students with diverse needs and learning styles;
2. ensure that kindergartens and schools receive adequate and sustainable financial support so that all activities and services are fully inclusive;
3. empower parents to assert their children's right to education in inclusive settings;
4. enable the entire community—including mainstream and special educators, social workers, parents, and students—to work together and participate in the design, delivery, and monitoring of education, thereby reframing inclusive education as a shared responsibility; and

5. hold the government responsible for implementing antidiscrimination legislation, legal mandates for inclusion, and policies to remove barriers.

The Expense of Inclusive Education. Making education inclusive is not a cost-cutting measure. Governments must be prepared to invest substantial resources at the outset on system reforms, such as teacher and staff training, improving infrastructure, additional learning materials, and equipment; and revising curricula to implement inclusive education successfully. However, by eliminating redundancy and the high costs of running parallel systems, such investments are an efficient and effective use of funds and have the potential of improving education for all students. Funding mechanisms must be reformed so that schools that enroll students with special needs receive the necessary additional resources. When students move from special schools to mainstream schools, the funding should also follow.

How to Support Inclusive Education. We can promote changes to policy and practice in these ways:

1. advocate for the recognition of children's legal rights, such as supporting organizations of parents of children with special educational needs and disabilities;
2. fund empirical research for documenting barriers to education;
3. support sustainable services such as teacher associations and parent groups for disabled children
4. strengthen civil society groups that give young people, parents, and educators a voice, including parent-led organizations advocating for the rights and inclusion of children with special needs;
5. engage with civil society and other actors in policy development by providing technical support to the development of key inclusive education-related laws, policies, and strategies at the national level; and
6. support government services to pilot models of successful inclusive education provision that could be scaled and replicated.

Grateful acknowledgement is due to Rukhsana Shah, former Federal Secretary, Ministry of Textile Industry, for her columns in Dawn.com on the subject of inclusive education, gender disparity, and poverty. Extractions of ideas from her writings have been helpful in constructing this essay on Inclusive Education.

5.8 The Empathy Gap

'Talent is universal, but opportunity is not.'
Nicholas Kristof and Sheryl WuDunn

In an online video course,[18] journalist and champion for global social change, Nicholas Kristof and his equally talented and socially conscious wife Sheryl WuDunn, discuss opportunity benefits to society at large from good quality universal education. 'Talent is universal, but opportunity is not. Expanding opportunities benefits not only those individuals but also enriches the entire society'. Kristof and WuDunn go on to say that the reason that nineteenth century America rose to global economic pre-eminence was because it invested in human resources, because the US became a leader in mass literacy, then in mass high school education. It was also one of the first countries in making tertiary education readily available on a mass scale, which benefitted not just those individuals who got educated but the entire American economy.

Kristof expounds also on the reality of an 'empathy gap' or insulation of the affluent from need and real poverty, a gap which can create narratives in which the poor are blamed for being poor, for personal irresponsibility, or other self-destructive behaviors. In fairness, the affluent are equally compassionate and kind as anyone else, and intellectually aware of the need. But they don't see the needs of the poor around them daily. The 'need' remains distant like a non-living object, not a human necessity. 'That's when that empathy gap arises and that's the basic obstacle in addressing inequity,' says Kristof.

Lottery of Life: The Rich-Poor Gap. The Kristof-WuDunn video narration continues with the statement that one of the most important reasons to expand opportunity and addressing the empathy gap is our own privilege, that we take things like security, food and clothing for granted even in tough economic times. 'With that good fortune comes great responsibility as well that if we win the lottery of life, we have some obligation to give back.'

The Rich-Poor Gap is just as evident in Pakistan as it is in America, the land of opportunity. It is this gap that is widening in both societies, with much less opportunity for those at the bottom. Many child enrichment opportunities are available in affluent families, from music, chess, sports, and healthy outdoor activity to books, personal computers, access to libraries, playgrounds, and parks. Early childhood intervention and college attendance are far greater in rich families, while merely having access to a school, *any school,* could be cause for celebration in a poor Pakistani family. To be born poor in America today is to have a much smaller chance of entering the middle class. The same has been true in Pakistan for decades, except for the few fortunate families who are finding a way out of poverty, beating the odds, because their children were blessed with a neighborhood school that gave them a foot in the door. Many of these Pakistani children are making it to colleges, universities, and better jobs. The numbers are miniscule but, in a few years, these educated children can make many times the income of their parents. They are successfully climbing the socioeconomic middle-class ladder, thanks to education. These life outcomes are as important as the cognitive gains of education for these children. A great deal more remains to be done. Transformation is imperceptibly sluggish in this young and difficult country. Progress for education in the court of social justice may be painfully slow but the struggle must go on. Again, Kristof's video narration says it well: 'We have been lucky in the lottery of life. We can move that balance by sharing all that good fortune we have with all those who didn't get that lucky.'

Educating a Family Begins with Education of Girls. More from Kristof's video narration: 'Education of girls and bringing them into the workforce—and into civil society—has a real impact on reducing radicalism and extremism, very likely because educated women have more voice in society, and women's voices are usually of moderation. Also, educated women have fewer children which has an impact on the "youth bulge" and contributes to unemployment, frustrations, and radicalization.'

One thing is certain: the myth has been busted that it is because of Pakistan's conservative culture that poor parents don't want their daughters to be educated. Recalling from Chapter 3, the amazing personal stories of Uzma, Sidra, and Iqra are evidence that girls from underprivileged families can successfully achieve their potential and do well in professional careers. Fortunately, and through their own personal struggles, these young women have created equity and opportunity by leveraging the education and life skills they have acquired. They are also living proof that there is no glass ceiling when equal opportunity for quality education is available. Such is the potential and the incredible power of good education.

The Out-of-School Children

To accurately measure the number of out-of-school children, we need to improve the accuracy of data on population, enrolment and attendance; refine consistency between population and enrolment data; and develop new indicators to measure exclusion from education.

The quote is from a milestone UNICEF 2015 report[19] that spotlights the barriers to education. First, half of the world's out-of-school children live in conflict affected countries. Second, deep-rooted gender stereotypes and cultural restrictions often influence whether or not a child starts and stays in school. Third, a household's dependence on child labor to supplement family income often conflicts with the child's educational needs. Fourth, many children are marginalized by education that is delivered in a language they neither speak nor understand. And, finally, there are barriers that prevent challenged children from participation in inclusive education. The UNICEF report reinforces the dire need for good data to inform educational policies and reduce the systemic barriers that stand between children and their fundamental right to an education. It also provides insights about the out-of-school population and the demand for education. There are equity gaps between the well-off and the poor, between those living in urban and rural areas, and between girls and boys. Together, the combination of gender, rural under-development and poverty keep some children out of school. The report also questions what keeps girls out of school: Is it gender related or because of poverty?

In 2001–2002, the populous South Asian region had 25 percent of the world's primary school-age children. The region also had the highest number of out-of-school (OOSC) children. In that period, 42 million of the 162 million school-age children in the region (or 26 percent) were out of school and South Asian boys and girls were more than a third (or 36 percent) of the global out-of-school children.[20] It is distressing to note that, despite the MDGs and global push for universal education in the last two decades, there has not been significant change in the region.

Estimates of the total out-of-school children in Pakistan run as high as 25 million. By itself, the country has more than half of the OOSC in South Asia. Balochistan province has the highest proportion of Pakistani OOSC and the greatest disparity by gender, household income, and the socio-economic gap of urban-rural living. There is also a high rate of child workers in the labor force. To supplement the family income, these at-risk working children often miss out on education during the ideal window of time for development in a school environment with more fortunate child peers.

Reiterating what TCF VP, Zia Abbas, has said (in Chapter 2) regarding persons who missed out on education, one of the TCF programs is:

> '...to look at the population who have missed the boat, so to speak, and see if we can provide a standardized, consistent, well-delivered and low-cost solution for men and women who are beyond the age of going to school—young adults, adolescents—and be able to provide not just literacy but basic life skills as well: how to open a bank account, how to deal with money, how to deal with the system, how to deal with government, and also how to run an enterprise perhaps and how to deal with technology. So, these are all themes which this population segment is not accustomed to or exposed to—and there is no enabling entity out there which provides information and guidance on this.'

In this context, it makes absolute sense that reforms must include literacy programs for those who were deprived of schooling in the early years.

5.9 The Global Challenge: Fixing the Broken Promise of Universal Education

Education is the most dependable course out of poverty and a pathway for healthier, more productive citizens and stronger societies. It represents the hopes, dreams and aspirations of children, families, communities and nations around the world. Education tops the list when people in poverty are asked what single factor could change the future of their families. Globally, about 258 million children are out of school, according to UNESCO data[21] for 2018. This includes 59 million children of primary school age and about 199 million of secondary school age. It is important to determine the reasons why children are not in school in the first place. As countries strive to achieve universal primary and secondary education by 2030, the UNESCO Institute for Statistics (UIS) provides detailed data and analysis on out-of-school children and youth to better identify who they are, where they live and the barriers they face.

My search for 'UNESCO children out of school' resulted in dozens of great sources worth deeper reading. The one to catch my eye was a news item[22] of September 13, 2019: 'UNESCO warns that, without urgent action, 12 million children [globally] will never spend a day at school.' Note that these are not dropouts. The news brief goes on to state that it will be difficult to ensure inclusive quality education for all by 2030, one of the Sustainable Development Goals. Can Pakistan contribute to the reduction of that number by implementing a system of good schooling for all Pakistani children by 2030? I believe it can be done. It will need strong, sustained civic leadership and a huge number of people behind the effort.

Notes

1. Stanford Encyclopedia of Philosophy, revision November 8, 2014, https://plato.stanford.edu/.
2. Universal Declaration of Human Rights, United Nations, http://www.un.org/en/universal-declaration-human-rights.
3. Amartya Sen, *Development as Freedom* (New York: Oxford University Press, 1999), p. 63.
4. Legatum Institute: https://www.li.com/.
5. The Legatum Prosperity Index™, 2018 (www.prosperity.com).
6. Pakistan Ranking, 2018, The Legatum Prosperity Index™, https://www.prosperity.com/globe#PAK.
7. In the latest report for 2020, Pakistan was ranked 137 among 167 countries. See The Legatum Prosperity Index™, https://www.prosperity.com/rankings.
8. Social Metrics Commission https://www.li.com/activities/publications/a-new-measure-of-poverty-for-the-uk-a-report-by-the-social-metrics-commission.
9. MDPI Report 2016 https://www.ophi.org.uk/wp-content/uploads/Multidimensional-Poverty-in-Pakistan.pdf.
10. Poverty and Shared Prosperity 2018, World Bank, https://www.worldbank.org/en/publication/poverty-and-shared-prosperity-2018.
11. http://pakhumanitarianforum.org/wp-content/uploads/2016/08/Caughtshort, Report, WaterAid.pdf. Note: The UNDP report Human Development 2018 Statistical Update verifies (in Table 8) that 45% of Pakistan's child population are stunted. http://hdr.undp.org/sites/default/files/2018_human_development_statistical_update.pdf
12. What is Childhood Stunting? The Borgen Project: https://borgenproject.org/what-is-childhood-stunting.
13. See Nicholas Kristof's column on malnutrition and stunting in *The New York Times*, 12 June 2019 'The World's Malnourished Kids Don't Need a $295 Burger' https://www.nytimes.com/2019/06/12/opinion/guatemala-malnourished-children.html?te=1&nl=nickkristof&emc=edit_nk_-20190613?campaign_id=45&instance_id=10155&segment_id=14250&user_id=1588f35a26d872a5cc778b9e5f3e195d&regi_id=5752450720190613
14. Almas Akhtar, 'Education and Inclusive Citizenship', *The Express Tribune*, 1 December 2017, https://tribune.com.pk/story/1573171/education-inclusive-citizenship.
15. Convention on the Rights of the Child, Unicef, 1990: https://www.unicef.org/child-rights-convention/convention-text.
16. Peter Mittler, *Overcoming Exclusion—Social Justice Through Education* (Routledge, 2013), p. xii.
17. https://www.opensocietyfoundations.org/explainers/value-inclusive-education?utm_source=news&utm_medium=email&utm_campaign=news_050617&utm_content=MFQ0zWmlUrqiSRjmPtoqLOh5VzsoGCqWn2j5YLNa7E4

18. How to Make A Difference, https://www.udemy.com/how-to-make-a-difference-by-nicholas-kristof-sheryl-wudunn.
19. 'Fixing the Broken Promise of Education for All: Findings from the Global Initiative on Out-of-School Children' (Reading is strongly recommended by author). https://data.unicef.org/resources/fixing-the-broken-promise-of-education-for-all-findings-from-the-global-initiative-on-out-of-school children/.
20. From UNESCO-UIS report (2005), 'Children Out of School—Measuring Exclusion from Primary Education'.
21. Out-of-School Children and Youth, UNESCO, http://uis.unesco.org/en/topic/out-school-children-and-youth.
22. UNESCO warns that, without urgent action, 12 million children will never spend a day at school, UNESCO, 2019, https://en.unesco.org/news/unesco-warns-without-urgent-action-12-million-children-will-never-spend-day-school-0.

Chapter Six

The Madrasa as an Institution of Education

As I set out to write about the education landscape, the misunderstood and often-maligned *madrasa* (pronounced 'mud-ruh-sa') began to emerge as an area of interest. The influence of Islamic culture in Pakistani society and its impact on education for the poor needs to be understood and discussed. The findings and views in the chapter are my own and may provide only elementary information about the system of madrasas. But some information may not be common knowledge even for people in Pakistan and readers elsewhere. I have provided brief translations of Arabic terminology or non-English words (see Glossary), my observations from visits to a couple of madrasas, and insightful conversations with two gentlemen in the madrasa system.

6.1 What is a Madrasa?

Contrary to common belief, the madrasa as an Islamic school system is struggling to find recognition as a viable institution of learning for youth in Pakistani society. The perception of the madrasa as a recent creation of political ideology or extremist teaching should be amended. Yes, there is evidence that extremist factions have used a few madrasas to recruit and radicalize youth to further their own political causes. However, most madrasas do not support militant teaching or violence and would probably like to offer a better blend of traditional Islamic teaching along with certain aspects of the mainstream curriculum of the country.

Madrasas have been around for ages and they are here to stay. A madrasa—derived from *dars*, a lesson, reading, or lecture—is a school or a place of learning. Interestingly, a *midrasha* in Hebrew is a Jewish seminary. Mr Jinnah, the first head of state, went to a regular school called the Sindh Madressatul Islam in Karachi, which is now a university.

Growing up in Karachi, I enjoyed going to the large New Town Masjid on Jamshed Road which had a madrasa where young boys and senior students were boarders or day-students, to learn about the faith, much like in seminaries or temples in other faith systems.

Ebrahim Moosa, professor of Islamic Studies at the University of Notre Dame, in his book *What is a Madrasa* answers the question as follows:

> In popular Western media parlance, the mere mention of the word "madrasa" conjures up an "us versus them" dynamic. [...] ...madrasas are the single, most widely used educational resource to cultivate religious learning in parts of the Muslim world. [...] Madrasas specialize in the study of classical theological and legal texts as well as commentaries on the Muslim scripture, the Qur'an.[1]

Dr Moosa goes on to say that madrasas place special emphasis on studying the life and teachings of Prophet Muhammad (PBUH), and the complex details of how rules and morals should regulate public and private conduct according to Islamic tradition. Madrasas also teach some secondary disciplines such as Arabic and Persian grammar and literature, rhetoric, logic, philosophy, and other subjects to gain proficiency in the primary fields of study. Dr Moosa describes the madrasa as a place of study where a sermon or lecture is delivered. In contemporary Arabic, *madrasa* is generic for any educational institution from preschool to high school. It can also mean a modern college, or academy, where lessons and lectures are addressed to the *talaba* (learners). Young children from most families all over the country—even those from middle-class and affluent families, going to regular schools—attend madrasas for an hour or so after school to learn how to read the Quran in Arabic and receive basic instruction on matters of faith. For more advanced Islamic learning, the madrasa is comparable to a theological seminary or similar religious school where scholarly experts in Islamic law and theology are trained in a structured eight-year curriculum.

From a 2017 report by the National Education Management Information System (NEMIS), there were 33,000 Deeni Madaris (religious schools) in Pakistan, of which only 3 percent were part of the public education system. The rest were privately funded and managed by local communities. It is commonly believed that larger madrasas receive funding from donors and possibly also from governments of the Arab countries, mainly Saudi Arabia. Total enrolment in the Deeni Madaris was about 2.26 million with male students making up 64 percent of the enrollment (NEMIS, 2017). Nearly 75,000 teachers were employed by madrasas, or an average of 2.2 teachers per madrasa, which seems about right as most madrasas in the country may have enrollments of less than a hundred students. The numbers of madrasas vary considerably depending on the source. These numbers from the NEMIS report are probably best estimates as the system functions loosely without strict reporting requirements. Included in the estimates are evening or 'after-school' madrasas that many thousands of children may attend for only an hour, primarily to learn recitation, until they 'finish' or *khatm* the Quran which may take a year or so, after which there is no further need to go the madrasa. Evening or after-school madrasas are common in cities and villages and it is interesting how these variables complicate the estimated total counts for type and capacity of the madrasa.

> It is to be noted that affluent and middle-class families will have a *maulvi sahib*, or a lady in the neighborhood, come to their homes to teach recitation to the children for a year or two, until the Khatm of the Quran, which is a family occasion for celebration. A relatively tiny number probably less than 5 percent children may, learn the meaning or interpretation of the entire Quran. – *Author*

Madrasas grew in numbers remarkably during and following the conservative General Zia-ul-Haq administration and are favored by poor families because many of them board and feed the students and enforce some 'discipline'. Most madrasas follow the Sunni doctrine of the Deobandi[2] school of thought and teach the essentials and principles of the Sunni majority version of Islam. Less than 10 percent of madrasas may belong to the minority sects of Islam, primarily the Shia sect, and there is a level of animosity and historical disagreement between conservatives in each of the factions, with hardly any middle ground.

For many families, especially in remote and rural areas, madrasas may provide the only option for *any* education. There are valid concerns by critics that many madrasas offer hardly any instruction beyond the memorizing and study of the Quran. But, in the absence of any school, madrasas may serve a purpose of at least providing 'some literacy' as long as the children are not being indoctrinated to adopt radical ideology. As a pragmatic step for change in such communities (the ones with no school, only a madrasa), these areas could be identified, and schools introduced there with community buy-in and support. With a school option available, parents can decide where their children belong, and both the madrasa and the school may have a place in the child's development, as it does in the larger cities. Over time, the madrasa may be gradually upgraded to deliver a hybrid and balanced education.

6.2 Islamic Scholarship

Dars-e-Nizami is an eight-year study curriculum in 'advanced' madrasas or Dar-ul-Uloom—literally, 'house of knowledge' for senior students—a system that originated in India in the early nineteenth century and can also be found in parts of South Africa, Canada, the US, the Caribbean, and the UK. The name of the Nizami Dars system is linked to its founder, Mulla Nizam Uddin As-Sihaalwi. The Dars syllabus comprises studies in

Tafseer	Quranic translation, commentary and explanation
Hifz	Memorization, Arabic syntax and grammar, Persian and Urdu languages
Taareekh	Islamic history
Fiqh	Islamic jurisprudence

The Dar-ul-Uloom offer a more advanced, broader level of study in addition to the usual Islamic subjects. For example, at the Jamia Dar-ul-Uloom in Karachi, the departments include math, economics, English language, politics, and information technology.

6.3 My Visits to Madrasas

In January 2017, Nadeem arranged for me to meet with Imam Mohammed Ibrahim from the neighborhood masjid in Ibrahim Goth, a dense settlement of about 30,000 in North Karachi. The Imam sahib took us for a Friday evening visit to two madrasas a few miles from Ibrahim Goth in the New Karachi area. We drove on dirt and asphalt roads, through long and open stretches of parched scrub-land, across four-lane 'double roads' with wide divider medians, and areas of sparse

Between the years of 13 and 16, I went through a short period of serious study of the faith, balancing life with excellent education at the St. Lawrence's Boys School, and—at the same time—with intense involvement in multiple sports and other activities, like the Boy Scouts. I was strongly influenced by the secular teachings of our school principal and resident padre, the Reverend Father Armando Trinidad, who taught a class in Sociology in grades 9 and 10. The class had replaced 'Character Building' for Muslim boys and religious instruction or catechism for Catholics. On most days, the Sociology class was just a few minutes of reading and more of open discussion, as we learned about world affairs and history and diverse ideologies—from Karl Marx and communism-socialism to Cuba and Fidel Castro, to segregation, social injustice, and race relations in the US. The discussion never strayed into religion or faith; if it did, Father Trinidad would stop it immediately. The memories are indelible and have shaped my thinking and my life in many ways. During that same phase, I was also regular with my five daily prayers and enjoyed other aspects of the faith—fasting, reciting and serious study of the Quran. I took it as being a normal part of life. My parents were secular and approved but I recall one occasion when my father expressed concern that I was 'turning into a mullah' (religious fanatic). For nearly three years, every morning—right after *fajr* (early morning prayers) and before school—I studied the Quran with Tashreeh which comprised detailed explanation, historical context, interpretations, and discussion with the teacher. In the tiny masjid of Patel Para, my teacher—the Imam sahib—was a respected and very knowledgeable Pashtun man from the scenic Swat region, a graduate of a Karachi madrasa in the New Town masjid. In his Friday *khutba* (sermon), Imam sahib would often include a few relevant couplets in Farsi by Maulana Rumi or Hafiz Shirazi, translate them in Urdu, and connect them to the theme of his khutba which added great value and made the sermons more pertinent to life and considerably more interesting for me. – *Author*

housing. There were signs of slow, planned development taking place in the area. Imam sahib said the entire area was changing and was part of a master-planned project of housing, commercial, and industrial development.

The first stop was Madrasa-e-Siddiqia.[3] We pulled into a gated, two-acre compound with a modest masjid structure that appeared unfinished but the grounds were clean and well-maintained. At the other end of the enclosed compound were rows of basic, flat-topped living quarters, the dorm structures for the boarder students. Closer to the masjid were a few housing units for the resident imam and some teachers. Being a holiday (Friday), no teaching was taking place. The campus had a relaxed level of activity, some children were playing football (soccer), others milled around curiously and came up to meet and greet our small group of visitors. The masjid had no doors, coverings or awnings over the entry ways and no furniture inside except for the low and slanted reading desks for study or reciting the Quran. This is typical of masjids and madrasas where all reading, study and prayer takes place on the floor. The large hall in the front was for prayers and probably doubled as an area where teaching was also conducted on mat-covered floors. In the back hall, I could see rows of bedding and personal items which belonged to student boarders who did not have living quarters in the dorms.

A spontaneous group conversation ensued with about a dozen boys ranging from 10 to 15 years in age, all boarders and mostly from the Khyber Pakhtunkhwa or Quetta, the major city of Balochistan province. Ethnically, most of the boys seemed to be of Pashtun origin but spoke Urdu comfortably. Inayatullah, one of the older boys from Quetta, who had been here for three years, took initiative as the spokesperson to answer our first questions. He was from a smaller madrasa in Quetta and all his education had been in madrasas; he had six brothers who were going to public school, not to madrasas. The madrasa teachers were off for Friday holiday but he pointed to a gentleman in the distance as the Naib Imam who also served as the Muezzin. The Naib Imam was also a teacher and occasionally led the prayers; the *asari-taaleem* at this madrasa was up to 8th grade.

Inayatullah described the normal day's schedule, starting at 8 a.m. with study periods for a combination of *deeni taaleem* and other general education classes until 12 noon, then a break for lunch and some rest, resuming classes for two more hours followed by about an hour for sports and recreation. In the evening, after *maghrib* prayers, they had another short session of study before dinner time, and discussion or study again after dinner, ending the day at about 11 p.m. Some students did their reading or study until later in the night. Another young man joined the group. He was from Sukkur and spoke Sindhi;

he had been at the madrasa for a year and was in his final year of the Dars-e-Nizami curriculum. The madrasa had about a hundred students enrolled. Because of the holiday, many were out in groups visiting relatives or friends in the area. Some groups went to nearby bazaars and communities of North Karachi, or the Clifton beach or parks in Karachi, perhaps for a meal and some clean fun.

I turned to Imam Ibrahim and asked for his thoughts:

> This is a sparsely populated area but for the *roohani* betterment of our society and to spread Islamic knowledge, madrasas like this one are doing what they can. As you heard from these students, there is awareness and desire for general *asari taaleem* and most madrasas are promoting that. The students in this madrasa all go through the general school program and that's a requirement. We believe that many different occupations and perspectives are needed in society. And *deeni ulema* are also needed to give guidance in an Islamic society. We do our best to teach peace and tolerance as well.

With that as a segue to the subject of tolerance and peace, I asked the Imam if there was any truth to what we hear of madrasas being breeding grounds for extremism and radicalism. Imam Ibrahim's calm response was:

> I think that is false and borders on evil rumors. The Prophet Muhammad (PBUH) preached a message of peace and tolerance. Islam is based on these principles. What is happening on the international scene is a geopolitical game of the great powers. The aim of these false rumors is to be divisive and, to a large extent, the rumors are believed only by those who have a bias against Islam and its followers. I firmly believe that in Islam and in the institutions of the deeni madrasas and masjids, there is no place for extremist teaching, violence, or terrorism. To the contrary, terrorism and intolerance is condemned in Islam. We believe in protecting our rights but not through terrorism. We must strive for our rights but only by deliberation and peaceful demonstration.

I asked Imam sahib to comment on 'peaceful jihad' and if that was a contradiction in terms. His response:

> Jihad is a struggle to find a solution. Unfortunately, it has become associated with violence and war but that is a biased view. Of course, we believe that finding a solution to any problem must be a peaceful process.

I don't see a contradiction. As a last resort, when there is the need to take up arms and go to war, that is an unfortunate kind of jihad in which there are no winners. Literally, jihad is a struggle to find solutions and it is always better to do it through a peaceful process. What we are doing through the dissemination of knowledge and education in madrasas is 'jihad' as a solution to human need for spiritual knowledge and moral guidance, with peace and harmony.

We moved on to our next madrasa, Jamia-tur-Rasheed.[4] Jamia is a university and this campus was elaborate and quite impressive. Again, it being a holiday, there was no teaching activity and students were trickling in after being out for the day. It was *maghrib* when we got there and, after quickly offering our evening prayers, we did a quick survey of the campus grounds and noted well-maintained lawns and gardens with spots to lounge and enjoy the surroundings. There was a large swimming pool and we were told there were other sports facilities as well. The three-story buildings for dorms and teaching classrooms were clean, built well, appropriately lit, and well-spaced. We met briefly with a person in administration who gave us a quick summary of the operations: a management committee oversees the Jamia; no tuition fees are charged for most Dars-e-Nizami programs but the BBA and MBA programs charge a fee which is much less than Karachi University; the 2,500 students are all male; the Jamia also operates a Matric (grade 10) school in a separate location and there is a fee of 800 rupees per month for the school program; passing the Matric exam is a requirement for being accepted to the Dars-e-Nizami. We were asked to go to the website[5] for more information.

The conversation with Imam Ibrahim continued on the way back to Ibrahim Goth and I asked:

Q. What type of education—*asari* or *deeni*—is important to solve the education problem in Pakistan?

Imam Ibrahim: The current system of education is based largely on *asari uloom*, but we must not forget our culture and roots of our civilization. Our environment is based on our faith and our culture but we, in the madrasa institutions, are open to learning from all sources of knowledge. Children in many private schools are taught English first, then other subjects. It would be far better if instruction was in the native languages—Sindhi, Balochi, Punjabi, Pushto—or in the commonly spoken Urdu language. The education policy must address these issues. Access to education is generally bad all over but it is so bad in the rural areas that it is hard to imagine how poorly informed and ignorant people can be. Illiteracy is a curse on us.

Q: **The social disparities are appalling, I agree. People from affluent parts of Karachi, the Defense and Clifton areas, have no idea that these communities even exist. They may never set foot in a madrasa or know much about the system. They would have no reason to come to this area in North Karachi and have scarce interest in knowing what's happening here, who lives here, or if the area could become a hub of large campuses of the madrasa system. So, how can they be sensitive to the needs of people living here, or be aware of what life is like in these communities, how the children here will be educated?**

Imam Ibrahim: You are absolutely right. Not only the people of Defense or Clifton, but people from our own Ibrahim Goth community have no idea of the surrounding *goths* and the madrasas we just went to. Unfortunately, it's because of unfounded fears and the stigma of the outlying areas—fear that they can be harmed or kidnapped for ransom. But such is life and there are many challenges. May Allah have mercy. Crime is prevalent with full knowledge of the police. The powerful are corrupt and part of the problem. They look after their own corrupt self-interests, not what is best for the people and the country. With honest law and order, free from corruption, we would not have the extremism and fear of terrorism that is so wrong and unnecessary. Many incidents are created by the police authorities themselves, for their own benefit.

Q: **What are your education and highest credentials?**

Imam Ibrahim: I completed the Dars-e-Nizami and passed the Wafaq-ul-Madaris[6] exam, a degree equal to a master's in Islamiat. I have also completed Takhassus-e-Fiqh or PhD.

The 'PhD' mentioned by Imam sahib was probably a brief 'post-graduate' period of deeper study of Fiqh or Philosophy not affiliated with a post-graduate or doctoral credential. – *Author*

Q: Do you plan further study?

Imam Ibrahim: I'd like to enroll in a four-year program at the International Islamic University in Islamabad. But I have to earn a living to support my family. I am also working hard at learning better English.

Q: Do you have any desire to get involved in politics or public service, to change policy?

Imam Ibrahim: Yes, I've given it some thought. The country needs better policies for equality and social justice, and we must do our part as compassionate Muslims to serve the country. We can, *Insha Allah*, make this a clean and peaceful country and a region of peace. We have been affected severely by geopolitical events in the region. First, we must educate ourselves and acquire the abilities it will take to influence the changes.

Q: Prophet Muhammad (PBUH) emphasized cleanliness and purity in all aspects of life—personal hygiene and grooming, in speech, in thought, and fairness in our actions and dealings with others. Are these thoughts and principles addressed in madrasas? And do you agree that being fair and truthful at all times could result in ethical conduct and reduction in corruption?

Imam Ibrahim: Absolutely. When a child shows up for classes at the madrasa, his personal grooming and cleanliness are noted, and he is advised accordingly. The madrasa environment, the classes and grounds, are kept neat and clean, free of trash and dirt. The Ulema impress upon the students that, with the education they receive, they will be role models and respected leaders of the future. They should practice and teach good values in society, not allow discord in their own communities amongst factions or sects, for example, stand against violence and always for peace and reconciliation. Politics and human emotions do creep into our actions and we must guard against them. Prior to 1974, things were not so bad. Then came the era of Zia-ul-Haq (1977–1988). He was a pious man, but he planted the seed of *firqa bandi* and, unfortunately, since that time, we've had more factions and differences and sectarian violence. We must be tolerant of differences between us and accept these differences which have always been there.

Q: But let's come back to corruption. Commonly, we think of the person taking a bribe as the evil one, and the person giving the bribe as the victim of circumstances. But isn't bribery a two-way transaction?

Imam Ibrahim: That's a good question. Yes, bribery and corruption are evil things in society. But things are not always quite that simple. For example, an educated and wealthy person knows his rights, and how to demand his right. A poor, uneducated person may not have any contacts, and does not know his rights or how to demand his rights. Often, he has to give in to a demand for bribe to get some work done in a government department because it is easier to take advantage of him. Unfortunately, it has become contagious.

6.4 Zeeshan Ahmed
Dean, Karachi School of Business and Leadership

For some time, I had looked for that special individual with a balanced blend of madrasa and modern university education. My patience was rewarded in January 2018 with an opportunity to speak with Dr Zeeshan Ahmed, a madrasa proponent and Dean of the Karachi School of Business and Leadership (KSBL). Zeeshan has a unique combination of education with a master's and a Doctorate in business related fields and has also done almost eight years of extensive study in the Dars-e-Nizami system.

If I were to characterize (dare I say, *profile?*) Dr Zeeshan Ahmed from a website photo—a full and untrimmed beard, a turban, and traditional garments—I would not guess that he is the dean of a business university. Instead, I would probably stereotype him as an ultra-conservative person, steeped in the teachings and practice of Islam, and very likely associated with a madrasa. Interestingly, Zeeshan

Ahmed is all of the above. He believes that it is possible to be a man of both worlds—*deeni* and *duniyawi*. I found him to be unassuming and easy to converse. He is eloquent in English and Urdu and I presume in Arabic as well. And he was comfortable speaking out on the curriculum and pedagogy in madrasas.

Zeeshan is a frequent speaker at community gatherings and some of his talks are documented videos. One video[7] I particularly like is where he talks about social conduct of parents in the context of raising children in modern-day Karachi, espousing parental values and teachings of the Islamic way of life. The video is in Urdu but worth sampling. I hope that the video will be translated with sub-titles in English.

Q: You have an interesting academic and professional portfolio. Please take me through your educational background, starting from early schooling to your PhD and professional development in academia, your education in the Dar-ul-Uloom madrasa, and your connection to the madrasa system.

Zeeshan Ahmed: I went to the BVS Parsi High School in Karachi, then to Government College of Commerce & Economics, Karachi, and did my MBA in marketing from IBA in 1995. I joined Ferguson—a prestigious accounting, audit and consulting firm, where I was a consultant for two years. I had a passion for teaching and learning for my own knowledge, so I joined the IBA faculty as a lecturer, and at the same time I took the course work and tests to become a Chartered Financial Analyst—a designation for international investment professionals. That was in 2001. I realized then that if I wanted to stay in academics, I should get a PhD. I was accepted at Mississippi State University (MSU)—it was the only application I had put in—and they offered me a teaching assistantship for a salary-stipend of $850 per month. After my first semester there, they increased it to $3,000. With that, my wife and I spent four good years at MSU and I returned to Pakistan in 2005 with a PhD in finance. My father and my father-in-law are both Chartered Accountants, same as a CPA or Certified Public Accountant in the US, and they encouraged me to get the American certification for CPA, so I took the CPA exam as well and passed it.

Upon my return to Pakistan, I rejoined IBA for a short time and then moved on to LUMS as an assistant professor and became director of the undergrad program. I was at LUMS for six years and returned to

Karachi in 2012. By this time, KSBL had been established and a few of my colleagues joined me at KSBL. I am currently the Dean at KSBL. My interest in Islamic banking and finance was the driver for me to take this position. Ideally, I would have liked to do my doctorate in Islamic banking and finance but there wasn't empirical data available at the time [in that field], and I didn't want to pursue theoretical research. So, I took this as an opportunity to pursue Islamic finance academically.

You may recall the corporate scandals in the US in 2002. That was the era of the Enron collapse. Consequently, the focus of my dissertation was on earnings management of corporations, how they can manipulate their earnings to a great degree, to look better during product recalls or crises, or to look better in the books, or to achieve 'other goals' and ulterior motives. My doctoral thesis was closer to accounting and market research as opposed to pure economics and finance research.

So, I was teaching Islamic finance at LUMS, and there was growing interest in that field, with new Islamic banks popping up all over the country. A renowned Islamic scholar, Muhammad Taqi Usmani Sahib, advised me to study and understand Islamic finance and banking in greater depth, I should study Fiqh and Arabic.

I've always had an intrinsic curiosity about Islam. In my youth, I had studied the Quran with *tashreeh*. I wanted personal resolution on a few things [in Islamic teaching] and how they were linked. Growing up, I also had an interest in Arabic. I had taken classes at the Dar-ul-Uloom, Karachi, one of the major madrasas, to learn Arabic and for deeper study of the faith. But, with the deanship at KSBL, I have not been able to finish my 8th year of study of the madrasa curriculum. I have about a half-year's study remaining to complete the Ulema eight-year course of madrasa graduation. So, yes—I've been involved in the madrasa system quite intensely.

Q: The statistics and qualitative data on madrasas in Pakistan vary considerably, depending on the source. What's your best estimate of the total number of madaris?

Zeeshan Ahmed: You see, there are various *wafaq* or boards that register the madaris, I think there are four such boards. Deobandi and Barelvi are probably the largest *wafaq*, and there is a common federation of the boards. I think there could be about 5,000 madaris in the country but there isn't an accurate count for any purpose.

Q: Among the madaris, is there consensus that there should be a balanced blend of religious and *duniyawi taaleem* or that madrasa education should be strictly religious?

Zeeshan Ahmed: I must point out that an 8th grade general education [based on the national curriculum] is a pre-requisite at most madaris. In many of the madaris, the pre-req is a Matric or 10th grade general education. In areas without public schools—and there are many such areas—many of the madaris have a school up to 8th grade which follows the national curriculum. Generally, the madrasa students come from regular public schools. Certain subjects like math, Greek philosophy, and Greek logic have been part of the madrasa curriculum for decades. Recently, there has also been discussion about other reforms in the madrasa curriculum. I have suggested integrating the developments that have taken place in the last 300 to 400 years. However, decision makers at the *wafaq* level are reluctant to make sweeping changes. But, reform-minded thinkers agree that changes should be made, and some madaris have introduced contemporary scientific theories of astronomy, the solar system, and so on. So, that's a beginning and change can be expected. It will be gradual, very slow.

If you ask someone who has studied in the conventional education and university systems—given the level of extraction and intangible concepts in theology, *fiqh* and *ilm-ul-aqaa'id*—the legal and philosophical arguments are rigorous even though they are not updated. There's a distinction between *asali* and *naqli dalaa'il*. *Asali dalaa'il* are gleaned from the Quran and Hadith and undoubtedly will contain authoritative and dogmatic statements, because if the Quran is the source of an exquisite statement—yes, the Quranic statement is authoritative—but there are many *naqli dalaa'il* with significant deduction, induction and reasoning. And these contribute significantly to sharpening critical thought processes.

These are the realities. Computer literacy, English, and modern-day science are taught in very few madaris at this time, but these are not yet a curriculum requirement dictated by the *wafaq* or the federation. There is an ongoing movement and effort to introduce these changes into all madaris, across the board, but this will come very gradually. Some progressive madaris in Karachi have taken the lead in this effort. For example, at some of the madaris, there is a rotation of a full year in which the students are immersed in English, learning only English, and they are enabled to study English literature and the sciences. The libraries are being populated accordingly. The objective is to produce madrasa graduates who are relevant for the existing culture in our present society.

> **Q: These are encouraging pieces of information and good signs that the madrasa, as an institution of learning, is opening up to blended and integrated education. But, are inquiry and critical thinking encouraged? Is there open debate and tolerance of non-dogmatic views and does it cause conflict?**

Zeeshan Ahmed: On the traditional side, the content of Fiqh or jurisprudence in Islam is quite rich in rigorous debate and arguments. When I was teaching at LUMS, the students would have a healthy debate and exchange of arguments, because the traditional teachings of Islamic scholars would neither convince nor excite that student population. And, to the surprise of many students, I entertained logical argument and debate. Now, applying this to the tradition that exists in the madrasa, some madrasa students are very sharp—especially if they go out in the world and get a mainstream job and balanced exposure, or get an additional master's degree or an MBA. Many of these madrasa graduates become recognized as highly capable individuals because they have rapidly developed logical thinking and intuition, ability to communicate and articulate, to link things—and these attributes make them stand out.

So, there is great potential but many of the madaris are slow in adapting to the realities and need of the times. *Tafaqquh* can only be achieved through debate and discussion and its *haq* in education can only be attained if teachers would—or if I could, as a teacher— integrate the traditional principles of Islam with current, contemporary knowledge. So, there is the potential to integrate traditional teachings of Islam with contemporary knowledge. And I feel that it can be done. But the madrasa pedagogy must evolve with the confidence that Islamic principles shall not be compromised. The sharper students who have a flair for higher level of thinking and understanding, who have the gift of examining the arguments and developing informed opinion, these are the ones who gain the most from open discussion. Some students can grasp the arguments, but they cannot appreciate its application and do not develop the ability to articulate a balanced position. Perhaps this shortcoming is because of their own limited capacity to learn, and the poor foundation of their general education in the early years. But, the 'high-quality' madaris are taking the lead and creating a model by which the madrasa student is enabled to overcome these shortcomings, and to develop the skills of communication and articulation through listening, comprehension, and practice of eloquent expression of their opinions.

In bank organizations, for example, there is excellent training and a stream for progression at the upper levels of management. But, at the lower levels of workers, it leaves a lot to be desired. However, if the madrasa teachers are pedagogically trained, provided a balanced model, and the teachers are open to teaching a blended and integrated curriculum, then madrasa education has the potential to really contribute a lot. A huge number of children would benefit from this, in addition to the multiple benefits to society at large. Because these are smart children and they have the potential to accomplish just as much as any other student from a non-madrasa elite education setting. In my case, the eight or nearly nine years that I have been associated with madrasa education and my PhD, along with my work and teaching experience, the combination has helped me to sharpen my thinking, my understanding of Islamic finance, and with my life, in general.

Another thing I should point out is that there has been significant damage from the 'split' that has existed between the stereotypical *maulvi sahib* and the 'Mr Khan' on the other side. If the systems had evolved side by side and in sync with each other—meaning the madrasa system and the mainstream education system—both segments of society would have truly benefited by that. The madrasa would have achieved a special quality and better understanding of world affairs and worldly knowledge. In many of the madaris, there is an often-quoted statement by an Islamic scholar, which I will paraphrase: 'Anyone who is not aware of what's going on in society is not an *a'alim*—he's an ignorant person'. The statement illustrates that madaris are encouraging broader knowledge of the world and greater awareness of what's going on around us.

At the Jamia-tur-Rasheed, they are making impressive inroads into modern education. In addition to the Islamic departments, they have an MBA program through their Institute of Management and Sciences, also a program in journalism, and they're exploring setting up a law department. They have an in-house newspaper with a business focus. They have invited me a few times for discussions on a future vision for madaris and I have made some suggestions for transformative thinking and curriculum changes. Their convocations are very elegant, with distinguished guests from mainstream occupations including bureaucrats and judges. The guests are given a high degree of respect and recognition, and their guidance and advice are solicited. The Jamia regularly invites speakers from various fields of expertise and different schools of thought. So, there are a few model madaris, but I think Jamia-tur-Rasheed is the most progressive and it plays a leading role in the transformation of the madrasa as an institution.

These are some examples of progress in madaris. Now, if I am to share with you the internal workings of the madaris (since I do have that access), I would say that the push for madrasa reforms by the government has been met by some resistance because madrasa leaders feel that changes are being imposed on them by the authorities rather than it being a collaborative effort with all the parties taking the time to discuss and plan, then implementing the actions in phases. I think there has been some dialog with the government, including the army, and what they have done in KP, especially in the Akora Khattak area, which has a conservative Taliban culture. The KP government has made the right moves by asking madaris to introduce math and English in their curriculum. These are isolated efforts but, gradually, transformation will take root. The few examples of change in the model madaris are there—but, to make sweeping changes, more resources are needed to hire good teachers.

Madrasa teachers are paid less than the minimum wage and the poor teachers work in madrasas as a service to the community and they are pleased that they have an opportunity to serve the faith. In that sense, the madaris in the rural and remote areas struggle to deliver what they can as part of their mission. Often, there are no public schools in the vicinity—and, of course, it isn't possible for TCF to be everywhere—so, the madaris are meeting a social need for education. But they don't have the ability to integrate the two systems of education. On the part of the madaris leaders, obviously, there is a shortage of resolve to make the change. There is poor awareness of the options as to how the change could be gradually implemented, and there is clearly a shortage of resources—which is also one of the reasons for the poor education system in the country.

Q: For the graduates from the madrasa system, the Ulema, what mainstream work options do they have, besides the traditional 'maulvi' or imam at a mosque, or teaching at a madrasa?

Zeeshan Ahmed: With Islamic banks evolving, Sharia advisor jobs are opening up with financial institutions. The Ulema would prefer to stay in occupations or jobs where they can have application of their expertise in Islamic knowledge. Even if they take up teaching jobs in schools or universities, they will probably stay in teaching subjects related to Islamic studies. The effort is picking up and progress is being made to see Ulema graduates employed in jobs other than at the *mimbar* or the madrasa. Another good thing is that many madrasas are now requiring Matric 10th-grade general education as a minimum before a student can enroll in the eight-year madrasa program for an *a'alim*. That will also add to the credentials of the students and help to open up more options for them if they want to go on to mainstream college education in parallel with their madrasa learning program. We have work to do in terms of employment opportunities for madrasa graduates.

Q: KSBL is a non-profit institution for business studies. How did you blend your business-finance expertise with your knowledge of Islamic principles? And who are the people behind KSBL?

Zeeshan Ahmed: My connection to KSBL[8] was very logical. My interest is Islamic finance, which is a business school subject, rather than a social science or theology or religious school subject. I was teaching at LUMS for six years in the business school and that was not related to Islamic studies. I haven't had a teaching or administrative job at the madrasa. KSBL is a non-profit and the board of trustees are prominent people from the business and professional community. As philanthropists and community leaders, they support KSBL as a service to business education in the country.

6.6 Supporting Education in the Madrasa

Beginning with its constitutional identity as an Islamic Republic, the prevalent culture in Pakistan is strongly Islamic. And it does influence many aspects of life in the country to varying degrees. The culture and lifestyle of Pakistani society has changed in the last few decades, leaning more toward religious conservatism, which has also percolated into mainstream education to varying levels.

It is a historical fact that churches, temples, and masjid-madrasas were among the first seats of organized learning. As education became organized and institutionalized, schools began to evolve as a system but remained under the influence of their respective religious orders. Societal changes spurred by the industrial revolution resulted in independent schools and universities, and eventually gave rise to public education.

Madrasas are a sizable segment of Pakistan's education landscape. From speaking with Imam Ibrahim and Dr Zeeshan Ahmed, it is evident that madrasas are striving to educate children in whatever ways they can, with the limited resources that they have. To the credit of the madrasa system, it is heartening to see that there is willingness— indeed, sincere desire—to integrate *asari taaleem* into the madrasa curriculum and that it is already being implemented in practice in the loosely-structured system, though not with quality or consistency. There is also acknowledgement on their part that more could be done for better quality and uniformity of *asari taaleem*. The range and quality of the present *asari taaleem* is probably a few notches below the quality of the public schools. And, that is where intervention can be offered, without meddling in the structure of the madrasa system or its *deeni* curriculum.

The aim of this discussion is to suggest practical solutions to the quality issue within the limits of resources. An idea worth exploring is a collaborative partnership between the madrasa system and mainstream education, so that beneficial changes may be achievable in madrasa education. The initiative can easily be attempted on a small-scale pilot.

Social change will come with the acceptance of madrasas as positive contributors to education in the community, not by imposing regulation, interference, or harsh action against the madrasas. Like the masjid, the madrasa is a social institution and an integral part of the community. Once established, madrasas cannot be abolished by decree. If offered support to improve their quality of general *asari* education, madrasas will probably be agreeable to work towards the common goal. It will be up to the mainstream private and public school systems to explore this opportunity to take the initiative and invite dialog with madrasas in order to design workable solutions for improving *asari taaleem*. The education landscape will be served if the mainstream systems could step up to facilitate transition of the madrasa towards a better hybrid system of *deeni* and *asari taaleem*. The proposition should be to gradually ease the madaris into teaching of science, social sciences, math, Urdu, and English; these are subject areas in which mainstream educators most certainly have the training, the pedagogical skills and teaching experience. The final curriculum and content of the *duniyawi taaleem* must, of course, be acceptable to the madrasas. Small changes can lead to transformative ones. And the children will be the beneficiaries.

Dr Pervez Hoodbhoy is a prominent educationist who is not comfortable with 'hybridizing' traditional madrasa *taaleem* and mainstream education and proposes 'a clear separation of religious and secular educational content'. His skepticism is understandable. He has expressed concern in a Dawn.com op-ed[9] of 27 October 2018, that blending of the two creates '…cultural and ideological choices but they do not mix together because they have different teaching methods, exemplars, and sources. Most importantly, they have totally different goals.' Professor Hoodbhoy asks:

'Which kind of education should a Muslim society encourage? Traditional or modern? This question created friction between the traditional *ulema* and Muslim modernizers during the colonial period. Since those times, things have changed somewhat. Today's religiously conservative middle-class Pakistanis do recognize the connection between modern education and worldly success. Hence, most do not send their children to madrasas. Instead, they seek out hybrid schools, which resemble the old system but with patches grafted from the new.'

Dr Hoodbhoy concedes that hybridization is a step forward for madrasas but rightfully complains that even science is taught without using scientific methodology. Another valid concern is that a conservative madrasa curriculum may not have the capacity to add new disciplines, such as computer science and biotechnology. To that end, I agree that very few madrasas may have that capacity (to add new disciplines) but the fact that *some* of the larger madrasas have added contemporary disciplines is evidence that there is willingness to change and move with the times. That trend could be further encouraged if assistance is offered by the mainstream institutions and systems.

I have great deal of respect and fondness for Dr Hoodbhoy who also has a bone to pick with teaching methods between traditional (madrasa) and modern systems. 'The traditional teacher is an authoritarian who may not be questioned. In most cases, the modern teacher is trained to promote learning through inquiry and welcomes questions [...whereas] critical thinking in learning is discouraged in madrasas.' Let me concede that Dr Hoodbhoy is essentially correct. However, I am convinced of a willingness to accept change on the part of the madrasa system and I base it on extracts from Dr Zeeshan Ahmed's narrative that:

> ... [madrasas] struggle to deliver what they can as part of their mission... they don't have the ability to integrate the two systems of education... obviously, there is a shortage of resolve to make the change. There is poor awareness of the options as to how the change could be gradually implemented, and there is clearly a shortage of resources.

Albeit somewhat awkwardly, madrasas have taken the first steps to include watered-down versions of *duniyawi* education. Many of the madrasas, already offer or require an 8th-grade or Matric education of the younger student before he or she can enter the senior Dars-e-Nizami program. That madrasas have moved in this direction of 8th or 10th-grade education, clumsy as it may be, is a welcome and significant detail but, for some reason, it has not been widely publicized and comes as a surprise to many. Admittedly, the present 8th or 10th-grade schooling in the madrasas is of questionable quality and disorganized. It would be prudent then, to work in partnership with the madrasa systems and offer to deliver a better 'blend' of *deeni* and *duniyawi* education, to enhance the quality of its *duniyawi* education component.

To summarize, madrasas are a large segment of education that primarily serves the needs of the underprivileged child. By 2017 estimates, there were 2.26 million children enrolled in madrasas, only about 36 percent were girls. The larger madrasas offering the Dars-e-Nizami curriculum have as many as 2,500 students on a single campus. These are significant numbers, large enough to warrant serious attention. The madrasa as an institution is here to stay. It is trying to establish a stronger identity and a role in the wider community. Many madrasas are requiring or providing at least an 8th-grade general education. But they are struggling to deliver quality in the non-religious or *duniyawi* component of the curriculum because, as stated by Dr Zeeshan, 'They don't have the ability to integrate the two systems of education'. That's where help is needed and heads need to come together for solutions that can benefit millions of children. It will be a significant step for reform of education and—if the madrasas agree—a major step towards reform, legitimization, and even greater social prominence for the madrasa. It will also mean the birth of a 'middle ground' between madrasa and schools, Dar-ul-Uloom and universities, a win-win for all, and most importantly for underprivileged children.

From 2001 to 2010, there were limited and unfinished attempts to introduce change in the madrasa system's curriculum and operations. It appears that the approaches employed were a plan to regulate and control them, not allow them to become legitimized or achieve broader acceptance. The futile approaches also seemed to aim for influence over the *deeni taaleem* and curriculum in the madrasas. There was international donor demand and political pressure to reform the madrasas. No surprise that it didn't get very far. Dr Zeeshan's words should have our attention, that the madrasa system is struggling to integrate the two systems of education, *deeni* and the *duniyawi* components. That's where the work needs to be focused. It will be a significant step for reform.

For decades, we—the elite and wealthy subscribers of mainstream education—have marginalized, sidelined, and disrespected the 'madrasa people' because they are 'different' to what we are used to. Let's get past that distinction. We are all one people. Let's all behave like adults and do the right thing. Let's unite and work *with* madrasas, for the sake of the country and for the children. Enough said ... and my apologies for the angry tone of these last few words.

The discussion and suggestions in this chapter are not intended as grand ideas for madrasa reform. The proposals are to encourage the acceptance of madrasas as modest institutions of education and to explore ways in which collaborative reform can benefit education of underprivileged children. It serves no purpose to marginalize or judge madrasas as basic, disorganized or 'regressive' in comparison to the advanced, modern, mainstream institutions of learning. Most underprivileged children do not make it to the best schools and universities. The state of the education landscape is what it is, and madrasas can have a positive role in the community. If assistance can be offered to madrasas to add 'quality' in the non-religious or *duniyawi* component of the curriculum, and a few madrasas are willing to accept the help—the beneficiary of the initiative will be the child. And that's what is most important.

6.7 Philanthropy in Islam: *Zakat*

Zakat (za-kaat) is a form of charitable giving as a religious obligation for Muslims who meet the criterion of being wealthy. It is one of the 'Five Pillars' of Islam, the core tenets. The payment and collection of Zakat vary considerably from one country to another and also by sect and local tradition. Zakat should not be considered a 'tax' paid to the state. It is purely an act of charity, out of concern for the well-being of fellow humans, and promotes sharing and redistribution of wealth to a very small degree. Zakat is calculated on income and the value of all possessions, customarily 2.5 percent or 1/40th of a person's total savings and wealth above a minimum amount known as *nisab*. Islamic scholars differ on how the *nisab* and zakat are to be calculated. Generally, the collected amount should be paid directly to the poor, or to reliable agencies that offer services to the poor. Today, in most Muslim-majority countries, Zakat contributions are 'regulated' by the state, but contributions are voluntary. In a few countries, including Pakistan, Zakat is mandatory and collected by the state, mostly by deduction from bank accounts, but the collection and distribution process are unreliable. Some scholars suggest that the idea of Zakat may have come to Islam from Judaism, with roots in the Hebrew and Aramaic word *zakut*.

Islamic financial analysts estimated in 2012 that annual Zakat-giving globally exceeded $200 billion, while scholars and development workers acknowledge that much of the Zakat practice is mismanaged, and most of the collections are wasted or ineffective. In a 2014 study[10] published in *Islamic Economic Studies*, Nasim Shirazi writes that widespread poverty persists in Islamic countries despite Zakat collections. Over 70 percent of the Muslim population in most Muslim countries is impoverished and lives on less than two dollars per day. In over ten Muslim-majority countries, over 50 percent of the population lived on less than $1.25 per day income. This suggests large scale waste and mismanagement by those who collect and distribute Zakat funds. *Waqf* is a form of endowment for charitable purposes, usually involving real estate. There are other forms of charitable giving which are optional; *Sadaqah* is one of them. Given the widespread poverty among Muslim-majority countries, the impact of Zakat in practice has been questioned by scholars. So far, Zakat has failed to relieve large scale poverty in most Islamic countries.

Re-directing Charitable Giving…to Education, for Social Change

It is commendable that the culture of charitable giving is well-established among Zakat givers, who donate regularly as a religious obligation. Donors have a wide choice of charities. There are numerous worthy causes. Each one vies for support and a piece of the pie. But, for lasting social change and greatest impact in relieving poverty, the need is to redirect the largest part of charitable giving to education for the underprivileged. Paraphrasing the age-old saying, 'teach a person to fish, and you feed him forever', holds very true when education is supported by Zakat and other forms of charitable giving. It's a gift that 'goes on giving' because lives are changed with education—for the family, the community, and for generations to come. Each one of us has an obligation to do our part, however small. Supporting girls' education is especially important.

* * * *

GLOSSARY

a'alim	A knowledgeable scholar who graduates from a madrasa; learned person
asali	Real, natural, divine
asari-taaleem	Contemporary or 'modern' non-religious education
azaan	Call to prayer
dalaa'il	Plural of *dalil*; evidence, proof; in the terminology of Islamic jurisprudence, the word refers to anything that is used to deduce and justify a ruling or *fatwa* from the Sharia, or Islamic Law
Deeni Madaris	Religious schools
deeni taaleem	Religious education
deeni ulema	Religious scholars
deeni	The spiritual, Islamic way of life
duniyawi	The 'worldly' way of life
fajr	Early morning prayers
Fiqh	Islamic jurisprudence; scholarly interpretation of the Quran and Sunnah
firqa bandi	Sectarianism

hafiz	A person—not necessarily a madrasa scholar—who has memorized the complete Quran, considered a high achievement and honor in Islamic culture
haq	Rightful position
ilm-ul-aqaa'id	Code of conduct
Imam or Maulvi Sahib	Usually a man, is commonly the worship leader in the *masjid* and may perform other functions as a community leader, much like the role of a Jewish rabbi or a Christian pastor or Hindu pundit. In more liberal masjid congregations, a woman may be the *imamah*—a rarity.
Insha Allah	If Allah Wills
Islamiat	Islamic studies
Islamic Banking and Finance	A system based on Sharia and Fiqh. Usury, interest or Riba is prohibited in banking and financial transactions. Islamic banks have been proliferating in Pakistan for the last few decades
Khatm	Completion
Khutba	Sermon
maghrib prayers	Prayers offered at sunset
Masjid	Mosque; a designated place of congregation and prayer
maulvi sahib	Islamic teacher, local preacher; a learned teacher or doctor of Islamic law—used especially in India as a form of address for a learned Muslim who ministers to the religious
mimbar	The pulpit
Muezzin	A man who calls Muslims to prayer
Naib Imam	Assistant Imam
naqli	False, artificial, man-made
qari	A person who recites the Quran according to rules of *qirat*, encompassing pronunciation, intonation and the beautiful, poetic *qirat* cadence, unique punctuations, and rules of Quranic recitation. Advanced level of *qirat* recitation is part of the eight-year curriculum and the title of Qari is bestowed by the madrasa
roohani	Spiritual
Sharia or Sharia Law	Derived from the religious precepts of Islam, particularly the Quran and the Hadith
Tafaqquh	Deep understanding of Fiqh
talaba	Learners
tashreeh	Detailed study and dissection

tulaba or *taliban*	Students in a madrasa. Literally, students or 'seekers of knowledge'
Sunnah	Teachings and practices of Prophet Muhammad [PBUH]
Hadith	A collection of traditions containing sayings of the Prophet Muhammad (PBUH) which, with accounts of his daily practice (the Sunnah), constitute the major source of guidance for Muslims apart from the Quran
Ulema	A body of Muslim scholars who are recognized as having specialist knowledge of Islamic sacred law and theology

Suggested Readings on Curriculum and Madrasa Reforms

'*A Missed Opportunity: Continuing Flaws in the New Curriculum and Textbooks After Reforms*'—a (2013) study for Jinnah Institute Islamabad, by A.H. Nayyar.

'*Another Approach to Madrasa Reforms in Pakistan*'—a Policy Brief (2012) by Syed Mohammad Ali / Jinnah Institute. https://jinnah-institute.org/opinions/policy-brief-another-approach-to-madrasa-reforms-in-pakistan/.

Notes

1. Ebrahim Moosa, *What is a Madrasa?* (University of North Carolina Press, 2015), p. 2.
2. Deobandi is a large sub-sect of Sunni Muslims. The name derives from Deoband, India, where the Dar-ul-Uloom Deoband is situated and has a significant following.
3. There can be several madrasas by the same name.
4. Kulliya Tush Shariah: http://www.kulyatushariah.edu.pk/index.php/en/.
5. Ibid.
6. Wafaq, the 'Board', is the certifying and examining body for madrasas.
7. Raising Children in Modern Times (Tarbiyat-e-Aulaad Daure-e-Jadeed Mein) https://www.youtube.com/watch?v=LF9royzGDVc&t=3210s.
8. KSBL website: https://www.ksbl.edu.pk.
9. Dr Pervez Hoodbhoy is a physicist who teaches in Islamabad and Lahore. He has been admirably bold and outspoken in his opinion on education reform and civic society issues, often drawing the ire of conservative thinkers. The Op Ed can be accessed at https://www.dawn.com/news/1441704/why-attempts-to-reform-pakistani-education-fail.
10. 'Integrating Zakat and Waqf into the Poverty Reduction Strategy of the IDB Member Countries' (Islamic Economic Studies, May 2014) by Nasim Shirazi. IDB is Islamic Development Bank.

Chapter Seven

Education Reform: The Essentials

7.1 THE ESSENTIALS OF REFORM

Education is everything. The state of education shapes the country. So, we need a societal shift in attitude about education. We need many more schools. And we need quality education. That just about sums it up. That's how simple and uncomplicated education reform can be. There's no mystery to it. But it's clear that the devil is in the detail. Reforming education in Pakistan is going to take systemic change. The clock is ticking.

It is said that intelligent people love problems. Well, we have an enormous problem with the broken education system. We will need capable people who are determined to find solutions to the dysfunctional and discriminatory system. Under the broad scope and umbrella of reforms, there will be issues ranging from universal access to language policy. In order to reduce inequities in education and promote policies that will even the playing field, we must also address the critical area of quality education, which incorporates *academic* quality in schools as well as *management efficiencies* of the school systems.

The convoluted maze of reforms must be simplified. Priority actions should be governed by plain common sense. We must be reasonable, willing to compromise, and eager to find solutions to our problematic challenges. We are so far behind that several reform ideas will appear to be equally important and demand equal priority. The focus and guiding force should be what is most important for *the child*—the millions of children who are not in school and just as many who are not receiving quality education. The key to achieving results is to tackle the problems in an organized, systematic manner with a realistic timeline for intended actions. Reasonable time should be taken for rapid analysis and planning but action must not be delayed by petty arguments aimed at achieving absolute perfection in the planning phase. Setting a direction and course will be important. Finer adjustments can be made once implementation commences.

My love for analogies is stoked by an esteemed music *ustaad*. I began Chapter 2 with a quote about unprecedented events by commercial pilot Captain Sullenberger. So, here's another flying analogy with regard to efficient multi-tasking: a pilot takes off in an easterly direction, on a heading of 090 degrees. Her planned course or direction of straight-line flight is 140 degrees from the take-off point, to her destination just a short distance away, say 100 miles. She banks right to the required heading, climbs to the desired altitude in compliance with terrain and airspace requirements, and she's on course, flying straight and level, until she starts her descent to land safely. Mission accomplished. But what we must realize is that, even for a relatively short flight, the pilot made adjustments for wind, traffic, navigational corrections, or communications from radar services and control towers. Yet, she was *on course* all the time. So, getting started with a plan is important. But multi-tasking and making adjustments on the way is an integral part of life.

Education reform will not be any different. Rapid reforms will not be a linear, unidimensional process involving the insertion of a few things here and there, or minor correction of others. Having given it considerable thought, we must strive to have the right education *systems* in place to achieve a solid foundational stage of reforms. The detail of refining and implementation will need a great deal of energy and commitment from civil society leaders and civic organizations who must remain in the game for a very long time to oversee, sustain, and improve upon the workings of the systems. There are technical aspects of reforms that will require special expertise. There's no doubt that Pakistan has the technical capability. Getting started is half the battle. The toughest challenge at every turn will probably be from vested political interests. That sums it up. And, most of it is plain common sense.

In Chapter 4, our celebrity friend Shehzad Roy said, 'Reform is going to be a series of small steps.' Those small steps must be in rhythm and all going in the same direction. Uppermost on the things-to-do list is to first stop the bleeding: *Get out-of-school children into schools* by building and staffing more schools. Every year of delayed schooling puts more children at risk of failure. Equally important is the *quality* issue that includes a plethora of items, starting with the long-standing *language* issue. A national policy on language should be in concert with all provinces and regions. *Registration* of all schools, including madrasas, is an absolute necessity for the very important functions of *monitoring, rating,* and *improving the quality* of education to be delivered. *Credentialing standards for teachers* and their *professional training* requirements need to be addressed and refined with buy-in from teachers' groups. The *curriculum* needs expert review and public acceptance, along with reformatting. Corresponding changes and revisions should be made in the *textbooks* at all levels. *Assessment of outcomes* is a key area that has been sorely mismanaged; it will need a set of tough teams to take on this task. The *management* systems will need solid structure and well-trained human resource cadres that are nimble, have fresh ideas, and are dedicated to reforms. Above all, reforms will need ongoing *advocacy* for public involvement and civic leadership by influential public leaders committed to reforms as a long-term national priority.

7.2 Language and Equity in Education

Education is a politically charged issue in Pakistan, as it is elsewhere. Even stronger cultural, emotional, and political forces are evoked when language policy in education is discussed. We love 'our' language and that's commendable as a positive social-cultural characteristic. It is also laudable that we are proud and possessive of our languages. We are easily upset when our languages are tampered with, ignored, belittled, or dominated by other languages, even if we are a small numerical minority.

The dominance and use of a language in a community, a country, or a region are influenced by political changes in the region. The commonly spoken language that makes communication possible between people of different origins or ethnicities is the *lingua franca*. Urdu is considered the *lingua franca* in Pakistan and serves as the common language of the environment (LE). Through history, the *lingua franca* has developed because of trade and for cultural, social, religious, diplomatic, scholarly, and administrative convenience. An international, world language like English is a *global lingua franca*. In the academic and scientific world, English is the most common means of exchanging information between scientists and scholars.

But, for most Pakistanis, English is a foreign language. The dominance of English as the medium of instruction in post-secondary education has crippled and severely affected the growth and maturing of social capital in Pakistan. We prepare the majority of our secondary school students in Urdu and then break their spirit and confidence by expecting them to abruptly switch to English in college and university. In college, we are 'teaching' in the wrong language, a beautiful but foreign language, English, instead of the beautiful and local languages of our own environment. For these reasons and others, our system is broken and dysfunctional. I must repeat that reform must include significant change in our language policy. Yes, writing of books and translation into Urdu or other local language will be a challenge. but well worth the effort and expense. In summary, I propose that, as long as we have a system of college education in English, we should consider these temporary and 'transitional' changes to partially balance the scales for parity in language:

1. In Urdu-medium schools: increase the intensity of English language teaching in grades 6 through 10 to enable better language competency although finding and training competent English language teachers is a huge challenge.
2. In English-medium schools: introduce requirements for higher skills in Urdu to reduce the language-equity gap between students from the public and private schools.

Ultimately, we must seriously consider adoption and transition to Urdu as the single language for higher education in all colleges and universities, with English only as a supplemental language for technical terminology, research, and learning of global information, as is the practice in most non-English speaking countries. The practice of a local native language for primary, secondary, and higher education should be adopted. This would be in the successful models of economic giants like China, Japan, South Korea, Germany, France, and a host of other countries that have retained their local languages as the pragmatic medium of instruction for education at all levels. The local or nationally spoken languages are a source of national pride for these countries, not a drag on the systems of education, international and domestic commerce, or normal daily life. These countries are comfortable using English terminology for technical explanations when necessary, without compromising the local languages.

European languages have evolved over centuries of geo-political changes in countries of the region. Borders and political maps have changed, but many local languages have been retained and preserved by individual cultures. Many countries in Europe have mixed usage of native languages and a working relationship with English. The Spanish colonial empire in Latin America resulted in most of the countries on that continent using Spanish as the primary language, except in Brazil where Portuguese is spoken. Sadly, indigenous native languages in South America, Central America, and North America struggle to survive. Pakistan's beautiful native languages must not go the same route. Can language be separated from how education is delivered, and from the policies and practices that govern the delivery of education? Zubeida Mustafa states articulately in her book:

> ... language is closely linked to socialization; it is something that develops in a community. The culture, political thought, and sociological dimensions of communities have a direct bearing on the language spoken...and the language chosen as the medium of instruction has far-reaching implications for a society.[1]

Zubeida Mustafa adds that political expediency, economic injustice, and class prejudice are the driving factors that have determined language policy in Pakistani education. It is appalling that language has not been a strong element in the foundation and reforms of our education system. And the void has resulted in flawed education policies and an ad hoc, arbitrary approach to language. On the rare occasions when a language policy has been framed, it has either failed or not been implemented. She states emphatically in her book that the worst impact of this ambivalence has been on the teaching of language.

We are a proud, multilingual people. To find a solution to our language issues in education, we must make choices. We cannot have it both ways. We must be willing to compromise and find a middle ground for the common good. Yet, we must retain the rights to foster native languages for early education, as well as for the importance of our heritage, culture, and linguistic identity.

OUR LANGUAGES—AND ENGLISH

In our globalized world, English enjoys a privileged status in the areas of business, science, and technology. The advantages of communication and technology may not be available to persons who are not familiar with English, which is probably the most widely spoken global language and continues to grow rapidly. It is learned and spoken by a large number of people as a second language. It is also recognized by its enormous geo-political influence because a few of the world's major economic powers have English as their national and business language.

The issue for Pakistan is not a three-way choice between the native language (L1, the mother-tongue or home language), the language of the environment (LE or L2), and English as L3. All languages are equally essential, as described in Dr Anjum Altaf's essay (see Appendix 3):

> The experience of the European Union, where the 'mother tongue plus two' mandate is widely accepted and where there is great emphasis on the acquisition of English, it [the EU experience] can provide very useful guidance on the stages at which each of the languages is best introduced and the points at which the language of instruction is switched, if warranted. There is little need to reinvent the wheel.[2]

Local community variations in language add to interesting challenges of language rights at the grassroots and language policy in education at the top. In most rural settings, populations are homogenous and use the same language with minor dialect distinctions. In the larger cities, especially in multicultural Karachi, dozens of languages and dialects can be heard because of the sizable communities of migrant families. But the common, ubiquitous language of the environment (LE) is generally Urdu.

Most contemporary language experts are in agreement that early childhood learning (pre-school, first and second grades) should be in L1, the home language—or, in the language of the environment, LE. There is some divergence in views about when exactly Urdu and English should be inserted and taught as 'a language' and what should be the medium of instruction (MOI) after grade three.

Zubeida Mustafa analyzes the language conundrum with research into the British Council 2010 report by Hywel Coleman and writings by other experts as well. Her recommendation is essentially that the child must learn up to grade 10 either in the home language L1, or in the language of the environment LE; starting in grade 3, Urdu and English should be taught as 'a language' or as a subject.

> Dr Anjum Altaf and I are fundamentally in agreement with this simplified approach. Depending on the linguistic composition of the regional communities, I feel that the timing of inserting Urdu and English are best left to the decision of the local communities and education managers. – *Author*

THE LANGUAGE DIVIDE

Zubeida Mustafa believes that the system of education in Pakistan is a class structure with the underprivileged suffering greater inequity. She eloquently writes: '... literacy in the context of education...calls for the ability to read and write in order to develop the mind and acquire knowledge. And in this context, language emerges as the key element because education...is a language related activity. The problem is that we tend to have a cavalier approach to human speech and the ability of humans to use language, although its numerous dimensions have direct bearings on our lives.'[3]

She regrets that English, as the language of the influential elites, 'has overshadowed other languages and stunted their growth. Worst of all, the privileged position bestowed on English [by private schools] ... has created the myth that good education can only be imparted in English... [and] public demand for English has been created to which the government does not have the capacity to respond. It [the government] has, therefore, chosen to be ambivalent on the language issue.'[4]

Addressing the class divide created by language, Zubeida Mustafa concludes: 'The class divide in Pakistan has become so wide that the "haves" who control education cannot...understand the basic issues which have a profound impact on the quality of education. Language, especially English, is not such a big issue for those who can afford to send their children to elite schools. *Since the parents are themselves educated and their children grow up hearing and speaking English, it does not even occur to them that for the underprivileged...language can become a major obstacle to progress in education.* That is [the reason] why this issue is hardly ever addressed in the discourse on education in Pakistan.' (Emphasis by author).[5] Language discrimination, whether perceived or real, contributes to insidious political demands for a separate state causing social unrest, worsening political disagreement and tensions. It is imperative to have agreement on language policy on the basis that all regional and native languages are considered important for their cultural value and no native language should be compromised. The steps for education reform must be built upon democratic solutions to a language policy that is fair and equitable.

The excellent and comprehensive SAHE 2014 report[6] addresses language as being *central to the process of teaching and learning* because it forms the communication bridge between teachers and students. Learning objectives are compromised and quality of education is undermined if the medium of instruction is a language in which both teachers and students have difficulty communicating. The medium of instruction also becomes an important feature of equity if children from different segments of society speak different languages, some more privileged than others.

As the language of success, English is associated with economic power and social mobility. The history of previous policies on language is a story of poor foresight on the part of policymakers and inadequate public participation in the decision-making process. An Education Conference in 1947 made Urdu 'the lingua franca of Pakistan'. The National Education Conference 1951 proposed Urdu to be taught as a mandatory language, while the place of mother-tongue instruction was explicitly acknowledged. Operationally, however, Urdu was adopted as the MOI for public schools and English was the choice for the elite private schools, contributing to the language divide along the socio-economic class-lines.

The 2009 National Education Policy (NEP) indicated steps to reduce inequities in the education system by suggesting changes in language policy. Regrettably, the language issue was muddled even more when (it is hard to believe) the NEP 2009 suggested using English as the medium of instruction in public schools '...to achieve greater equity in the education system'. The ludicrous reasoning was based on the premise that proficiency in English would even the playing field and provide equal access to opportunities. Going along with this strange logic, more recently (early 2000s, I think), Punjab introduced English as the medium of instruction from grade 1 in all public schools. The KP province followed suit by adopting a similar language policy. Supporters of the policy applauded the move as a means to bridge the divide in the education system. Others found it to be detrimental. This is a classic example of flawed language policies. As expected, it failed and was reversed in both provinces.

Since those early years, the language policy has vacillated but come to no conclusion for the role of the home language L1, the mother tongue. The strongest case is of Sindh which has firmly stood ground and insisted on Sindhi to be taught in more than 80 percent of the K-10 schools as L1. In areas where Urdu is L1 (most of Karachi and surrounding regions), Sindhi is required and taught as L2. Other provinces are further behind and do not have a consistent policy, skirting around the issue of language, leaving it up to local communities and education managers to work things out. Adding to the prevailing confusion, in KP province for instance, is the teaching of an Arabic version of *deeniyat* (religion studies) in Arabic.

EDUCATIONAL ROLE OF ENGLISH IN DEVELOPING COUNTRIES

Hywel Coleman[7] has discussed his research commissioned by the British Council on the educational role of English in developing countries based on case studies from Indonesia, Gabon, and Pakistan.[8] He reports on the British Council's aim in commissioning the research was 'for a better understanding of the use of English language' in the education system, in line with its Charter to 'develop a wider knowledge of the English language' around the world, and to 'promote the advancement of education.' As Coleman explores the sociolinguistic framework in the countries he studied, he asks the following questions:

- What other languages are used and what roles do these languages play?
- Are any of the languages given an official role by the government?
- How do people perceive their own languages, the national language, and English?
- Do speakers of certain languages enjoy privileges not available to others?
- Where does English feature in this ecosystem of languages, and does English threaten the existence of native languages?

Coleman also considers the total number of English language teachers, their qualifications, and whether the number is sufficient for the number of learners. He enquires about other relevant elements of education: how much time do the teachers spend in school; the proportion of children who finish school; whether girls drop out more than boys do; and how parents perceive education.

Specifically related to the teaching of English as a subject, Coleman asks about the number of hours allocated to teaching English.

- Is it an important, high-stakes subject in assessment and tests for learning outcomes?
- Are the teachers confident in the language and appropriately trained through pre-service and in-service training?
- Are there English language experts who inspect and visit the schools to observe teaching; and,
- Where do learning materials come from?

Lastly, he questions *why* English is being taught, and if there is a clear purpose for it, and whether stakeholders (parents, policy makers, community leaders) are aware of the reasons. He also enquires which language is the medium of instruction in schools:

- Is it the home language, or is it the 'national language', or the former colonial language, English?
- And to what degree is language policy truly fulfilled in the classroom?

It is imperative that Pakistanis ask these pertinent questions raised by the distinguished language scholar.

In 1947, Pakistan adopted Urdu as its national language. Though most widely used, Urdu is the mother-tongue of only 5 to 7 percent of the population while English continues to play an important role in government and commerce. English is virtually the primary language of the elite class, the military, in higher education institutions, and elite private schools.

At the time of Coleman's 2010 study, Sindhi was the medium in primary schools in Sindh, and Pashto was used in some schools in Khyber Pakhtunkhwa, but other indigenous languages had no role. Even in upper Sindh, Seraiki-speaking children were learning in Sindhi because the policy was not based on teaching in the mother-tongue in early grades. Indigenous languages were thought of as constraining a child's development and most primary education was provided in Urdu, not in the home languages. English, on the other hand, was believed to facilitate higher education and employment in the civil service and was touted as a panacea for wider social inequalities.

Various adverse outcomes are attributed to negative attitudes towards indigenous languages. These (adverse outcomes) include high dropout rates and poor educational achievements. The use of Urdu and English as languages of instruction run the risk of marginalization of certain ethnic communities and, over the longer term, a risk of language death. 'Pakistan is considered to be one of the countries most exposed to these risks.'[9]

Among the underlying factors contributing to the weakened state of education are language policy, widespread misunderstandings about language learning, the very role of language in education, and specifically the role of English. There is urgent need for awareness-raising public advocacy about the importance of the mother-tongue in the early years of schooling. Furthermore, there should be open discussion regarding the privileged status of English speakers, as the discriminatory landscape of education calls for societal transformation.

In a subsequent 2012 report,[10] Coleman and Capstick recommend that every child should have equal opportunity to access high-quality education, regardless of socio-economic status, gender, or home language, and that 'Urdu and English should be introduced only when children are ready'.

The outstanding reports by Hywel Coleman have contributed to engaging debate and helped to advance public understanding of language issues in Pakistan. But, in Coleman's words, 'substantial longer term impact seems…elusive'. It is hoped that this discussion will compel public interest to address the language issues and that civic leadership will play a greater role in seeing it to fruition as a vital component of education reform.

POLICY ON LANGUAGE: ANJUM ALTAF

Early education using the mother-tongue as the medium of instruction improves a
child's ability to learn. There is ample evidence to support this claim. Given
this evidence…the mother-tongue should not be ignored as the medium of
instruction in early education. This does not rule out learning other
languages either later or simultaneously.
– Anjum Altaf

A liberal thinker, educator, and articulate writer with immense love for country and for the Urdu language, Dr Anjum is a brilliant scholar whom I have the privilege of addressing as a friend and respected mentor. He has strongly influenced my views on education reform, especially on language in education. Professionally an economist and development specialist having served at World Bank, he has published several writings on a range of subjects including education, language, development, inequality, and social and political change. Anjum has written extensively on language in education. In this volume, Appendix 3 is a compilation of five of Anjum's best essays that I have selected (it wasn't easy). One of the essays is titled, *Functional Arguments for a Rational Policy on Language.* Though it results in a minor redundancy, here are a few relevant extracts from the essay to whet the appetite for more of Anjum's eloquence and thoughts:

- In 2015, the Supreme Court of Pakistan ruled that Urdu should replace English as the national language of the country. Our experience with the politics of language has been so traumatic that we need a dispassionate analysis of this decision in the context of the functions of language and the current situation in Pakistan.
- The evidence pertaining to [the transfer of knowledge]…has become scientifically more rigorous over time and is by now overwhelming. It has been shown repeatedly that the mother tongue is the most effective vehicle for instruction during the early years of education.
- The choice of the mother tongue as the medium of instruction in the early years and Urdu as the second language does not rule out the acquisition of English at a later stage. The evidence regarding development from countries like Japan, South Korea and China that use their national languages as the medium of instruction is so stark as to make it impossible to overlook.
- My recommendation, keeping very clear the distinction between learning a language and learning in a language, would be to have the early years of education in the mother tongue, introduce Urdu second, followed by English.
- The efficacy of the first language for early education is now irrefutably strengthened by additional evidence that the acquisition of additional languages is easier for those whose early education is in their first language because their ability to learn is stronger.
- The case for Urdu as the second and shared language for horizontal and vertical communication is dictated simply by the reality of its wide familiarity across the country.

7.3 Quality Education

The common assumption among Pakistani families is that, wherever English is the medium of instruction, the education delivered must be of 'good quality', whatever the connotation of good quality might be in that context. Without a rating system or reliable criteria to objectively evaluate school quality, the higher tuition fee in supposedly 'English medium' schools probably leads to another erroneous assumption that the higher cost (and visibly better amenities than public schools) must mean better education quality as well. The baseline yardstick is that the 'free' education in Urdu-medium public schools is of poor quality.

For most families, there is no benchmark for quality of the education their children are expected to receive. And, the choice of a school (if there is a choice) usually depends on word-of-mouth recommendations and factors such as what's affordable for the family, which school is more conveniently located, and whether the school is 'English-medium'. Most parents do not have the ability or take the time to evaluate or compare important quality inputs of teacher credentials, professional training, textbooks, curriculum, school facilities, management, or extra-curricular programs at the schools being considered. In many cases, there may be no other choice except the single school in the area. Given a choice, the decision is based on subjective accounts of quality, or what's affordable, or the convenience of distance from home.

The standards in education, how education is managed and delivered, and *what* is being taught in the curriculum, will have serious consequences for Pakistan's future. The statement should be taken seriously, and I suggest we read it once again: 'The standards in education, how education is managed and delivered, and what is being taught in the curriculum, will have serious consequences for Pakistan's future.'

Quality in education comprises a great deal more than what is being taught in the classroom. There are numerous behind-the-scenes 'inputs' that go into the making of a quality education environment. We will discuss the various elements of education inputs and see how they come together under the canopy of *quality* education. For instance, having good textbooks does not ensure quality. It also takes good teachers and sound pedagogical practices to deliver quality education. The effort to achieve quality must begin with a straightforward, reasonable and robust policy that improves the *systems* of education at the national level, regardless of devolution. The present 'non-system' will not alter the quality of education.

Quality has been overlooked in the zealous impulse for universal education, a politically expedient and more visible undertaking. However, *quality* must be the overarching focal point of education reform, debates, and policy decisions. The crisis in education is a multi-faceted challenge: having all out-of-school children going to school will be a remarkable achievement but it addresses only the access and enrollment issue. Until universal education is inseparably bonded with delivering *quality* education for all children, it does not accomplish the goal of producing well-educated, good citizens with marketable skills and a sound knowledge base. Sadly, there is general consensus that the level of learning taking place at the present time is far below acceptable standards. And adding more children to a sub-standard system is a recipe for disaster and surefire guarantee to create additional and indefinably miserable challenges down the road.

The best things in life take skillful preparation, patient nurturing, and careful monitoring. So, let me digress for a yummy side note. *Biryani* is a popular Pakistani-Persian-South Asian menu item with rice, meat, and potatoes cooked in mild, special spices and steamed in the irresistible aroma of saffron. For generations, it has been served exclusively on special occasions. The best *biryani* has the right blend of ingredients and is made with an unhurried process of preparation. Quality education is like *biryani* in a child's life, requiring the initial investment and commitment of the right ingredients and methodology in place. Like good *biryani,* quality in education requires careful and continuous monitoring. The recipe (curriculum) must be endlessly improved with a fine balance of ingredients (innovations, technology) and culinary expertise (pedagogy). For a connoisseur's palate, 'great *biryani*' are inseparable two words, just as 'quality education' should be joined-at-the-hip twin essentials. And, like well-prepared *biryani,* the outcomes of quality education will be many times more gratifying than the cost and effort invested in it. Final thought: education sans quality should not have a place on the menu. Mediocrity should not be acceptable. *Biryani* should always be great and perfect, no exceptions. End of that thought.

The question of equity rises against the backdrop of this salivating analogy because quality education must be uniform and universal. Quality education must not be selectively available only to those who can pay the high price for it. The option to buy an expensive car is fine for the person who can afford it, but it is not a given right. Education, on the other hand, is a constitutional right and should always be delivered with quality. And, let's not forget that higher quality does not come cheap. If education reform is worth doing at all, it must be done well. Without *quality*, 'education' is reduced to an empty, meaningless misnomer and an obvious contradiction. The quality of education must be objectively measurable and ratable by acceptable standards. Educators, school systems, and teachers must be provided technical assistance and management support to improve the quality that is to be delivered. As a serious professional responsibility, educators must accept their obligation for improvement of quality and the effort must be consistent, continuous, and enduring. Education quality is a win-win strategy. Everyone gains when quality education is delivered: the child, the family, the community, the educators, the management and operators of the school system—whether public or private. And, everyone loves to win. Everyone stands to lose when quality in education is compromised. The registration of schools and madrasas is the first step to ensure monitoring, rating, and improvement of quality in education.

Quality in education cannot be taken lightly, or as an optional 'add-on value' for a price. All education institutions must be *expected* to deliver quality education and vigorously participate in implementation of quality improvements or, very bluntly, get out of the business of education. Pakistan's children have been constitutionally guaranteed the right to quality education and high-quality standards must be deemed binding on the managers of education delivery. It cannot be a choice. And the standards must be supported by enforceable, corrective measures put in place by federal authority, and strictly applied.

I concede that I am not an 'expert' in education. I am not an educator or an academic. But I am comfortable in saying that I am an expert layperson and activist in the area of Pakistan's education. To advance the debate on quality improvement and enforcement parameters, I propose a no-nonsense, straightforward, and bare-bones framework which I have briefly discussed with some friends in education—Irfan Muzaffar, Abbas Rashid, Salman Humayun, and Nadeem Hussain. With deference, I propose these ideas after careful thought. These are not prescriptive, rigid concepts. However, I feel strongly that the evaluation, rating and enforcement of quality is one critical national issue that must not be left up to the provinces—at least, not initially and not until the program is firmly established. For uniformity and, as a serious country-wide concern, quality standards must be enabled by appropriate policy and enforced by federal mandate. The quality standards should be honed and refined initially under a federal umbrella with public-private stewardship and transferred to the provinces in five years but conditional upon continuing federal and public oversight. The five-year period should give the provinces sufficient time to prepare for the transition and administration of this critical feature of education.

Proposed Framework and Rationale for 'Quality Improvement Program and Rating Authority' (QIPRA)[11]

The foremost concern of education reforms must be the Pakistani child and the community. Across the country, possibly 70 percent of school-going children 5 to 16 years in age, are enrolled in public schools or low-cost private schools. Probably 30 percent are in mid-range private schools or high-cost, elite private schools. Since there is no reliable database of schools in the country, these are loosely defined segments of the education population. Generally, there is no dependable, single agency that has even close to accurate numbers aggregated into actionable information on important aspects of education, as it relates to quality. The systems and data collection vary considerably from one province to another. The data is typically outdated and relies on extrapolations of inconsistent surveys of questionable methodology. In turn, the poor data makes it difficult for thoughtful planning to take place in timely fashion.

It is imperative that the present frustration of 'guesswork' in education planning is eliminated, starting with a single, authoritative, nation-wide registration process of all schools and madrasas. Common sense dictates that planning cannot happen in a vacuum. It cannot proceed without accurate inventory of assets, needs, and goals. For starters, the planning and implementation of quality programs must have, as its first requirement, an accurate and relevant count of schools and madrasas, the numbers of students by gender, the numbers of teachers by their teaching disciplines, and basic information of the space and facilities of the school or madrasa. The baseline collection of additional relevant data should be considered to study future changes and trends.

The data collection process can be refined as needed, without making it a cumbersome and meaningless exercise. It is important that the information gathered should serve a useful purpose and that the school owners and managers see value in cooperatively providing accurate data.

REGISTRATION FUNCTION OF QIPRA

With laser-like focus on improving quality in primary and secondary education—including K-10 Matric, K-12 'A' level programs and all madrasa programs, a federal agency QIPRA should be created as a public-private collaboration and administered by a federally appointed commission. The agency's mandate should be for an initial period of five years and it should be the sole agency to register all schools and madrasas in all the provinces and federal territories. The provinces should be prepared to administer QIPRA in their respective jurisdictions after the initial five-year period.

Rationale for Registration of all schools and madrasas

(1) QIPRA to maintain a uniform database of all K-10, K-12 schools and madrasas;
(2) the day-to-day operations of schools and madrasas would not be affected;
(3) to ensure transparency of the agency and its operation, there should be participation and oversight provided by civil society organizations and public members;
(4) for madrasas: the action provides an opportunity for madrasas to be included in the education system, to improve quality of education, and transition to mainstream education at a reasonable pace.

Expected argument against national Registration

(1) education has been devolved to the provinces;
(2) quality of education can be managed by school operators and management;
(3) madrasas are registered with *wafaqs* (boards or councils) which offer guidance to madrasas.

Counterargument for Registration:

(1) quality in education is a national priority for education reform and must not be left up to the options of provincial policymakers;

(2) historically, the quality of education has not been a priority of school operators and management;

(3) registration is the first step to ensure monitoring, rating and improvement of quality in education;

(4) uniform quality inputs should be available, monitored and given high importance in the rating process;

(5) authority and operational functions for quality and curriculum standards shall be transferred to the provinces at the end of five years;

(6) all madrasas are not uniformly registered with *wafaq* boards;

(7) *wafaq* boards may continue to offer guidance to madrasas;

(8) madrasa curriculum shall not be affected by the QIPRA registration process;

(9) registration and participation in QIPRA's monitoring program shall be mandatory for all schools.

MONITORING AND RATING OF EDUCATION QUALITY BY QIPRA

Reiterating what's been said in Chapter 1, enormous amounts of time plus large sums of money are invested into education by parents and students, in the hope that children are receiving quality education in the schools. In this era of technological advances and objective evaluation methodologies, parents and students should not have to rely on subjective, word-of-mouth recommendations for 'quality'.

Pakistan's education system has been almost totally void of operational standards for quality assurance and quality improvement in education. As a vital component of quality education, standards for quality and implementation of the quality inputs must be put into effect. There needs to be a well-resourced system in place to monitor quality and to objectively rate the quality on a scale that is consistent, easily understandable and usable by the consumer population, namely parents and students. I propose that national quality standards should be designed, organized, and managed by one centrally authorized agency

QIPRA and all K-10 and K-12 'A' level schools, and madrasa programs should be monitored and rated by QIPRA on a bi-annual schedule.

Rationale for Monitoring and Rating by QIPRA

(1) QIPRA to be the single, unified agency for monitoring and rating of all schools and systems;
(2) QIPRA shall not affect the curriculum or quality of education delivered at 'O and A' level schools;
(3) With defined standards of education quality and with an objective rating system, parents and students shall be able to obtain information related to quality of education being delivered at any registered school in the country.

Expected argument against Monitoring and Rating:

(1) Monitoring by QIPRA may duplicate monitoring by the Cambridge system already in place;
(2) Rating will be detrimental to schools that are rated low.

Counterargument for Monitoring and Rating (M&R):

(1) M&R by QIPRA shall have no conflict or duplication with Cambridge standards;
(2) high ratings can be expected for Cambridge 'A' level schools;
(3) uniform quality rating standards shall be applicable to all systems—matric, Cambridge and madrasas;
(4) schools that have a low rating shall have incentives to improve their education quality.

SALIENT OPERATIONAL POINTS FOR THE QUALITY IMPROVEMENT PROGRAM (QIP)

– Registration and participation in the M&R and QI programs shall be mandatory for all schools.
– Services provided by QIPRA shall be charged to the school management; *no services shall be free.*

- All schools, including public schools, shall pay for Registration, M&R and QI services.
- Through federal funding, QIPRA shall subsidize the cost of its programs and services to schools.
- For operators and management of private schools, total cost of Registration, M&R and QI programs shall not exceed 5 percent of the tuition fee revenues of the schools.
- For public schools and institutions that are free or charge no fees, a nominal cost of say, Rs. 100 per student shall be assessed as the Annual Registration Fees (ARF).
- Private schools shall pay an ARF based on the school's tuition fees, enrollment numbers and other factors; a sliding-scale schedule of fees shall be developed.
- The ARF shall include the cost of Monitoring and Rating (M&R).
- For the first year only: as incentives to participate in the QIP and to improve the quality of education, low-cost and medium-cost schools may request a 50 percent reduction in the ARF and cost of QI programs.
- Schools shall be monitored biannually, i.e. twice in each academic cycle, for implementation of quality improvements through uniform Learning Outcomes Assessment (LOA).
- The first M&R evaluation shall establish the baselines for each school.
- Each subsequent biannual M&R evaluation shall be conducted in thirty days from start of the semester.
- Schools shall be rated on a scale of 1-Star (Poor) to 4-Star (Excellent).
- The goal is to have all schools achieve a minimum 3-Star (Good) rating in the shortest possible time.
- Poor or mediocre performance in quality improvement shall be penalized.
- Schools rated 1-Star (Poor) or 2-Star (Fair) for three consecutive evaluations shall be assessed a penalty of 10 percent; the penalty shall be added to the ARF for the next year.
- Incentives shall be offered to schools that achieve a 3-Star or better rating.
- Schools rated 3-Star (Good) shall be given a 25 percent reduction in the ARF the next year and a 25 percent reduction in the cost of the QI program.
- Schools rated 4-Star (Excellent) shall be given 50 percent discount in the Registration Fees for the next year and a 50 percent reduction in the cost of the QI program.

- Schools rated 1-Star or 2-Star shall be placed immediately on First Notice of Probation (FNP).
- Low-rated schools that do not advance to a 3-Star rating after three consecutive M&R evaluations shall be put on a FNP for one year.
- In the event that a low-rated school does not advance to a 3-Star rating at the end of the one-year Final Notice period, the Registration of the school shall be cancelled, and the school shall be closed down by court order.
- Schools closed down by legal decree may reopen upon application to QIPRA with a new charter and reorganized operating plan that ensures the management's ability to deliver quality education at a 3-Star or better rating within a probationary period of one year (an academic cycle).
- QIPRA shall assist the school in the re-opening process and offer the same incentives that are offered to schools registering for the first time (reduction of ARF and QI costs for the first year).
- All prior penalties and past arrears must be paid in full before registration is granted to a school requesting re-opening.
- As an integral component of the Quality Improvement Program, QIPRA shall provide quality input tools, learning materials, and coaching services for improvement of the quality of education.
- QI services shall include curriculum review, teacher training, textbooks and lesson plans, and management training.
- Low-rated 1-Star and 2-Star schools to get 25 percent off on QI services.
- The child and parents would benefit from receiving a better product in terms of quality education.
- Parents would have a simplified 1-Star to 4-Star system to objectively evaluate quality of education.
- The entire education system would benefit from better student learning outcomes.

ESSENTIAL ELEMENTS FOR QUALITY IMPROVEMENT

Continuously looking for innovative ways to improve quality is a normal practice in progressive countries that have the highest levels of quality education systems. Unfortunately, quality is often neglected where a national culture of mediocrity prevails and an attitude of *kaam chalta hay* (it's working) is the norm.

So, what are the essential inputs for quality improvement? Specific standards for the curriculum, books and learning materials; pedagogy; teacher's education and certification credentials; evaluation of the teacher's content knowledge; training and professional development of teachers; and a top-notch system of management: these are the bare essentials. The QIPRA Registration, Monitoring and Rating System and Quality Improvement programs should become a normal part of education delivery and the quality assurance apparatus. And this may be just a partial list of systemic, essential inputs needed. Parental voice and demand for quality education should be added to the list.

Emphasizing the need for quality in education, my friend Irfan Muzaffar states in the next chapter that the public demand should be not only for increased attention to education but just as strongly for '...a favorable change in policy to expand quality education for all.'

Regarding QIPRA—Abbas Rashid, Director of SAHE and CQE has suggested in a personal communication:

1. Participation need not be mandatory and schools delivering a certain quality of education would, in any case, want to be a part of such an initiative. [*Author: see my concern below*].
2. The rate at which schools improve matters almost as much as where they are at any given point. So there has to be some room in the system for tracking trends. [*I agree. QIPRA should also track, analyze and report trends for improvement of quality*].
3. There should be some means of measuring the quality of inputs as well. Various surveys in Pakistan have measured student outcomes repeatedly without there being much improvement in these outcomes. [*I agree. QIPRA should develop methodology to evaluate quality inputs as well as learning outcomes*].

Abbas is a good friend and respected leader in education research. His efforts for reform are unmatched and his comments are highly valued. With deference, I take slight exception to the suggestion that 'participation need not be mandatory'. I readily accept that quality improvement takes place voluntarily in the elite private schools where parents *expect* quality and the cost is passed on to the affluent parents who can easily afford it. But, historically, without incentives for improvement of quality, the school operators of public and low-cost private schools have not shown interest in making investment in quality education. And we must agree that quality is far too important to be left to chance, or to the notions of school operators, provincial policy makers, or agencies who have no incentive to deliver quality education.

It is also apparent that essential inputs for QI are not uniformly available to all schools so inequity in quality will continue to be an issue without the incentive to achieve a better public rating, coupled with penalties for poor performance and eventually, closure of 'poor quality' schools that show no improvement in quality. For QI to be taken seriously, a federally mandated 'QI and Ratings' program is needed as proposed in the QIPRA framework which emphasizes the agency's role also in QI through better inputs. And I reiterate: if education reform is worth doing at all, it must be done well. Without *quality*, 'education' is reduced to an empty, meaningless, misleading term, and an obvious contradiction. The quality of education must be objectively measurable and ratable by acceptable standards.

We must not take a chance. Quality must be part and parcel of education delivery. And quality does not come without a price tag. Ignorance, illiteracy, poverty, and economic stagnation have a much greater social and financial cost which will grow exponentially with time as Pakistan continues to pay a hefty price for negligence in quality education. Our future generations deserve better.

The consumerism culture, as it is known globally, has effectively reached the area of education, both public and private. Local, regional, state-wide, and national ranking of schools and universities benefits all consumers of education because the rankings stimulate competition for quality improvement in the systems. Parents, students and counselors in the US can readily access the rankings, descriptive narratives, and reviews of all schools prepared by reliable research done by consumer groups and publications like *US News & World Report* and *Consumer Reports*. Along these lines, I see the value of QIPRA partnering with prestigious publications and education groups to produce annual reports on the ranking of schools.

7.4 Credentialing and Professional Training of Teachers[12]

Teaching is the quintessential skilled profession that can make and shape, or waste and impair the lives of many young adults. And the development of a teacher in a suitable system is paramount to her (his) effectiveness as a mentor, knowledge expert, and personal role model for a young person. Many of us have fond memories of our own best teachers and how we wish to discard memories of mediocre or poor teachers that we somehow survived, hopefully unscathed. For many children, bad teaching is the only choice they have. It is the child who pays the price when the choice is limited or unaffordable, or the parents are unable to identify good quality inputs in education.

In a country that has a serious short supply of 'educated' people, perhaps less than 50 percent, it comes as no surprise that the pool of potential teachers is significantly smaller than ideal numbers. Consequently, the recruitment standards and required criteria for teachers take a nose-dive. The quality of teaching suffers and the vicious cycle of poor education and poor teaching continues.

Pre-service teacher education (PSTE) programs are entry points for careers in the teaching profession. The programs must impart specific knowledge of pedagogical skills as well as the content knowledge required of teachers in the various disciplines. The programs must also include adequate observation and supervised teaching experience in an interactive classroom setting. The value of this early training has lasting influence on professionalism and effectiveness as teachers. The professional education and timely grounding of a new teacher become the foundational basis for quality of education.

Formal teacher-education programs in Pakistan have ranged from one-year certificate or diploma courses to professional degrees, including a bachelor's or master's degree in education. Efforts have been made to replace the earlier, shorter duration pre-service programs with fresher, more rigorous education for teachers. Several efforts to reform teacher preparation have been led by international development partners; some details of the programs are in the SAHE report[13] (EM 2014). PSTE programs intended as an improvement on the short certification programs have been criticized as having the same shortcomings as the older programs, i.e. lack of interactive teaching, encouragement of rote memorization, limited period of study, and poor content knowledge for teaching.

IDEAS FOR EDUCATION AND CREDENTIALING OF TEACHERS

So, we are readily convinced that teaching quality in Pakistan is not at the desired level. But what can be done to standardize the profession of teaching? First, I must agree with Shehzad Roy (in Chapter Four) that credentialing of teachers is key for quality improvement as it is the basis for the standards of teaching and reduces discrepancies in education and qualification requirements for teachers.

A flexible approach to credentialing may be needed for the short term, say five years. In large sections of the country, particularly in the remote and rural areas, there are few schools and universities where aspiring teachers can receive the quality of education or develop the interactive professional skills and content knowledge required for teaching well at primary and secondary level schools.

Here are a few thoughts on how the teaching profession can be elevated and teacher education can be incentivized with continuing professional development and credentialing as the standard to be achieved:

- Uplift the status of credentialled teachers: yes, teachers are respected members of the community. But more can be done. Are teachers paid proportionate to the investment in professional preparation, ongoing professional development and their valuable contribution to society?
- Provide professional perks, incentives, conveniences and essential rewards: in addition to base salaries, what can be done to provide teachers (especially credentialled teachers) with incentives to deliver better education? Examples of perks or conveniences are health insurance benefits, transport and childcare.
- For teachers who have given their best years to the profession but do not have the required credentials, the cost of training classes and testing to obtain the credentials should be compensated.
- For aspiring teachers with minimal college education, the cost of college classes and transport can be compensated to incentivize further education and credentialing as the goal.
- Credentialing: there are existing standards for credentialing and certification of teachers, at least on paper. These standards and certification requirements need to be reviewed and revised by experts with focus on achieving better quality in teaching. Should a four-year degree in education be the minimum requirement for credentialing of all teachers? Or, for persons with a bachelor's degree in other fields, should a two-year program in education be sufficient for credentialing?

- Temporary exceptions: obstacles should be removed for the person who wants to make teaching a professional career. The system may temporarily accommodate the aspiring teacher to join the teaching cadre on condition that, in addition to the teaching job, she (he) will diligently pursue the education and other requirements for full credentialing in a defined period of time.
- 'Apprentice' or Student Teachers: fresh 12th grade or undergraduate aspiring teachers should be considered for starting jobs as Apprentice or Student Teachers, to work under supervision of an experienced teacher. School networks and operators should formalize an apprenticeship system. QIPRA and other agencies should help in developing guidelines for teacher apprenticeship programs.
- I would remind the reader that credentialing is essential to establish standards of quality in teaching with focus on benefit to the child.
- Pre-service and continuing professional development programs should be required for all teachers. School management should provide frequent (at least monthly) in-service training for prompt problem-solving and attention to any weak areas in teaching.
- Standards for Continuing Professional Development of Teachers (CPDT) should be established and implemented by all schools. CPDT standards should be monitored by QIPRA as part of its mandate to oversee quality assurance and inputs. The process of school ratings shall consider compliance with the CPDT in the overall quality standings of all schools.

Reform efforts must also consider that teachers do spend most of their work time in a classroom setting. A pleasant classroom and congenial school environment play a significant role in teacher enthusiasm and motivation to perform at a higher level. Teachers appreciate in-service training and support from management, with freedom to be creative in delivering the curriculum. Teachers also crave a collegial relationship with fellow teachers in the school team. A healthy facet of the teacher's job is the school-community leadership by well-trained principals or head teachers who have the support of system managers. The principal's role is significant in developing good community and parent-teacher-school relationships, contributing to better quality in school education.

Box 7.1 LUMS School of Education offers M.Phil program

LUMS has added (2018) a School of Education offering a 2-year M.Phil in Education Leadership and Management program of research, policy, and practice which shall 'provide strategic direction to the educational landscape in the country [...] focused on producing educational decision-makers with a strong foundation in research'.

The program has attracted extraordinary individuals from classroom teachers, nonprofit workers, social entrepreneurs, consultants and corporate employees—all with a passion to lead education reform.

The student interests include curriculum development, education technology, teacher training, early childhood education, accessibility, educational psychology, skills development, special needs education, arts education, and education assessments. – *from LUMS website*

7.5 Curriculum and Textbooks[14]

There is, on paper, a national curriculum which is essentially, guidelines or drafts of what should be taught in schools. Since the 2010 devolution to provinces, the curriculum has become the responsibility of the provinces and the territories of AJK and Gilgit-Baltistan. There is a federal Ministry of Education (MOE) which has administrative responsibilities in the Islamabad capital area and some federal territories. Its role in the current 'national' curriculum is ambiguous, nor is it clearly understood how the MOE interacts with provincial agencies that control development of the curriculum and textbooks. It can be assumed that the national and provincial curricula have not been reviewed, modified, updated or modernized since[15] the last National Education Policy 2009 or since devolution in 2010. The MOE has tied its own hands, while the provinces are embroiled in games of political survival and have not developed the enduring capacity to do much about improvements in the quality of education, or the curriculum.

A different approach to curriculum development will need a wide range of both seasoned and fresh experts, balanced but innovative, and creative yet traditional professionals, to review the curriculum content with full transparency and vigorous public participation in the process.

Corresponding change, revision, and reformatting of the content will be needed in the textbooks that have been published by outdated and non-functional provincial agencies or textbook boards. Also, in the mix, a fair number of Pakistani tech-based education platforms have been field tested and are ready to ramp up their products in the local languages. These technology options are poised to prove their value and contribute to reforms with large-scale application in public systems and private school networks. With reform as the goal and *the child* as the beneficiary, we must encourage and welcome bold changes in education.

The curriculum and books used in schools are among the crucial, load-bearing cornerstones of quality education. Once these blocks and associated elements are set in place, they are very difficult to dismantle, amend, or re-engineer. Curriculum and textbook reform will be 'the mother of all challenges' to be taken on in the battle of quality improvement. We can expect these to be the hardest nuts to crack because the participants in these enterprises are entrenched bureaucrats and colluding businesses who will fight tooth and nail to retain control. But, if we care for *the children* and place high value on quality education, the battle must be fought head-on, and the battle must be won with democratic strength, public advocacy and support, patience and determination. The controls of the curriculum must be with civil society. There is no other choice.

It is entirely feasible that all aspects of quality inputs for education can be planned and implemented outside of the government bureaucracies. TCF is evidence of that. And it makes no sense to continue with the same teams, the same processes and strategies inside government bureaucracies when they have failed miserably and repeatedly. Rhetorically, if the functions devolved to provinces have not worked, shouldn't it be the responsibility of the federal government to intervene, correct the problems, and find solutions? One such critical area of failed devolution is education curriculum and its overriding importance in quality improvement. Radical correction by urgent federal intervention is the way forward.

By federal mandate (and all provinces will see good reasoning in this), I propose the development and implementation of a new national curriculum, related textbooks and learning materials to be assigned to a new Commission on Curriculum and Textbook Development (CCTD), for a period of five years. The defunct provincial agencies of the existing 'curriculum wings' and textbook boards should be closed down for good and the CCTD should implement the curriculum and textbook operations in the interim five years. After five years, the provinces must be ready with improved capacity to take on the responsibilities of the curriculum as modeled by the CCTD. The business of publishing textbooks should be totally privatized with a transparent and public bidding process, and contracts should demand top quality products. For their professional expertise, publishing and technology enterprises should be invited to become key partners in the effort to achieve quality in Pakistan's education. We have an impressive number of capable people with requisite technical expertise in development of academic curricula. These experts can be called upon to serve on teams for curriculum reform, and I am confident that many will happily take on the assignment if it is a part of comprehensive reforms.

The SAHE Report 2014 defines curriculum as a plan that includes strategies for achieving desired learning goals. The curriculum determines the aims of the education, the content and its organization, the processes of teaching and learning, the activities and learning experiences that are to be emphasized, and the textbooks and evaluation procedures. The report recommends that the curriculum 'should have substantial input from those entrusted with delivering it'. The most important stakeholders in education and the best source for ideas, feedback and input are the education planners, the teachers, school operators, academics, language experts, textbook writers, parents, non-profit and other education entities, think tanks, research organizations, and others concerned about quality education. The most appalling neglect has been that these stakeholders, perhaps by design, have had no say or any influence in curriculum planning and development. The curriculum is simply given to teachers to be taught.

The curriculum and textbook bureaucracies appear to be in charge and in full control of the large amounts of revenue transacted both in the development of curriculum and production of the textbooks. There is no human consideration for education and its quality, or for *the child* who pays the ultimate price of poor education quality. In a perverse manner, the politics and the underground economy in the public departments that produce curriculum and textbooks are the strongest, most active, and probably the best organized. Political appointments to these departments are aggressively sought because these departments are regarded as moneymaking enterprises that operate with deviant efficiency for huge personal gains flowing proportionately to the entire network. With that said, I searched online for a better understanding of 'political economy' and found a site[16] that defines it as '…the study of how economic theory and methods influence political ideology'.

In his articulate essay 'Politics of Education' (see Appendix 1), Irfan Muzaffar says: 'The literature on political economy of education suggests that lack of investment in education is part of a strategy of political survival in Pakistan.' It makes me wonder if Irfan's statement can also be interpreted to ask, rhetorically: for political survival, does one have to be part of a crooked system?

SAHE adds: 'Most textbooks suffer from poor quality. […] the curriculum has undergone several modifications over the years…it was revised [2006–2007] to make it more objectives-based, outcome driven, and responsive to current needs. Improvement in textbook development can play a critical role in improving the quality of education.' One of the hallmarks of the 2006 revision was the inclusion of Student Learning Outcomes (SLOs) for each grade and subject level. It was on the basis of SLOs that assessments and textbooks were to be developed. In reality, textbook development has not kept pace.

Post-devolution Curriculum and Textbook Development

The devolution of education to the provinces in 2010 resulted in substantial changes of federal and provincial relationship in governance, with significant impact on the process of curriculum and textbook development. In theory, the authority to develop curriculum and textbooks now rests with the provinces and the roles relating to writing, reviewing, approving and publishing textbooks vary considerably. Sadly, the resulting chaos and deteriorating quality of education have been the embarrassing outcomes.

One agency in each province (known by different names) is in charge of developing the curriculum and approving textbook development. Another agency, usually a textbook board, is in charge of overseeing the development and printing of textbooks. These agencies, their functions and mandates also vary in each province and details are described in the EM 2014 report.

SAHE: 'Generally, textbook writers are in-service [employed] high school teachers, university professors or retired educationists. They are expected to have a good academic background, experience of textbook development and specific knowledge of the subject they are working on.' Regardless of the specific criteria for textbook writers with respect to education qualifications, teaching experience and relevant specialization, the criteria are not rigorously applied and the textbook writers selected often lack in expertise or appropriate subject specialization.

In addition to management staff, textbook boards are expected to have editors, proofreaders, and subject specialists on staff. But, the agencies remain understaffed. Subject-specialist writers are scarce and receive no organized training for insight into the curriculum. They also struggle with interpreting the curriculum and aligning it with SLOs. As a result, textbook manuscripts often to do not meet the review requirements, causing delays in publishing, or the schools receive embarrassingly poor quality textbooks.

For ongoing curriculum and textbook development (after the reformative interim period of five years), I propose the best recommendations from SAHE-EM 2014 combined with a few of my own suggestions:

1. First and foremost, biased content and contextual misrepresentation shall be eliminated.

2. For quality education, the importance of an appropriate curriculum cannot be overstated. Textbooks shall be based on excellence in curriculum design which shall be reviewed and updated with annual regularity, and with public participation and monitoring by watchdog groups and the media.

3. Robust new agencies for curriculum and textbook development shall be established along with coordinated review and input from important stakeholders: competent teachers, subject specialists, writers, planners, academics, language experts, parents, education organizations, think tanks, research organizations, members of civil society, and others. The scope of curriculum planning shall be expanded in accordance with the new criteria and national curriculum standards.

4. The new process of curriculum development shall enable innovation and encourage teachers to actively participate in curriculum change at every juncture. Teachers shall contribute to *what* is to be taught, *how* it is to be taught and *why* it should be taught.

5. A close link and working relationship between curriculum planners and the stakeholders is vital for the success of curriculum goals. Teachers and textbook writers should be enabled to understand the principles and value of the curriculum development process. All stakeholders should become familiar with the objectives of the national curriculum to ensure and oversee its implementation.

6. Perfect coordination and clarity of responsibilities is needed between curriculum and textbook development agencies. There shall be no confusion or overlap in terms of authority.

7. Appropriate resourcing and training of staff shall be a priority for the curriculum and textbook departments for smooth functioning of these agencies, for the timely selection of writers and publishers, and avoidance of delays in the review and production process.

8. The selection of textbook writers, reviewers, publishers and others engaged in the curriculum and textbook agencies shall be in accordance with established criteria and managed by a public panel of subject specialists. The selection shall be transparent and without political interference.

9. Textbook writers and reviewers shall undergo appropriate training and orientation to improve their capacities in the preparation of high quality textbooks. Ongoing training programs shall be offered to sustain the quality of textbook writing and review processes.

10. As an interprovincial and national body to oversee education quality, QIPRA should be the regulatory authority to promptly resolve issues between institutions and agencies and avert the bogging down of curriculum development and other matters related to quality.

11. SAHE-EM 2014 recommends a regulatory authority to oversee the distribution and execution of roles at the curriculum and textbook agencies; to introduce interprovincial standardization in curriculum and textbook development; and to oversee training and capacity building of institutions responsible for curriculum and textbook development. Perhaps this function can also be assigned to a division of QIPRA as curriculum development and textbook production are also deemed quality inputs.

The devolution process has faltered severely in a number of areas related to education, and specifically in the space of quality education and curriculum development. As a strong, prominent and sensible conclusion, SAHE-EM 2014 judiciously recommends: 'In the absence of a structured regulatory authority, the process of devolution, which is still markedly at a preliminary juncture, may continue to falter and struggle. The involvement of the federal government ... may not be an unfamiliar move in a devolved set up. In most countries where education is decentralized, curriculum and testing remain centralized... whereas functions such as the selection of teachers, textbooks, and other instructional materials, and facility construction and maintenance, are being left increasingly to the school.'

The SAHE report wisely adds that developing a national curriculum saves time and effort and that such skills are not present at the provincial level. 'In decentralized set ups, therefore, some authority can still rest with the central government. In China, which has also undergone educational decentralization, the central government reserves the mandate to approve textbooks published by any Chinese publisher. The provincial governments select the textbooks to be introduced in the respective province and county level governments decide what to use in local schools. Thus, there could remain an involvement of a centralized regulatory body (perhaps with provincial representation) in terms of providing standardization in what students learn in schools till the time the devolved setups develop the capability to function on their own.'

The engagement of competent, specialized personnel for curriculum and textbook development and review is emphasized again by SAHE. 'Producing developmentally appropriate, relevant and engaging materials is the prime responsibility of the material developers. Professional curriculum and textbook development and reviews can only take place if relevant people with the necessary skills and knowledge are involved.' The report rightfully scorns the practice of individuals becoming reviewers only by virtue of their 'noteworthy positions' in government.

Finally, publishers and others must not be allowed to ignore important quality control measures. There should be zero tolerance for typos, grammatical errors, or poor visual quality. Textbooks and electronic content should be appealing and engaging for students. The vital components of textbook production are the development of materials, content presentation, physical layout, and contextual appropriateness. These elements should be the responsibility of the publishers together with the writers and textbook agencies. It is important for government agencies to engage private publishers who can develop high quality textbooks. But first, the government institutions need to be free of political interference and unburdened from the prevailing, entrenched nepotism to ensure that private publishers follow appropriate protocol for producing better quality textbooks.

7.6 Assessment and Testing of Learning Outcomes[17]

One measure of education quality is the objective assessment of learning outcomes. Though not exclusively, learning outcomes also reflect teaching practices and other inputs that contribute to quality education and can serve as an analytical tool for evaluating the effectiveness of reforms. The SAHE 2014 report recognizes the importance of examinations and assessments in driving teaching and learning practices but the report is critical that 'Very little focus has been on reforming the examinations that shape much of what students learn. If anything, emphasis has been on removing instances of cheating rather than improving the quality of the exam and its associated processes.'

Types of assessment currently in use are either classroom based; periodic or final examinations; and system level assessments. Classroom assessments provide continuing information on learning taking place. Examinations are largely cumulative and useful in making decisions about a student's progress, hence often high-stakes. Finally, system level assessments provide information on school or system performance and can be used to hold certain groups (teachers, principals, managers) accountable. In high performing systems, there is a greater emphasis on school-based assessment, whereas external exams are meant to compliment or validate the assessment.

Schools develop their own internal assessments for promoting children to the next grade. Such practices vary from one school to another and do not adhere to any assessment frameworks or standards. Moreover, teachers are not trained to make and score classroom-based assessments. This pitfall has been recognized; however, not much has been done in this regard.

In Pakistan, annual or final examinations are the most common form of assessment, certainly in the public system. SAHE 2014 report: 'In high performing systems around the world, assessment is viewed as part and parcel of the learning process. Assessments have become closely aligned with learning objectives and, to some extent, with instructional strategies. Assessment strategies also privilege [or favor] higher order thinking skills, rather than merely test students for memory recall [rote learning]. Finally, the newer assessment systems prioritize providing feedback to students, teachers and schools about what has been learned, shape future learning by informing practice and help students make decisions about career paths and college choice.'

SAHE 2014 adds: 'Examinations...are high-stakes for students; they determine promotion into the next grade, entrance into university and have a bearing on job prospects. In some instances, they also carry high stakes for teachers. Teaching to the test is the norm as teacher performance is evaluated on the basis of exam results. Thus, examinations as a specific form of summative assessment are important to students, parents, teachers, schools and other education stakeholders.' Examinations shape quality of education as an important element of inputs. In the context of examinations, these suggested questions should be asked: Are examinations organized in a technically sound manner? Are they helping to improve quality of education? How can they be reformed and improved on a regular basis? And, is the testing environment conducive to the technical quality of the examinations?

SAHE traces historical trends related to assessments in Pakistan: 'Increasingly, education policies have recognized the need to enhance quality in the existing assessment systems and the crucial role they can play in uplifting quality at the level of classroom practices.' Policy documents have discussed the kinds of assessments required and the need to balance annual examinations with some form of internal classroom-based assessment or periodic testing. 'For instance, the education policy in 1970 put a great deal of emphasis on the need to train teachers in educational measurement and curb unfair means.' The report emphasizes the need for: better alignment between test content, curriculum objectives, teaching-learning processes and efforts to improve the capacity of personnel working in the specialized area of examinations; automating the process of compiling and finalizing the exam results; revising the examination format to include objective, short-answer and essay type questions; and efforts to discourage rote learning (a major problem).

There is recognition that appropriate adjustments in assessments can promote much needed critical thinking among students. However, better standards need to be developed for: the conduct of assessment and examinations; alignment of assessment with curriculum design and planning; alignment of textbook development and teacher professional development; ongoing improvement in the capacity of specialists who design the tests and examinations; the use of assessment data to inform decision making, policy and operational functions; and reducing multiple types of assessments conducted by various boards (more than twenty nationally).

Through pre-service training or specialized courses, teachers must acquire the ability to develop personal skills in conducting assessments and using them for quality improvement. The emphasis—for students, teachers and schools—must shift from 'passing the test' to acquiring knowledge of the subject matter, to enable student confidence in taking the test in any format. The use and application of technology to organize, conduct, process, aggregate and report large-scale data on student testing and outcomes must be a high priority in the effort to streamline the system of examinations. Technological interventions must be introduced and aligned with all aspects of reform and improvement of education quality.

The steps must begin with a proposed one-year campaign to revamp and replace the current examinations system. While other aspects of reform are underway (as part of the interim five-year program), a team of experts should be appointed as an independent Commission on Examinations and Assessments Systems (CEAS). The CEAS should be assigned responsibility to study and redesign the examinations system with substantial application of database technology and integration with other systems. Again, the projects must be seamlessly coordinated with other functions of quality improvement and reform.

Readers are encouraged to examine and study details in the SAHE-EM 2014 report.[18]

7.7 Management Systems in Education[19]

Governance and management are the processes by which policies are developed, priorities identified, reforms implemented, and institutional relationships created to link the multiple actors in education. These are important tasks which shape all aspects of education delivery. Pakistan's education system faces a daunting governance challenge in delivering education to all children. And governance reform has to be at the root of change in processes by which decisions are made and implemented to deliver quality education. Because there are opportunities for greater participation by public stakeholders in education, it is important that the stakeholders understand the governance and management structures of education: the various actors, influences, and issues in the approaches adopted and the limitations within the realities of provincial variations.

In the stir of the 18th Amendment and devolution, an unrealistic (almost utopian) feeling was given birth that universal education would finally be achieved, and that everything was magically going to be just fine in Pakistan's education system. A great opportunity to meet the enormous challenges of education reform was lost at the time of devolution, when the requirements for new governance and management should have taken on intense reorganization. That has not happened. What must happen will be the discussion and the narrative in this section. The citizen's attention, understanding, and participation will be most important because of the serious implications of the challenges in governance and management.

The education departments are the largest public employers in each of the provinces and possibly the federal territories as well. Combined, these departments equal or outnumber the personnel employed in Pakistan's defense services. The numbers are staggering in terms of human resource management (which is ineffective). The mandates are unclear. The challenges of political interference, financial mismanagement and systemic inefficiencies are overwhelming and severely limit personnel capacity. The system is broken. It is not possible for children to be learning very much in such an environment.

Fragmented reform processes, often initiated with help from international donors, have not been sustainable. SAHE reports: 'Over the last few years, a number of donors and those involved in reform, have pushed the case of public private partnerships in education to help [underprivileged] students benefit from the services of a private school. Punjab Education Foundation runs the largest such program. Other provinces also have their models managed by [similar education] foundations.' The report questions long-term effectiveness in making quality education available through such strategies but presents a more optimistic tone that (at the very least) 'the continued democratic process has seen an increased prioritization of education in the political arena.'

The SAHE report sums it up: 'The inadequacy of reforms and [along with] political interference afflicts routine management decisions and consequently the internal drivers of behavior in organizations. A stark symptom of low faith in the public sector school system has been the mushroom growth of private schools all over the country.' In the face of new challenges, the provincial governments have not responded to the changing landscape and private sector growth by enhancing their own capacities in public education.

There are some positive examples of cross learning and adaptation among provinces. SAHE adds: 'Success of these reforms will, however, depend on sustained political will, continued prioritization of education and continued financial support...*Effective implementation of the 18th Amendment would require a complete overhaul of the education system.'* (Emphasis by author).

A clear education policy remains elusive for all provinces. A mix of arbitrary political decisions, donor-backed priorities, and some 'policy documents' comprise the policy framework under which the provincial education departments function. The national policy documents have been shelved, with parts being implemented by random prioritization of certain programs, or possibly at the command of private interests. Generally, no national policy has been followed by effective implementation. The current policy environment is substantially influenced by donor agencies. Some donor ideas have urged broader reform. But their acceptance has been tepid in government circles and the ideas have not been usefully employed.

SAHE: 'As a result of inertia in the traditional organizations [bureaucracies], donors have bypassed them by creating parallel reform units. Initiated as temporary support to specific donor interventions, parallel reform units have continued to function and have attained a near permanent status. Officials in these units, normally from the government, have better salaries and privileges than their counterparts in the traditional bureaucratic setup. This has created an incentive structure leading to certain level of attrition [from the bureaucracy to the donor entity].'

Private schools have emerged as a significant element in the education landscape and provinces have been slow to acknowledge this change. Their policy response to this growth has been largely silence. Donors have supported public-private partnerships in the belief that private schools perform better than the public sector. A comparative study of low cost private and public schools in Punjab provided empirical support for this theory. However, based on the low benchmark set by public schools, the low-cost private schools perform only 'relatively better' than their public sector counterparts.

In the present situation, where the government has not been able to monitor the quality of public sector institutions, the possibility of regulating standards in the private sector seems unrealistic. SAHE laments the inequities: 'The risks of a laissez-faire growth of private schools without state oversight on content and learning remain high in a country faced with sharp inequities...The growth of the private sector is also not entirely due to a perception of poor quality of education in public schools. The governance limitations in the public sector are also responsible for it. In many urban areas the demand arises more from a lack of public schools. *No major urban center has seen a [public] school constructed in years despite enormous growth in the population.* In many cases the expenditure on transport to the nearest government school is higher than the fees of low-cost private schools in the vicinity. In the case of girls, safety considerations also add to the incentive to enroll in private schools closer to home.' (Emphasis by author).

More from SAHE: 'The most glaring gap lies in the implementation of policies. This is due to the lack of implementation plans, inadequate planning capacity, insufficient ownership of donor interventions, donor bypassing of traditional structures and the lack of coordination in donor interventions.'

So, what does all this percolate down to? I believe it is evidence that the governance and management of education in Pakistan is fragile, exhausted and—for the most part—broken, like other aspects of the system. This truncated section on Corruption and Cheating is directly from SAHE-EM 2014: 'The endemic corruption in Pakistan's public sector also plagues the education sector. Major incidences of corruption can be found in procurement, deductions from salaries where these are paid in cash, bribery for transfers and postings and covering up of absenteeism. The most sinister form of corruption has been institutionalized cheating in public examinations. Entire examination centers are sold and cheating support provided to candidates. [...] In places with endemic cheating there appears to be acceptance of the practice across the board. While the eventual onus lies with the political leadership, societal collusion makes it a difficult area for successful intervention. Irrespective, failure to prevent cheating reduces the quality of education even further and makes a mockery of reform efforts.'

Sadly, that does not shock the country. Extortion and corruption are commonplace and carried out with impunity. Though it should not be an excuse for unethical conduct and malfeasance, the challenges of governance and management efficiency are partially due to the huge scale of education services. The capacity to adequately address governance challenges is hindered by systemic failings as well as political interference. These fundamental governance and management issues must be addressed and resolved if reforms and full implementation of the constitutional 18th Amendment are to occur.

Technical and operational improvements have resulted from programs funded by donors but the fundamental capacity of provincial governments to deliver quality education remains dismally low. There must be sustained public demand for a much higher level of commitment on the part of political leadership, to assume greater ownership of this critical area of national development. Both political champions and public leadership are needed, with clarity on educational needs. The SAHE report says it well: 'Governance models are only as good as the outputs they pursue, the processes they use and the quality of inputs they employ.'

Bold actions are needed for change and reform. And time-limited commitments are needed to prioritize the actions under a new approach to governance and management. Here's a partial list of suggestions for what should be done both rationally and operationally:

1. Transfer requests take up enormous time of managers and executives in the provincial secretariats of education. To reduce the day-to-day demands of time, all transfers/postings must be frozen for two years with rare exceptions in limited and genuine hardship cases. This would help to refocus attention on radical reforms and quality inputs.
2. Political interference must come to a complete halt and reported under protection of anonymity.
3. Reforms and quality education must be the overriding principle of every action and conversation in education agencies.
4. As guiding principles and focus of its operations, the governance and management model must respect the civil, human and constitutional rights of *the child*.
5. The multiple unnecessary agencies (with unchecked duplication of programs and personnel) must be systematically weeded out.
6. Non-essential agencies must be closed down; personnel must be reduced, terminated, transferred, or retrained for new positions.
7. Relationships between agencies must be redefined with clarity of purpose and mandated authority.

8. The erosion of clarity, effectiveness and quality of management in education must be halted.

9. Personnel capacity and key processes must improve through concerted and sustained effort.

10. Insertion of essential quality inputs must be a high priority to ensure better learning outcomes.

11. Education managers and general administrators must receive ongoing relevant training.

12. Cadres of education specialists (for teacher training, textbooks, curriculum, and examinations) must be developed through high-quality, specialized training programs.

13. Contribution of expertise and participation in decision-making must be invited from bold and competent public leaders and stakeholders in education who are capable of expressing independent opinions and have the courage to democratically debate or disagree on sensitive issues.

14. The governance model should require a panel of civil society leaders to control (be in charge of) the education system, just as an effective board of directors does in a business or non-profit setting.

15. The governance group must demand efficiency in management performance of the managers and public employees and demonstrate a 'culture of quality' in the entire education ecosystem.

16. Data collected from ongoing surveys, studies, and other statistics or outcomes must be utilized for decision-making at policy level; professional services shall be engaged for valid recommendations and analysis of raw data.

SAHE appropriately alleges 'institutional inertia' of the education agencies and that the inaction has created a set of systemic shortcomings. We can look back and agree that not much has changed in the last five decades. Details vary but there is absence of quality benchmarks across the provinces. A model for monitoring quality assurance is nowhere to be found. The current wisdom is that the quality of inputs and processes influence the outcomes. However, the politically visible inputs of budgets, personnel, and materials have far greater relevance than the quality of essential inputs and processes. 'No benchmarks for achievement have been developed [...] outputs such as learning outcomes, dropouts and standards do not drive the decision making.' A new system of management must have high-priority on quality inputs which should be diligently monitored along with corresponding focus on outputs (student learning outcomes and others). In the absence of a clear mandate, the provincial agencies have become lethargic.

Data is used mainly in project planning but not used effectively in decision making. Most decisions are finalized by high ranking officials after cursory discussions with specialists and experts in the field. The data collected is often presented in the form of tables or raw data, not as analytical reports or relatable analyses for examining the impact of school improvement on learning outcomes.

To conclude the section, I refer readers, particularly decision makers, to Chapter 2 for review of how TCF has modeled its governance and management to run a large system and network of schools. It is an entirely homegrown and people-generated set of solutions that presents an opportunity to learn and replicate successful practices, and confidently discard obsolete or ineffective ones. The talent and brains to deliver quality education are present in Pakistan. The expertise should be garnered and given the chance. We should also be open to new ideas but there is no dire need to consult and gain the endorsement of 'foreign experts'. Huge mistakes have been made. It is time to learn from them and do the right thing.

7.8 Political Advocacy and Civic Leadership

Shortly after takeoff, an engine on the aircraft sputters and fails. It's an emergency. This is where training and procedures kick in. With cool heads, the captain and crew quickly assess and manage the situation. The other engine is working fine and the auxiliary engine has fired up. There's sufficient altitude to turn and make it back to the airport. Three things need to be done. First, aviate—*fly* the airplane and keep it safely in the air. Second, navigate—*know* where you are in relation to the airport and the shortest, safest way to get back and land. Third, communicate—*talk* to the tower, declare the emergency and let others know what you plan to do. The decisions made are the right ones. Lives are saved and all is well. Pakistan's education system is the airplane with the failed engine. We're keeping it in the air, but just barely. We know where we are. Now, we must maneuver the airplane to land, fix or replace the faulty engine, and make it safe to fly again. (Regular preventive maintenance will help).

The broken education system has failed the country and its people, especially *the children*. Our youth are maturing but without satisfactory education, and millions are not receiving any formal education at all. That in itself is a shameful acknowledgment, in this day and age. In the course of this book, several essential and technical steps have been suggested to start the fixing process. Everything is open for discussion. But, as stated in section 1.9 'Civic Leadership Needed for Reforms to Succeed', we will need solid civic leadership to re-build our education systems to ensure lasting change. The bureaucracies, policymakers, and planners have failed us. We, the people, must take control of the limping aircraft and find civic leaders who can make it airworthy to fly again.

Education reform is a never-ending process and, in all seriousness, we have not even scratched the surface. For reforms to succeed, there has to be a focused effort on a national level, with strong civic leadership and unwavering commitment to sustain the effort. Let's get started.

POLITICAL ADVOCACY

The education reform initiative must be a people-driven movement and one that works closely with the entire education landscape, without segmentation. In terms of equity, what's good for one should be good for all Pakistani children. The systems should be inclusive, with no child or community overlooked, neglected or abandoned. There are thousands of expatriates in the Diaspora population, myself included, who are eager to pitch in for the recovery and reform programs. And there are thousands of well-wishers and friends of Pakistan who would like to see the country make leaps of progress in its education and social development programs. With that said, I propose the creation of an International Coalition for Education Reform in Pakistan (ICERP). Stay tuned for details and how you can participate.

Through the narratives and stories of changemakers and the outstanding work of TCF leading the change, this book has presented multiple facets of school education in Pakistan. The highlighted Agents of Change are extraordinary individuals who continue to contribute to transformation. Tugging at our humanity, personal insights have been shared and powerful emotions revealed. Bold (perhaps audacious) ideas and arguments have been proposed. Thoughtful suggestions have been framed and presented for discussion. A roadmap has been laid out for direction and to arouse debate.

As all books do, this one too will come to an end. But the discussions and ideas contained, I hope, will, stir your thoughts and be in your conversations to ignite action for reforms. Hopefully, you've been inspired to do your part for Pakistani children and for the country's prosperity. I hope also that the book has created greater awareness of the issues and inequities, made you more conscious of the realities and politics that we live with, and also given you optimism that the education system can be fixed. Finally, it is my hope that the book has moved you to join us in the vigorous effort of supporting quality education and national reforms. If you're reading this, thank a teacher. Reading this is sufficient proof that you have an interest in helping Pakistan with education reform.

Oprah Winfrey[20] wrote, 'It takes only one candle to light a whole room of darkness. ...Don't underestimate your power. ...Get woke to how you can be an agent for change.'[21]

The suggested ICERP initiative and other ideas are not set in stone. They may be easily expanded or replaced with a better set of ideas. But here's a proposed framework for ICERP, why it should be supported and why you should join by signing up, online (at ICERPak.org):

- Initially, ICERP shall be an online platform for public information and political advocacy to support education reform in Pakistan.
- ICERP shall be non-partisan and shall be an open platform for all persons and organizations concerned with education reforms.
- It shall seek support of committed and influential civic leaders who can effectively contribute to changes in policy and practices to advance education reforms.
- It shall also seek support of education organizations and others, including government agencies, to advance education reforms.
- The objectives of ICERP shall be:

  1. to support public efforts for education reform through the sharing of information about education plans and projects, trends, surveys, academic research studies, legislation, policy and practices related to quality education in Pakistan;
  2. to work in close coordination with government agencies at all levels, to advance education reform; and
  3. to serve as a vigilant watchdog group, to monitor fiscal and operational functions of education systems.

Closely aligned with its primary objective of political advocacy (and contingent upon the direction of its leadership and the feelings of its supporters), I also foresee a role for ICERP as a credible think tank or policy and research institute, with a body of experts as the premier resource of evidence-based ideas to be developed and proposed as policy in specific areas such as curriculum. Other inputs for quality education may also be pursued by ICERP.

To sustain public efforts for comprehensive reforms, and for the sharing of relevant current information, ICERP will have an effective and unpretentious system of two-way communication with supporters. The platform shall be a central point to mobilize support for public campaigns and for the expression of public and political voice, either in praise or protest. With a sizable database, opinion surveys may be conducted on matters of concern and innovative ideas fleshed out.

ICERP shall be a people's initiative for public and political advocacy, tapping into the ideas and energies of the millennial youth generation as well as the seasoned experience of the senior generations. The founding of ICERP will be a volunteer effort. To sustain its programs and advocacy, ICERP shall transition from an online platform to an organization registered as a non-profit in Pakistan and elsewhere, employ competent staff for management and operations, and seek operating funds through grants and other sources.

CIVIC LEADERSHIP

In section 1.9, the discussion is about the need for robust civic leadership to sustain education reforms. Past assignments to address reforms have been in the form of appointed task forces which typically did not have enforcement authority, or clear mandate to make bold recommendations and see them to completion. The result has been no solution and virtually no change in strategy, policies or practices. Wrapping up the 2010 Task Force, Michael Barber stated that the Task Force had no intention of writing yet another report and that 'The challenge of education reform in Pakistan is not a lack of ideas or experiments; it is one of scale, capacity to deliver and political will to tackle longstanding binding constraints.'

We can casually dismiss Barber's statement as not exactly fresh news. But it has profound meaning and depth when unpacked and thoughtfully assessed. The second part of the statement is what got my attention: that the education reform challenge is one of scale, capacity to deliver, and political will to tackle longstanding binding constraints. It became obvious that even though these elements are separate, they are interconnected. Allow me to analyze.

The scale of any country's challenges is in direct proportion to its population. To top that, Pakistan has a significant number of persons living in poverty and squalid conditions, not receiving adequate education. 'No education' or poor education means there's meager opportunity to get on the generational path to relative prosperity and progressive, incremental improvement in the quality of living conditions. But, more to the point, we—the affluent and powerful—have not recognized the human needs of underprivileged people or done enough about the challenge of equity in Pakistani society at large. Let's face it: we have been callous, indifferent, and busy with our own lives. We have chosen to neglect the quality of life in the larger society of humans, our fellow inhabitants.

It is a no-brainer that Pakistan's capacity to deliver quality education has been stunted and severely paralyzed by the mismanagement and dysfunctional non-systems that have seen large amounts of funds disappear, with nothing to show. Freedoms and abilities to steer policy and societal direction have been somewhat limited by political events but also by how we have tacitly allowed our governance to be shaped and administered. We have paid the price for negligence. Now is the time to turn things around.

For the longest time, I have thought of political will as the lack of motivation of our political leaders, the decision makers. I realize how wrong I have been. Today, I interpret political will to mean *the people's* desire for change expressed through democratic processes, for the continuous building and re-shaping of our civil society. We have not done that adequately. We have not raised our collective voice in demand for equitable quality education for all children. We have not truly rolled up our sleeves and done what's needed. Instead of standing ground, we gave up the fight.

And, as examples of longstanding and binding constraints, we must resolve the important battles over language policy, curriculum content, quality inputs, management, and the discriminating systems that result in education inequities. Reforms cannot succeed unless these fundamentals are addressed in open forums and resolved democratically, with fairness for all—especially for the children.

It is likely that earlier reform efforts were not successful because broader civic leadership and public demand were not effectively mobilized. The lesson to be learned from past failures is that, to achieve lasting impact, effective civic leadership is essential. I suggest earnest review of section 1.9.

7.9 Perceptions of Quality Education in Silicon Valley, USA

Around the world, people assume that education at all levels in the US is top-notch. That is true for the university, professional, and research programs. But, is it also true for the K-12 system of public schools, in the entire country? Not necessarily true, not across the board. However, most elementary, middle and high schools in the public systems are generally delivering fair-to-good quality of education; some are clearly outstanding and highly ranked year after year. Though not in all cases, private schools do generally rank higher than public schools. The better-rated public schools are typically in the more affluent and pricy suburban neighborhoods with proportionately fewer minorities of Latino, African-American, or migrant families. In most communities, these minorities combined make up less than 20 percent of the population. Public schools that are ranked lower are typically in the less affluent suburban and inner city areas with proportionately higher number of minorities. But how can that be the case in the richest country on the planet—and why do inequities exist at all?

Discriminatory practices in the US have been checked and reduced significantly through laws pertaining to civil rights and effective activism for desegregation of schools in the last sixty years. But true equity in education still has a long way to go. Even with funding resources being allocated proportionately and fairly, inequities do exist in school education because of unequal demand, uneven expectations, and inconsistent quality inputs. Simply put, and regardless of minority factors, I think affluent communities have higher expectations. And they are more effective in their demand for better quality inputs. That's how better outcomes are achieved and better school rankings are reached.

So, is money the only underpinning for quality education? It helps to have appropriate funding but, that being fair and equal by law, I believe the game changers in education are higher expectations and more effective demand for better quality inputs. This is evident in affluent communities. And education systems in the US are not perfect. If the systems were perfect, why would high-achieving students need extra help? Why do college-preparatory coaching centers do a roaring business, and private tutors get paid as much as $75 an hour? Answer: because more is expected of college-bound youth in affluent communities, that's why.

The cities and counties that make up Silicon Valley and the greater Bay Area—from San Francisco to Berkeley-Oakland to San Jose and the suburban communities—have some of the highest ranked schools and most expensive housing market[22] in the country. I am very fortunate to live in the heart of Silicon Valley, California. Within a ten-mile radius, I estimate there are at least *fifty* tutoring businesses to help with SAT or ACT preparation, the standardized tests for college admission. Students with high GPA, from expensive private schools and from highly rated public schools, pay good money to these coaching centers to better their SAT or ACT scores—or for other needs like difficulty with math, or reading comprehension, or science interpretation skills.

The observation made here is that even the highly rated education systems—Finland, Germany, England, Singapore, and others—cannot be complacent or rest on their laurels. Every system is in constant pursuit of quality improvement because the expectation is to be better and not allow regression. Attaining a system of excellence and near perfection and then astutely sustaining the high standard are the desired goals of aspiring education systems. In that respect, Pakistan has a formidable journey ahead with its program of reforms.

Legislatively, we are not in a bad spot. Constitutionally, we do have equal access on the books. Our governance and management need total overhaul. Language policy issues must be resolved. Operationally and in management efficiency, we severely lag behind. In the area of public demand for quality education, we must strive for better public participation and strategic political advocacy. As I said at the top of the chapter: we need a societal shift in attitude about education. And we need quality education. Education reform can be simple and uncomplicated. The devil is in the detail. Tick-tock, tick-tock, tick-tock. The clock is ticking.

Notes

1. Zubeida Mustafa, *Tyranny of Language in Education: The Problem and Its Solution* (Karachi: Oxford University Press, 2015), p. 2.

2. Appendix 3, Essay No. 5: 'Functional Arguments for a Rational Policy on Language'.
3. Zubeida Mustafa, *Tyranny of Language in Education*, p. 1.
4. Ibid., p. 4.
5. Ibid., p. x.
6. Society for Advancement of [Higher] Education Report, Education Monitor 2014, Chapter 7, http://www.sahe.org.pk/wp-content/uploads/2014/12/EM-I-Reviewing-quality-of-key-education-inputs-in-Pakistan-Part-7.pdf
7. Hywel Coleman is Honorary Senior Research Fellow in the School of Education at the University of Leeds, UK. His edited books include *Society and the Language Classroom* (Cambridge, 1996) and *Dreams and Realities: Developing Countries and the English Language* (British Council, 2011).
8. Hywel Coleman, '"To be consulted, to encourage and to warn": The impacts and the limits of language-in-education research in the developing world,' in Robert Lawson and Dave Sayers (eds.), *Sociolinguistic Research: Application and Impact* (Routledge, 2016).
9. Hywel Coleman, 'Teaching and Learning in Pakistan: The Role of Language in Education' (Islamabad: The British Council, 2010). https://www.researchgate.net/profile/Hywel_Coleman/publication/265186454_Teaching_and_Learning_in_Pakistan_The_Role_of_Language_in_Education/links/5512738b0cf268a4aaea51b0/Teaching-and-Learning-in-Pakistan-The-Role-of-Language-in-Education.pdf
10. Hywel Coleman and Tony Capstick, 'Language in Education in Pakistan: Recommendations for Policy and Practice' ((Islamabad: British Council, 2012). This is a follow-up to the earlier report of 2010. The earlier document was subjected to public scrutiny through a series of policy dialogs, conferences, high-level discussions, and radio programs with community participation. The second report describes the disappointing consultation process, analyses the findings, and makes recommendations regarding further development of policy for language in school-level education in Pakistan. https://www.academia.edu/31726335/Language_in_education_in_Pakistan_Recommendations_for_policy_and_practice?auto=download
11. QIPRA is a suggested name and acronym. The actual name may be different, but it is strongly recommended that 'Quality Improvement' and 'Rating' remain an integral part of the name of the agency to identify its purpose and functions.
12. Much of the content in this section is gleaned from the excellent SAHE Education Monitor Report 2014, 'Reviewing quality of key education inputs in Pakistan' (Chapter 3, Professional Preparation of Teachers) http://www.sahe.org.pk/wp-content/uploads/2016/01/4.-EM-I.compressed.pdf.
13. Ibid.
14. Copious amounts of content in this section are gleaned from Chapter 6, *Curriculum and Textbooks* in the comprehensive and excellent SAHE Education Monitor Report 2014 (EM 2014), 'Reviewing quality of key education inputs in Pakistan', http://www.sahe.org.pk/wp-content/uploads/2016/01/4.-EM-I.compressed.pd
15. SAHE EM 2014 reports: 'The new curriculum was promulgated in 2006 with the intention that the textbooks would be developed according to the newly available guidelines. However, to date many textbooks are still published in accordance with the old curriculum framework.'
16. Political Economy, Investopedia, https://www.investopedia.com/terms/p/political-economy.asp
17. Much of the content in this section is extracted from the SAHE Education Monitor Report 2014 'Reviewing quality of key education inputs in Pakistan' (Chapter 8, Examinations), http://www.sahe.org.pk/wp-content/uploads/2016/01/4.-EM-I.compressed.pdf
18. Ibid.
19. Significant portions of content in this section are taken from the SAHE-Education Monitor Report 2014 'Reviewing quality of key education inputs in Pakistan' (Chapter 9,

Governance and Management) http://www.sahe.org.pk/wp-content/uploads/2016/01/4.-EM-I.compressed.pdf.

20. Born in poverty in rural Mississippi, Oprah is an iconic American woman—a media executive, actress, talk show host, television producer and philanthropist who also supports girls' education in Africa. She is best known for her Oprah Winfrey Show which was the highest-rated television program of its kind in history and ran in national syndication for 25 years. Dubbed the 'Queen of All Media', she was the richest African American of the 20th century and North America's first black multi-billionaire. She has also been ranked as the most influential woman in the world. (Source: *TIME*)

21. Oprah Winfrey, 'Oprah on Why She Thinks "We're in Trouble and Need a Collective Reckoning"', 5 December 2018; https://www.oprahmag.com/life/relationships-love/a25401249/oprah-coming-together/.

22. Higher property values translate into higher real estate tax revenues collected by the counties, thus more funding for schools and higher quality of education. Affluence and better-quality lifestyle lead to the expectation of superior education quality and incremental improvement in public schools.

Appendices

The Appendices herein are by recognized academics who are enthusiastic supporters of education reform. Readers are asked to adapt to the academic styling of these chapters. The insights by the writers are invaluable to understanding education reform and nation building in a broader context. Appendix 3 comprises thoughtful and timeless essays by Anjum Altaf.

Appendix 1

Politics of Education in Pakistan

Irfan Muzaffar, PhD, is an educator and researcher who has been involved in teacher education, policy analysis, and program design for education reform. As a teacher educator, Irfan has conducted math education courses at the Ali Institute of Education, Lahore, and at Michigan State University. His research interests include history of education reforms and connections between research and policy related to public-private education. He is a consultant and research team member for reform programs in Pakistan and is a founding member of Campaign for Quality Education in Pakistan. He is also co-author of *Educational Crisis and Reform: Perspectives from South Asia* (Oxford University Press, 2015).

* * * *

A paradox has long been puzzling observers of education reforms in Pakistan—that while there appears to be a very high level of demand for quality education, there is no impact of this demand on Pakistan's education policy and the country's spending on education remains one of the lowest in South Asia and the world. Failure to increase education spending and accountability render constitutional guarantees such as those enshrined in the 18th Amendment (which mandates compulsory education) vacuous and meaningless.

The failure of policy to respond to public demand lies in the inability of the political process to aggregate parental demand for education. In a perceptive response to a blog post by me on this subject, Professor Faisal Bari, an eminent economist and supporter of education reforms, observed:

> ... [the] failure is that the political system is not aggregating demands well, is not responding to the needs of the parents…it seems that if policies followed by governments are supposed to be somehow reflections of the public demands that have been aggregated, that process is not working very well in Pakistan (Bari, 2011a).

This essay is motivated by these conversations about public demand in education and the failure of politics to adequately aggregate in ways that result in an increase in public spending on and subsequent improvements in public education. It is argued that while parental demand for education may inevitably lead to the creation of an education market place, as it has in the case of Pakistan (see Andrabi, Das, and Khwaja, 2008), it does not necessarily lead to decisions by the political elite to increase public spending on education. Such increases happen under very specific political and economic conditions that do not exist in Pakistan. In fact, the rhetoric of demand and supply of education does not work very well to explain the political inaction towards educational issues. If education is a right, it does not have to be demanded and supplied by the market, rather it should be secured through legal and political means. Furthermore, the right to education is unlikely to be achieved without increased levels of public spending to ensure equity in access and quality of primary and secondary education. History of education reforms in countries that have successfully universalized education reveals the use of a wide variety of instruments by stakeholders, including legal and political activism, to force governments to increase public spending on education.

Why Do Societies Decide to Educate Everyone?

The idea of *Education for All* has not always been with us. Greeks, Romans, not even Islamic civilizations entertained the idea of universal education at the expense of the state. It was only in the last three hundred years or so that universal education emerged and became consolidated as a necessary precondition for development of any society. The reasons behind universalization of education have been both political and economic but have differed widely across different countries.

For example, during the eighteenth century, King Fredrick William I made education compulsory for all children who did not have access to private schools as part of his attempts to supply the Prussian state with a nation to match it (Ramirez and Boli, 1987). The King's decision was based on a strategic rather than a moral imperative. It certainly did not represent an aggregation of public demand for education. That is to say, it did not really matter whether there was demand for education or not, the sovereign power just declared it compulsory for all children. The goal of such education was to inculcate a sense of 'nationhood'. Also, the state did not have to target children from the families of Prussian elites who already had access to private education. It is important to note for subsequent discussion that the advantage enjoyed by Prussian elites was not threatened in any way due to compulsory education of the Prussian masses.

In contrast, public education in British India was introduced to serve an entirely different set of imperatives. While there may have been differing motivations for its public provision, the one that has been acknowledged as the most dominant was the instrumental use of a highly differentiated education system to facilitate the colonial government of a highly diverse polity (Allender, 2006). Different kinds of education(s) targeted different social classes in British India, reinforcing distinctions between people along language and socio-economic lines. An important way in which power differential was experienced in India was through a kind of linguistic exclusion. The British preserved and reinforced this tradition of linguistic exclusion by immersing Indian elites in English who sought to preserve their status and influence through so-called 'modern' education. As argued by Ara (2004: 35), the Aligarh Movement for modern education spearheaded by Sir Syed Ahmad Khan in the late nineteenth century was meant for a small group of Muslim elites and not for the Muslim masses. Education in the 'vernacular' became the preserve of the commoners. Such education spending provided for the education of the masses under the British Raj did not interfere with the advantage enjoyed by the small elite secured through linguistic exclusion. British government subsidies for education of the elite were welcomed by segments of the population that benefited from such support.

In the US, unlike Fredrick William's Prussia and British India, education was delivered primarily in what was conceived as a *common school* (Cremin, 1951). The American *common school* movement drew its impetus from the American Revolution. The early coming together of liberalism and democracy in America imbued this movement with contradictory political goals (Labaree, 1997). The American polity decided to levy taxes to pay for the common school through a political tug of war. This tug of war continues to this day but it has turned into a debate about whether education should be provided by the private sector and paid for by the state or paid for by the public schools. The spending on education, however, has been steadily increasing in the US irrespective of this debate. In fact, education was termed as a 'civil right' by civil rights activists (Perry, Moses, Wynne, Cortes Jr, and Delpit, 2010), a source of American pre-eminence among other nations, and a highly effective instrument of social mobility. High levels of demand for education in the US have found robust political expression forcing the left and right-wing policy elite to increase public spending on education throughout the twentieth century. Furthermore, it is important to note that in an economically ascendant US of the late nineteenth and early twentieth centuries, expanding educational opportunity enhanced the advantage of the elite rather than diminishing it. Thus, in the case of the US, both democracy and the economy worked in favor of educational expansion.

Public Spending on Education: The Role of Policy Elites

In all three cases, educational policy was ultimately decided by a handful of policy elites who under different pressures made different spending decisions in different settings. This aspect of educational policy making processes, as Ansell (2010) argues, is true under all dispensations. It is always a small policy elite who typically makes decisions to increase or decrease educational spending.

Imagine a society which consists of two segments of population, a small educated segment—the elite or rich—and a large inadequately educated semi-literate or illiterate segment. Assume further that expanding educational opportunity in this society will increase the life chances of everyone in it. Add to this picture the small segment of policy elite, irrespective of whether this imagined society is ruled democratically or by authoritarian means. This elite segment has the wherewithal to influence policy decisions. The question is: under what circumstances will it use its power to expand educational opportunity? It would be perfectly rational for them to block such expansion if it is likely to render them worse off. Also, the political office holders amongst them will only increase education spending if such an increase in spending brings political benefits to them. If the economy of this society is such that a redistribution of resources aimed at making the disadvantaged better off would leave the rich worse off through taxation and meritocracy, it would make sense for the elite to do everything they can to block education spending in order to preserve their advantage. Thus, low levels of public accountability (autocracy) and weak economic conditions contain incentives for the elite to block education funding.

Conversely, high levels of public accountability (democracy) and strong economic conditions contain incentives for the elite to invest more in education.

Thus, when governments undersupply public education they do so not because they are unable to aggregate high levels of demand, but because those who control the government *do not want* other peoples' children to become educated (Ansell, 2010). He proposes an explanation in terms of the strong distributive effects of education, providing the following three reasons for the elite's attitude towards public spending on education:

1. The elite typically earn more and thus have to pay more in taxes to educate other peoples' children.
2. The elite accrue advantages from the scarcity of education; fewer the university-educated people, the stronger their monopoly on highly paid jobs that require skilled labor.
3. The elite also dislike increased education spending because it increases meritocracy at the expense of heredity and thereby threatens the transmission of their wealth legacy from generation to generation.

The Role of Pakistan's Policy Elite

Do the reasons mentioned above hold true for the policy preferences made by the elite in Pakistan? This essay argues that they do. A cursory examination of nearly all education policy documents, except for the 1972 Education Policy, shows a tendency by the policy elite to block public spending on education. Take for example, a quote from the six-year plan for education (1951–57) and another from the Sharif Commission Report commissioned by Ayub Khan's dictatorial military regime in 1958. In both quotes, the commitment toward increased public spending is avoided by appealing to the private sector. In the first quote, Minister of Education Fazl-ur-Rehman stridently declares education as compulsory, but also renders it unachievable without contribution from the private sector. Private voluntary contribution, not compulsory taxation, is depicted as an expression of patriotism. As he puts it:

> During British rule, private enterprise in [the] Indo-Pakistan subcontinent has greatly assisted the development of education. If in

the past, education could generate such remarkable enthusiasm in the people, I do not see why the achievement of independence should not release all the latent forces of patriotism and initiative for the task of educational advancement...I am, therefore, confident that they [the private sector] will come forward in a true spirit of patriotism to bear a share of the burden which the present plan imposes on us, and, as far as primary education is concerned, provide free land, buildings and equipment. Unless this is done, the execution of the programs of free, compulsory primary education (Emphasis by author), which have been and are being adopted by the provinces, will be retarded. (Government of Pakistan, 1951: 11)

In 1958, the Sharif Commission made recommendations about how education should be organized. The report of this commission minced no words in making a case for less public spending on education:

The services provided by the government must be paid for eventually from their [the people's] own resources [...] our citizens must also depend on their own spiritual and material resources and not expect the benefactions of government to provide them with the environment and institutions they desire for themselves, their children, and their community... In education...it is impossible to escape the economic reality that one receives largely what one pays for. Good education is expensive, and educational expansion means more expense. The people must accept the fact that since it is they and their children who benefit most from education, the sacrifices required must be borne primarily by them (emphasis author's). (Government of Pakistan 1959: 8)

These quotes are typical and representative of policy positions throughout Pakistan's history and emphasize the consistency in a policy position against increasing public spending on education. They show that the policy elite identified expansion in education as a precondition for progress, even used the ideal of compulsory education, but stopped short of taking practical steps to provide the resources needed to expand educational opportunity for all citizens.

While earlier, the policy elite grounded their argument for less public spending in appeals to patriotism or in an economic rationale—those who utilize education as a good must also pay for it—the present-day elite justify their lack of attention to issues of education in terms of an absence of demand by the people they want to serve. Recently some politicians were asked as to why they did not make education an important issue within their parties. They agreed that education should get a very high priority, but also said that it was hard for them to turn education into one of the top issues as their constituents did not demand delivery of education (Bari 2011b). So, the bottom line is that issues pertaining to education are never registered at the leadership level of the political parties as a top demand from the people.

Tracing the Roots of Political Inaction about Education, Using the Logic of Political Survival

There are two things happening here. First, the political [or policy] elite are unwilling to invest in education. Second, they have an incentive to block funding for education. Therefore, a rhetoric that construes their inaction in terms of *lack of tangible demands by the public* makes invisible the possibility that politicians have no stake in education of the masses due to the small size of the electorate. Isn't it puzzling that the demand for education, which is so palpably visible to the economists of education, remains invisible to the politicians? What is going on? It has been argued that the categories of demand and supply work to provide the policy elite with a sort of alibi for not working toward expanding quality education to the masses (Muzaffar 2011). The assumptions about elite preferences from Ansell's model provide further support to this assertion which argues that it is not in the interest of the elite to expand education to the masses under all conditions (Ansell 2010).

Yet, it is in their interest to project themselves as helpless champions of education only because of unanimity of opinion about education as a necessary ingredient of modern nation-statehood. Therefore, it is perfectly rational for the political elite in a country that has a claim to modern nation-statehood to not take an explicit position against educating the masses. It makes sense, therefore, to develop a rhetoric that at once expresses an aspiration for it as well as an inability or lack of capacity and resources to realize it. This rhetoric is designed to project a certain sense of helplessness on the part of policy elite. In the past, Pakistan's policy elite have employed this rhetoric frequently in policy documents. The language of demand (or the lack of it), however, has added another element to an existing position of helplessness in matters of education. The upshot of this discussion is that the decisions to block public spending must be justified with appeal to one or the other discourse. In the past, the elite grounded their lack of enthusiasm for public spending in education in an appeal to voluntarily provide education rooted in philanthropy and patriotism, now they do it in an absence of public demand for education.

Let us extend this discussion to describe ways in which the discourse of *demand* works to keep educational preferences of the poor from appearing on policy registers. To do this, the essay will use key features of the educational scene of Pakistan, both its supply and demand, as presented in a policy brief by Andrabi, Das and Khwaja (2011). This scene is described by the supply of drastically inadequate and low quality public education, a booming but credit-constrained market of private schools, and a strong parental preference or demand for education. Here, though, demand is not meant to be *precursor to a political action* to increase public spending in education, but rather as a basis *for informed consumption of education* in a dynamic market place. The *demand* is seen as merely existing and, therefore, also playing a vital role in the expansion of the market of affordable private schools. In such a market situation, no one explicitly voices his or her demand. Instead, people express it by purchasing education from one vendor or another. The market does not require collective action, only individual choice-making for its operation.

So, the *market* positions education as a private good or service, which may be in high demand. But such demand does not need collective public action for it to be fulfilled. Rather, it assumes for it to be fulfilled as the individual is assumed as the consumer.[1] Surveys aimed to assess parental preferences may validate the existence of parental demand for education, but it is not paradoxical when the preferences do not turn into a source of public outrage. The market scene does not offer individuals the position of a citizen or an activist or a demander in the political sense of the term. Rather, it only provides them a choice to be, at the very best, an *informed consumer*.

The mere existence of *demand* does not necessarily imply political action, but rather an informed choice to consume a particular good or service. Political systems do not aggregate demand—markets do. Demand aggregation is not necessarily about collective political action inasmuch as it is merely an objective measure of total demand for particular goods and services.

But when the rhetoric of demand is used within the realm of democratic politics, it leads to confusion and fails to achieve the ends for which it is mobilized, i.e. increased attention to education and a favorable change in policy to expand quality education for all. The reason this rhetoric fails is because it casts the ordinary 'citizens' in the role of inarticulate demanders, and politicians in the role of suppliers of education. The worrisome consequence of the logic inherent in the demand/supply narrative when applied to public education is that the disadvantaged parent takes a beating at both ends, first by being already deprived of quality education for her children and secondly for not adequately articulating demand. The elite may be blocking educational spending for other reasons. However, in this simplistic narrative, they are let off the hook simply because it describes them as passive responders to public demand.

Political inaction has other possible reasons. Two interrelated theoretical insights, which are also supported by empirical evidence, are important to consider in order to move forward with this discussion. The first is the idea of *Selectorate*. This notion conceptualizes active politicians as actors who do not want to let go off their privilege [in an autocracy] and their elected position [in a democracy]. Selectorate is defined as a set of people *who have a say* in choosing leaders and with a prospect of gaining access to special privileges doled out by them once they [the elected leaders] are chosen (Bueno de Mesquita, Smith, Siverson and Morrow 2005: 42). The *winning coalition* is a sub-group within the selectorate '*who maintain incumbents in office and in exchange receive special privileges*' (Bueno de Mesquita et al. 2005: p. xi). They argue that in the case of authoritarian states, the size of the selectorate and the winning coalition is too small. The implication of this, they argue, is that *what appears to be a bad policy from a rational standpoint is actually good politics inasmuch as it helps keep the incumbents in power*. Their ideas get further support in Ansell's empirically tested model that provides a statistically significant correlation between the form of government and the levels of public education spending (Ansell 2010). His findings show that public spending on education increases under a shift from autocracy to democracy. Theoretically, this increase is ascribed to an increase in the size of the selectorate and, by implication, that of the winning coalition.

So ordinarily, one would expect public spending on education to respond to popular demand for education and, therefore, increase under democratic dispensation. That has been the pattern in countries like Philippines or India[2]. But according to the World Bank 2012 indicators, this does not seem to be true in the case of Pakistan whose public spending on education remains consistently low. Providing every child quality education requires redistribution of public resources. But unlike other countries transitioning to democracy that have registered significant post-transformation increases, Pakistani policy elite have consistently opted to maintain low levels of public spending.

Following Bueno de Mesquita et al. (2005) and Ansell (2010), we may hypothesize that the transition to democracy does not have a significant effect on the size of winning coalitions. Malik (2010) uses the former to explain the inability of successive Pakistani governments to institute land reforms and extract taxes from agricultural incomes. With a low tax base, politicians are not in a position to increase spending on public services such as education. Democracy in Pakistan has not translated into an increase in taxation on the rich and redistribution of wealth, which is a basic condition for expansion in quality education. More research is needed to shed some light on the hypothetical explanations that emerge when we ground failure to increase education spending in a *logic of political survival*.

Where Do We Go from Here?

One way out of this dilemma is to work with actors at both ends of the spectrum, that is, by helping both the citizens to demand better education and the politicians to recognize that educating the masses is in their interest.[3] This approach then introduces another actor into the scene who occupies the position of neither the citizen nor the politician but a mentor of sorts for both. The trouble with this approach is that it seeks to target the behavior of the *potential demander* and the *potential responder* without changing the conditions that enabled their existing apathies in the first place. Those who suffer because of lack of educational opportunity are also conditioned to *demand less* by their deprivation, which has its own 'logic of survival'. As Sen (1999) puts it:

> The deprived people tend to come to terms with their deprivation because of the sheer necessity of survival, and they may, as a result, lack the courage to demand any radical change, and may even adjust their desires and expectations to what they unambiguously see as feasible. (P. 63)

Therefore, populations that have endured deprivation long enough tend to naturalize a state of educational deprivation[4]. Expansion of educational opportunity, therefore, cannot wait for its demand to become explicit. There are some innovative interventions that attempt to help citizens articulate their demand for education and also help politicians and political parties become more responsive to them. We will learn more about their effects with time.

Can civil society by proxy—and erroneously so, NGOs—help to change this situation? According to the model articulated by Bueno de Mesquita et al. (2005) and Ansell (2010), we will need to ascertain if well-intentioned NGOs are part of the *selectorate* or *winning coalitions* aspiring for political office. More research is needed to make credible claims about the role of NGOs in influencing the course of education reforms. But from the anecdotal evidence we know that the path to change in educational policy does not pass through chest beating advocacy campaigns run by NGOs as time bound projects.

Over the last two decades or so, NGOs or Civil Society Organizations (CSOs) have become part of a well-defined development sector. They actively seek time bound social development projects as contractors to one or the other donor. Such time bound contracts are likely to weaken the public sphere in which the politics of education must happen. Political philosopher Hannah Arendt argues that unlike architectural structures that continue to exist beyond human *actions* that developed them in the first place, the public sphere depends on constant nurturing and action. It disappears when the action that produced it disappears. As she puts it in the *Human Condition* (1958):

> Unlike the spaces which are the work of our hands, it [the public sphere] does not survive the actuality of the movement which brought it into being but disappears not only with the dispersal of men—as in the case of great catastrophes when body politic of the people is destroyed—but with the disappearance or arrest of the activities themselves. Whenever people gather together, it is potentially there, but only potentially, not necessarily and not forever. (P.199)

NGO-led, time-bound campaigns for education are one of the many illustrations of this flashing appearance and disappearance of the public sphere in Pakistan. Social and political movements, such as the recent 'lawyers' movement' to reinstate an 'independent judiciary' in Pakistan is another example. The other is the recent 'education emergency.' There are also people and organizations that are engaged in public efforts to get the right to education enforced for Pakistani children. All of them are worthwhile efforts. But unfortunately, much of this work is based on time-bound funded projects which are useful work of constituting public spaces where politicians and public office holders can be held accountable, but which disappear as soon as the funding that created them is exhausted.

A way out of this dilemma is to keep reminding politicians of the positive externalities that follow from quality education for all citizens. Public intellectuals in Pakistan have been doing this for some time through the print and electronic media. But there are, as argued above, very objective historical conditions under which the elite have favored expansion of education; sermonizing the political elite does not seem to be one of them. The first and the foremost is genuine democratization, and the second is economic development. The autocracies in which the very small elite determine policy outcomes have expanded education spending when their economies integrated within the global system. Singapore, China and Malaysia are examples of such autocracies. None of these conditions seem to exist in Pakistan and time-bound efforts to convince politicians and citizens can only go so far.

Finally, let us raise the issue of a distinction between education as a good or service benefit and education as a basic right, to reflect on the irrelevance of the idea of public demand to the reforms in public sector schools. The former view (of a good or service) lends education for analysis in demand and supply terms; but the latter (a basic right) leads us to view the problem of education in political and legal, rather than economic terms. It is mutually contradictory to speak of education in the same breath as a basic right that must be guaranteed irrespective of individual circumstances, and as a good or service that is procured in accordance with the individual circumstance. If it has been secured as a justiciable basic right, then we should not expect the public to demand it. Rather, we should expect the legal and executive branches of the state to 'protect' it. Basic rights are not supplied. They are demanded as long as they have not been constitutionally secured. After they have been politically secured, activism should focus more on finding legal ways of ensuring that the constitutional provisions are delivered in their letter and spirit.

It is crucial to emphasize also that education has not been a sufficiently political issue and, therefore, needs to be politicized (Drèze and Sen 1999). As they put it:

> There is no question that, even in a country as poor as India, means can be found to ensure universal attainment of literacy and other basic educational achievements, at least in the younger age groups. There are important strategic questions to consider in implementing that social commitment, but the primary challenge is to make it a more compelling political issue. (P. 139)

Turning education into a political issue in Pakistan, however, will require a healthy public domain which has been weakened due to time-bound projects in the social development sector. However, political debates about proposals that seek to preserve public interest, as defined by the Constitution, ought to occur in robust public spaces (Marquand 2004):

> Public domain is both priceless and precarious—a gift of the history, which is always at risk. It can take shape only in a society in which the notion of a public interest, distinct from private interests, has taken root; and, historically speaking, such societies are rare breeds. Its values and practices also do not come naturally and have to be learned. Where the private domain of love, friendship, and personal connection and the market domain of buying and selling are the products of nature, the public domain depends on careful and continuing nurture. (P. 2)

Without cultivating spaces which are constantly available and populated with debates about education reforms in Pakistan, the public demand for education is not likely to find a genuinely powerful political expression.

CONCLUSION

Lack of education reforms or increase in educational spending in Pakistan cannot simply be attributed to the lack of capacity, or lack of public demand, or lack of competence. The literature on political economy of education suggests that lack of investment in education is part of a strategy of political survival in Pakistan. When the size of winning coalitions and 'selectorate' is small, as it is in the case of authoritarian and military regimes, and in the case of a weak democracy in Pakistan, political office holders only need to protect the interests of the members of their winning coalition.

And while the rhetoric of public demand and supply works best in describing market settings, it is not necessarily applicable in the case of political decision-making. That is to say, in making policy choices, elite policy makers are prone to respond to the demands from their winning coalitions, rather than from the public. The logic of demand also posits parents as autonomous, self-contained, agentive, and individualistic consumers. This logic is not necessary when education is described as a fundamental right guaranteed by the Constitution of the state. Basic rights are not goods to be traded in the market place and politicians are not their suppliers. Once secured constitutionally, rights need to be guaranteed and protected, just like any other provision of the Constitution. It sounds contradictory to speak in the same breath about education as a 'right'—which requires activism aimed at its protection through political and legal guarantees—and a 'good or service'—which is subject to the logic of demand and supply. When politicians occupy the position of suppliers of education, they can always find an alibi in the absence of demand which does not find political expression largely because of what Amartya Sen views as the conditioning of the deprived.

When the deprived do not explicitly ask to end their deprivations, the political elite turn around to say, 'Look, no one is knocking at our doors, so what do we do?' This response is not appropriate or acceptable from the protectors of basic rights guaranteed by the Constitution. But such a response is wholly appropriate if the policy elite are positioned as suppliers of education. Once positioned as protectors of basic rights they, as well as state institutions in general, need to be held accountable irrespective of demand or its aggregates. The policy elite will only take expansion of quality education seriously if positioned and held accountable as guarantors of constitutional rights.

The 18th Constitutional Amendment, by providing constitutional guarantees for universal education, provides a window of opportunity for legal and political activism. Constitutional litigation against office holders and the government can compensate for the lack of public demand and eliminate, or at least lessen, the need for expensive time bound advocacy campaigns with a history of failure. If quality education is to become a reality, development interventions will need to target attitudes of the policy elite a lot more than the quick fix technical interventions that are currently in vogue.

References

Allender, Tim. 2006. *Ruling through Education: The Politics of Schooling in the Colonial Punjab.* Asian Studies Association of Australia and South Asian Publication Series No. 14. New Delhi: New Dawn Press Group.

Andrabi Tahir, Jishnu Das and Asim Ijaz Khwaja. 2008. 'A Dime a Day: The Possibilities and Limits of Private Schooling in Pakistan.' *Comparative Education Review* 52(3): 329-355. Retrieved December 17, 2013. (http://www.hks.harvard.edu/fs/akhwaja/papers/PrivateSchool_CER.pdf).

———. 2011. 'Students Today, Teachers Tomorrow? Identifying Constraints on the Provision of Education.' Policy Research Working Paper No. 5674. Washington, DC: The World Bank, Development Research Group, Human Development and Public Services Team. Retrieved December 17, 2013. (http://elibrary.worldbank.org/doi/pdf/10.1596/1813-9450-5674)

Ansell, Ben W. 2010. *From the Ballot to the Blackboard: The Redistributive Political Economy of Education.* New York: Cambridge University Press.

Ara, Arjumand. 2004. 'Madrasas and Making of Muslim Identity in India.' *Economic and Political Weekly* 39(1): 34-38.

Arendt, Hannah. 1958. *The Human Condition.* Chicago: University of Chicago Press.

Bari, Faisal. 2011a. 'Reform Society First.' *Just Questions* Blog. Retrieved December 10, 2013. (http://just-questions.com/2011/06/14/reform-society-first/).

———. 2011b. 'Public Demand for Education Reform.' Comment, *Daily Times*, July 27. Retrieved December 10, 2013. (http://www.dailytimes.com.pk/default.asp?page=2011\07\27\story_27-72011_pg3_5).

Bueno de Mesquita, Bruce, Alastair Smith, Randolph M. Siverson and James D. Morrow. 2005. *The Logic of Political Survival.* Cambridge, Mass.: The MIT Press.

Cremin, Lawrence Arthur. 1951. *The American Common School: An Historic Conception.* New York: Bureau of Publications, Teachers College, Columbia University.

Drèze, Jean and Amartya Sen. 1999. *India: Economic Development and Social Opportunity.* New York: Oxford University Press.

Government of Pakistan. 1951. 'Proceedings of Educational Conference to discuss Six-Year National Plan of Educational Development for Pakistan.' December 4-5. Karachi: Government of Pakistan.

Government of Pakistan. 1959. 'Report of the Commission on National Education.' Karachi: Ministry of Education.

Labaree, David F. 1997. 'Public Goods, Private Goods: The American Struggle over Educational Goals.' *American Educational Research Journal* 34(1): 39-81.

Malik, Anas. 2010. *Political Survival in Pakistan: Beyond Ideology.* Abingdon: Routledge.

Marquand, David. 2004. *Decline of the Public.* Cambridge: Polity Press.

Muzaffar, Irfan. 2011. 'Education Reform in Pakistan: Through Popular Demand or Political Activism?' *Social Science and Policy Bulletin* 3(2): 10-14.

Perry, Theresa, Robert P. Moses, Joan T. Wynne, Ernesto Cortes Jr. and Lisa Delpit, eds. 2010. *Quality Education as a Constitutional Right: Creating a Grassroots Movement to Transform Public Schools.* Boston, MA: Beacon Press.

Ramirez, Francisco O. and John Boli. 1987. 'The Political Construction of Mass Schooling: European Origins and Worldwide Institutionalization.' *Sociology of Education* 60(1): 2-17.

Sen, Amartya. 1999. *Development as Freedom.* New York: Oxford University Press.

World Bank. 2012. 'Public Spending on Education. Total % of GDP.' Retrieved June 6, 2012. (http://data.worldbank.org/indicator/SE.XPD.TOTL.GD.ZS).

Notes

1. Note that a distinction is being made between a consumer and citizen.
2. For more details on the Philippines and India, see Ansell (2010).
3. There are many within the government who seriously relate the contribution of education, particularly technical and professional education, with labor productivity and general competitiveness.
4. There is a physiological analogy that helps in elaborating this argument. Some children are born with a condition called Amblyopia or lazy eye. That is to say, one of their eyes does not work as well as the other at birth. However, these children have no way of recognizing that they suffer from a condition, as they have never experienced better vision. It is only when their eyesight deteriorates further that they realize that they have a problem with their vision.

Appendix 2

Education Governance and Political Advocacy: A Case of Punjab

Salman Humayun, PhD, is an accomplished public policy expert and executive director of the Institute of Social and Policy Sciences (I-SAPS) in Islamabad. He has managed, designed, and delivered technical assistance and reform programs especially focusing on governance in the education sector in Pakistan. He started his career as a faculty member at Quaid-e-Azam University, Islamabad. He later joined the Research Triangle Institute in North Carolina and worked as deputy chief of party of Education Sector Reforms Assistance Program for Pakistan. He is also an alumnus of regional and international policy think tanks, and co-editor of the Journal of Social and Policy Sciences.

Ehtisham Adil, M.Phil., is a public policy practitioner and research fellow at the Institute of Social and Policy Sciences (I-SAPS) in Islamabad. He has extensive experience of working with technical assistance and reform programs in the education sector. He also has considerable experience with developing and executing development projects for educational, social, and economic development of communities. In addition to working in Pakistan, he has also worked extensively in the education and social development sectors in Bangladesh. Before joining I-SAPS, he was working with BRAC International, overseeing the education portfolio in Punjab, Sindh and Balochistan.

* * * *

Preamble

The puzzle of improving the education sector in Pakistan is complex at best, and perplexing at the least. Significant increases in financial resources available for education and ambitious reforms have resulted in only marginal improvements in the situation. Clearly, more money and frequent reforms cannot transform the education sector on their own. Political and policy advocacy by primary beneficiaries—parents and communities—must assume a major role in designing and delivering effective reforms agenda. Articulating, aggregating, and leveraging the voice of practitioners and parents can ensure that the reform processes and the institutional apparatus remain responsive to the manifold challenges of education.

Introduction

Pakistan is faced with numerous challenges in delivering universal access to quality education for all children between 5–16 years of age. In a bid to tackle these challenges, the response from the state during the last decade has been multifaceted and can broadly be divided into three streams of initiatives where various components often seek to reinforce each other.

The first stream of initiatives include the constitutional amendment which facilitates provision of education in an effective manner. The amendment made the right to free and compulsory education justiciable, as an issue which can be settled by law or by legal action. It also reconfigured the legislative and executive roles of the federation with regard to the provinces and devolved various functions relating to education to them, the provinces. As a result, subjects which had been on the concurrent list with the federation taking precedence over provinces in these matters such as policy, planning, curriculum, and standards came to fall into the exclusive domain of the provinces.

The second stream includes the substantial increase in the fiscal space available to the provinces due to the revised National Finance Commission (NFC) awards that resulted in increased allocation of financial resources to education. An analysis of budget allocations show that the resources going into education sector in Pakistan increased by 147 percent between fiscal years 2010–11 and 2016–17.[1]

Thirdly, the provinces have also initiated a renewed reforms agenda for effective education policy, planning and service delivery during the last decade. These include, inter alia, a steady shift towards using data and evidence as the basis for policy and planning; Public Private Partnerships to expand the access to quality education; empowering the district tier of education administration for improved service delivery;

school-based financing to improve learning environment and quality etc.

Notwithstanding multifaceted and multilayered engagement of the state with the challenge posed by the education sector, key education indicators have shown no improvement, or at best limited improvement, over the past decade. For instance, literacy rate at the national level shows an increase of merely 2 percentage points between 2010–11 and 2014–15.[2] Around 23 million children of school going age are still out of school, as compared to 26 million children out of school in 2012–13. In percentage terms, around 44 percent of children of school-going age are still out of school in the country.[3]

In addition to access, quality also remains a major challenge as the overall performance of students between 5–16 years of age seems to have stagnated, or even declined steadily over the last few years. For instance, in Punjab, only 42 percent of children in this age group were able to read a story in Urdu in 2012. This dropped by 5 percentage points over the next five years to 37 percent in 2016. The drop in students' performance is rather significant for English where compared to 40 percent children in 2012, only 33 percent children were able to read sentences in English in 2016.[4] The decline in quality presents an alarming situation as besides the substantial number of children out of school, those who are enrolled learn little while they are at school.

In view of the present performance of the education sector, it is confounding to witness that even significant shifts in the design and execution of education reforms have yielded limited results so far. It is difficult to point out one or even a range of factors responsible for the state of affairs, as it is rather a complex interplay of many factors that has arrested the improvement in the education sector to this point. This includes the disconnect between evidence and policy, the political economy of reforms, limited usage of technological innovations, and effective political advocacy.

To us, effective implementation of education reforms towards envisaged results has been compromised by weak governance and management on one hand, and the lack of capacity of parents and citizens to engage with the system for effective service delivery, on the other hand.

The effectiveness of the reform processes is a function of the governance and management infrastructure that serves as a vehicle for the implementation of reforms. In other words, reforms are invariably as effective as the governance processes in place for their operationalization. However, a review of the existing governance and management infrastructure for education service delivery at the district tier reveals a number of challenges ranging from the insecurity of lack of tenure to the capacity gaps among incumbents at various positions. In this scenario, even the well-grounded reforms designed to address specific needs highlighted by data and evidence tend to fall short of attaining the desired outcomes.

In addition to the effective governance and management, evidence-based political advocacy by parents and citizens helps ensure that the reform processes have wide ownership of the government departments concerned, public representatives, and local and international development partners. It also helps to continuously refine the reform processes so that these remain responsive to the emerging challenges and opportunities. However, a cursory look at various advocacy initiatives by parents, communities and civil society at large reveals limited success in engaging with the system for effective design and implementation of reforms agenda as well as improving service delivery.

In this backdrop, the chapter aims to discuss various reform processes in Punjab from a standpoint of effective governance and management. The chapter also aims to understand the role of parental and citizen's engagement and voice towards effective oversight and engagement with the reforms processes and the system at large.

The chapter comprises three sections. The first section presents the legal and policy framework in Pakistan, with a focus on Punjab, that constitutes the context in which various reforms processes operate. The second section discusses the governance and management infrastructure of education in Punjab with a focus on key challenges that diminish or have the potential to undermine the effectiveness of the agenda of reforms in the province. The third and final section deals with the way parents, communities and civil society at large engage with the system for design and implementation of the reforms processes. It briefly looks at various models of political advocacy that have so far been leveraged to restore parental and community voice. It also highlights key ingredients which must inform the approach to political debate and policy to make reform processes more accountable, and responsive to system-wide as well as local-level challenges.

1.1 Legal and Policy Framework

In the broader landscape of governance in Pakistan, the 18th Constitutional Amendment is a critical branch-point in the relations between the federation and the provinces. It profoundly altered the sphere of legislative as well executive jurisdiction of the federation with respect to the federating units. The concurrent list which included the subjects of joint responsibility of federation and provinces, with the federation having precedence in case of disagreement, was abolished as a result of the amendment. Hence, it transferred more than 47 subjects exclusively to the legislative and executive domain of the provinces. The amendment also caused reconfiguration of the Federal Legislative List (FLL) Parts I and II to make the second part more reflective of subjects of common interests among the provinces and federation.

The amendment also resulted in far-reaching changes for the governance and management of education across the country. From being a subject predominantly governed by the federation, education came to fall within the sole legislative and executive domain of the provinces, with the federation still retaining a few functions. These include matters relating to education of foreign students in Pakistan and Pakistani students in universities abroad,[5] standards of education in institutions of Higher Education, scientific and technical institutions[6] and implementing the treaties and agreements relating to education.[7]

Other than these, the roles relating to policy, planning, curriculum and syllabus, standards of education, centers of excellence, area study centers, Pakistan study centers and higher education have been devolved to the provinces. Along with the devolution of the roles, the associated administrative apparatus has also been devolved to the provinces. For instance, the Bureaus of Curriculum which were the field formations of the Curriculum Wing of Ministry of Education, were devolved to the provinces for performance of all functions relating to development of curriculum. In addition to the institutional and functional devolution, the Amendment also necessitated administrative reconfiguration in the provinces to perform the newly devolved functions.

The 18th Constitutional Amendment not only significantly altered the relation between the federation and provinces, it also made the federation and provinces responsible to provide free and compulsory education to all the children aged 5-16 years. Article 25-A, inserted in the constitution through the amendment, calls upon the provinces and the federation to legislate on the form and manner of provision of education to all children in this age group, without discrimination. Even before the insertion of Article 25-A, the constitution recognized the right to education as a fundamental right of the citizens; however, the recognition of this right did not necessarily make it justiciable. The element of justiciability is now a part and parcel of the right—empowering the aggrieved to seek legal remedies against infringement of their right to free and compulsory education by holding accountable the federal or provincial governments. Indeed, since the insertion of Article 25-A, civil society has filed many public interest litigations in the high courts across provinces and the federal capital.

Now that the policy, planning, curriculum, standards and service delivery have devolved entirely to the provinces, there is active debate on the role of federation in education, post-18th Amendment. Proponents argue that the federation must lead a national response to the challenge of providing free and compulsory education to every child across the country, that the right to compulsory education enjoys constitutional guarantee, and it is the state that is responsible to ensure its provision to all children regardless of the province or territory of their residence.

Moreover, it is argued that the role of the federation is also required because the state is the signatory to international treaties and agreements relating to education including MDGs, SDGs and various covenants. The federation must exercise considerable influence and oversight in keeping the progress of provinces on-track relating to goals, targets and commitments subscribed to by the state.

The support for greater role of the federation also arises from the perspective of national integration. With provinces now responsible to design and implement their own curriculum, there are concerns among various quarters that provincial curricula might over-emphasize local cultures and languages, even to the detriment of national integration, cohesion and harmony.

In addition to curriculum, the devolution of the standards of education has also caused equity concerns relating to the all-important quality of education across provinces. In the absence of the role of federation in maintaining minimum standards, the students could be receiving varying quality of education depending upon the province or territory of residence.

It does not, therefore, come as a surprise that the 18th Constitutional Amendment received two notes of reiteration relating to the role of the federal government in the governance of education in the post-amendment scenario. The two notes of dissent highlight the need of a federation's role in matters relating to curriculum, standards of education, and policy and planning by placing these functions in Federal Legislative List (FLL) Part II, thus effectively bringing these in the domain of the Council of Common Interest.[8]

Since the Amendment, the debate for a greater role of the federation vis-a-vis governance of education in the provinces seems to be gathering momentum, particularly as far as curriculum, syllabus, and standards of education are concerned. Proponents argue that the fundamental premise underlying the devolution, i.e. oppressive federation and weak provinces, does not adequately address the need of the federation's role in carrying forward the agenda of quality education. Perhaps, in a bid for wholesale devolution, many functions which could best have been performed together by the federation and provinces were also devolved to the exclusive provincial domain without sufficient consideration for efficiency and national interest.

In the absence of these functions in the FLL Part II, what are the other forums which the federation may leverage to further the goals of national harmony and integrity, and the minimum standards of education, without trampling over the provincial autonomy, post-18th Amendment? The National Curriculum Council (NCC) is an initiative by the Inter-Provincial Education Ministerial (IPEM) to draft a National Curriculum Framework outlining the curriculum aspects which would be taught across the country in all provinces and territories. In addition to drafting the National Curriculum Framework, the NCC has also drafted and approved the Minimum Education Standards to be adhered to by all provinces. For effective implementation, however, it is important to note that the design of the curriculum framework and minimum standards, significant accomplishments as these are, will still need to negotiate with provincial administrative and political differences. It will be critical to see how the NCC and IPEM are positioned to monitor and manage the implementation in the face of challenges that emerge during the process.

Even after devolution, the National Education Policy 2009 formed the policy framework for the federation as well as the provinces in the absence of province-specific education policies. Since the Education Policy of 2009, significant changes in the local as well as international education milieu have taken place, including the 18th Constitutional

Amendment, Article 25-A, Sustainable Development Goals, and a drive across provinces (although to varying degrees) to strengthen the service-delivery tier of education management and governance. These developments necessitate that Education Policy 2009 be reviewed and updated to bring up-to-speed the national response to the education question in Pakistan. In view of these developments, the IPEM unanimously decided in favor of revising the National Education Policy in its meeting held in 2015. The draft Education Policy 2017 is ready, and the Ministry of Federal Education and Professional Training is holding consultations with various stakeholders in order to solicit their feedback on the draft.

It is important to note that the National Policy 2017 comes at a time when there is debate on whether the provinces should devise education policies at all or let the developments in the education sector be guided by overarching policy frameworks. The education policies, although very comprehensive in their scope, have several components which remain beyond implementation through the life-term of the policy, and these are then carried forward to the next policy. On the contrary, the policy frameworks may guide the development of strategic documents such as sector plans and similar reforms agenda with time-bound targets, budgets and cost analysis for various initiatives within the overarching policy framework.

1.1.1 Legislative Developments in Punjab: Article-25A, where it empowers the citizens to hold the state accountable, has also resulted in wavering of various provincial governments in enacting legislation on free and compulsory education. In Punjab, the legislation was enacted in 2014, four years after the Amendment. Despite the passage of the 'Free and Compulsory Education Act' (FCEA) legislation, the province has exhibited reluctance in notifying the rules of business which would essentially operationalize the FCEA.

In this regard, it is important to note that after the insertion of 25-A in the constitution, there has been only limited political advocacy in the province and that too largely to the extent of legislation on free and compulsory education. However, the advocacy and sustained engagement of parents, communities, and civil society with the system to have the rules of business notified by the government has been conspicuously missing. As mentioned earlier, curriculum, standards, and policy and planning were devolved to the exclusive legislative and executive domain of the provinces. This necessitated the provinces to legislate and evolve administrative mechanisms to perform the devolved functions. Notable examples in this regard include, among other things, the Punjab Curriculum and Textbook Board Act to perform functions related to design and implementation of curriculum as well as the production of textbooks; Punjab Examination Commission Act, for conducting examinations for elementary education; revamping of Directorate of Staff Development to establish the Quaid-e-Azam Academy of Education Development (QAED) to cater to the training and capacity needs of teachers and head-teachers. In addition to these legislative and administrative developments, Punjab is also mulling over enacting legislation to deal with a number of other issues and challenges. For instance, the government is set to table a bill before the assembly, Truancy Bill 2018, that will penalize parents for voluntarily keeping their children away from schools. Similarly, in a bid to improve quality of education, the government has developed a bill that will provide legislative cover for certification of teachers and teacher trainers in Punjab.

At the same time, it is important to note that while there have been substantial legislative and administrative developments in Punjab, there is still a lot more that needs to be done. For instance, the private education sector, which constitutes around 38 percent enrollment[9] in Punjab, continues to operate largely without the administrative and legislative oversight of the government or any agency of authority. Existing legislation on private education intuitions[10] deals largely with the registration of private schools with the government and the fee increases. There is little focus on the curriculum, quality of teaching, minimum standards of education, basic facilities in the schools and the performance of students enrolled in these schools.

1.1.2 Enhanced Finances for Education: In addition to empowering the provinces with legislative autonomy, the 18th Amendment facilitated more finance resources to be made available to the provinces from the Federal Divisible Pool. The wholesale devolution of a wide range of functions and corresponding administrative apparatus at the provincial level necessitated that the provinces are also given increased resources to shoulder the challenge posed by the amendment. In this regard, the 7th NFC Award substantially changed the share of provinces vis-à-vis the federation—up from 47.5 percent under the previous arrangement, the provinces have now come to receive 57.5 percent of the Federal Divisible pool in the post-amendment scenario. For Punjab, the budgetary allocation of resources has increased on average by 13 percent each year between 2010–11 and 2015–16.[11] Figure 1 provides the yearly increment in Punjab's education budget since 2010–11.

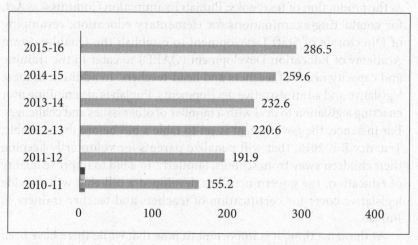

Figure 1: Trend in Allocations of Provincial Budget for Education
(in billions, Pak Rupees) Source: I-SAPS Calculations

While there has been a significant increase in the allocation of resources for education, the absorptive capacity of the province has remained rather poor. This also questions the prevalent notion that a major challenge of the education sector in Pakistan is under-financed and that increasing financial allocations will automatically yield sector-wide improvements in education.

It is important to note that much of the advocacy efforts surrounding financing of education in the province, as well as across the country, have revolved around the premise of increasing the education budget. There are notable exceptions to this where technical evidence has been generated to show that the issue of education financing is complex and requires more than just continuing to increase resource allocation. However, the discussion on enhancing absorptive capacity of the system has received limited advocacy support in the post-amendment scenario.[12] Figure 2 illustrates the gap between the allocation of resources and the expenditure incurred in Punjab between 2010–11 and 2015–16.

Moreover, the allocation of finances must also be responsive to the needs highlighted by the data. In this regard, analyzing financing decisions in the backdrop of student achievement in Punjab offers valuable insight. Comparing students learning achievement for PEC (Punjab Examination Commission) exams at the district level with the per-student expenditure reveals a significant disconnect between the resource distribution and student learning. Districts within the red circle (Figure 3) perform poorly in PEC results, yet these districts receive lower resources in terms of per student expenditure.

Student learning outcomes are merely one aspect of needs to which financing decisions must respond while allocating resources. There are other factors as well, including the incidence of poverty, incidence of out- of- school children, gender parity, etc. which must also inform the allocation of resources in order to improve allocative efficiency of resources. Although there has been substantial increase in the financial resources for education, their effective utilization continues to be a challenge in the province. The challenge is aggravated in the absence of parental voice and engagement with the system. The inability of the parents is largely due to the technical nature of education financing as a subject, and the remoteness of parents from the mechanisms that govern resource planning, allocation and utilization in most cases.

Furthermore, the existing advocacy efforts are largely in disconnect with the nuanced challenges of education financing in the province, as well as across the country. These efforts and campaigns have reduced the education finance challenge which are largely due to the paucity of funds available for the education sector. Consequently, there is increased demand to raise the funding for education to 4 percent, or even 6 percent of the GDP. As discussed, this entry point into the debate of education financing offers limited potential to address the multi-faceted challenge of education financing in the province, as well as in the country. The advocacy efforts must adopt a nuanced approach to improve the absorptive capacity of the system, allocative efficiency of existing resources, and campaigning for additional resources for the education system.

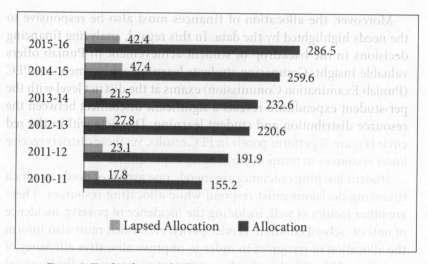

Figure 2: Total and Lapsed Allocations (Punjab, in billions Pak Rupees)
2010–11 to 2015–16. (Source: I-SAPS Calculations)

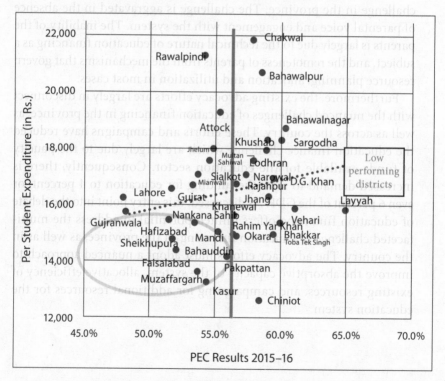

Figure 3: Per Student Expenditure and Students Learning Achievements 2015-16.
(Source: I-SAPS Calculations)

1.1.3 Renewed Reforms Design: Effective delivery and implementation of reforms depend on the robustness of governance and management mechanisms in place. Reforms agenda of the government may be well-conceived and propose technically sound solutions to the challenges at hand; however, in terms of their actual ability to address the challenges, these proposed solutions may only go as far as the limits imposed by governance and management infrastructure through which they are delivered.

Punjab has witnessed a wave of renewed reforms agenda during the last decade. The province has experimented with a series of reforms under the rubric of the Reforms Roadmap 2010–18, Education Sector Plans 2013–17, Mid-Term Education Sector Plan 2016–18, and Punjab Growth Strategy 2015. In a bid to improve service delivery and access to education, Punjab has also experimented with reforms including empowering the district tier of education administration, conditional cash transfers, school-based financing, and other initiatives. However, these reforms have not been able to deliver optimum results due to insufficient support from effective governance teams and management infrastructure. In this regard, the case of Literacy and Numeracy Drive (LND) in Punjab provides important insights.

The (Punjab) Chief Minister's Reform Road map which began in 2010, focused on improving access and quality of education at the primary level and remained the major emphasis of the School Education Department (SED) until recently. To measure the improvement in student performance, the SED started six-monthly assessments which were sample based and provided information on student achievement in 3rd grade across SED as well as PEF schools. And, in order to improve the six-monthly assessment results, the SED started conducting Literacy and Numeracy Drive (LND) across all SED schools.[13] Moreover, it was made a target of the reforms roadmap for each school, and by extension for each district, to score at least 75 percent in the literacy and numeracy test held by the MEAs every month.

Like other indicators of the reforms roadmap, the LND results were also discussed during the chief minister's quarterly stock-take sessions. The fear of repercussions and censure for missing the quarterly target for LND compelled the officials, particularly at district level, to check off essential boxes without much emphasis on the deeper issues around quality. Consequently, across a large number of SED schools, the head-teachers and district education officials placed disproportionate emphasis on LND preparation for 3rd grade relative to the curriculum. Moreover, it is important to note that LND tests were based on the literacy and numeracy related learning outcomes of 1st and 2nd grades.[14] Consequently, a well-intentioned reform initiative which aimed to improve quality of education in 3rd grade ended up in reducing teaching and learning in 3rd grade to test-centered preparation of students, and that too for a test based on 1st and 2nd grade outcomes. All this, largely because the mechanisms instituted to deliver the reforms introduced a perverse, intimidating structure of incentives for the district officials.

Furthermore, a significant body of evidence has been produced since the inception of the Literacy and Numeracy Drive on the quality of education in public schools across all levels. However, policy advocacy on the ability of assessments or examinations to inform policy and planning processes on one hand, and to feed into teacher training, textbooks and materials development on the other has largely eluded the advocacy efforts from civil society.

Despite greater provincial autonomy over policy and planning, and significant increase in resources available for education, and a renewed reforms agenda in the province since the 18th Amendment, the education sector has shown only marginal improvement in terms of access and quality of education in the province.

This has largely been due to absence of voice from parents and the inability of civil society to help steer the reforms agenda through advocacy efforts. The advocacy efforts have not been entirely absent during this time but they have lacked nuanced, calibrated and strategic engagement with the policy, planning and delivery of reforms and various initiatives. The important areas missing from the focus of these efforts are rules of business to operationalize the Free and Compulsory Education Act; learning achievements of children on standardized national and provincial assessments; intra-region disparities in student learning outcomes; and absorptive capacity of the system. Furthermore, the inability of reforms to achieve envisaged results is also the result of ineffective governance and management mechanisms which are essential to deliver these reforms. The next section discusses the key aspects of governance and management of education at the service delivery tier in the province.

2. Governance and Management of Education—A Case of Punjab

As mentioned in the preceding section, Punjab has implemented a set of renewed reform initiatives to improve service delivery of education in the province. However, the ineffective governance and management processes at various tiers, particularly at the service delivery tier, places significant constraints on the ability of reforms to produce the desired outcomes. Consequently, we witness that a number of sound policy recipes and reforms including conditional cash transfers, formative assessments, and review and accountability forums have yielded limited results instead of their envisaged potential.

In this regard, it is important to outline key aspects of governance and management processes that mediate the ability of reforms in improving the service delivery. This section takes up this probe and explores key aspects of the processes in place that have the potential to comprise the renewed reforms agenda of the government. As political advocacy by civil society (or the lack of it) also have significant bearing on the ability of governance and management to deliver the reforms effectively, the section will also comment, where possible, on these to highlight space for advocacy to improve service delivery.

2.2.1 District Education Authorities: Establishing District Education Authorities (DEAs) across Punjab under the Punjab Local Government Act (PLGA) 2013 marked a welcome and significant milestone towards empowering the district tier of education administration for improved service delivery. The DEAs were established in response to the challenge of service delivery which stemmed from inadequate financial and administrative autonomy and capacity deficits of the staff running the education offices at district and sub-district tiers. However, several years after their establishment, the DEAs exist largely in the legal sense alone with business going on as usual. In most respects, the DEAs continue to have no more financial and administrative autonomy than the previous set-up, and the routine operations of the DEAs mirror that of the district education administration prior to the institution of the DEAs.

An important case in this regard is the appointment of a chief executive officer who is to serve as the principal accounting officer of the DEA and is to be recruited from the market on a competitive salary package. The incumbents were expected to infuse corporate spirit in the working of the DEAs and bring valuable experience of working with the education sector. However, the gains which were envisioned with the recruitment of such officials could not materialize as no such recruitment has been made by the education department to date. In fact, the senior district officials have been given an additional charge of the post with an additional monthly charge allowance. Similarly, the post of the chairman of DEA is also vacant across districts, with the respective deputy commissioners holding additional charge of the post.

Furthermore, the DEA structure envisages a number of branches[15] under the DEA-setup to facilitate various administrative operations and activities at the district tier of education. These include streamlining budget formulation and execution, administration of education affairs at Tehsil (district) and Markaz (local council) levels, and effectively dealing with court cases. However, these branches are barely functional owing to staffing gaps. A substantial number of posts sanctioned for the new DEA-setup are still vacant, while those which have been filled are largely a result of internal transfers and postings.[16]

The DEAs are also constrained by the capacity gaps of the staff at various levels. The staff lack requisite skill set to effectively perform the roles and responsibilities of their positions. Given the capacity gaps, it is mostly a few select officials who often have to shoulder the burden beyond the call of duty. The capacity gaps are a significant disabling factor for the DEA in performing the functions as envisaged by legislation.

In short, the establishment of the DEAs, which was considered an overarching structural reform in empowering the district tier to improve service delivery itself continues to be an unfinished agenda. Although the DEA setup has been rolled out, the aggregate set of interventions which would culminate into fully functional and empowered DEAs continue to be missing even five years after the PLGA 2013. In this backdrop, the service delivery tier effectively lacks the administrative and financial autonomy as well as the requisite human resource required to oversee successful implementation of any reform agenda at the district and sub-district levels.

2.2.2 Monitoring and Evaluation: Monitoring is carried out in two streams across public schools in the province. The first stream involves daily visits of schools by the Monitoring and Evaluation Assistants (MEAs). The data collected by the MEAs is used for follow-up and accountability of district education officials for monitoring the progress on various reform initiatives under the 'reform roadmap'. In order to ensure that the data captured by the MEAs is accurate and free from any bias, it is made accessible to all stakeholders including schoolteachers, education managers and the communities. Any of these stakeholders can challenge the data if they find discrepancy between the report and the actual situation in schools.

As a policy recipe, it is a significant step to involve all stakeholders in the data collection process to enhance the accountability of monitoring officers as well as to ensure greater validity of the data collected. However, there are a few constraints which limit the efficacy of this mechanism in flagging discrepancies in the data collected by MEAs. First, not all head-teachers and schoolteachers at primary and elementary levels are aware of this policy initiative to check, validate and contest the data. Although the Assistant Education Officers (AEOs) are aware of the policy initiative, it has not fully permeated to the school level across all Marakiz[17] (centers) in Punjab. This has the potential to render the initiative ineffective as the data discrepancies will come to fore, if at all, in only a limited number of schools. Secondly, there have been a number of instances where the MEAs have taken recourse to retaliatory measures against the school administration for flagging discrepancies. These measures include influencing school performance in Literacy and Numeracy Drive tests, being overly particular about attendance of teachers even when they are away from school on official business, and other such unfortunate incidences. In other words, although the system to involve school administration in the data collection and validation exercise is established, the ability of various stakeholders to engage with the system is limited on the one hand; and, on the other, there is insufficient insulation of the school administration from retaliation by the data collection agents, i.e. the MEAs.

The second stream of monitoring involves visits by the education managers of the district education authorities including AEOs, Deputy DEOs and DEOs.[18] Presently in the district education administration, only the AEOs are required to complete a certain number of school visits each month.[19] Officials at the higher levels, i.e. Deputy DEOs and DEOs are exempt from this requirement of mandatory school visits. In the absence of mandatory visits, the managers of education authorities are unlikely to adequately monitor the status of implementation of various reforms or to identify and address various issues and challenges at the service delivery level.

Furthermore, the school visits of district education officials remain unstructured insofar as the activities during the visit. Only a handful of activities are carried out during the school visit by the officials, mostly concentrated around record checking, communication of instructions from higher officials, resolving staff related matters, and a round of the school. This runs contrary to the lofty agenda that officials can accomplish through their school visits including, among other things, classroom observations for various grades; content specific support to teachers; community mobilization, and; checking the status of the Non-Salary Budget (NSB),[20] School-Based Action Plan, and learning materials with the students.

In the absence of structured school visits of education officials, it becomes a challenge to ensure that school visits by the education administration are geared towards accomplishing targeted and measurable progress on various aspects of teaching and learning at school level. Consequently, the education officials have greater room for exercising individual discretion on what they observe, or what they accomplish, and report related to the school visits. At the system level, this gap in the management of education reforms is likely to erode the ability of reform processes to improve service delivery.

2.2.3 Tenures: Secure and predictable tenure of officials are a pre-requisite for continuation of reform processes at the service delivery tier. It helps to ensure the ownership and accountability of incumbents engaged with the delivery of reform. Frequent transfers of officials result in administrative and operational inefficiencies which affect the delivery of reforms at the service delivery tier. It also slows down the pace of reforms as new officials require time to get up to speed with on-going initiatives, challenges and constraints.

In the context of Punjab, the challenge related to security and predictability of tenure is more pronounced at the top-tier of district education administration. For instance, between 2012 and 2015, district Mianwali and Vehari saw more than 10 different EDOs within a period of three years. Similarly, there were 20 districts in the province where 6 to 10 officials were transferred during the same period.

Service rules prescribe a minimum tenure of three years at a given post before the staff can be transferred. However, the rule has a caveat, that 'in public interest,' staff can be transferred before completing their mandatory term[21]. This renders the service rule ineffective as evidenced by frequent transfers and postings at the top-tier of district education authorities.

An effective way to curtail the excessive use of 'in public interest,' is by operationalizing the term so that the incumbent official and other stakeholders can objectively ascertain observance of the public interest. As important as it is to define 'public interest,' it is also crucial to have transparency and a semblance of consensus whether the transfers in question are actually meeting any public interest. In this regard, a committee may be established at the provincial level, given that the transfers and postings beyond the Basic Pay Scale (BPS-9)[22] now fall in the domain of Directorates of Secondary and Elementary Education. This committee may include representatives from civil society as well as representatives from the local government of the district for broad-based consensus on the public interests being served by the transfers before completion of the mandatory term.

3.3 POLITICAL ENGAGEMENT AND ADVOCACY: INFORMING POLICIES, REFORMING PRACTICES

A major element that characterizes the context in which education reforms have largely operated in Pakistan can be expressed in Hirschman's terms, as 'exit and absence of voice' by opinion leaders in the policy sphere as well as at the service delivery level. These opinion leaders primarily include the parents and communities at large on the one hand, and public representatives and politically influential members of the community, collectively referred to as political capital, on the other.

Parents from the middle class have opted out of the public education system, leaving the children of disenfranchised people in the government schools who have little voice or means to articulate their demand for reforms. Similarly, given the lack of any effective entry point i.e. evidence on performance of the system at the service delivery level, the communities at large have also not been able to engage with the system even from the standpoint of ensuring effective delivery of basic services by the education department.

In the absence of voice from the parents and communities, the political capital at the local as well as the provincial level have come to acquire a rather narrowly defined set of interests which often does not account for improving the effectiveness of reforms or the service delivery at the local level. The political capital largely remains distant from any meaningful discourse on reforms related to access or quality; however, it responds more often to the structural and operational reforms that involve award of contracts, visibility and political mileage.

The situation calls for a nuanced approach to political advocacy to engage with the system and with various stakeholders within the system, to ensure that the reforms agenda delivers the envisioned outcomes and improvements in service delivery. Such an approach needs to be cognizant of the central role of the voice of parents and of the communities at large—in design, implementation and continuity of reforms. Indeed, there have been many efforts in Punjab, and more generally in Pakistan, where civil society has attempted to bring back the voice of parents and communities, by creating incentive structures to make education politically relevant and a means of value for its potential political capital.[23] The initiatives covered substantial ground and made significant gains, but much more is needed to build upon the gains made by these campaigns. In this regard, there are a few essential ingredients to the design and execution of an effective political advocacy campaign, which may ensure not only the voice of parents and communities in reform processes, but also make education a political priority for the political capital at provincial, district and local levels.

3.3.1 Education Reforms—Interface between the Technical and Political: The advocacy efforts around education reforms can broadly be traced back to two distinct assumptions. The first assumption is that education reform is largely a technical issue and requires the government to figure out what is required in terms of capacities and resources for improving the service delivery. Once the government has it figured out, the next step is to make these resources available, and given time the range of education indicators will start to show improvement. Based on this assumption, it would seem fairly simple to address the challenge of teacher-supply across the province. After all, it merely involves transferring teachers from schools having oversupply to the schools facing a shortage of teachers. However, in reality, anyone who has had the experience of working with education reforms knows quite well how enormously difficult it is to undertake rationalization with teachers. It is largely because the teachers are one of the most organized groups operating in the education ecosystem, enjoying considerable influence with the political capital at district and provincial levels. Such is the case with all other reforms. All reforms are political.

This brings us to the second assumption—that education reform is not only a technical issue, it is deeply political as well, where different stakeholders aim to pursue their own narrowly defined interests. For instance, the allocation of block-grants is a significant policy issue from the standpoint of transparency and efficiency. Block-grants have been quite prevalent in budgetary allocations in Punjab. The approach to tackle this issue involved, on the one hand, generating technical evidence on block- grants, i.e. their size, repercussions for efficiency, and global best practices. On the other, it involved bringing creative pressure on the political dispensation by sharing evidence with the political capital across the entire political spectrum. By building an interface between the technical and political side of reforms over the period of several budgetary cycles, the campaign[24] was effective in substantially reducing the size of block grants in Punjab.

3.3.2 Standards for Evidence: Advocacy without evidence seldom leads to concrete results. When speaking of evidence, a crucial consideration is the level of rigor required to have discourse with various stakeholders, particularly those who have the wherewithal to influence reform processes. It has far reaching implications in terms of both human and capital resources required, and the ability of evidence to feed into the reform processes in a timely manner. In this regard, it is important to note that the standards for evidence required to inform debate on reforms in policy and planning spheres are often significantly different from those required for publication in international peer-reviewed journals. Technical soundness of reforms in dealing with issues at hand, compliance with principals of public finance management, and the ability of reforms to navigate the political milieu are some of the major aspects on which affirmative evidence sets the stage for discussion with the political dispensation, and policy and planning spheres.

Different standards of evidence for policy and political advocacy also provide opportunities for engagement on reform processes. There are a number of easy opportunities (or low-hanging fruit) where evidence can be generated rather swiftly and within limited resources, and an effective political and policy engagement can significantly improve governance and management processes, as well as policy and planning. An opportunity which has not been capitalized upon so far, and one that has tremendous bearing on management of reforms, is the lack of secure and predictable tenures of officials at provincial and district levels. This is one of the areas where sound evidence can be generated and leveraged through political and policy advocacy to improve implementation, continuity and pace of reforms.

3.3.3 Contextualized and Relatable Evidence: Evidence that is contextualized and relatable is key for an effective debate on education reforms at the provincial, district and constituency levels. For a parent or local leader to hold the system accountable for out of school children or missing facilities is of limited utility. However, equipping a parent and other stakeholders with contextualized and relatable evidence sparks meaningful engagement around reforms. There have been a number of campaigns[25] around the time of general elections in recent years where district and even constituency level situation analyses on education performance were shared with the parents and political capital at the constituency, district and provincial levels. These campaigns were aimed essentially at the political capital to use this evidence on education performance as a political resource in their debates on why one should or should not vote for a certain candidate or political party. These campaigns also aimed at restoring voice of disenfranchised parents whose children went to public schools. The campaigns culminated in acquiring public acknowledgement as well as signed declarations from candidates across the political spectrum on their commitments to initiate reforms and to improve service delivery once the candidates were in public offices.

3.3.4 Identifying and Engaging with the Political Capital: Political capital at the constituency level includes all politically active players at the constituency and district level. It comprises not only the public representatives and the candidates for national or provincial assemblies, but also those who play a key role in the election of these candidates. These include the local elders and/or the candidates who might never have won an election by themselves, but play an important role in making, breaking and shifting political alliances at the local level.

While the local political capital may or may not have a direct stake in education, they do have a stake in the politics that surrounds education. For instance, the political capital when engaged through contextualized and relatable evidence, uses the evidence as a political resource to support or undermine a candidate running for the assembly. For the candidate who has represented the constituency in the past, the evidence serves as a score-card of their efforts on education reforms in previous years, while it serves as a baseline for the aspiring public representative.

3.3.5 Leveraging Evidence through Procedural Activism: Generating and disseminating the evidence is not an end in itself. Rather, it is a crucial component of the process where the evidence enables the political capital and various stakeholders to engage with the reform process. Using the evidence base, the political capital and stakeholders can select from a range of entry points to trigger certain procedural responses from the system that governs education at district and provincial levels.

For instance, procedural activism at the provincial level involves equipping public representatives with evidence on the status of education in particular constituencies. The public representatives, in turn, can be expected to present the evidence through various motions to draw attention of the provincial assembly to the state of education in their constituencies. The representatives can also ask a direct question of the Minister of Education regarding the state of education in their constituency which then, makes it binding upon the minister, and by extension the school education department, to furnish a response to the member of assembly. The same can be done at the district level as well by sharing the evidence with the political capital who would then, collectively write issue-based letters to the officials of district education officials and follow-up on their requests through their public representatives. Appreciating and capitalizing on the potential of the public representatives and the political capital in initiating a debate on education reforms and eliciting a response from the system is a hallmark of this approach to advocacy.

* * * *

The role of political and policy advocacy in effective design and implementation of reforms agenda cannot be over-emphasized. It ensures that the reform processes remain responsive to the challenges and opportunities at the service delivery level. While considerable ground has been covered through advocacy campaigns, there is still the need to empower, equip and mobilize the parents and communities-at-large towards restoring their voice in reform processes. Restoring voice by parents and communities will be a strategic win in the long run to ensure that the reforms processes, as well as the governance and management mechanisms which act as the vehicles to deliver these reforms remain responsive to the challenges and needs at the service delivery level.

Notes

1. Institute of Social and Policy Sciences, Education Financing Report 2010–11 to 2016–17.
2. Pakistan Bureau of Statistics, Labor Force Survey 2010–11 to 2014–15.
3. AEPAM. Pakistan Education Statistics 2012–13 and 2016–17.
4. Annual Status of Education Report 2012–2016, Punjab.
5. Entry 17 of Federal Legislative List Part I.
6. Entry 12 of Federal Legislative List Part II.
7. Entry 3 of Federal Legislative List Part I.
8. One note of dissent came from Jamaat-e-Islami and the other came from PML-N. Senator Khursheed Ahmed of the Jamaat-e-Islami argued that a uniform curriculum is crucial to ensure national identity and solidarity, and the Council of Common Interest should be renamed the Council of Common Interests. Ahsan Iqbal from PML-N argued that Entry 38 (Curriculum, syllabus, planning, policy, centers of excellence, standards of education) may be moved to Federal Legislative List Part II.
9. Private School Census 2016, Program Monitoring and Implementation Unit, Punjab Education Sector Reform Program, School Education Department.
10. Punjab Private Educational Institutions (Promotion & Regulations) Act 2017, Amended.
11. I-SAPS Budget Calculations 2010-11 to 2015-16.
12. See 'Education Financing 2010–11 to 2017–18' by Institute of Social and Policy Sciences (I-SAPS), and 'Financing Education in Pakistan: Opportunities for Action' by Rabea Malik and Pauline Rose.
13. PEF schools performed much better than the SED schools in the six-monthly assessment, hence LND targeted only the SED schools for improvement in the six-monthly assessment.
14. 'Transforming Primary Education in Punjab: The Journey of Punjab's Education Roadmap' by Chief Ministers' Special Monitoring Unit.
15. These include the following branches: General branch; Budget and Accounts; Planning and Development; Administration; and Litigation branches.
16. Education Sector Analysis for Education Sector Plan 2019–23 by the Institute of Social and Policy Sciences.
17. Marakiz (plural for Markaz; literally 'center' or nucleus) are the cluster that comprises primary and elementary schools in Punjab.
18. Assistant Education Officer (AEO) is responsible for Primary and Elementary Schools at Markaz level and reports to the Deputy DEO who is responsible for Primary and Elementary Schools at the Tehsil level. Deputy DEO report to the DEO Elementary who supervises all the Deputy DEOs in a given district. For the Secondary and Higher Secondary Schools, the head-teachers and principals of these schools report directly to the DEO (Secondary) through the Deputy DEO (Secondary).
19. An AEO is presently assigned 10 to 12 schools at the Markaz level and is required to visit each school at least twice in a month.
20. The Non-Salary Budget is a formula-based allocation of funds to facilitate smooth operations at school level in Punjab. In addition to fixed amount for specific levels of school (primary, elementary, high and higher secondary), the formula accounts for enrollment, retention and furniture needs of schools for funds allocation under the NSB.
21. Civil Service Rules, Government of Punjab.

22. Basic Pay Scale is a system that defines salary structure of government officials based on factors such as position, rank, years in service, and education level of the incumbent. The Basic Pay Scale ranges from BPS-1 to BPS-22.
23. These advocacy efforts include media campaigns by Alif Ailan, District Rankings and Education Financing of Education reports and policy advocacy by Institute of Social and Policy Sciences, ASER Surveys and subsequent campaigning by Idara-e-Taaleem-o-Agahi, and Public Interest Litigations by Punjab Coalition of Education.
24. The campaign on effective education financing was run by Institute of Social and Policy Sciences. It was titled Effective Education Budgeting Initiative.
25. I-SAPS and Alif-Ailan ran notable campaigns.

Appendix 3

The Social, Political and Economic Imperatives of Education: A Systems Perspective

Anjum Altaf, PhD, is a social scientist. He was a dean at LUMS and provost at Habib University. He is the Weblog moderator of THE SOUTH ASIAN IDEA—A LEARNING RESOURCE FOR COLLEGE STUDENTS IN SOUTH ASIA* where participants share opinions so that they may express and defend them elsewhere with expertise and conviction. The blog is an academy of learning and investigational thinking to encourage the development of ideas through discussion, a job that ought to be done by schools and colleges in Pakistan. The blog provides a substitute by offering a forum for learning where each issue is looked at from many angles. He describes the blog as a resource for learning, not a source of expert opinion. 'The posts on the blog are starting points for classroom discussions and the position at the end could be completely at odds with the starting point. Thus, the blog simulates a learning process and does not offer a final product.' Readers are invited to explore the blog and help improve understanding of important contemporary issues through critical thinking and expression of informed views.
*https://thesouthasianidea.com/

* * * *

I. Ten Big Questions[1]

1. Why is Pakistan still half-illiterate?

The lack of political will or of money are not convincing answers. There is not enough political pressure to make education a high priority issue for governments. Ruling elites tolerate only as much mass education as is necessary because it is subversive of the status quo especially in societies based on oppression.

2. Can NGOs fill the gap?

The arithmetic does not support this contention. The issue of scale is important. The problem is too large and growing at a rate faster than the capacity (physical and financial) of the NGOs to eliminate it. The only effective solution is reform of the public education system.

3. Is illiteracy the main problem in Pakistan?

All management and decision-making has been in the hands of the educated and it has been abysmal. Blaming the illiterates reflects either the ignorance or the callousness of the literate.

4. Why are the educated increasingly bigoted and intolerant?

The content of education and the style of pedagogy are both problematic and need attention. A literate individual taught to accept falsehoods and prejudice unquestioningly would be more dangerous than an illiterate person. There is a difference between education and indoctrination.

5. What is the problem with the content?

In the worst case, the content has been subverted to promote ideological objectives. In the best case, it is oriented to the job market and is overly information and skill oriented. The humanities that inculcate critical thinking are considered a waste of time and poorly taught. The product is either an unthinking ideologue or technician. The technician could be very competent but not likely to be innovative or flexible.

6. What is the problem with pedagogy?

The pedagogical style rewards memorization and suppresses critical thinking. This can be by intent, by self-censorship motivated by fear of persecution, or by capacity constraints imposed by very large class sizes.

7. What is wrong with philanthropy in Pakistan?

NGOs set internal goals like doubling the number of students enrolled in five years and celebrate their achievement even though such goals have no relevance to the scale of the problems they wish to address. In unequal societies, philanthropy is primarily a vehicle for feeling good not for effectively solving problems. Charity is laudable if the objective is to be charitable. It should not be conflated with problem solving.

8. What is the ideal role of NGOs?

NGOs have a vital and critical role to play but it is not one of filling the resource gap. NGOs should be experimenting with new content, pedagogy, incentives, and financing mechanisms to be mainstreamed into the public education system. They should be acting on behalf of citizens as a lobby to raise the political priority of education and presenting effective models for reform of the public education system.

9. Can the existing problem be solved in the traditional way?

The resource gaps, especially in teaching capacity, are now too large and the vested interests too entrenched to allow traditional approaches to succeed. Recourse to modern technology (Internet and mobile phones) is needed to leapfrog barriers of state resistance, mass illiteracy, and low incomes. Note that mobile phone is a technology that will scale to the magnitude of the problem and become more functional at the same time. By 2020 almost every individual is expected to have access to a mobile phone and the ability to afford it. Experiments have confirmed that illiteracy is not a bar to the acquisition of knowledge and information.

10. What is the bottom line?

Access to education and control of content are as much political issues as social or financial ones. They need a political strategy spearheaded by NGOs and backed by technological innovations overcoming state resistance, capacity constraints and income limitations.

* * * *

II. Are NGOs Relevant?

Non-Governmental Organizations in Pakistan remind me of Iqbal's poem *Aik Pahar Aur Gilehri* (the Mountain and the Squirrel) in *Bang-e-Dara*, a compilation of his popular poems. In terms of the scale of the problem, they are insignificant just as the size of the squirrel is insignificant relative to the size of the mountain. In terms of the ability to think, the roles are reversed—the brain of the squirrel is vastly superior to the non-existent brain of the mountain. So, clearly NGOs can be irrelevant or relevant depending on whether one looks at their brawn or their brain.

Take education in Pakistan as an example. The public school system in the country is the mountain; the NGOs are the squirrel. It is quite clear to anyone who has looked at the numbers that the public school system has broken down. Leave aside the quality of education being imparted in the schools (it should best be called 'indoctrination'); between 2004 and 2010, the number of dropouts from the primary grades is projected to increase from 11 million to 14 million children.[2] Now look at the scale of the NGOs. If you add all of them together, the schools they operate will not exceed a few thousand and the total number of students enrolled will not be more than a few hundred thousand. In terms of the scale of the problem, NGOs are irrelevant to the solution of the national crisis.

If NGOs are realistic (and many of them are), they should be able to see that they cannot replace the public school system or even come anywhere close to filling the gap left by the latter's collapse. The numbers don't add up. Such NGOs have other objectives that can be equally laudable.

But not all NGOs are realistic, and this reminds me of another story about the elephant and the mouse. The elephant is toying with the mouse with its foot; the mouse looks up contemptuously at the elephant and says: *chotey hondian, bimaar riyaan* (I was ill when young, otherwise...)

So, there are NGOs that get puffed up, lose sight of their scale, and begin to believe they can take on the elephant. You can see that in the targets they set for themselves—doubling the number of schools in five years, tripling the number of children enrolled, etc. They spend vast amounts of time and energy raising funds to meet these targets without taking into account the real costs per unit of output and go into self-congratulatory raptures when the targets are achieved.

> ## So, what should the NGOs be doing?
>
> What else but leveraging the aspect where they have an overwhelming superiority! The NGOs are driven by a civic motivation, a concern for children, and have some of the most thoughtful minds in their ranks. The public school system is run by tired bureaucrats and infiltrated by retrograde ideologues.
>
> The NGOs should be using their brainpower to figure out how to make the public school system perform better because only if the public school system performs better will the national crisis be resolved. NGOs can use their schools to experiment with new content and learning methods and teaching techniques. But in the end, these have to impact the system itself to yield meaningful results on the scale required.—Anjum Altaf

But if filling the gap left by the public school system is the objective, these kinds of targets are irrelevant and meaningless. NGOs can double or triple or quintuple the number of their schools and it will not make a dent in the problem.

There is no denying that NGOs make a huge difference to the life chances of the children they reach. But, to repeat the arithmetic, they are irrelevant to the scale of the problem. The question NGOs have to ask themselves is whether they desire to derive their satisfaction from acts of charity or from contributing to the solution of a national crisis. There is room for both, but the clarity is necessary. A mouse can be a very noble mouse (and there is no shame in being one) but the nobility will not turn it into an elephant. A mouse that thinks of itself as an elephant, on the other hand, makes for a sorry spectacle and gets in the way of solving the problem. It needs to shed the illusion.

There is another analogy that comes to mind that illustrates this point. In the 1960s, American automobile manufacturers were making unsafe cars, a practice that was noticed by Ralph Nader who had a sort of consumer NGO. Imagine Nader going into the business of manufacturing safe cars—ten cars the first year with a target of doubling output every year. All those who would have received Nader's safe cars would have been better off but Nader would have been irrelevant to the scale of the problem—the manufacturers were putting millions of unsafe cars on the roads every year.

Instead, Nader used his knowledge and intelligence (Princeton, Harvard Law School) and his group of committed consumer activists

(Nader's Raiders) to force the manufacturers to make all cars safe. His 1965 book *Unsafe at Any Speed* and his mobilization campaign are still considered classics of effective NGO action.

And this also makes the point that NGOs in the field of education should teach poetry and the liberal arts in their own schools and lobby for them to be an important part of the curriculum of all schools. Students in the age of information and technology feel all such subjects are a waste of time. But if they had *Aik Pahar Aur Gilehri* explained to them with care, they would have found it easy to understand why Nader preferred brain to brawn in his quest to solve a major problem.

* * * *

III. Beyond Literacy: The Problem and Directions for the Future[3]

Sixty years after the creation of the country, half of Pakistan's population is still illiterate. This is a major problem, but it is not the most major problem. It is only an outcome of the major problem. This distinction is important because the identification of the problem defines the nature of the solution. If we think of illiteracy as a major problem caused by the inattention of the state, we will immediately think of a course of action in which all the NGOs get together, construct schools, and deal with the problem one school at a time. I will argue that this will send us off on the wrong track.

Think of it this way. If you go to a physician with fever and rashes, the physician does not treat you for fever and rashes. The fever and rashes are not the disease; they are just the symptoms of a disease. And the disease is unidentified till there is a diagnosis which is the real job of the physician. Only when the underlying cause is identified can the appropriate treatment be prescribed. And this prescription will be very different depending on whether the fever and rashes are due to malaria as opposed to chicken pox.

The social scientist is the physician of the social system and his/her real task in this case is to identify the underlying cause whose symptom is 50 percent illiteracy in Pakistan. Before we begin to address that question, we should also clarify that just as illiteracy is not the problem, the 50 percent illiterate citizens are not the problem. They are not the ones holding back the development and prosperity of the country. Blaming them would be akin to blaming the patients and the victims.

The fact of the matter is that Pakistan is a grossly mismanaged country. And the ones who have been in charge of mismanaging the country are its literate—not its illiterate—citizens. Let us grant for the moment that it is part of this mismanagement that is manifested in the illiteracy of half the population. So, the question we have to ask is why the literate managers have failed to impart literacy to the still illiterate citizens?

The two explanations that one hears all the time are lack of political will and lack of money. But these are not convincing explanations. Why is political will needed to spread literacy? Who in the country is opposing the spread of literacy? Why does political capital need to be expended for this cause? There is no satisfactory answer.

And why is there a lack of money for education? There seems to be a lot of money for everything else from the making of nuclear bombs to buying F-16 planes to building the highest water fountain in the world. Why is it education that is starved for money? Once again there is no satisfactory answer.

The only plausible conclusion seems to be that spreading literacy amongst the illiterate has a very low priority for the literate managers of the country. And so, we push back the question further to ask why is that priority so low? Let me try to present a hypothesis with a few examples. Take the tribal *sardars* [feudal leaders] in Balochistan. The population of Balochistan is only 10 million and only half of those are ethnic Baloch. We know that a number of Baloch sardars have been paid millions of dollars for the use of natural resources on their lands. So why have the sardars not used this revenue to educate their tribesmen? When you pose that question almost everyone in Pakistan is quick to inform you that the sardars do not wish to educate or otherwise develop their tribesmen because they want them to remain dependent.

We can conclude from this that there is at least one type of political-economic system in which the rulers are positively not interested in educating their constituents.

Have I picked an outlier, the only such system of this type in the world ruled by barbaric tribal sardars? Think again. Recall that in the American South before the Civil War many states had passed laws making it a crime for slaves to learn to read and write and for others to instruct them. The punishments included flogging for slaves and heavy fines for the teachers.

Why was this necessary? Because if the slaves had been able to read the Constitution, they would have noted that it began with the statement that all men were born equal and, one presumes, they would have been curious to know why the equality did not apply to them.

So, we can begin to believe that there are indeed political-economic systems, especially those based on oppression, where the rulers do not wish the ruled to develop the ability to think and question because that questioning would lead to a questioning of the legitimacy of the systems themselves.

Do you believe that such things just happen by themselves without conscious thought? Once more you will have to think again. Most people in the subcontinent are familiar with the name of Lord Macaulay made famous by his 1837 'Minute on Education'. Here is what he said in a remarkable speech in the British Parliament on the Government of India Bill in 1833: 'Are we to keep the people of India ignorant in order that we may keep them submissive? Or do we think that we can give them knowledge without awakening ambition? Or do we mean to awaken ambition and provide it with no legitimate vent?'

What happened in India later is a fascinating digression, but I will not get into that. The point to take away is that the decision to educate or not to educate the subjects is a political decision, that education policy is an element in the political calculus, and that there are some political-economic systems, of which I have provided three examples, where the decision of the rulers is not to educate the ruled beyond the minimum that is necessary for the functioning of the system.

Of course, not all systems are like that. Here in the Silicon Valley you have a sub-system that puts a great premium on learning and that even pays you to acquire more knowledge. Why? Because this system is part of a globally competitive environment in which it would die if it didn't remain ahead of its competition. So, one can conclude that it is the needs of a political-economic system, not good will, that determine its attitudes towards education.

Note that one cannot even generalize from the Silicon Valley sub-system to the US as a whole. You might agree that the US does not really want its citizens to learn more than it feels necessary about the Iraq war, for example. And it does not strongly enough wish the same kind of thinking to be taught in inner city schools as it does in the schools of

Palo Alto. Do you attribute that in the richest country of the world to lack of political will or lack of money?

So, here is the first major conclusion: Education is a political issue; political-economic systems are in general inimical to enabling their citizens to think; they enable only as much thinking as is necessary for the survival of the system; and systems differ in how much thinking-power they need to survive.

You can even apply this perspective to attitudes towards the education of women within families if you think of a family as a political-economic system. When we see the issue in this perspective, we can better understand why education has such a low priority in Pakistan for the managers of the system. They sense a very low need for innovative thinking that is satisfied by a handful of elite institutions whose teaching methods have never trickled down to the vast majority of schools and colleges. On balance, the dangers posed by critical thinking far outweigh its benefits to the status quo.

Now, of course, there are occasions when populations rebel against this kind of oppression. We can think of the warlords in China, the Tsars in Russia, and the capitalists in Cuba as the equivalents of our Baloch sardars. Their populations under Mao, Lenin, and Castro rebelled against the oppression and were able to win universal literacy for themselves.

But does this stop education from remaining an instrument of politics? No, the politics just moves up to the next level—that of the content that comprises education and literacy. So, the Chinese were made literate with the Little Red Book, the Russians with Marxism-Leninism, and the Cubans with the Socialist Man. The object was to concede the hard-won right of citizens to learn but to ensure that they thought in a particular, state-sanctioned way. Many would call that indoctrination, not education.

The second major conclusion is that literacy is important, but the content of that literacy is even more important. Let me give you an example from closer to home. Ashis Nandy, a leading political psychologist in India, recently got into a lot of trouble for writing an article in which he laid the blame for the ethnic cleansing in Gujarat on its educated middle class. Remember that this ethnic cleansing is alleged to have been incited and encouraged by Narendra Modi, the very literate Chief Minister of the state.

Related to this, Dr Asghar Ali Engineer, a leading scholar of ethnic conflict working in Mumbai, asked a very profound question: Why is the educated middle class more bigoted than the illiterate masses? And he had a very simple answer: because it is educated.

Think about this. If you take the mind of a child as an empty vessel and make the child literate while filling his or her mind with hate and lies, what will you get? You will get a literate young person who is infinitely more dangerous than an illiterate one.

So, if you teach numeric literacy in a Gujarat school by asking how many *kar-sevaks* [social activists] would it take to demolish 7 mosques in 3 days if one kar-sevak can demolish one mosque in two days, you will certainly achieve literacy but at a very heavy cost to society.

Of course, this political use of education is not confined to India. The curriculum wing of the ministry of education in Pakistan retains very tight control over what is to be taught in public schools in Pakistan. An analysis of the content is available on the web in a report prepared by the Sustainable Development Policy Institute in Islamabad. When you see it, you will be convinced that this is indeed not education but indoctrination.

So, this is what we mean by the term 'beyond literacy'. Education is not pouring propaganda into empty minds but enabling those minds to think for themselves. And thus, we have a twin struggle: first to ensure that our citizens obtain their basic human right of education; and second that the education they get enables them to think for themselves.

Once we have diagnosed the problem and placed it in its political context, only then can we begin to think how we can get from where we are to where we want to be. The first part is obviously a political struggle. We have to mobilize the citizens to demand their right to a good education—no one is going to give it to them as charity. But this also requires us to see the role of NGOs in a realistic perspective. The arithmetic does not support the conclusion that NGOs on their own can fill the gap left by the omissions of the state.

NGOs are doing a commendable job in changing the life chances of the proportionately very few people they are able to touch. But all the statistics confirm that the overall gap in Pakistan is widening despite the heroic commitment of the NGOs. The NGOs need at the same time to act as awareness-raising groups to mobilize citizens around their rights and as pressure groups to force the state to discharge its responsibility to its citizens.

Second, we must contest the struggle over the content of education and the pedagogy of critical thinking, aspects we have ignored to our detriment by allowing ideologues to capture and enfeeble the educational arena since the time of [military dictator] Zia ul Haq. Here again, NGOs have a vital role in the evolution of new content and learning methods that they can experiment with in their institutions. But we must realize that the conventional approach to improving the quality of education is no longer possible. Quite apart from the opposition of the state and of those who control educational institutions today, there is no way we can get the thousands of trained teachers we need in the schools and colleges spread over the rural areas, the small towns and the secondary cities of Pakistan. We have to think of a way to leapfrog this limitation.

Here we have an opportunity provided by the emergence of technologies that did not exist even a few decades ago. Recall that Ayotallah Khomeini toppled the Shah by using cassette tapes to educate Iranians about the oppression in the country. We may disagree with the political content of this education but here we only want to note the leverage provided by new technology and the weakening of state controls because of it.

Since that time digital technology has made remarkable inroads. The cell phone has now penetrated into the remotest villages and reached amongst the poorest of the citizens. And if you in Silicon Valley continue what you are doing, the digital content that would be available on cell phones tomorrow cannot even be imagined today.

It is this democratization of access to information not subject to state control (recall the attempts to ban dish-antennas a few years back) that holds out the biggest hope for the future. It would be technological forces supported by civic action that would be the driving force of this transformation. Our job would be to find the content that would take advantage of these technological opportunities. So, the ball is very much in our court.

On our part, we have started a modest initiative to provide content in a thought-provoking format for college students in South Asia. It is still in an experimental stage seeking to find the right mix of content, format and complexity. We hope to turn this into a major e-learning platform grounded in specific nodes in South Asia with the content transferred to local language blogs. I invite you to take a look at this initiative, to provide your inputs, and to participate in the experiment to see if we can really make a difference in the sense that I have outlined in this presentation.

I think we can and I am excited by the challenge. If we pool our strengths—mastery of technology, familiarity with content, and motivation for civic action—we can make our presence felt and make a decisive contribution to the cause of education and liberation in Pakistan.

* * * *

IV. Education Reform in Pakistan and the Role of NGOs[4]

NGOs are doing a remarkable job in changing the life chances of the children in Pakistan—the children they are able to reach. In this perspective their role is to be commended and supported.

What are the other roles that NGOs can perform? And what can be the role of NGOs in the reform of the education system in Pakistan?

The term reform implies that the system is functioning reasonably well and improvements are required at the margin. In this perspective, there is agreement that improvements in content and teaching methods are at the top of the agenda. NGOs are already playing a role in experimenting with more effective teaching methods and more learner-friendly content in their schools.

The NGOs can consciously strengthen this function by using their schools as laboratories and by holding joint workshops to discuss and evaluate the innovations. The most important next step would be to then work towards having these innovations adopted in the public school system. This task remains to be done and is one where NGOs can play a greater role by taking on a greater responsibility as the cutting edge of education reform.

The conference was titled 'Education Reform in Pakistan' and TCF prefaced the opening of the conference by placing it in the context of the state of education in Pakistan. The summary from the State Bank of Pakistan's report and information from the National Education Foundation highlighted the crisis situation and confirmed that the gap between demand and supply continues to widen. Thus, while dropouts from the primary school system totaled 11 million in 2004 the figure was projected to rise to 14 million by 2010.

The total number of schools run by NGOs is of the order of a few thousand and the total number of students reached of the order of a few hundred thousand. In this perspective, it is obvious that NGOs cannot see themselves as substitute service providers that can hope to fill the gap. NGOs have to do the arithmetic and realize that they cannot set this task for themselves. The most effective role for NGOs is to act as an advocacy group to lobby the state to discharge its responsibility to the citizens.

However, it is also clear that education is a right that has to be won—there will be no supply without effective demand of the right. Therefore, NGOs also need to act as consciousness raising groups to mobilize excluded citizens around their basic right to a good education.

In this context, both the state and international donors claim to have invested a very large amount of funds in education in Pakistan. This effort has been very high in visibility but very low in impact. This identifies another role for NGOs—to act as watchdog groups on behalf of citizens to ask for greater accountability. Collaboration with the media to investigate into the outcomes of specific projects would generate the pressure to improve delivery.

An international coalition of key NGOs and all interested individuals is the best next step in this situation. The objectives of the coalition should be to raise the consciousness of citizens regarding their right to a good education, to experiment with new content and teaching methods in their own schools, to exert pressure on the state to deliver more and better education based on these innovations, and to institutionalize mechanisms which improve the accountability of funds invested in education by the state and by international donors.

Further Reading

- *The Subtle Subversion: The State of Curricula and Textbooks in Pakistan, SDPI, Islamabad, 2002.*
  http://www.sdpi.org/whats_new/reporton/State%20of%20
  Curr&TextBooks.pdf
- *The South Asian Idea*—an e-learning resource for college students in South Asia to promote critical thinking based on contextually relevant content. http://thesouthasianidea.com

* * * *

V. Functional Arguments for a Rational Policy on Language

In 2015, the Supreme Court of Pakistan ruled that Urdu should replace English as the national language of the country. Our experience with the politics of language has been so traumatic that we need a dispassionate analysis of this decision in the context of the functions of language and the current situation in Pakistan.

Language is recognized as having three primary functions: First, it is a tool to facilitate the transfer of knowledge from one generation to the next; second, it serves as a means of communication among people at any given period in time; and third, it constitutes the repository of wisdom that provides the foundation of a sound and meaningful education.

Language for Instruction

The evidence pertaining to the first function has become scientifically more rigorous over time and is by now overwhelming. It has been shown repeatedly that the mother tongue is the most effective vehicle for instruction during the early years of education. In the specific case of Pakistan, a 2010 report on education by the British Council offered the following major recommendation:

> Early years education must be provided in a child's home language. The dangers of not doing so include high dropout levels (especially among girls), poor educational achievement, poor acquisition of foreign languages (such as English), the long term decline and death of indigenous languages, and ethnic marginalization leading to the growth of resentment among ethnic minorities. Pakistan is considered to be one of the countries most exposed to these risks.

In the light of this evidence, it should be obvious that as far as the learning function of language is concerned the choice is not between Urdu and English but between either of these languages and the mother tongue. The real policy question is at what stage in a child's education should a second language be introduced and whether it should be Urdu or English.

One should not lose sight of the fact that the choice of the mother tongue as the medium of instruction in the early years and Urdu as the second language does not rule out the acquisition of English at a later stage. The evidence regarding development from countries like Japan, South Korea and China that use their national languages as the medium of instruction is so stark as to make it impossible to overlook. If facility with English had been the preeminent requirement for development, Pakistan and India should have been global leaders and if lack of facility in English had been a genuine hindrance Japan, South Korea and China ought to have been laggards.

The fact is that facility with English in non-English speaking countries is very poorly correlated with any index of development. Pakistan's elite, responsible for all its policy decisions, is fluent in English and yet what do Pakistan's rankings reveal: the sixth largest country in the world ranks 146 out of 187 countries on the Human Development Index, which measures health, standard of living, and education and 136 out of 144 countries in primary education according to the World Economic Forum's Global Competitiveness Report. Arguing that this abysmal plight would improve if the entire country learns English is the kind of pie-in-the-sky thinking that has plagued our education policies to date. More seriously, it also ignores the evidence that even the acquisition of English depends on sound early education in the mother tongue.

Language for Communication

Communication at any given point in time is the second primary function of language and this has two dimensions. First, horizontal communication amongst citizens and second vertical communication between elected representatives and citizens. Clearly, the existence of a common language greatly facilitates communication across both dimensions as we can observe again from the examples of Japan, South Korea and China.

Of course, this quest is greatly complicated in multi-lingual countries like Pakistan and India when the choice of a single language becomes politically fraught. But the situation in Pakistan today is very different from what it was in 1947. It remains the case that it would be politically impossible to mandate any one of the sub-national languages as the language for horizontal communication. However, by now everyone in the country has some familiarity with Urdu that far exceeds familiarity with English. If the only choice of a common language for communication is between Urdu and English, then Urdu has a huge advantage over the latter in terms of familiarity.

Therefore, the fact that Urdu is understood to some extent by the majority of the population makes the case for its acceptance as the language of horizontal communication very strong. This would not confer any special privilege on native Urdu speakers. Amongst the educated cohorts, the native Urdu speaker today has virtually no advantage over the native speaker of the other sub-national language— all of them communicate equally well or equally poorly in a mangled hybrid of various languages because of the deterioration of primary and secondary education in the country.

The function of language for vertical communication is much more important in some senses and here the situation has deteriorated to a critical pass. Inclusive development calls for a common medium of communication and its absence is stark in countries like Pakistan and India where the ruling elites communicate in English while the majority of citizens is unfamiliar with the language. Ministers and experts pronouncing in English leave virtually the entire population out of the national discourse at great cost.

Given this communication gap, the choice of Urdu as the official language would be the sensible and far-sighted one in the concrete situation that exists in Pakistan today. The debate should really be on how to operationalize the transition. My recommendation, keeping very clear the distinction between learning a language and learning in a language, would be to have the early years of education in the mother tongue, introduce Urdu second, followed by English. This would yield a sound instructional foundation, a common language for communication, and a facility with English when the study of science and technology requires its use.

The experience of the European Union, where the 'mother tongue plus two' mandate is widely accepted and where there is great emphasis on the acquisition of English, can provide very useful guidance on the stages at which each of the languages is best introduced and the points at which the language of instruction is switched, if warranted. There is little need to reinvent the wheel.

It is an added advantage that this transition does not take away the option of the provinces to conduct their parliamentary procedures in their own language or to make information available to their citizens in the language with which the latter (the citizens) are most comfortable. Indeed, this is what they should be doing in any case just as in the US most material related to citizen-state interaction is made available in Spanish as well as English.

Language for Education

It is the third function of language, as the foundation of a good education, that is both the most critical and the most complex to understand. Close contact with students has left no doubt in my mind that our language policy has had an extremely debilitating effect even on the best students in the country simply because the majority are not solidly grounded in any one language.

Why should that be a problem? Why is it not good enough to know a language just sufficiently enough to undertake everyday transactions and to buy and sell whatever it is that one might want to transact? Indeed, one should ask what being solidly grounded in a language means and why it is of any importance for students.

I believe an understanding of this dimension is vital for the discussion we should be having keeping in mind that at this time we are talking not of the entire population but about students attending the leading universities in the country. These are the students from among whom will emerge the decision-makers of tomorrow and we should have a very great stake in the creativity and intellectual ability of this cohort.

The process of education, as opposed to skill acquisition, can be characterized as one of osmosis through which an individual imbibes the accumulated wisdom of the past. This conceptualization of education needs some elaboration.

One can readily accept that a great number of extremely learned and gifted human beings have been part of human history and that their accumulated wisdom is enshrined in the texts they wrote and the commentaries that have been written on those texts subsequently. Access to this storehouse of wisdom, and the ability to interpret it, is an essential starting point for all those who aspire to contribute to human progress. This is best exemplified by the saying attributed to Newton: 'If I have seen further than others, it is by standing upon the shoulders of giants.'

Examples of the creators of wisdom abound—Plato, Aristotle, Ibn Khaldun, Ibn Sina, Panini, Buddha, to name just a few. It was the wisdom of the Greeks, kept alive by the Arabs, which re-lighted the lamp of knowledge in Europe. In our region, an incredible amount of wisdom resides in the legacy of Mirabai, Guru Nanak, Bulleh Shah, Shah Latif, Ghalib, and Iqbal down to our times. Creativity is enhanced by being able to draw upon this knowledge in the performance of our everyday tasks. In a way this is reflected in the positive aspect of a question like 'What would Jesus do?' You have to know what Jesus did in order to answer that question. A useful analogy is of a plant that, without conscious effort, draws nourishment from the soil. If the soil is dry, the plant withers in no time.

Our linguistic heritage is akin to the soil that nourishes our ideas, that makes possible the spark that can connect disparate thoughts and thus lead to new ways of seeing things. If we lose access to this nourishment, we weaken the source of our creativity and thereby the ability to draw upon the wisdom of the past in deliberating intelligently on current problems and their possible solutions.

When I come across students who cannot read their first language, whose second language, in most cases Urdu, is barely adequate for verbal communication, and whose English is only proficient for essential reading and writing, the critical dimension of our dilemma becomes obvious. In no language are they equipped to access the many storehouses of wisdom. This difficulty is compounded in our region because the wisdom of our vernacular traditions is not adequately translated into English, the one language in which our best students can read with any proficiency. This is unlike the West where, say, the wisdom of the Greeks, is kept alive by continuous reinterpretations in local languages so that some access is possible for those who are educated in those languages, say the French in France or Germans in Germany.

I am being generous in conceding that our students are proficient in reading English—the ability to truly understand a language comes from being imbued in its culture. It is not possible for our students to pick up, say, Milton's *Paradise Lost* and get the same out of the poem as a peer whose native language is English. One needs to be steeped in a culture to make sense of its literary allusions; for example, much of English literature has its roots in the Bible. But we do have similar wisdom couched in more familiar and accessible metaphors in, say, Noon Meem Rashid's *Hasan Koozagar* or in Kabir, Bulleh Shah, and Ghalib that can be much more readily accessible because the allusions and metaphors belong to our own lived reality. We do need to ensure a solid grounding in our first language and/or Urdu to get to the point where we can access this wisdom.

There is a very sound intellectual case for the need to ensure mastery in at least one language and if we are convinced of this objective, its translation into reality is actually quite easy. The choice of language is not the political one between English and Urdu. Rather, it is the balance between languages and their sequencing that ought to be at the heart of the policy discussion. Evidence for the efficacy of the first language for early education is now irrefutably strengthened by additional evidence that the acquisition of additional languages is easier for those whose early education is in their first language because their ability to learn is stronger. The case for Urdu as the second and shared language for horizontal and vertical communication is dictated simply by the reality of its wide familiarity across the country. A good knowledge of Urdu would also make accessible the storehouse of wisdom that is essential to a sound and equitable education for all its citizens. Finally, English as the third language would facilitate access to the global integration that is considered essential by many primarily for practical and material reasons.

There is really no convincing argument to sacrifice the very essential functions of language that are better served by the first language and an easily shared second language for the utilitarian advantages conferred by English, a language that can be learnt on an as-needed basis as it is in many other advanced nations in the world. As mentioned earlier, learning a language and learning in a language are very different propositions and losing sight of the distinction comes at a very high price.

Note: This essay is a synthesis of arguments articulated in a number of earlier writings by the author. These writings are archived at
https://thesouthasianidea.wordpress.com/#Language

References

Altaf, Anjum. 'Macaulay's Stepchildren,' Himal Magazine, January 2010. http://old.himalmag.com/component/content/article/35-macaulays-stepchildren.htmlColeman, Hywel. 'Teaching and Learning in Pakistan: The Role of Language in Education,' British Council Pakistan, 2010.

Coleman, Hywel and T. Capstick. 'Language in Education in Pakistan,' British Council, 2012.

https://www.teachingenglish.org.uk/sites/teacheng/files/Language%20In%20
Education%20in%20Pakistan.pdf

Supreme Court of Pakistan. Order on Urdu as the official language of Pakistan,
August 26, 2015.

http://www.supremecourt.gov.pk/web/user_files/File/Const.P._56_2003_E_
dt_3-9-15.pdf

Wright, Wayne E., Sovicheth Boun and Ofelia Garcia, Eds. The Handbook of
Bilingual and Multilingual Education, Wiley Blackwell, 2015.

https://books.google.com.pk/books?id=KG_-
CAAAQBAJ&pg=PR3&source=gbs_selected_
pages&cad=2#v=onepage&q&f=false

Enhancing Learning of Children from Diverse Language Backgrounds:
Mother Tongue-Based Bilingual or Multilingual Education in the Early
Years (UNESCO, 2011)

https://www.observatoireplurilinguisme.eu/images/Recherche/enhancing%20
children%20unesco.pdf

* * * *

VI. Some Reflections on the Nature of Economic, Social, and Political Change

This essay is the text of the 16th Hamza Alavi Distinguished Lecture delivered in Karachi on 16 December 2017, under the auspices of the Irtiqa Institute for Social Sciences and the Hamza Alavi Foundation. The lecture was delivered in Urdu and does not follow the order of the formal written version. A video of the lecture in Urdu is accessible at the Irtiqa Institute Facebook page.[5]

An important strand of Hamza Alavi's work was about change and the agency for change as attested by the two well-known hypotheses associated with his name—those of the middle peasantry (1965) and of the salariat (1987) [salaried white-collar workers]. I intend to use these as the point of departure to offer some tentative reflections on the nature of change and on the scenarios facing us today in Pakistan and more generally across the world.

Economics, the Importance of Rules, and Collective Agency

My own academic interest in the subject arose not with reference to politics or sociology but via a study of economics. In preparing for doctoral work, I was struck by the centrality of rules in our lives. Everything we do is governed by rules, some of which, such as those enforced by organizations and legislatures, are relatively short-lived, while others, like cultural norms, have comparatively longer lives. Any number of examples can be offered by way of illustration. The most obvious case of the application of rules to action is in the realm of games like chess, cricket and hockey. Industrial behavior is circumscribed by laws pertaining to labor and the environment, commercial transactions by rules of taxation, social interactions by rules of inheritance and marriage, and history by rules of succession. Extending the argument, it is asserted that all institutions can be characterized as sets of rules that define and govern behavior (North, 1990).

Once I realized the centrality of rules, it occurred to me that mainstream economic theory was limited in the way it incorporated this fact within its corpus. Recall that in the theory of the firm, for example, the highest virtue is efficiency. A producer is expected to maximize efficiency in the production process within the given set of rules applicable at the time. The last part, however, is left unstated and implicitly assumed as a datum.

I started my doctoral work abroad, but my formative experiences had been in Pakistan and this conceptualization of the production process did not ring true to me. I was quite aware that producers in Pakistan cared little about efficiency while investing a lot of time and money in manipulating rules to their advantage. It was an easily observable fact that windfall gains, many times those resulting from being efficient, could be achieved by manipulation of rules. There were examples that I had experienced personally. Consider a rule change that made it mandatory for motorcycle riders to wear helmets. This could multiply the demand for helmets overnight increasing their price in the market. Consider another rule that would prohibit the import of helmets. That would yield another bonanza for domestic producers.

Given this fact, it was quite clear to me that rational economic agents would invest more in trying to change rules to their advantage than in being efficient within existing rules. It was also obvious that rules were not fixed but liable to change and often the object of conscious efforts intended to induce change and that one could differentiate various situations by the relative stability of their rule regimes.[6] Based on these insights, I set out to investigate how rules impacted economic behavior by incorporating the rule regime explicitly into the theoretical framework of mainstream economics from which it had been excluded (Altaf, 1983).

A major conclusion followed immediately. The kind of rule changes mentioned above, e.g., mandating the use of helmets, cannot, in general, be engineered by any individual producer in the market. However, we encounter such rule changes quite often. This means that economic theory resting on methodological individualism, i.e., taking the individual as the unit of analysis, could not account for such dynamics. It needed to figure out a way to resolve this limitation.

But let us step back for a moment. Does the fact that an individual is unable to engineer a rule change imply that he or she has no agency? Not at all, because the individual always retains the agency to violate a rule, e.g., to not stop at a red light. The instances of individual firms violating safety and environmental rules are so flagrant that there is no need to belabor the point. Suffice it to say that the economics of cheating is a major area in its own right though not of primary importance for the subject of this discussion.

But consider the flip side—while individuals cannot change rules, groups can. In the realm of economics, these are lobbies associated with various industries like textiles, automobiles, healthcare, hedge funds, etc. Thus, an economic theory desirous of incorporating the reality of rule changes would need to take the group as the unit of analysis— only then would something like the economics of lobbying become an integral part of the theory rather than an add-on.

Let us reiterate at this juncture the immense significance of rule changes. The point can be driven home vividly by reference to the mundane sport of hockey. Many people claim that just two rule changes—that of the playing surface from grass to Astroturf and the off-side rule—put paid to [confirmed, facilitated] the dominance of subcontinental teams [of India and Pakistan] in favor of European and Australian ones. The changes lessened the importance of artistry and close ball control in favor of stamina and long passes in which Europeans [and Australians] had a comparative advantage.

In weightier domains, one can think of the differences over rules of political succession that were at the bottom of the schism in Islam right at the very outset. The inability to agree on rules of succession continued to plague Muslim empires throughout history—recall the fact that during the Mughal empire each successive emperor had to eliminate all his brothers to establish dominance. In our own times we see a recurrence of something similar in the emerging rift between Maryam Nawaz and Hamza Shahbaz—different sets of courtiers informing each of them that they are intended for the same role.

Here I would like to recall a fascinating hypothesis I heard first from the late G.M. Mehkri (Altaf, 2009a). He posed the question of why Muslims were the poorest community in India despite over a thousand years of Muslim rule. His speculation was that Muslims in India had persisted with a law of inheritance, one that was appropriate in a desert economy where reproducible assets like animals were the principal source of wealth, after migrating to an agricultural economy in which the principal source of wealth was land, a non-reproducible asset. He surmised further that the reason Memon, Khoja, Ismaili and Bohra communities were more affluent amongst Muslim communities was because they had retained their caste laws of inheritance on conversion [from native faiths in early India] to Islam. While I am not in a position to validate these specific hypotheses, they do illustrate vividly the possibility of deep and long-lasting impact of rules and rule changes on society.

One of the extensions of this line of thought is the realization that some of the most important interactions in our world ('games' in the game-theoretic sense) are played not within given rules but over the rules that are to govern transactions. One needs only to think of global negotiations over rules of trade, intellectual property, and climate change to realize this vital truth. This opens up many issues that are of great interest. For example—who has the power, authority and legitimacy to make rules, how do groups form and sustain themselves to challenge rules, how do groups opposed to each other interact in the struggle over rules, and what is the role of the rule-maker, often the state, in such struggles? Is the rule-maker a neutral umpire or an active player with interests of its own?[7]

The bottom line of this argument for me was the following: that the relevant unit of analysis is the group (including the state as an identifiable group) and that groups are not averse to using all means, not just economic ones, to change rules in order to maximize their self-interest. Even within the discipline of economics, restricting ourselves to *Homo Economicus* [economic man] was to limit the analysis without adequate justification. Humans are really political animals—Zoon Politikon, in the characterization of Aristotle. Thus—for the phenomena that interested Hamza Alavi—economics, sociology and politics come together in a unified social science that sees history as the struggle over rules of games that are continuously played out amongst contending groups aiming to optimize their respective self-interests.

Consider in this light the motivations of Hamza Alavi's middle peasantry and the salariat. At the conceptual level the characterization presented above would make sense quite independent of whether or not the groups were capable of effecting the changes attributed to them. Between the motivation and the ability there are intervening variables that we will address later in this discussion.

Provincializing Europe

Before doing so, I would like to flag an issue that would hopefully nuance the discussion. This pertains to the default backdrop of Enlightenment Europe as an exemplar of the type of change we often implicitly have in mind with its salience regarding the rights of individuals—the transition to an age characterized by the transformation of subject to citizen along with corresponding notions of social contract, citizenship and civil rights. We need to remain aware that the European experience emerged out of the confluence of a very particular set of developments (Johnson, 1999) that need have almost no parallel in our part of the world. Differences matter even within the colonial context as Andre Beteille (2013) observed regarding the evolution of democracy:

> In both India and the United States—unlike in England or France— democracy grew in response to the challenge of colonial rule, but the responses were not the same in the two cases. America was a new nation characterized by social conditions that were very different from the social conditions prevalent since time immemorial in India.

Even the transformation of subject to citizen in Europe had a particular history modulated by the rise of capitalism. Marshall (1950), in a classic essay, has elaborated the peculiarity of the development in England of the civil, political and social dimensions of citizenship, in that order, each taking around one century to consolidate.

Marshall's thesis on the sequential development of citizenship rights (Cohen, 2010) is embedded in the specificities of the emergence of capitalism in Europe with its imperatives to protect privacy (of property) and to promote individualism (to make labor a freely tradable commodity). The unintended outcome of these imperatives was the concession of civil rights extending the sanctity of property to the body of the worker, his or her primary asset. This concession of the equality of all bodies, in turn, led to a demand for political rights, an equal say in the election of political representatives. And the need to protect the capitalist system from the pressures for redistribution from below generated by the exercise of civil and political rights led to the progressive yielding of socioeconomic rights.

In the colonies, by contrast, political rights took precedence, being virtually gifted in the historical process, and are still significantly more legitimated than individual and civil rights. Khilnani (1997) observes that 'most people in India had no idea of what exactly they had been given. Like the British empire it supplanted, India's constitutional democracy was established in a fit of absent-mindedness.' Mehta (2003) adds that India's democratic experiment 'was not the object of ideological passion, it was not born of a deep sense of conviction widely shared, but it was simply the contingent outcome of the conflicts amongst India's different elites, or an unintended by-product of the British having produced too many lawyers adept in the idioms of modern politics.'

Dr Ambedkar (1949), the author of the Indian Constitution, was under no illusion regarding the nature of the evolution of rights in India:

> 'In politics we will have equality and in social and economic life we will have inequality. In politics we will be recognizing the principle of one man one vote and one vote one value. In our social and economic life, we shall, by reason of our social and economic structure, continue to deny the principle of one man one value. How long shall we continue to live this life of contradictions?'

Teresa Caldeira (2000) has argued convincingly that scholars of

> the history of the countries that invented the liberal-democratic model (France, England, and the United States) ... have tended to generalize the history so that it becomes the history of the development of rights and discipline in general and the model of what citizenship and democracy should look like.
>
> One of the effects of this generalization is to link certain elements as if they always occur together and in a certain sequence. Countries such as Brazil, but also others with different histories (usually colonial histories) and that today have disjunctive democracies, force us to dissociate the elements of that history and to question their sequence.

They force us to see the possibility of political citizenship without the control of violence, of a rule of law coexisting with police abuses, and of electoral democracies without civil rights or a legitimate justice system... Looking at these histories, we realize that what we think of as the norm—the European history of the control of violence and development of citizenship rights—is only one version of modernity, and probably not even the most common one. When we look at other histories we realize that multiple modernities are produced as different nations and peoples engage with various elements of the repertoire of modernity (monopoly of the use of force, citizenship, liberalism and so on).

The European historical model of social change referred to above encapsulated what we can call a progressive expansion of the rights of individuals modulated by groups seeking to change rules to extract privileges from other groups standing in the way of their advancement. One can begin with the iconic example of the Magna Carta before progressing through social revolutions characterized by the rise of the bourgeoisie against the aristocracy, political evolution marked by the prolonged struggle of citizens to extend the electoral franchise, and economic amelioration exemplified by the efforts of workers for improved working conditions.

As opposed to the European experience modulated by the rise of capitalism and the politics of economic growth, there were no social revolutions in South Asia which moved from pre-modern to modern forms of governance, midwifed by the British, with the same social classes remaining in charge and reinventing themselves in new roles. A more defining phenomenon in the colonies was the waning of imperial power and the politics of decline and economic scarcity in which dominant minorities struggled to safeguard the erosion of their privileges.[8] In India after 1857, the British resorted to rule changes that would weaken the nationalist opposition by privileging the divisive salience of religion in governance. This threatened some segments of the Muslim aristocracy when governance inclined towards dependence on electoral representation. Suddenly numbers became a critical factor and the Muslim aristocracy, in turn, sought rule changes (like separate electorates and over-representation) that would protect its privileges despite its lesser numbers. In this framework, the failure to reach an agreement with the dominant community on the rules of the game resulted in the division of the subcontinent.

A similar pattern, but without a similar outcome, was repeated in Sri Lanka in the case of the Tamils and later in Pakistan with the erosion of the dominance of the Urdu-speaking group concentrated in urban Sindh, another phenomenon that was of interest to Hamza Alavi (1989). The point to keep in mind is that such rearguard movements to safeguard against the erosion of privileges, although of immense political significance, do not necessarily lead to progressive change in the rights of individuals. They can sometime, but not always, result in political fragmentation in which a smaller clone of the larger territory can exercise sovereignty within similar sets of rules.

This tendency is strengthened by the fact that civil rights remain weak in South Asia and the primary identity is not the acquired one of an individual citizen, but that of subjects subscribing to ascriptive social affiliations related to religion, ethnicity, language, etc. The difference can be illustrated by reference to Marx's appeal that formed the core of the European class struggle, 'Workers of the World Unite.' While workers, an acquired identity, were not able to form coalitions across nations, they were able within nations to wrest many individual concessions encapsulated in rule changes like the length of the working day, minimum wage, unemployment insurance, etc. In the subcontinent, by contrast, the solidarity of workers was much more easily negated by the state's recourse to divisive ascriptive affiliations of religion, ethnicity and language.

This situation, peculiar to our types of countries, has been formulated conceptually by Chatterjee (2001) in a recategorization of the population between a small civil society comprised of citizens motivated by individual rights and a large political society comprised of marginalized subjects motivated by the acquisition of collective rights. The argument is advanced that civil society has tended to align itself with the state while political society has struggled to find effective means to assert its numerical power.

The bottom line that emerges from this discussion is that in all cases there is a collective agency at play, but the dynamics are very different depending on historical specificity. The changes in Enlightenment Europe were driven by the interests of rising economic powers in the context of the emergence of capitalism leading to progressive gains in a particular sequence in the rights of individual citizens. In most colonies, on the other hand, the driver of change was either rearguard action by privileged minorities to safeguard their entitlements or demands by marginalized subnational groups for collective rights leading to repression and/or political fragmentation.

It is of interest to note, if only in passing, the recent emergence of the politics of economic decline in the West consequent upon the playing out of the globalization of capital. One can see the election of Donald Trump in the US and the gains of far-right political parties in Europe in this light. The decision of the UK to quit the European Union also conforms to the predicted pattern.

By contrast, the prospects of progressive politics in present-day Pakistan seem to have faded over time. The labor movement has weakened considerably and while there are numerous disaffected groups in political society, their ability to form effective coalitions resistant to countervailing measures of the state is yet to be demonstrated.

Here one must return to the salience of identity as a variable in the effectiveness of collective agency via the ability to craft coalitions united in a political struggle. A number of scholars (see Lilla, 2017) have noted that almost all politics in the West has now reduced itself to identity politics. But it may be this very factor that has resulted in the remarkable progress of some struggles that have overcome the barriers of co-existing primordial loyalties, the LGBTQ movement being the most recent example. The nature of the outcome is in some measure a result of the choice of identity that has traction in a particular situation, the choice arising (or being induced) because, as Amartya Sen (2006) has pointed out, identity is multidimensional. Recall that there were few takers for the concerns of the Muslim aristocracy in India till 1937 and it was only the projection of an arguably exaggerated existential threat to religious identity that gave momentum to the movement in the 1940s.[9]

Prospects for Change in South Asia

What can one conclude about the prospects of change in Pakistan today? Given the nature of political society and the dominant markers of identity one can foresee the continued festering of demands for ethnic recognition and regional autonomy along lines we are familiar with in South Asia—demands of the Baloch, Seraiki and Hazara come readily to mind. These could be resolved in better or worse ways but are unlikely to proceed to the outcomes exemplified in the past by either Pakistan or Bangladesh for reasons articulated later.

As for progressive change, the prospects along stereotypical revolutionary lines appear slim. However, there is an emerging perception that sees a different way forward in working with elements within political society.[10] It has been noted that of the many disaffected groups in political society there are some, like trade and community associations, that have functioning democratic structures. A number of civil society activists are working with such associations to pressurize the state to deliver on the legitimate entitlements of the latter. Marginalized groups are vulnerable because they often have to break rules to engage the state, e.g., by encroaching on state land and then demanding the regularization of the status quo. But there are other rules defining legal entitlements that remain unimplemented. These pertain to benefits like overtime, disability pay, etc. that are evaded by employers and rights that are promised in the Constitution. The *de jure* [rightful] representative state is forced into a delicate balancing game with such groups and it remains to be seen what will transpire if and when such movements threaten to shift the balance of power. It is still likely but not *a priori* inevitable that the state might be able to finesse these emerging coalitions by recourse to divisive primordial identities as it has in the past.

It is useful to highlight the existing and potential differences between contemporary Pakistan and India in the context of change. While India has also had its demands for regional autonomy they have been handled relatively better except for the states on the peripheries. Marginalized groups have achieved a measure of access to rights to education, employment, food, and information. However, the major difference could lie in the quest for social and civil rights. While one sees virtually no identity-based movements in Pakistan likely to lead to decisive progressive change, the same may not be true in India where one could plausibly envision an alternative scenario. The access to political rights via the vote and the existence of marginalized primordial, caste-based identity groups (Dalits) with significant electoral power has resulted in the latter securing some economic rights through affirmative action to rise up the economic scale. These economic gains have yet to be translated into gains in social status and one can see a collective movement that could evolve in that direction in a period of continued economic growth. The recent surge of campus activism has encouraged the possibility of potential coalitions of such caste groups with more traditional factions of the Left in the struggle for civil rights.

As a necessary caveat, one should note that in thinking of the prospects of change the influence of background events such as the Black Death [the Great Plague, fourteenth century]—that hastened the end of feudalism, or the growth of capitalism in Europe—cannot be ignored. Three major factors could be mentioned in the case of Pakistan. The first has been the safety valve of emigration out of the country— the actual numbers belie the psychological significance of the fact that till today both the elites and the marginalized have concentrated their efforts on trying to maximize their self-interest by leaving the country rather than fighting to change it.[11]

The first academic paper I wrote (Altaf, 1982) articulated the likely political implications of this phenomenon. My conclusion was that 'the process may well leave in its wake a newly arisen small-property owning class that could side more readily with narrow reaction than with progressive change.'

The second major factor, evolving under the radar as it were, is that of continuing urbanization. It could foreshadow a non-revolutionary model of change akin to that of Latin America where numerically significant urban middle-class groups demanding better access to essential services like water, power, health, and education were able to wrest concessions from the state and ultimately displace military rule with more representative governance.

The third factor is the displacement of labor from agriculture which would continue in Pakistan. In the absence of the kind of rapid economic growth that marked the Industrial Revolution in Europe or the later industrial transformations in East Asia, we might end up with a huge population parked in the never-never land between agriculture and industry. Given a demographic profile skewed towards the young, this disaffected population would be a potential agent for change but many doubt that its mobilization would be along progressive lines. Just thinking whether the ideology of the 'revolution' of such groups would be of the Right or the Left and whether it would be armed or not is sufficient to yield serious misgivings. A thought-provoking dimension of such a prospect is the contemporaneous bankruptcy of ideas that might motivate a revolution in Pakistan today. When one thinks of the social revolutions of Europe, one is inspired by the intellectual debates of the times and the stature of the public intellectuals who participated in the debates. The entire foundation of the European Enlightenment emerged out of the contestation of ideas that are studied in academia to this day.

This thought leads me to highlight a seemingly unrelated fact—that almost all progressive change we have experienced in the world has been accompanied by a huge amount of literature in the form of treatises, novels and plays that have paved the way for the acceptance of change by the often subliminal projection of alternate realities.[12] The latest example of that has been the phenomenal speed with which the LGBTQ movement has been accepted in the West by populations that were viscerally opposed to its demands on doctrinal grounds a mere few decades ago. The relative dearth of such literature in Pakistan means that a very powerful lubricant of progressive social change is missing.[13] On the contrary, the hardening of regressive views continues apace.[14]

A Modest Conclusion

In conclusion, it does appear that we are in a bind. A social revolution is warranted but one can sense that the time for old-style social revolutions of the disenfranchised could well be gone; modern states have too much firepower, instruments of control, and technologies of rule at their disposal to be overthrown in the ways of the past—history rarely repeats itself like that.[15] One can also sense that any revolution of the traditional types we are familiar with, in which one class upends all the rules of the game in one go, could easily end up as a horror story.[16]

One can infer from this discussion that a major revolution occurred in the West with the transition of people from subjects to citizens. This transition, in turn, irrevocably altered the nature of the playing field on which future battles would be enacted. In brief, the terrain became rule oriented in which the rulers and the ruled were bound by legally protected rights and entitlements. All future changes would be marked by a struggle in this domain over the nature of rules that would be chosen to govern society.

A most vivid example of this phenomenon would be the evolution of capitalism itself. Instead of the outright overthrow of capitalists by workers, a much more gradual process followed in which workers extracted concessions one entitlement at a time. The end result, if one sees the Scandinavian countries as an exemplar, was the virtual attainment of the same quality of life of workers that was posited as an objective of the overthrow of capitalism by socialism.

The situation in South Asia is complicated by the fact that, as Partha Chatterjee has conceptualized, society remains fragmented between subjects and citizens which means that the struggle for justice and a better quality of life would tend to be a composite of rights-based movements for change, insurrections of the kinds marked by the increasing frequency of *dharnas* [protest sit-ins] and more typical local modes of protest like fasts-to-death. Whether subjects and citizens, responding to quite different tensions in society, can unite in the struggle remains to be seen. Their fragmentation provides the major weapon to the ruling class to prolong the status quo via a strategy of divide-and-rule.

Given the above, it can be argued that the most optimistic scenario is for civil and political society coalitions to realize that in parallel with whatever else they may be doing, they cannot but gain by raising the stakes in a more pragmatic joint strategy focused on identifying rules for change that would yield benefits for all. It is not inconceivable that some of these, like those mentioned earlier in the context of hockey, while apparently innocuous could well trigger developments that tip the balance of forces over time. The myriad rules that go into forming the Constitution—recall that institutions are nothing but rules—could provide possible targets. As one example, changing the first-past-the-post rule for elections could well begin sending more responsive representatives into the legislature with a snowball effect (Altaf, 2008). Instead of allowing the state to manipulate developments to its advantage, coalitions could identify and struggle for non-controversial rule changes that could redound to their benefit.

This may sound like a less than heroic conclusion, but it may be a pragmatic complementary approach and a worthwhile endeavor to be adopted in the given circumstances. It would be a decided improvement over either lamenting the existing state of affairs and giving up on the future or being dismissive of small but cumulative gains in the quest of a chimerical revolution.

References

Alavi, Hamza, 1965. 'Peasants and Revolutions,' The Socialist Register.

_____, 1972. 'The State in Post-Colonial Societies: Pakistan and Bangladesh,' New Left Review, I/74.

_____, 1987. 'Pakistan and Islam: Ethnicity and Ideology,' in Fred Halliday and Hamza Alavi (eds), State and Ideology in the Middle East and Pakistan. Monthly Review Press, New York.

————, 1989. 'Nationhood and the Nationalities in Pakistan,' Economic and Political Weekly, Vol. 24, No. 27.

Altaf, Mir Anjum, 1982. 'The Political Implications of Migration from Pakistan: A Note,' South Asia Bulletin, Vol. II, No. 2. Accessed at: https://thesouthasianidea.wordpress.com/2010/06/27/imaginings-retrospective-on-pakistan/

————, 1983. The Strategic Implications of Varying Environments: Aspects of Decision-Making Under Instability, Unpublished PhD dissertation, Stanford University, Stanford, California.

————, 2008. 'Democracy in Japan—Electoral Rules Matter,' The South Asian Idea Weblog. Accessed at: https://thesouthasianidea.wordpress.com/2008/02/22/democracy-in-japan-%E2%80%93-electoral-rules-matter/

————, 2009a. 'On the Poverty of Indian Muslims,' The South Asian Idea Weblog. Accessed at: https://thesouthasianidea.wordpress.com/2009/05/23/on-the-poverty-of-indian-muslims/

————, 2009b. 'Justice, Power, and Truth,' The South Asian Idea Weblog. Accessed at: https://thesouthasianidea.wordpress.com/2009/10/18/justice-power-and-truth/

————, 2015. 'Muslim Women and the 1946 Elections in India,' The South Asian Idea Weblog. Accessed at: https://thesouthasianidea.wordpress.com/2015/10/16/muslim-women-and-the-1946-elections-in-india/

Ambedkar, Bhim Rao, 1949. Speech to the Indian Constituent Assembly. Accessed at: http://indialawyers.wordpress.com/2010/01/24/speech-of-bharat-ratna-dr-bhim-rao-ambedkar-detailing-the-accomplishments-of-the-constiuent-assembly-of-india/

Beteille, Andre, 2013. 'The Varieties of Democracy,' Economic and Political Weekly, Vol. 48, No. 8, pp. 33-40.

Caldeira, Teresa, 2000. City of Walls: Crime, Segregation, and Citizenship in Sao Paulo. University of California Press, Berkeley.

Chatterjee, Partha, 2001. 'On Civil and Political Society in Postcolonial Democracies,' in Civil Society: History and Possibilities, Sudipta Kaviraj and Sunil Khilnani, eds. Cambridge University Press, Cambridge, pp. 165-178.

Cohen, Mitchell, 2010. 'T.H. Marshall's 'Citizenship and Social Class", Dissent Magazine, Fall. Accessed at: http://www.dissentmagazine.org/article/t-h-marshalls-citizenship-and-social-class

Dey, Debatra, K., 2017. 'Contextualizing Five Decades of Naxalbari,' Economic and Political Weekly, Vol. 52, No. 42-43.

Hirschman, Albert, O., 1970. Exit, Voice, and Loyalty. Harvard University Press, Cambridge.

Johnson, Ian, 1999. 'On Hobbes' Leviathan,' accessed at: http://records.viu.ca/~johnstoi/introser/hobbes.htm

Kamal, Daud, 2006. O City of Lights: Faiz Ahmed Faiz—Selected Poetry. Oxford University Press, Karachi. A rendition of the poem by Iqbal Bano can be accessed at: https://www.youtube.com/watch?v=dxtgsq5oVy4

Khilnani, Sunil, 1997. The Idea of India. Hamish Hamilton Ltd., London.

Lilla, Mark, 2017. The Once and Future Liberal: After Identity Politics. HarperCollins, New York.

Marshall, Thomas Henry, 1950. 'Citizenship and Social Class,' in Inequality and Society, Jeff Manza and Michael Sauder, eds. (2009). W.W. Norton, New York. Accessed at http://delong.typepad.com/marshall-citizenship-and-social-class.pdf

Mehta, Pratap Bhanu, 2003. The Burden of Democracy. Penguin Books, India.

North, Douglas, 1990. Institutions, Institutional Change and Economic Performance. Cambridge University Press, Cambridge.

Qasmi, Ali Usman and Robb, Megan Eaton, eds., 2017. Muslims Against the Muslim League: Critiques of the Idea of Pakistan. Cambridge University Press, India.

Sen, Amartya, 2006. Identity and Violence: The Illusion of Destiny. W.W. Norton, New York.

_____, 2009. The Idea of Justice. Harvard University Press, Cambridge.

Notes

1. This is an edited version of the submission 'Education in Pakistan: Ten Big Questions' made at an event organized by students at Harvard and MIT. The questions are intended to stimulate discussion.
2. State Bank of Pakistan report From The South Asian Idea (26 September 2008).
3. This is the text of a keynote presentation by Anjum Altaf at a conference on 'Education Reform in Pakistan' hosted by The Citizens Foundation, USA in San Jose, California, on 30 August 2008. Participating organizations included the leading Pak-American non-profits supporting education in Pakistan: Human Development Foundation (HDF), Developments in Literacy (DiL), Central Asia Institute (CAI) and The Citizens Foundation, USA (TCF-USA). The USAID was represented by the Officer in Charge of the Pakistan Desk in Washington, D.C.
4. Conclusions from the Conference (San Jose, CA, August 30, 2008).
5. A video of Anjum Altaf's lecture in Urdu is accessible at the Irtiqa Institute Facebook page: https://www.facebook.com/682259595183576/videos/1556960391046821/.
6. In the dissertation, I posited that rule regimes could be stabilized by the introduction of 'meta-rules', i.e., 'rules to make rules' that would procedurally be relatively more difficult to change.
7. The role of the state was another important strand in the work of Hamza Alavi (1972).
8. All the four theoretically possible scenarios—those resulting from economic growth and decline in developed and developing countries, respectively, are

discussed in Altaf (1983). The socioeconomic processes likely to emanate from each are separately articulated.

9. Even then, not all Muslims subscribed to the position of the Muslim League (see Qasmi and Robb, 2017). For the strikingly different attitudes of Muslim women which were given short shrift in a patriarchal society (see Altaf, 2015).

10. Private conversation with Sarwar Bari, Pattan Development Organization, 2017.

11. A theoretical formulation of this phenomenon is to be found in the celebrated 'Exit, Voice, and Loyalty' hypothesis of Hirschman (1970).

12. Note the salience accorded in the feminist movement to the writings of Virginia Woolf, Simone de Beauvoir, Betty Friedan, Germaine Greer, Kate Millett, Shulamith Firestone, etc.

13. It is fascinating to speculate that genre might matter in this context—that genres like novels, plays, and films work on attitudes one mind at a time while poetry in a largely oral culture works on the collective psyche. Does the fact that we have a much greater output of poetry—intended to be heard not read, compared to the other genres—signify anything in this context? I don't feel competent enough to answer this question but leave it as a subject for discussion.

14. Based on limited information, my understanding is that a considerable quantity of such literature is now emerging in local Indian languages. It may also exist in local languages in Pakistan unknown to those not familiar with them. Also recall the Russian and Chinese literature that was relatively abundant in the early years of Pakistan.

15. Consider the trajectory of the Naxalite movement in India (Dey, 2017) and the ephemeral Arab Spring and Occupy Wall Street Movement.

16. Along the lines of the Cambodian revolution which was initially welcomed by a number of leading intellectuals in the West. But note that in the popular conception the old style revolution remains dominant in Pakistan, kept alive in the imagination by our poets—see the classic 'hum dekhenge' [We shall see ...] by Faiz immortalized by Iqbal Bano with its stirring lines 'sab taaj uchaaley jaaenge/sab takht giraaey jaaenge [The crowns shall be tossed/the pedestals toppled (translation by author)] (Kamal, 2006).

Postscript

Postscript

Final Thoughts and a Call to Action

The conceptual birth of this book took place in 2016. It has taken three years to collect, compile, write, and refine the content plus almost another year to prepare the manuscript for review and publication. As I write my Final Thoughts in late 2020, we are in the midst of the severe Coronavirus pandemic which has disrupted life everywhere, with millions of lives affected, and economic havoc around the world. As bad as the recent natural disasters and armed conflicts have been, the pandemic is worse in many ways. Education too has taken a big hit. In Pakistan, education can suffer a severe setback when it is already struggling to find a footing as an essential, national institution. But, as we return to normal, we must ensure that education reform in Pakistan is also back on track. The status quo is worrisome for the country's future—and the need for comprehensive reforms is urgent. We are all complicit either by action or inaction, in giving rise to substandard public education in favor of the inequitable private education.

This **Call to Action** is a chance to take the right action.

In a few more pages, this book is about to end. But the battle for education reform in Pakistan must go on because the work is far from done. Now that we have a better understanding of the education landscape and its complex challenges, our commitment to comprehensive reform must take on a greater sense of purpose, with clarity and laser sharp focus on the mission to change the education environment. Our motivation must be based on compassion for the deprived, the needs of the underprivileged, our obligation for social justice, and for equitable opportunity in education as a human right. The unequivocal long-term vision must be that education is the best pathway from poverty to prosperity for Pakistani children. Likewise, education is important for the robust development of the country's social capital institutions—to be suppliers of a proud, productive, and diverse workforce that is mature, technically knowledgeable, generally well-informed, and globally competitive.

The bedrock foundation of development and equitable prosperity is equal opportunity for education. Inter-woven threads of society make up our communities and the collective order in Pakistan. Let us honestly check and ask ourselves: is the fabric of our society unraveling because of our own destructive behaviors—corrupt practices, cheating, intolerance, feudal attitudes, injustice, inequity, thoughtlessness, the educational and economic apartheid, and lack of compassion for the underprivileged? To reverse many of these severely damaging attributes, education reform must be the starting point for a major social correction. Our aspiration for education reform must be that we will thread the needle this time and get it right with astute leadership provided by influential stakeholders and with strong public support. It will take organized action and the changes will be incremental. Dedicated influencers will need to serve as stakeholders for sustained change and reform in education for the long term. Without question, it will be a multi-generational, ongoing effort.

Participation in education reform is an act of ultimate patriotism, an opportunity to lead the change and to be a part of history. Because of its dynamic nature, education reform may remain a moving target and adjustments will be needed. The first goal should be to start rebuilding the system with collaborative civic action, with a plan to establish a system of quality education for all Pakistani children. That will be the courageous and patriotic thing to do because we all do better when the poor do better.

This **Call to Action** is an invitation to join a coalition as a supporter of education reforms. (Simply go to www.ICERPak.org and sign up online). The proposed charter for the International Coalition for Education in Pakistan (ICERP) is not rigidly set in stone. The framework may be expanded and remain open to better ideas. To serve as a catalyst in driving the reforms, ICERP should be adaptable to re-modeling as needed by prevailing conditions. But here is a suggested initial structure for ICERP, why it should be supported—and why you should join.

ICERP shall be the central point and a platform for free and open expression of public and political voice to mobilize support for education reform. It proposes to be a grassroot people's coalition of multiple organizations and individuals to advocate for reforms and serve as a clearinghouse of communication with supporters of education reform. As the initial organizers, we plan to reach out and mobilize a core of influential persons as stakeholders and rally a large number of public supporters as well. Every single voice of support will be valuable. There is strength in numbers and it will take a significant number for the successful implementation of reforms and their long-term effectiveness.

We will share relevant and current news related to education to keep you informed, stimulated, and motivated. As the online source for public information and a platform for political advocacy, ICERP shall be a democratic voice and catalyst for education reform. It shall be non-partisan, apolitical and open to all persons and organizations concerned with education reforms. As outlined in Chapter 7, the fundamental objectives shall be to initiate and support public efforts for comprehensive education reform; to work in close coordination with government agencies at all levels; and, to serve as a vigilant watchdog group to monitor fiscal and operational functions of the education systems.

Aligned with its primary objective of advocacy, we foresee a future role for ICERP as a think tank and policy research institute, with a body of experts who could contribute as a resource of evidence-based ideas to propose as policy. As a collaborative intervention, research may be pursued by ICERP in areas such as curriculum, language policy, professional development, and pedagogy.

ICERP shall be a people's initiative—tapping into the ideas, energies, and resources of the millennial youth generation as well as the seasoned experience of the middle and senior generations. The founding of ICERP will be a volunteer effort. To sustain its programs and advocacy efforts, ICERP should rapidly transition from an online platform to a structured organization registered as a non-profit in Pakistan and elsewhere, employ competent people for management and to seek operating funds through grants and other sources. All of this will be up to its leadership and supporters.

Education is an enormously complex undertaking. There is much more to know than could possibly be fully described in a single volume. The cultural barriers to education are huge, especially for girls and the underprivileged. The issues of quality education and other elements such as management, curriculum, books, assessment of outcomes, etc. are also in the mix. Through public demand and with solid civic leadership, the comprehensive process of reforms must be under public control. Because reforms cannot be left entirely to bureaucrats and task force committees. Suggested essentials for reform and their rationale have been discussed in Chapter 7.

I reiterate that the purpose of the book is to stimulate open conversation on the education landscape and initiate civil society action for sustainable change. The book has presented the dysfunctional and feudal political environments which have impeded reforms for more than seven decades. The highest measure of the book's success will be the achievement of public participation in the reform effort with strong civic leadership. The concluding thought, then, is that incremental social change must begin with a sound education system, led by a sustainable program of reforms effectively steered by civic society leadership.

The facts are before us: the highest absolute number of out-of-school children (OOSC) in the world is in the South Asia region.

The highest share of OOSC in South Asia is found in Pakistan, where roughly 40 percent of school-age children are out of school.

The future of Pakistan's children, indeed the country's future, is in our hands.

Let's not be our own worst enemy. Time is not a luxury we have. Tick-tock, tick-tock, tick-tock.

Acknowledgements and Gratitude

Nadeem Hussain, an energetic and intellectually amazing young man has been my partner, co-author and without any doubt the most valuable asset in this project. Nadeem is already a mature leader in his own right and I owe him a huge debt which I will never be able to repay. We make a great pair and I thank Nadeem for all his help and untiring effort and for his time on the long phone calls at all hours of the day and night. Our collective reward shall be the success of education reform and equitable opportunity for quality education of all Pakistani children. *Shukriya* for everything, Nadeem.

The kind foreword and valuable assistance by my friend Shashi Buluswar is genuinely appreciated. For their most valuable counsel and excellent contributions, the four authors—Irfan Muzaffar, Salman Humayun, Ehtisham Adil, and Anjum Altaf—deserve high praise and my most sincere gratitude. My thanks also to those who gave time to speak with me and contributed to this effort, even those who could not be included in the book which, again, I deeply regret.

The professional team at Oxford University Press, Karachi, have been extremely helpful in providing guidance and I am grateful for their patience and understanding throughout the publishing process, with special thanks to Arshad Saeed Husain, Raheela Baqai, and Sunehra Mehmood.

A big shout-out to the prominent people who have contributed comments and endorsements despite multiple demands on their time. Thank you for being supporters of education and advancement of Pakistani people. The endorsements are of tremendous value for wider distribution and support of the core message of the book.

I would also like to thank the interviewees who consented to speak with me, knowing that the text of the interview would be published.

I thank all Agents of Change—from parents, teachers, students, planners, managers, innovators—to the thousands of supporters, education reform leaders and all others who patiently work in the trenches, day in and day out to achieve the mission and objectives of quality education. I am hopeful that the book will add to that ongoing effort.

Finally, with much love—my dear wife and life partner Najma and our entire family are thanked profoundly for their patience and restraint during the book project. I am overwhelmingly grateful. I could not have done it without their encouragement and understanding that the cause is worth much more than the tiny price we may have collectively incurred.

Index